The Negotiation
Process and
the Resolution of
International Conflicts

The Negotiation Process and the Resolution of International Conflicts

P. Terrence Hopmann

UNIVERSITY OF SOUTH CAROLINA PRESS

To Alexander and Nicholas

Published 1996
First paperback edition 1998

©1998 University of South Carolina

Published in Columbia, South Carolina, by the
University of South Carolina Press

Manufactured in the United States of America

02 01 00 99 98   5 4 3 2 1

ISBN 1–57003-293-9

Library of Congress Catalog Card Number 95-41777

Contents

Preface

This book has been some twenty-five years in the making. I began working on it in the summer of 1970, which I spent in Geneva with the assistance of a grant from the Office of International Programs at the University of Minnesota. There I concentrated on reading verbatim transcripts of the Conference of the Committee on Disarmament at the Palais des Nations and interviewing delegates to that conference about the process they utilized to negotiate on arms control and disarmament issues. I was immediately struck by the wide gap between abstract, academic conceptions of bargaining that dominated the literature at that time and the perceptions of the process held by practitioners in a multilateral negotiation setting such as that found in Geneva. I became convinced that it was both possible and desirable to bridge that gap and to bring together the best of the insights of academic research on negotiations and the understandings of some of the most experienced practitioners of that art. This book is in part an effort to bridge that difficult gap.

Throughout the subsequent twenty-five years, therefore, I have immersed myself in this subject. I have read as widely as possible in the theoretical literature, including many diverse theoretical perspectives ranging from mathematical game theory, through experimental social psychological research, the work of political scientists on the domestic and international politics of international negotiation, to the many contributions made by anthropological studies about the impact of culture and communications on negotiation. I have also read widely, but by no means have mastered, the vast number of case studies of historical negotiations, both recent and past.

I have been increasingly persuaded as I have read through the literature and watched it develop over the past twenty-five years that no one approach or perspective is sufficient to understand a process as complex as international negotiations. On the contrary, it seems to me that only the integration of these different perspectives can enable both the analyst and the practitioner to get a grasp on such a multifaceted topic. That has become another major objective of this book. Rather than contending that I have discovered the best way to achieve success in international negotiations, I argue that there are many factors that contribute to successful negotiations. And there remains an element of uncertainty about which techniques and approaches may work best in any concrete negotiation; it is in this domain that the conduct of successful negotiations retains an element of "art." Someday our theory may progress to the point where we can make these complex discriminations and learn systematically which approach works best under which specific conditions. But we are far short of achieving such certainty at this point in our theoretical development, and it is better to remain modest about our claims than to assert with certainty that one and only one approach works best in virtually all conditions. Our theoretical understanding has advanced considerably in the twenty-five years during which I have been researching this book, but I am equally impressed with the important questions that remain to be answered by future researchers.

While reading widely in the theoretical and empirical literature on negotiations, I have also tried to maintain contact throughout my research with the "real world" of international diplomacy. I have interviewed literally hundreds of diplomats engaged in international negotiations of many different kinds and in many parts of the world. Because of my personal interests, I have concentrated mostly on negotiations in the realm of international security, especially arms control and disarmament. That focus is reflected in the central case study of this book, the negotiations on the Partial Nuclear Test Ban Treaty of 1963. But I have focused most heavily on negotiations on European Security and Cooperation in Europe, on Mutual Balanced Force Reductions and subsequently Conventional Forces in Europe, and on Intermediate-Range Nuclear Forces in Europe. I have benefited particularly by the opportunity to spend a half year at the Carnegie Endowment for International Peace's office in Geneva in 1974 and two years on Fulbright-Hayes Fellowships in Belgium in 1975–76 and 1982–83 and by many subsequent trips, especially to Geneva and Vienna to interview negotiators in these settings. Although some examples from these negotiations appear in this work, most of that material is being saved for a subsequent, more substantive book on the negotiation of European security from 1973 through 1992.

My knowledge of the "real world" of international negotiations has also benefited tremendously from the opportunity afforded me from 1986 through 1991 by the United Nations Development Program (UNDP) and the UN Economic Commission for Latin America and the Caribbean (ECLAC) to offer a series of workshops on negotiations throughout Latin America to experienced diplomats as part of their mid-career training programs and at diplomatic academies of Argentina, Brazil, Paraguay, Chile, and Guatemala. This gave me an opportunity to work in a different setting, Latin America, and on a different set of issues than those on which I had devoted most of my research. It would perhaps surprise most of the "students" in these workshops to know that I learned a great deal more from them cumulatively than they could have possibly learned from me in two weeks. These also included six multinational workshops in Mexico and several in Costa Rica and Uruguay. In connection with these workshops, I developed an early and much shorter version of this book which was published by ECLAC in Spanish for use in these courses, and the feedback from the workshop participants about this "text" has been invaluable in writing the present book. I am especially grateful to the project coordinators for the UN, Luciano Tomassini and Carlos Eduardo Mena, and to the two principal coordinators of the FLACSO program in Costa Rica—both distinguished negotiations scholars themselves—Manuel Araya Incera and Francisco Rojas Arevena. From all of them I learned a great deal about how international negotiations operate in Latin America, and I must thank them for helping me to make contact with so many excellent practitioners and thoughtful students of negotiation throughout Latin America and the Caribbean.

Throughout this twenty-five-year period I have benefited from the advice and assistance of numerous individuals and institutions. Until 1985 I received a great deal of support from the University of Minnesota, including the Office of International Programs, the Harold Scott Quigley Center of International Studies, and the Stassen Project for World Peace in the Hubert H. Humphrey Institute of Public Affairs. Also occurring at Minnesota is the partnership with my former colleague Chuck Walcott in much of my early work on negotiation, for which I am especially grateful. Chuck is the primary author of the Bargaining Process Analysis (BPA) system that I used to content analyze many negotiations, and he also assisted me greatly in developing simulations for both teaching and research about negotiations. We literally launched this project together, and I could not have gotten it off the ground without his intelligence and dedication to the subject and to our students. I also benefited on numerous occasions from the advice and constructive criticism of many colleagues, including John Turner, Dave Bobrow, Bob Kudrle, Brian Job, Bud Duvall, and Martin Sampson.

Of special importance, however, to the development of this book during my Minnesota years was the collaboration I experienced with many graduate students. Several worked closely with me on research on negotiations, and I have been honored to publish some of this work in collaboration with Tim King, Theresa Smith, and Jo Husbands. Without the contributions of students such as these this book would never have been possible.

Since coming to Brown in 1985, I have benefited especially from the assistance of the Center for Foreign Policy Development (CFPD) and the Thomas J. Watson Jr. Institute for International Studies, with which I have been associated. I am especially grateful to my predecessor and the director emeritus of the CFPD, Mark Garrison. Having come to Brown after a distinguished career in the U.S. Foreign Service, Mark demonstrated time and again the value of integrating the perspectives of the academic analyst and the practitioner of the diplomatic art. In his own personal life he provides the ideal embodiment of this integration. I am also grateful to the support of the late Howard R. Swearer, president of Brown when I arrived and subsequently the first director of the Watson Institute, and I will always remember fondly the kind and supportive environment that he provided for my work.

This book has also benefited from the comments and advice of several other Brown colleagues, including the late Eric Nordlinger of the Department of Political Science and the late Richard Smoke of the Center for Foreign Policy Development. I valued them highly as colleagues, and I miss them both greatly. I also appreciate very much the support of the current Watson Institute director, Tom Biersteker, with whom I have had the great pleasure of working closely the last few years since I have been director of the CFPD. Also, this book has been improved greatly by the feedback to an early draft of it from my students in Political Science 149, "International Negotiations," in 1992–93 and 1993–94. I also want to thank José Juara, a former undergraduate from Florida International University who served as my assistant during the summer of 1993 under the auspices of Brown's early identification program that encourages minority students to enter academic careers. José read and commented on the entire manuscript in detail, he checked references and footnotes, and he helped to prepare a preliminary index. I am pleased that he is now in graduate school and on his way toward a career in academic international relations. Finally, I want to acknowledge the support from the staff of the Center for Foreign Policy Development at Brown, including Leslie Baxter, Sheila Fournier, Brenda Menard, and Patricia Monahan, who have done so many little things to make this manuscript cumulatively better. Also Agnes Gasu, secretary for many years in the International Relations Program at Brown, has been an invaluable source of assistance and warm enthusiasm from the first day she joined us.

I also owe a great debt of gratitude to many people outside of the two institutions where I have taught over the past twenty-five years. First, I want to acknowledge the encouragement of my graduate mentor at Stanford, Ole Holsti, who first introduced me to the subject of international negotiation. I also owe a great deal to the warm support throughout this project of Harold Guetzkow of Northwestern University, who is one of the real pioneers in integrating political science and social psychology to enhance the systematic study of international negotiation and conflict resolution. Although I have no personal relationship with him, I also owe a great intellectual debt (as will be evident to all who read this book) to Anatol Rapoport, one of the great minds of our era, whose writing inspired me greatly to work in this area.

I have benefited greatly over the past twenty years from a close collaboration with Dan Druckman of the National Academy of Sciences. Dan, who came out of the experimental social psyvchology tradition, and I, trained in political science and international relations, have developed a natural partnership in research in which our interests overlap and our training complements one another's. The result has been two decades of research collaboration and numerous jointly authored works in which many of the ideas contained in this book were developed and tried out. Dan was also kind enough to read and offer helpful comments on an earlier draft of the manuscript, and his insights are to be found on virtually every page.

I was also fortunate for a number of years to be able to participate in regular seminars of the Harvard Program on Negotiations. Regular interactions with some of the major scholars in our field, including Roger Fisher, Jeffrey Rubin, Howard Raiffa, Herbert Kelman, William Ury, James Sebenius, Robert McKersie, and Lawrence Susskind, provided a great deal of intellectual stimulation for my work in this field. Similarly, I have participated for the past five years in the Processes of International Negotiation (PIN) project at the International Institute of Applied Systems Analysis (IIASA) in Laxenberg, Austria. There I have profited greatly from interactions with many international scholars, including Bert Spector (the former director of PIN), Victor Kremenyuk, Raymond Cohen, Bill Zartman, Jeffrey Rubin, Dean Pruitt, Otomar Bartos, Guy Olivier Faure, Christopher Jönsson, and Arild Underdal.

I also wish to acknowledge my close collaboration over the past ten years with Jean Freymond, director of the Center for the Applied Study of International Negotiation in Geneva. I have had the privilege of codirecting negotiation-training workshops in Mexico for six years and more recently at IIASA with Jean and of working with him on numerous occasions. I am also grateful to his associate, Brook Boyer, who also read and gave me detailed comments on an earlier version of this manuscript, and to Jean's wife and collaborator, Guadeloupe Sanchez de Freymond, who participated in our Mexico workshops and who prepared the Spanish-language version of my text on negotiation for the Latin American workshops. I also wish to mention the valuable insights and fine collaboration during many workshops in Central and South America with my former Minnesota colleague Gary Wynia. Gary played an indispensable role in helping me to understand negotiations in a Latin American and North-South context, aiding me to get beyond my Eurocentrism and prior exclusive focus on East-West negotiations during the cold war.

At the University of South Carolina Press, I would like to thank the series editors, Chuck Kegley and Don Puchala, who were patient with me while this manuscript "matured." I also very much appreciate the help of the acquisitions editor, Joyce Harrison, and, on the editorial staff, Jamie Brown and Bill Adams. They have all been a delight to work with.

I would like to conclude this preface by expressing my gratitude to my wife, Marita, and out two sons, Alexander I. Hopmann and Nicholas E. Hopmann. This book is dedicated to our two boys, who both literally grew up along with this project, and I have profited from their company, encouragement, and insights throughout. They have provided pleasant diversions from work as well as enjoyable company on numerous research trips to Russia, Europe, and Latin America. I only hope that this book will contribute in some small way to assist their generation to do a better job than their predecessors of settling international conflicts peacefully through diplomatic negotiations rather than through violence and war. It is to Alexander and Nicholas and the hopes of their generation for a more peaceful future that I dedicate this book.

*The Negotiation
Process and
the Resolution of
International Conflicts*

Part 1
Introduction

Chapter 1

The Role of Negotiations in Contemporary International Politics

As we approach the end of the twentieth century, the system that has structured international relations since 1945 appears to be undergoing a fundamental transformation. The bilateral cold-war confrontation between a communist bloc led by the Soviet Union and a western bloc led by the United States dissolved in the concluding years of the 1980s; by 1991 the leading state of one of the two postwar blocs, the USSR, had fragmented into a group of independent and sovereign states.

It is particularly notable that this is perhaps the first time in the history of the modern state system, dating back at least to the Treaty of Westphalia in 1648, that the international system has gone through such a fundamental transformation in the absence of a major war. Whether as an effect of the Napoleonic wars of the early nineteenth century or World Wars I and II in the first half of the twentieth century, all previous large-scale system changes have been preceded by major war among the great powers in the international system. Yet the transformation that occurred in the international system in a brief span of three years from 1989 through 1991 took place peacefully, with popular action at the domestic level and diplomacy rather than force at the international level as the primary forces driving this change.

The newly emerging system as we look ahead into the twenty-first century is much more likely to be characterized by complex multilateral relations roughly of the kind described as "complex interdependence"[1] rather than one characterized by an emphasis upon military competition and confrontation. This is not to say that security issues will disappear from the agenda of international politics, but rather that these issues are likely to take on many new dimensions—including economic, environmental, cultural, demographic, and social components along with the traditional military ones. Nuclear weapons, whose traditional purpose has largely been to insure mutual deterrence between the two superpowers, are likely to become far less central to international politics (the problem of nuclear proliferation not withstanding). Nuclear weapons have never been useful instruments for the conduct of warfare, but only for its deterrence. As Bernard Brodie pointed out at the very beginning of the nuclear era, "Thus far the chief purpose of our military establishment has been to win wars. From now on its chief purpose must be to avert them. It can have almost no other useful purpose."[2]

Yet the very presence of nuclear weapons and the danger that any conflict might somehow escalate to the nuclear level is likely to continue to make the resort to military force a very risky and unattractive option in all but the most desperate situations. If force is likely to be an even less effective instrument for settling international disputes in the future, then it follows that diplomacy is likely to become relatively more important by comparison as a process for resolving international conflicts. Indeed, diplomacy has already increasingly become the central focus of international politics over the past several decades, and, despite the war in the Persian Gulf in 1991, it is likely to become even more prevalent in the future.

If diplomacy grows in importance, then the process of negotiation, the central activity of contemporary diplomacy, is also likely to increase in importance. Whether practiced formally in large multilateral conferences, informally in private bilateral exchanges, or in many diplomatic encounters falling between these two ends of a continuum, negotiation already has become the primary mechanism through which states solve common problems and resolve international disputes. All major international problems, such as nuclear disarmament, resolution of debt problems, and improvement of the global environment, rely heavily upon the process of negotiation to improve the conditions of life for all of the peoples of our planet.

Furthermore, a state's policies can be successful in the current international system only insofar as its diplomats are skilled practitioners of the art and science of negotiation. Without such skills, most states will be doomed to frustration as they try to advance their interests on the international stage, perhaps resorting to violence out of an inability to achieve their major goals through other more peaceful and less dangerous means. Good diplomacy alone, of course, will not guarantee success in achieving one's national objectives in a world still characterized by a great deal of anarchy, but it is an absolutely necessary condition for being able to advance one's interests.

The importance of the negotiation process also transcends the interests of any particular state. In an interdependent system, violent conflict anywhere threatens the very stability of the system, and thus effective diplomatic processes are required to prevent the outbreak of widespread violence and chaos within the global system. Furthermore, in a world of complex interdependence where a variety of nonstate actors and transnational organizations crisscross the traditional state system, and in which many of the states created in the aftermath of the two world wars in the first half of the twentieth century are fragmenting into rival ethnic communities, the practice of negotiation must extend beyond its traditional focus on state-to-state diplomacy. Indeed, Keohane and Nye have emphasized that "any analysis of the politics of interdependence requires a sophisticated conception of bargaining."[3] International negotiations, therefore, may increasingly bring together disparate groups of people who identify with one another on ethnic, cultural, linguistic, and religious grounds or as members of nongovernmental organizations such as the International Red Cross or Amnesty International, as well as representatives of states and intergovernmental organizations that have traditionally been the sole focus for the study of international negotiations.

Any analysis of the future role for diplomacy and negotiations, however, must necessarily be founded upon an understanding of how this process has operated in the past and upon an investigation of those factors that seem to have contributed most to the attainment of mutually beneficial, fair, and enduring agreements among states versus those conditions that have tended to produce stalemate and the intensification of conflicts. Distinguishing between these two opposing sets of conditions is a major task of a theory of international negotiations, especially of a theory that aspires to provide sound prescriptive advice to policy makers and diplomats interested in resolving conflicts and improving the outcomes of negotiated settlements of disputes.

The purpose of this book, therefore, is to provide a comprehensive framework for the analysis of the negotiation process in all of its many dimensions. Rather than suggesting a single approach or theory that might claim to explain all negotiations, my task will be a much broader one. I shall identify a wide range of candidate explanations and try to elucidate some of the conditions in which various explanations may be more or less valid or useful in understanding the process in any particular negotiation. Although the effort here is to provide a general framework, any general framework will be useful only insofar as it can be applied to explain the process and account for outcomes in any particular international negotiation.

Therefore, I shall begin this analysis by presenting such a case—namely the negotiation of the Partial Nuclear Test Ban Treaty of 1963. My goal throughout the vast majority of the remaining chapters of this book will be to develop a framework that will help us to understand, explain, and draw lessons from this single important negotiation that may be useful in future negotiations, even in the very different world of the post-cold-war period. I shall also return to this case in part 4, where I shall attempt to demonstrate the utility of the analytical framework developed in the intervening chapters by applying it explicitly to this important case.

Although at the time of this writing more than thirty years has elapsed since the signing of the Partial Test Ban Treaty in 1963, this remains one of the most important watershed negotiations in the history of the cold war. From the very dawn of the nuclear age in 1945, the issue of nuclear disarmament had been widely debated and negotiated, with notable lack of progress. Throughout the most difficult years of the cold war, from the Berlin crisis of 1948 through the second Berlin crisis of 1961 and the Cuban missile crisis of 1962, the world appeared to be poised on the brink of potential nuclear catastrophe and diplomacy seemed helpless to slow down, much less reverse, the spiralling nuclear arms race. Coming just nine short months after the nuclear confrontation over the Soviet missile deployment in Cuba, the Partial Test Ban Treaty, signed in July 1963, represented the first breakthrough in negotiations intended to slow and eventually to bring a halt to the race toward nuclear Armageddon. Furthermore, it brought about a significant turning point in Soviet-American relations that ushered in a period often characterized as détente between the two cold-war rivals.[4] Few negotiations, therefore, have had a comparable impact upon the course of post-World-War-II history.

Furthermore, the test ban negotiations provide a case study of a negotiation that is long since completed, and where the results and long-term effects are readily visible. Since my goal is to develop a framework that will explain and evaluate how the negotiation process affects the outcomes of negotiations, and since outcomes can only be evaluated over a period of time as agreements are implemented, this provides a particularly useful case study against which the framework developed in this book may be applied. In spite of the fact that this represents a classic state-to-state negotiation between superpower rivals in a bipolar international system, I shall attempt to show that it has considerable relevance as well to understanding the negotiation process in the contemporary international system. I shall try to realize this goal both by identifying features of this negotiation that seem to be generic to the negotiation process in general, and also by developing explanations that will enable us to extend our analysis to more multilateral cases and more complex issues where nonstate and supranational actors are involved.

In the next chapter, therefore, I shall present a brief historical account of the test ban negotiations. This will provide us with a concrete case upon which subsequent analysis may be built. I shall then return in part 4 to apply the theoretical framework (developed in parts 2 and 3) to the negotiation of the Partial Nuclear Test Ban Treaty of 1963. This case study will provide both an empirical foundation to validate the framework and an opportunity to evaluate the utility of the framework in elucidating how the negotiation process affected the outcome reached in one of the most important negotiations of the second half of the twentieth century.

Chapter 2

A Brief History of the Test Ban Negotiations, 1962–63

O ne important purpose of theory in international politics, as in all social sciences, is to help us to explain events in the real world and, in the light of our values, to enable us to provide prescriptive advice to practitioners about how best to proceed in an uncertain future. Therefore, the major test of the value of any theoretical framework, such as that to be developed in this book, is its ability to be applied usefully to real world cases. In order to understand the substantive subject I wish to apply my framework to, I shall begin in this chapter with a descripitive, historical overview of the negotiations leading up to the Partial Nuclear Test Ban Treaty signed in Moscow on 5 August 1963–the first major arms control agreement of the cold war period.[1]

THE NUCLEAR TEST BAN NEGOTIATIONS PRIOR TO 1962

Beginning with the Manhattan Project, in which the United States developed the atomic bomb that first exploded on Hiroshima in 1945, the United States, followed by the Soviet Union, Great Britain, and later France and China, frequently detonated nuclear warheads both to test new weapons developments and confirm the reliability of stockpiled warheads. For several decades the major medium for testing these weapons was in the atmosphere, usually in relatively isolated locations. However, the wisdom of atmospheric testing came into question following a test in 1954 by the United States of a nuclear weapon on the Bikini Atoll in the Pacific, which produced a far larger yield than had been planned and spewed radioactive fallout across the Marshall Islands and over fishing vessels in the region. This incident provoked the first serious discussions of a ban on nuclear testing, but it also provoked proponents of weapons testing to develop procedures for the underground explosion of nuclear warheads in which radioactive debris would not be released into the atmosphere.

By 1957 international protests against atmospheric nuclear testing began to mount. Yet in that same year, Great Britain tested its first hydrogen bomb. These events prompted the Soviet Union to propose a moratorium on nuclear weapons tests, which was quickly rejected by the United States as unenforceable. However, in 1958 Soviet Premier Nikita Khrushchev announced a moratorium on Soviet nuclear tests in a letter to U.S. President Dwight D. Eisenhower, as long as others did not continue testing. Eisenhower quickly dismissed this proposal, leading to a public furor in the United States and around the world. As a consequence, Eisenhower proposed calling a conference of experts to study methods to verify compliance with a nuclear test limitation. Somewhat to the surprise of U.S. policy makers, Khrushchev agreed to this proposal. The result was that a Conference of Experts began meeting in Geneva on 1 July 1958 and completed its deliberations on 21 August. After much scientific debate about the difficulties of monitoring a test ban, especially about whether or not on-site inspections would be required to verify suspected violations, the committee concluded that "it is technically feasible to set up, with certain capabilities and limitations, a workable and effective control system for the detection of violations of a possible agreement on the world-wide cessation of nuclear weapons tests."[2]

On the basis of these findings, President Eisenhower proposed a conference among the three nuclear powers of that time—the United States, the Soviet Union, and the United Kingdom—to negotiate a test ban treaty. He also agreed to a one-year moratorium on nuclear testing while the negotiations took place. Thus, the Conference on the Discontinuance of Nuclear Weapons Tests opened in Geneva on 31 October 1958. At the outset, all parties seemed to be in general agreement about the desirability of reaching a comprehensive ban on the testing of all nuclear weapons in all environments. Almost immediately, however, the obstacle that was to plague the negotiations throughout their history arose prominently in the deliberations. The differences concerned details of the system of verification, especially how to distinguish between underground nuclear tests and earthquakes.

The system decided upon in Geneva called for an extensive global system of seismic monitoring stations that could detect seismic activity anywhere on the globe. However, the United States and Great Britain continued to assert that these stations could not accurately discriminate between earthquakes and at least some underground nuclear tests, especially if those tests were of low yield or were conducted either in soft surrounding materials or in a high cavity below the earth. The only reliable means of determining for sure that a seismic event was actually a nuclear test according to the two Western delegations was to conduct an on-site inspection of the suspected location to search for evidence of intense radiation. In addition, they wanted the power to conduct such inspections to reside in an international commission that would operate by majority vote. The Soviet Union countered that such inspections were not necessary to detect suspected violations since seismic stations based on the Geneva system would be adequate for that task. They also argued that the Western insistence on on-site inspections was simply a pretext for the conduct of espionage in their territory. Finally, they insisted that the veto principle should apply in the international control commission, so that the Soviet Union would have to authorize all inspections of Soviet territory and that Soviet personnel would have to oversee any inspections that might take place.

Within this new conference it appeared that both sides had stepped back slightly from the findings of the Conference of Experts. The United States had grown increasingly uncertain about the ability to distinguish nuclear tests from earthquakes after some experiments with U.S. nuclear tests had shown how these tests could be concealed from the seismic detection systems. At the same time the Soviet Union seemed to place greater faith in these detection devices than seemed justified on the basis of the technical report. Once the question about on-site inspections became politicized the Soviets were also able to construct an enforcement procedure that would not guarantee the other countries the right to inspect Soviet territory.

In an effort to try to overcome this stalemate, British Prime Minister Harold Macmillan visited Moscow in late February 1959 and proposed to Khrushchev that there should be an annual quota of on-site inspections. Soon thereafter President Eisenhower wrote to Khrushchev to suggest a ban on atmospheric tests of nuclear weapons less than 50 kilometers above the earth's surface "while the political and technical problems associated with control of underground and outer space tests are being resolved."[3] Khrushchev rejected this proposal because it would permit the United States to continue testing in the environments not covered by this ban, where the United States probably had a technological advantage. He countered by returning to the proposal discussed with Prime Minister Macmillan, namely a relatively small quota of annual on-site inspections. The two Western leaders agreed to explore this idea further. Immediately thereafter the Soviet ambassador in Geneva proposed a small fixed quota of annual on-site inspections that would not depend in any way on voting in the International Commission. The Soviet veto principle had clearly been dropped and the positions of the two sides seemed to be converging.

A subsequent technical conference in Geneva also reached the conclusion that a limited number of satellites would be sufficient to detect any nuclear weapons tests in outer space. Eisenhower tried to pressure the negotiators by announcing that the United States would no longer consider itself bound to abide by the moratorium on testing after 31 December 1959, although he indicated that the United States would announce its intention to resume actual testing well in advance. Khrushchev replied by reasserting that the Soviet Union would not resume testing as long as the Western nations did not do so. At the same time efforts to negotiate an agreement based on a technical consensus among the experts from the three nuclear powers proved fruitless, so the search turned in 1960 to look for a more political basis for a settlement.[4]

The United States tried a new tack at the Geneva negotiations in February 1960. The essence of the new proposal was that the test ban treaty would be implemented in phases. It would start with a ban on those environments in which control by external technical means was viable and proceed step-by-step to additional environments as the technical verification capabilities improved. The United States illustrated this proposal with the suggestion that such a ban could include in its first phase an atmospheric ban to a given, but unspecified, altitude and a ban on underground tests producing seismic shock waves greater than 4.75 on the Richter scale. This threshold on atmospheric tests in space could be raised as satellite reconnaissance improved, and on underground tests it would be lowered as seismic detection improved. The ban would be further enforced by an annual quota of on-site inspections calculated as a percentage of the unknown seismic events detected during the year. In practical terms, this would have generally yielded about twenty annual on-site inspections of Soviet territory.

The Soviets responded favorably to these proposals, with three minor exceptions. They wanted the ban on tests in space to be unlimited; an initial moratorium of four to five years on underground tests below the specified threshold; and the determination of the quota for annual on-site inspections would be on a political rather than a technical basis. Eisenhower and Macmillan agreed in principle to these suggestions, except they wanted the moratorium to be limited to two years. Remaining differences were to be negotiated in a major summit scheduled to begin in Paris on 16 May 1960. However, shortly before the heads of state of the three nuclear powers joined President Charles de Gaulle in Paris, Khrushchev revealed that the Soviets had shot down a U-2 spy plane of the United States and captured its pilot, Francis Gary Powers. When he arrived in Paris, Khrushchev refused to continue discussions until he had a full apology from Eisenhower and his pledge to cancel all future flights of this nature. Since Eisenhower continued to insist on the importance of continuing these missions due to the closed society that characterized the Soviet Union, the Paris Summit collapsed and with it hopes for a speedy agreement on a nuclear test ban.

When the Kennedy administration arrived in Washington in 1961 the attainment of a test ban agreement immediately became a high priority. They submitted their proposal as a formal draft treaty coauthored with the United Kingdom to the Geneva Conference on 18 April 1961; however, this proposal deviated only in minor respects from the most recent positions taken by the Eisenhower administration before the failure of the Paris Summit. The Soviets countered by retracting some previous offers and generally by toughening their negotiating position. They proposed that the International Commission should be governed by a "troika" in which the main groups of states—Western, socialist, and nonaligned—would be equally represented and each group leader would be given veto power over the actions of the Commission. Soviet Ambassador Semyon Tsarapkin also raised the touchy issue of French nuclear tests, which had recently begun in the North African desert. He contended that, as a member of the North American Treaty Organization (NATO), France could continue to test nuclear weapons on behalf of the United States and Great Britain—even if these two countries ceased testing altogether. Finally, the Soviets indicated that the maximum annual quota for on-site inspections would be three, far below the figure of twenty per year proposed by the United States and the United Kingdom.

This toughening of the Soviet negotiating position also accompanied a general intensification of the cold war. President John F. Kennedy's first summit with General Secretary Khrushchev in Vienna in June 1961 was a sobering one for the new president, since he found the Soviet leader in no mood to be conciliatory on any of the major issues dividing the two superpowers. Furthermore, in August 1961 the East Germans began constructing the wall around Berlin, cutting off emigration from East Germany and touching off the Berlin crisis—one of the most serious crises of the postwar period. Then on 30 August 1961 the Soviets used French nuclear tests as a rationale for announcing that they were terminating their moratorium on nuclear testing, and a new Soviet test series began the very next day. Kennedy was deeply hurt, but he refused to announce an immediate resumption of U.S. nuclear tests; instead he proposed an immediate atmospheric test ban. When the Soviets rejected this, he announced that the United States would resume underground tests immediately. By the beginning of November he also indicated that the United States was preparing to embark upon a series of atmospheric nuclear tests in early 1962.

Despite a continuing series of meetings in Geneva, the Conference on the Discontinuance of Nuclear Weapons Tests came to a desultory conclusion on 29 January 1962. Shortly before adjournment, the Soviets had argued that changed conditions required a comprehensive ban on all nuclear weapons tests to be monitored exclusively by national detection systems, with no mention of any international commission or on-site inspections; they also insisted that France, as a new nuclear weapons state, must be brought into any future negotiations. In effect, the Soviets rejected the conclusions of the Conference of Experts and retracted most of their major concessions in the Geneva Conference since that time. When the negotiations adjourned, they seemed to be hopelessly deadlocked. In this context, President Kennedy announced his intention to resume atmospheric tests on 25 April 1962, setting off a storm of protest internationally and within the United States. As the Geneva Conference concluded, however, the Western countries proposed that the test ban discussions be transferred to a new forum created by the U.N. General Assembly to discuss general and complete disarmament. This new forum was scheduled to begin meeting in Geneva on 14 March 1962 and was to be called the Eighteen Nation Disarmament Conference.

THE EIGHTEEN NATION DISARMAMENT CONFERENCE (ENDC), MARCH 1962–JUNE 1963

The Eighteen Nation Disarmament Conference was created by the United Nations with a mandate to negotiate on general and complete disarmament. Although created by the United Nations, it had a semi-autonomous status and was cochaired by the United States and the Soviet Union. It was supposed to be composed of five members of the Western alliance system, five of the socialist bloc, and eight neutral or nonaligned countries (although one of the Western members, France, refused to take its seat until many years later). It was intended that the eight nonaligned countries would serve as a kind of mediating group between the two superpower alliances. During 1962, however, the test ban negotiations took place primarily in a subcommittee composed of the three nuclear powers, in effect recreating the old test ban negotiations under the new umbrella.

When the conference opened, the United States repeated its familiar proposal for a comprehensive test ban and an extensive system of on-site inspections, only slightly modified from the proposals introduced almost one year previously. However, the Soviets seemed to harden their position by now insisting that even underground tests could be adequately distinguished from earthquakes on the basis of national detection systems, so that no intrusive inspections would be required to enforce a comprehensive ban. They rejected the Western proposals outright as founded on an "utterly discredited basis."[5]

The major new element in the ENDC was the addition of the eight nonaligned nations. These countries collaborated to draft a document that attempted to bridge the gap between the two superpower blocs, although it was itself the outcome of intense negotiations among these eight countries. In the end, their disagreements also caused them to introduce some ambiguity into the document. The major provisions of the

Eight Nation Memorandum, introduced on 16 April 1962, included enhancing the existing system of national detection devices and establishing an international commission of scientists to monitor these devices to determine when a suspicious event occurred. In case of a suspicious event, the country on whose territory this event was detected *could invite* the Commission to inspect its territory. It further stated that all nuclear weapons states had an "obligation to furnish the Commission with the facts necessary to establish the nature of any suspicious and significant event," and consult with the Commission about any methods, "including verification *in loco*," which might help to establish the nature of these suspicious occurrences. On the basis of the Commission's evaluations, parties to the treaty would be free to decide what action they would take with regard to the treaty, presumably including the right to withdraw from the treaty if a major violation had been uncovered.[6]

In an effort to gain the support of the nonaligned countries, both sets of nuclear powers accepted the Eight Nation Memorandum as a basis for negotiation. However, they both interpreted it very differently. The United States and the United Kingdom referred to the obligation to provide the International Commission with the information necessary to determine the nature of suspicious events, including on-site inspections, as evidence that this envisaged a full system of international control and verification including obligatory on-site inspections. The Soviet Union, on the other hand, emphasized the fact that the suspected countries *could invite* the international control commission as being evidence that the proposed inspections were essentially voluntary—at the invitation of the country to be inspected. Both asked the nonaligned countries to amplify their intention in the memorandum to resolve this difference of interpretation, but they refused to do so. Obviously the eight nations were themselves divided over this matter, and they had employed this somewhat ambiguous formulation to overcome their own differences; but for that very reason it failed to overcome the differences between the nuclear powers. Long debate about this issue within the ENDC failed to resolve these differences, and the ENDC recessed on 14 June 1962 with no evident progress having been made toward a test ban agreement.

Furthermore, tensions were enhanced by the fact that the United States began its long threatened series of nuclear tests, known as operation DOMINIC, on 25 April 1962; this included a series of atmospheric tests on Christmas Island (a British possession in the Pacific) and tests in space launched by missiles from Johnston Island. The entire series lasted over six months and was met by a wave of protest from around the world, especially in Japan. At the same time the United States began to consider a reformulation of its position for the Geneva negotiations, influenced in part by some of the test results and by the seismic research project known as Project VELA. This project revealed that seismic detection capabilities were perhaps greater than had previously been believed. Indeed, U.S. ENDC Ambassador Arthur Dean declared somewhat prematurely at the Geneva airport in July that this might make it possible to have a test ban without any international stations situated on Soviet territory.[7] The nonaligned states continued their effort in Geneva to bridge the gaps on the basis of this new information. On 25 July the Brazilian delegate observed that the major differences between the two sides concerned only the verification of underground tests, whereas there appeared to be far fewer problems with verification of the testing of weapons in the atmosphere and space. He proposed concentrating efforts on halting nuclear tests in these two environments, which presented the greatest dangers to humanity.[8] The United States did not react negatively to this statement, and indeed the Italian delegation supported the Brazilian proposal.

At the same time the Kennedy administration began a thorough reappraisal of its negotiating position, which led to the introduction of two alternative draft agreements submitted jointly by the United States and the United Kingdom in the ENDC on 27 August 1962. The first was a comprehensive test ban treaty, a modified version of the proposal set forth on 18 April 1961 taking into account both the discussion surrounding the Eight Nation Memorandum and the new technical information. They proposed creating an International Scientific Commission, composed of fifteen members. The United States, United Kingdom, and Soviet Union would be permanent members, and twelve other countries would be elected for three-year terms—three nominated by the USSR, two by Britain, two by the United States, and the remaining seven would be jointly nominated (presumably nonaligned countries). Thus, the overall ratio of Commission members would be 4:4:7 and give a far larger role to the nonaligned countries than in previous Western proposals. This Commission would be equipped with an international staff. The verification system would include stations located on the territories of all nuclear weapons states and elsewhere in the world where nuclear tests might be detected. Some of these would be presently existing stations, but new stations would be constructed and maintained by the International Scientific Commission. In order to investigate events the Commission could not identify with certainty, an equal and annual quota for on-site inspections would be established for the three nuclear powers. Although the quota was left blank in the draft treaty, U.S. and British delegates declared that it would be fewer than the twelve to twenty inspections required by previous Western proposals.

The second draft agreement submitted by the United States and Great Britain on 27 August 1962 called for a partial ban on tests "in the atmosphere, above the atmosphere (in space), or in territorial or high seas" or "in any other environment if such explosion causes radioactive debris to be present outside the territorial limits of the State" conducting the test.[9] This draft did not foresee the creation of an international commission or a system of verification. Ambassador Dean argued that this treaty could be accepted immediately, while negotiations continued toward a comprehensive test ban agreement.

Both of these draft proposals were immediately and firmly rejected by the Soviet Union. The comprehensive draft was opposed because of its insistence on obligatory on-site inspections rather than the system of inspections by invitation proposed by the nonaligned bloc. The Soviets also objected to placing control posts under an International Scientific Commission rather than relying solely on a system of national control posts. Soviet Deputy Foreign Minister Vasily Kuznetsov rejected the partial agreement on the grounds that it legalized underground nuclear tests, where militarily significant advances could still be made. He also contended that it would do little to halt nuclear proliferation, and that the dangers of radioactive fallout were rather minor in comparison to the dangers of nuclear war, which would in no way be made less likely by this agreement.[10] Thus, the ENDC recessed again on 7 September to report to the annual session of the U.N. General Assembly with little actual progress having been achieved on a test ban agreement, although the subcommittee on the test ban continued its work in Geneva throughout this period.

During this recess in the main negotiations, tensions between the United States and the Soviet Union reached an all-time high due to the Cuban missile crisis. The crisis began on 15 October 1962 when American U-2 spy plane flights over Cuba discovered evidence that the Soviets were constructing a site for medium-range missiles capable of striking at much of the U.S. territory. After receiving the report and taking almost one week to deliberate on his response, President Kennedy announced to the world this discovery and the imposition of a naval quarantine around Cuba on 22 October. For a week tensions mounted as Kennedy and Khrushchev bargained over the status of these missiles, until Khrushchev announced over Radio Moscow on 28 October that he had ordered the missiles to be crated and returned to the USSR. In a letter to Kennedy on that day, Khrushchev referred to the necessity of making new progress "on the prohibition of atomic and thermonuclear weapons," and Kennedy replied by calling on Khrushchev to join him in making progress on arms control, especially in giving "priority to questions relating to the proliferation of nuclear weapons . . . and to the great effort for a nuclear test ban."[11]

When the formal negotiations reopened in Geneva on 26 November Soviet Ambassador Tsarapkin introduced a proposal that had emerged from the Pugwash Conference (an unofficial meeting of scientists from

East and West) in London the previous September. The idea was to employ a series of automatic seismic stations, known as black boxes, on the territories of the nuclear states that did not need to have personnel stationed nearby to maintain them. These boxes would be tamperproof and their instruments would be read at regular intervals by international scientific personnel. Tsarapkin proposed employing three such devices on the territory of each of the nuclear powers to supplement the national detection devices. The United States agreed to study the idea further through technical discussions, which the Soviets later rejected.

Another crisis struck the negotiations on 19 December 1962 when Khrushchev wrote to Kennedy and proposed again that three automatic seismic stations be deployed on the territory of each nuclear weapons state. He also referred to a meeting in New York between U.S. Ambassador Arthur Dean and Vasily Kuznetsov, the first deputy minister for foreign affairs of the USSR. In that meeting Ambassador Dean allegedly had indicated to Kuznetsov that "two to four onsite inspections a year in the territory of the Soviet Union would be sufficient" for the United States, and that he would "be prepared to agree to two to three inspections a year being carried out in the territory of each of the nuclear powers, when it was considered necessary, in seismic regions where any suspicious earth tremours occurred."[12] Ambassador Dean subsequently denied having agreed to fewer than eight to ten annual inspections, and Kennedy thus replied to Khrushchev on 28 December that the United States was not prepared to reduce its quota for annual on-site inspections below that figure which had been publicly discussed for some time.[13] Khrushchev also mentioned several months later in a conversation in Moscow with Norman Cousins, editor of *Saturday Review,* that Jerome Wiesner, special assistant to President Kennedy for science and technology, had told a Soviet scientist and advisor to the delegation, Yvegeni Federov, that the United States was ready to accept a few annual inspections. These reinforcing comments had caused Khrushchev to argue for a new proposal on annual inspections, despite considerable opposition from his own military and from the Chinese. When the United States then denied these reports, Khrushchev acted with anger and embarrassment, as expressed to Norman Cousins: "People in the United States think that I am a dictator who can put into practice any policy I wish. Not so. I've got to persuade before I can govern. Anyway, the Council of Ministers agreed to my urgent recommendation. Then I notified the United States I would accept three inspections. Back came the American rejection. They now wanted—not three inspections or even six. They wanted eight. And so once again I was made to look foolish. But I can tell you this: it won't happen again."[14]

Thus, when the three nuclear powers met in Washington in January 1963, the Soviet delegation appeared to be in no mood to make further concessions beyond three black boxes on Soviet territory and a maximum of three annual on-site inspections. Glenn Seaborg, director of the U.S. Atomic Energy Commission, in an account of the negotiations, summarizes the situation at the time: "The momentum generated by the missile crisis had produced some concessions from both sides. But the high hopes that both President Kennedy and Premier Khrushchev seemed to have entertained that the world's brush with catastrophe might hasten a test ban agreement were, for the moment, not realized. The situation was to get worse before it got better."[15]

The Eighteen Nation Disarmament Conference reconvened in Geneva on 12 February 1963 although the subcommittee on nuclear weapons tests was dissolved and all negotiations on the test ban issue now took place in the plenary sessions with all seventeen members present (excluding France, which still refused to take its seat at the Palais des Nations). A few days thereafter, in a private meeting with Deputy Foreign Minister Kuznetsov, William Foster, director of the recently created U.S. Arms Control and Disarmament Agency, responded to Khrushchev's offer of three black boxes on Soviet territory and three annual on-site inspections with a U.S. offer to accept seven black boxes and seven on-site inspections per year. Indeed, he had been authorized by President Kennedy to lower that number to six if the Soviets seemed interested in negotiating over specifics. In exchange, he presented a new U.S. proposal for inspections that assigned a greater role for the United States and the United Kingdom to inspect USSR and vice versa—a slight hardening of the previous position which had granted a more extensive role to the nonaligned members of the International Scientific Commission. The Soviets refused to discuss these new proposals, and the two sides seemed deadlocked at seven versus three seismic stations and on-site inspections. This was the closest that the two sides came to one another's positions on a comprehensive test ban, at least until the late 1970s. As Seaborg suggests, the differences were greater than just the distance between the two sets of numbers, since the difficult issue of modalities and procedures for inspections probably would have created additional obstacles had the two sides reached agreement on a specific number of inspections.[16] Still this failure to close the final gaps remains one of the great missed opportunities of early East-West arms control negotiations.

While the Geneva negotiations remained stalemated, a good deal of back channel activity was taking place between the two sides. As noted earlier, Norman Cousins of *Saturday Review* met with Khrushchev on 12 April 1963, and he conveyed to Kennedy the message that Khrushchev accepted the incident of the previous December about the U.S. position on the number of inspections as an honest misunderstanding, which he was willing to put behind him. However, he insisted that the next move was up to Kennedy. He also added a threat in an interview with an Italian journalist in late April, noting that if the West did not accept his offer of two to three annual on-site inspections he might retract the offer and return to the previous Soviet position of refusing on-site inspections altogether.[17]

At about the same time British Prime Minister Macmillan had become more actively engaged in seeking a solution to the impasse. At his urging, he and Kennedy sent a joint letter to Khrushchev on 24 April offering to send to Moscow "very senior representatives who would be empowered to speak for us."[18] Khrushchev replied on 8 May accusing Kennedy of having acted in bad faith, but also agreeing to receive the British and American representatives in Moscow. At the suggestion of Ambassador David Ormsby-Gore, British representative to the United States, and following a precedent set during the Cuban missile crisis when the United States had responded to positive Soviet offers while ignoring negative ones, Kennedy proposed sending representatives to Moscow in late June or early July. Kennedy then set in motion once again a substantive re-examination of the U.S. negotiating position within the government. This was stimulated in part by a Senate resolution introduced by Senator Thomas J. Dodd of Connecticut, an announced opponent of a comprehensive test ban, calling on the administration to negotiate with the Soviets for a ban restricted to the atmosphere and oceans, where on-site inspections would not be required. On 8 June Khrushchev wrote a hostile letter to Kennedy, but he did agree to receive the Western delegations on 15 July in Moscow. In addition, on 10 June he met with Harold Wilson, leader of the British Labour Party, and suggested that the Soviets were withdrawing their offer of two or three annual on-site inspections from the negotiating table in Geneva.

Kennedy's next move was one of the most important in his administration. He had been invited to deliver a commencement address at American University in Washington, D.C., on 10 June 1963, and he decided to use the occasion to make a major pronouncement about relations with the Soviet Union. The ensuing speech is viewed by many analysts as the most important of Kennedy's presidency, and indeed as one of the most important presidential speeches of the postwar period. In this speech the president spoke of the narrow brush with nuclear war in Cuba just a few months before. Despite acknowledging many differences between the United States and the Soviet Union, he stressed that the two countries shared in common their "mutual abhorrence of war. Almost unique among the major world powers," he noted, "we have never been at war with one another."[19] He also emphasized the importance of avoiding future confrontations like the one in Cuba, where the choice might boil down to one between accepting a humiliating defeat or initiating a nuclear conflict. He then announced publicly the proposed meeting in Moscow agreed upon among Prime Minister Macmillan, Premier Khrushchev, and himself. He declared that the United States would refrain from conducting nuclear tests in the atmosphere so long as others did the same.

Khrushchev responded very positively to the American University speech, calling it the "greatest speech by any American President since Roosevelt."[20] Even though it included some criticisms of Soviet policy, it was published in its entirety in the Soviet press. Furthermore, the Soviets immediately ceased jamming broadcasts of Voice of America and the British Broadcasting Corporation directed to the Soviet Union that had been occurring for the previous fifteen years. The Soviets dropped their prior objections to safeguard procedures to be undertaken by the International Atomic Energy Agency at nuclear facilities throughout the world at the meeting of that body's Board of Governors on 20 June 1963. On that same day, the United States and the Soviet Union signed an agreement establishing a "hot line"—a direct communications link between the White House and the Kremlin that would enable the two leaders to communicate directly and instantly in the event of a future crisis. Finally, in a speech in East Berlin on 2 July Khrushchev criticized the Western position on a comprehensive test ban, but he agreed publicly for the first time to accept an agreement "on the cessation of nuclear tests in the atmosphere, in outer space, and under water,"[21] in conjunction with a nonaggression pact between NATO and the Warsaw Pact. With this rapidly improving international atmosphere, the stage was set for the endgame negotiation in Moscow.

The Moscow Conference, July 1963

The negotiations opened as scheduled in Moscow on 15 July 1963. The United States was represented by Under Secretary of State W. Averell Harriman, an experienced diplomat who had served as U.S. ambassador to the Soviet Union during World War II. The British were represented by Lord Hailsham (Quinten Hogg), who as minister of science was better versed in the technical than in the diplomatic aspects of his assignment. Finally, the Soviet Union was represented by Foreign Minister Andrei Gromyko, although Premier Khrushchev himself opened the negotiations. The U.S. delegation was rather small, although all major agencies were represented. The principals back home were also small in number—Secretary of State Dean Rusk, Under Secretary of State George Ball, Secretary of Defense Robert McNamara, Central Intelligence Agency Director John McCone, Ambassador Llewellyn Thompson, and Arms Control and Disarmament Agency (ACDA) Director William Foster— and the president met with them daily. All communications with the delegation in Moscow were supervised by President Kennedy himself.

The U.S. delegation had been instructed to pursue a comprehensive test ban agreement, with adequate controls, but if they failed to generate any new Soviet responses they were authorized to move rapidly to the partial test ban proposal.

When Khrushchev spoke at the opening session, he began by tabling a draft agreement on a partial test ban in the atmosphere, outer space, and under water, and a second draft agreement calling for a non-aggression pact. The former included a provision for other states to accede to the treaty, but it contained no withdrawal clause or provisions for peaceful nuclear explosions. The Western delegations replied by re-submitting their 27 August 1962 proposal to the ENDC for a partial test ban. They also tried to press hard for the comprehensive ban, but ran into Khrushchev's strong opposition to accept any on-site inspections, although he was willing to accept a greater number of black boxes on Soviet territory than in previous discussions. When it became evident that no progress was likely on this issue, on 18 July Harriman requested and received permission from Kennedy to effectively drop the comprehensive proposal from the discussions. Therefore, the actual negotiations focused almost exclusively on the partial test ban.

In the endgame negotiations, which centered around the Western draft of a partial agreement submitted almost eleven months before, three major issues were debated. First was the Soviet desire to obtain a non-aggression pact between the two major alliances linked to the test ban agreement. Since this involved all members of the NATO alliance and not just the United States and Great Britain, Harriman and Hailsham had strong instructions to resist this approach. After a period of resistance, Gromyko finally conceded to the Western compromise of including a statement in the final communiqué about this issue and promising to consider it for future negotiations.

Second, was the issue of so-called peaceful nuclear explosions, those that might be used for such purposes as oil and gas exploration or digging canals. The draft that the United States and the United Kingdom had submitted to the ENDC in 1962 would have permitted such explosions if unanimously agreed to by the parties and if carried out in accordance with certain specific procedures designed to limit their utility for weapons development. The Soviets argued that such a provision might be undesirable because some such activities could still take place through underground explosions; any explosions that produced significant fall-out would probably weaken the treaty in the eyes of world public opinion and arouse suspicion on the part of nonnuclear states about possible collaborative cheating on a ban by the nuclear powers. The Western delegation essentially agreed with the Soviets' concerns, and accepted abandoning the peaceful use provision in exchange for Soviet acceptance of the Western position on the third issue—withdrawal from the treaty.

The issue of withdrawal revolved around a section of the 1962 Western draft that the United States and the United Kingdom thought to be of critical importance because it provided a deterrent to violation by other signatories and simultaneously assured the signatories of their right to withdraw in the event that proliferation of nuclear weapons by nonsignatories presented new security threats. The West was concerned about retaining the right to withdraw if nuclear proliferation on the part of nonsignatories necessitated reconsideration of abiding by the treaty's provisions. The Soviets insisted that the right to withdraw was inherent in national sovereignty and thus did not need to be mentioned in the treaty itself, and that calling attention to the possibility of withdrawal might again appear to weaken the treaty in the eyes of public opinion. However, the Soviets eventually conceded on this point in exchange for the West's agreement to drop the provision about peaceful nuclear explosions. Some disagreement still remained, however, over the specific wording. The Western draft called for withdrawal in case of "a nuclear test by a signator or nonsignator" of the treaty. The Soviets preferred much more general language, calling instead for the right to withdraw if a country decides that "extraordinary circumstances jeopardize the supreme interests of its country."[22] Kennedy found this language to be too general, so Harriman proposed substituting the notion that a state could withdraw in case "any nuclear explosion has occurred in the prohibited environments" which might jeopardize its national interests. Gromyko objected to specifying "nuclear explosions," and Harriman then threatened to walk out if the Soviets objected to a specific withdrawal clause.[23] Gromyko then counterproposed making the reference somewhat more specific by referring to "extraordinary circumstances related to the contents of this treaty." Harriman urged Kennedy to accept this since he felt that the Soviet bottom line had been reached, and Kennedy agreed provided that the word "circumstance" was changed to "event" in the English translation only. When Gromyko accepted this final fine-tuning of the draft language, the endgame was over and the agreement was ready for initialling.[24]

On 25 July the three representatives in Moscow initialled the agreement, and it was officially signed in Moscow on 5 August 1963 by Foreign Minister Gromyko, Secretary of State Rusk, and Foreign Secretary Lord Home. After a somewhat tense debate in the U.S. Senate, during which the Kennedy administration had to give assurances about a vigorous program of continued underground testing, that body gave its advice and consent for the administration to ratify the treaty by a vote of eighty to nineteen on 24 September. The Presidium of the Supreme Soviet of the USSR gave its approval one day later. President Kennedy signed the treaty on 7 October, and the treaty entered into force on 11 October 1963. The first arms control agreement of the post-World-War-

II period was successfully completed after a long and difficult series of negotiations. The arms race was hardly stopped by this measure, and both superpowers continued a high rate of underground testing. However, there were undoubtedly a number of significant limitations placed on the arms race by this agreement, and several other beneficial side effects also resulted.

First, the agreement probably slowed nuclear proliferation by making it more difficult to test nuclear weapons in the prohibited environments, since underground testing often was too expensive and technically complicated for many potential nuclear proliferators. It also inhibited the development of antiballistic missile (ABM) technology by making it impossible to conduct live tests of ABM systems equipped with nuclear warheads, so that the reliability of these systems could never be demonstrated with any degree of confidence. Second, the treaty produced a number of positive environmental consequences, especially by reducing dramatically the radioactive pollution of the atmosphere from testing above ground. The entry of these radioactive substances into the food chain through fallout was also significantly reduced. Third, it produced important political consequences by paving the way for a number of other significant arms control agreements, especially in nuclear proliferation, nuclear free zones and environments, and eventually strategic arms limitations and reductions. Sadly it did not, however, lead to an agreement on a comprehensive test ban; indeed, it is certainly arguable that it significantly reduced the political pressures on national leaders to achieve such an agreement. Nonetheless, it did also have the more general political effect of initiating the first major era of East-West détente, which grew fairly steadily, if somewhat erratically, through about 1975. This détente lasted more or less until late 1979 when the world entered into another decade of cold war prior to the eventual collapse of the communist bloc. In spite of its limitations the Partial Nuclear Test Ban Treaty of 1963 must still be viewed in historical perspective as an extremely important accomplishment.

Toward an Explanatory Framework

The explanation of the results obtained in Moscow from negotiations among the United States, the Soviet Union, and the United Kingdom requires a broad and supple analytical framework rather than a single, rigid theoretical perspective. Such a framework is even more important if we want to move beyond a single case study such as this one and develop truly comparative analyses that can be applied to many different negotiations in diverse settings, and involving different parties. The primary task of the vast majority of the remainder of this book will be to develop such an analytical framework. I will identify some factors that can be useful in explaining the outcome of this long and difficult negotiation process, and I also plan to suggest other factors that may be of little utility in evaluating this particular case, but may be valuable for analyzing other, quite different, negotiations. By the end of part 3, I shall have presented a comprehensive set of conditions and factors that may explain the difference between negotiation processes that successfully reduce international conflicts and produce mutually beneficial, fair, and stable agreements, on the one hand, and processes that fail to break through stalemates and that may, in some cases, even deepen the conflicts they were seeking to ameliorate, on the other hand. In the final section, part 4, I shall return to the partial nuclear test ban case in order to evaluate the capability of the intervening theoretical framework to explain in a systematic way the results of the specific negotiation I have described in this chapter.

Before turning to an analysis of the many factors affecting the impact of the negotiation process on outcomes, I will first define more precisely the subject of our analysis. It is especially important to define both what is meant by the negotiation process, the central concept under analysis, as well as how I evaluate the outcomes of that process in order to understand just what it is that a theoretical framework about the negotiation process seeks to explain. It is to that task that I shall turn in the next chapter.

Chapter 3

Negotiating for Mutual Benefits: The Process and Outcome of Negotiations

Although negotiation has been discussed in academic texts for centuries, there has been little systematic analysis of this topic until the decade of the 1960s. Since that time a substantial set of academic literature and systematic studies has been created and a coherent and cumulative picture of the negotiation process and its effects on the resolution of international conflicts is beginning to form. Numerous theorists of international politics have sought to explain the differential effects that the negotiation process has on outcomes, especially on the success or failure of the process in resolving conflicts and enhancing mutual benefits.

Early work on the negotiation process tended to be framed largely within the realist tradition of international politics, with its emphasis on state-to-state diplomacy in which individual and autonomous states seek to advance their own national interests, often at the expense of other states. Much of this work tended to be influenced heavily by models derived from economic theory, with their emphasis upon rational actors bargaining with one another to realize their goals. This literature provided an essential foundation upon which most subsequent theories of negotiation have been constructed.

However, the more recent focus on theories of interdependence, usually developed within a more liberal paradigm of international politics, as well as the demands placed on negotiation theory by the changing nature of the post-cold-war world, have all contributed to a substantial reconceptualization of the international negotiation process. In this new light negotiation is increasingly viewed as a tool in which conflicts may be resolved in such a way as to produce mutual benefits for the parties rather than exclusive benefits for one at the expense of others. The emphasis of this contemporary perspective on international negotiations is that one negotiates not primarily to achieve a victory for one's own country, but rather to solve problems that affect the relations among countries in a highly interdependent world. The international system in the last years of the twentieth century has evolved to the point where the self-interest of individual nation-states cannot take precedence over the needs of an interdependent global community. Reliance upon national self-interest will cause the system to remain in a state of essential anarchy, where, as Thucydides put it so well some twenty-five centuries ago, "the strong do what they can and the weak suffer what they must."[1]

On the other hand, as the cold war dissolves and as the international community redirects its attention to problems such as pollution and environmental decay, poverty, debt, overpopulation, famine, and the spread of arms races around the globe, it is clear that such a competitive approach to negotiation based on narrowly defined national self-interest has become an anachronism. Therefore, our task is to develop an approach to diplomacy for the next century that will improve the ability of the global community to coordinate its efforts to solve common problems rather than trying to win short-term, but essentially meaningless, victories in disputes with other states or nonstate actors on the global stage.

DEFINING THE NEGOTIATION PROCESS

Before proceeding further with the development of a theoretical framework, it is necessary to define the central subject of our analysis— the negotiation process. Perhaps the most basic definition of international negotiation was put forward in one of the earliest systematic works in the 1960s by Fred Charles Iklé, who defined negotiations as "a process in which explicit proposals are put forward ostensibly for the purpose of reaching an agreement on an exchange or on the realization of a common interest where conflicting interests are present."[2] This definition emphasizes what I shall call the mixed motive nature of negotiations, namely that negotiations always take place in situations involving some combination of common and conflicting interests. We may conceive of relations between any two parties as falling along a continuum from completely identical interests to totally incompatible interests. At the one end of this continuum, if the two parties have identical interests, then they do not need to negotiate to arrive at an acceptable solution. Each party can behave as it prefers, and the behavior of the two parties should be in complete harmony even in the absence of any negotiation. Of course, communication might be helpful to enable them to discover or to locate the common interests that they share, but this would not normally be considered to be a process of negotiation. At the other end of the continuum, where the interests of the two parties absolutely cannot be realized simultaneously, there also is no basis for negotiation. In this situation, there are no common interests around which an agreed solution may be fashioned. Thus, the dispute will almost inevitably be resolved by force or coercion rather than by diplomacy.

However, few if any, issues in international relations fall at either end of this continuum; most fall somewhere along it. Even two countries with such common interests as the United States and Canada have occasional disputes over issues such as environmental pollution and trade policy. At the other extreme, even during the most intense fighting of World War II, the opposing sides had a common interest in avoiding the introduction of poison gas into combat, and this restraint was more or less tacitly observed by all parties in that intense and violent conflict. Thus, even in the midst of war, opposing parties may still have common interests, and the closest of allies almost always have some significant differences of interest. Therefore, virtually all of international relations takes place along this continuum, perhaps at times tending toward one or the other end of the continuum, but always somewhere other than at either extreme end. And it is, of course, within this middle territory where Iklé's essential condition for negotiation is met: conflicting interests exist in this territory, but so does the possibility for the realization of a common interest.

A second key feature of any definition of negotiation is that it entails a situation of interdependent decision making, where two or more parties must each make decisions and where the outcome for the parties is not exclusively under their own control, but is a result of their joint decisions. This aspect of negotiations is emphasized by I. William Zartman, who notes that, "negotiation is considered one of the basic processes of decision-making. . . . That is to say, it is a dynamic or moving event, not simply a static situation, and an event concerning the selection of a single value out of many for implementation and action. This decision-making event is a sociopolitical process involving several parties, and not simply one individual's making up his mind."[3]

As Zartman emphasizes, the study of negotiation is very much a part of the analysis of decision making, through which national leaders select from among a set of options a single policy they believe will enable them to achieve their goals at the least cost. The major difference from the analysis of foreign policy decision making, however, is that in this case the result of one's decision is not strictly under one's own control. Since other parties have an influence on the outcome, it is necessary to negotiate with those other parties in order to create conditions in which one's decision will produce a beneficial outcome—a result that enables all parties to realize their vital national interests.

Since each party also seeks outcomes that will be beneficial in terms of its own national goals, it follows that an acceptable agreement resulting from negotiations must be mutually beneficial for all of the parties participating in the negotiation. Of course, in an interdependent system it is no longer possible for any one party to optimize its outcome, since the result will in part be influenced and constrained by the behavior of others. But it usually is possible to design joint decisions, such as negotiated agreements, that will at least serve the fundamental interests of all of the parties affected by the decision. This, then, is the goal of negotiation: to achieve mutually beneficial outcomes that will at least serve the basic interests of all parties affected by a particular decision.

The jointness of the process of decision making is further emphasized by Richard Walton and Robert McKersie, who have worked primarily in the area of labor-management negotiations in the United States. They define negotiations as "the deliberate interaction of two or more complex social units which are attempting to define or redefine the terms of their interdependence."[4] In this analysis they stress the nature of the social and psychological (attitudinal) relationship among the parties, and they emphasize that negotiations are very much a part of an ongoing social relationship that precedes the formal negotiation and will continue to exist long afterwards. Indeed, the central role of negotiations in their conceptualization is to define the nature of this continuous and dynamic social relationship. This aspect of negotiations has been applied to the international arena by Roger Fisher. He stresses that the objective of negotiations is to create a good and enduring relationship among the parties that will enable "conflicting interests to be accommodated as well as possible and . . . shared interests to be advanced."[5]

Such a relationship cannot be constructed upon a win-lose approach to negotiations in which one party seeks victory at the expense of the other. Agreements that are essentially one-sided cannot endure indefinitely. This is due to the fact that parties that have been coerced into accepting agreements that do not serve their interests will invariably resent those agreements and the parties that imposed them. Furthermore, they will have every incentive to avoid, fail to implement, or even cheat outright on such agreements. So even the victorious party loses if an agreement intended to serve its interests fails to be fully implemented. Indeed, an agreement is worth preserving only if it serves the long-term interests of all parties. Not only must specific agreements be based upon mutual interests, but they must help to create a mutually beneficial relationship among the parties that will assure their long-term adherence.

Throughout much of history diplomats have pursued agreements to serve their narrow national interests, but the results of such agreements are generally short lived and unsatisfactory. Agreements imposed by one set of parties on another, such as the treaty reached at Versailles in 1919, invariably create resentment and fuel conflicts rather than ending them. Far from resolving violent conflicts, the result is often even more severe and destructive conflict. Despite the frequent historical examples of failed international negotiations based on the pursuit of narrow national interest, many approaches to negotiation continue to emphasize strategies for winning over the opponent. Analogies with sporting events are frequently utilized—"the ball is in the other player's court" or "we seek a level playing field"—all of which tend to suggest that diplomacy is rather like an athletic contest where one party wins and the other loses.

The essential thesis of this book, by contrast, is that this approach in the long-run creates situations in which everybody loses. What is needed is a negotiation process that produces outcomes in which all parties believe that they have won in some meaningful sense or feel that they have constructed agreements which serve their most fundamental interests. This approach to negotiation is difficult to realize, but a reorientation that emphasizes the role of diplomacy to solve common problems and produce mutually beneficial results is essential if diplomacy is going to be able to cope with the difficult problems of the increasingly interdependent world we are entering at the dawn of the twenty-first century.

OUTCOMES OF THE NEGOTIATION PROCESS

An analysis of the negotiation process would not be complete without an evaluation of the results of that process—the outcomes of negotiations. Before proceeding to a more extensive analysis of the process, it is useful to define more clearly the outcomes that serve as the dependent variables, the effects that I hope to explain through an analysis of the process of negotiating. Outcomes may be defined in at least four different ways, all of which are important for an evaluation of the impact that the process has on the results.[6]

First, the mere fact of agreement itself constitutes an outcome. In this sense, I am only concerned with the binary result of whether or not a negotiation results in agreement or stalemate. Indeed, some agreements may be of intrinsic value, largely because they may positively affect a long-term relationship. States may thus seek agreements not because they produce immediate, concrete benefits, but because they will improve the political relationship with other countries. All agreements, however, will be assumed to provide some benefits to the negotiating parties, whether tangible or intangible, immediate or long term. This is not the same as arguing that any agreement is intrinsically valuable no matter what its terms. On the contrary, I assume that an agreement is worthwhile and likely to be consummated only if it produces an outcome in which all parties perceive that they are better off with the agreement than they would be without it. Agreements that result from pure coercion, such as the imposition by the victors in a war of terms upon the defeated party, will not be considered to be a negotiated agreement. Although there may some element of coercion in all negotiations, I will exclude from consideration agreements that are imposed by brute force, where one party has no choice but to accede. Agreement outcomes are, therefore, assumed to be accepted by the parties as being better than their alternatives, although, if the alternatives are very unattractive, an agreement may not necessarily reflect significant absolute gains. Under this heading, however, it is not important whether or not the outcome represents the optimal benefits that could be achieved, if it is fair, or if it will endure. I am only concerned with whether or not the parties reach an agreement as a result of the negotiation process.

Second, we may examine the efficiency of the outcome. An agreement will be considered to be optimally efficient if it is the best agreement that the parties could achieve jointly under the circumstances. That is, if under given conditions the parties could have found alternative agreements in which all would be better off than under the present agreement, the present agreement will be considered to be inefficient or suboptimal. If, on the other hand, there is no way in which all parties may improve their result simultaneously, that is if gains by one party must necessarily come at the expense of other parties, then the negotiation may be considered to have reached the optimal joint outcome possible under the circumstances. When the parties have achieved an agreement in which there are no more mutually beneficial changes available in their positions, then they may be considered to have done the best possible within the constraints under which they are operating. Such an outcome may be considered to be efficient; on the other hand, as we will see later, most agreements in international negotiations fall far short of this criterion of efficiency.

Third, one may evaluate the stability of outcomes. An agreement may be considered to be stable if no party has an incentive to defect or to undermine the agreement. Defections may include renunciation of the agreement, cheating on the agreement, or willfully failing to implement the agreement with reasonable vigor and diligence. In order for an agreement to be stable, all parties must believe that they are better off with the agreement in force than without it, for whatever reason. If for any reason, they can find a short-term or long-term rationale for defecting from the agreement, it is considered to be unstable. Furthermore, stability may be viewed in dynamic as well as static terms. Agreements may create conditions that lead to their expansion, as in the process of spillover in which agreement in one functional area may be generalized into other areas of activity, and the scope of cooperation and agreement may consequently expand.[7] Indeed, as Underdal notes, there may be four states of stability in negotiation outcomes: "(1) stable, which does not provide incentives to expand cooperation or to defect; (2) unstable, which does not provide incentives to expand cooperation but does provide incentives to defect; (3) stable and dynamic, which provides incentives to expand cooperation but does not provide incentives to defect; and (4) empty, which provides incentives to expand cooperation and incentives to defect."[8]

Fourth, the outcomes of negotiations may be evaluated in terms of the distribution of the benefits. This basically refers to the extent that the gains from an agreement are spread equally or unequally across the parties to the negotiation. There may be many different criteria for evaluating the distribution of these gains. We may compare the absolute gains by the parties to a negotiation, or we may examine their relative gains in comparison with their next best alternative if the negotiations had failed. We may look at the change from the opening positions and compare the magnitude and frequency of concessions by the parties. Obviously the standard for a fair agreement is highly subjective, and parties to the negotiation may apply very different criteria for evaluating the fairness of alternative outcomes. But, assuming that we could agree upon a common standard for fairness, we could then array negotiation outcomes along a continuum from symmetrical, where the benefits to the parties are approximately equal, to asymmetrical, in which one or more parties gain a great deal of benefits while others benefit less.

GOALS OF THE ANALYTICAL FRAMEWORK

In summary, I want to be able to explain the outcomes of negotiations as a consequence of the process of negotiating. Yet these outcomes are multidimensional. I will start with a binary distinction between agreement and nonagreement. Within the class of agreements, I then look at three other criteria: (1) an optimally efficient agreement and a range of more or less suboptimal possible agreements; (2) a two-by-two classification of the stability of outcomes (stable versus unstable arrayed along with static and dynamic); and (3) a continuum ranging from symmetrically to asymmetrically distributed gains from agreement. In attempting to develop a theory of negotiations, therefore, I will consider not only what factors seem to contribute to the simple attainment of agreement rather than stalemate, but I will also consider a wide range of process variables that may affect the quality of the agreement achieved according to the criteria of efficiency, stability, and distribution.

In parts 2 and 3, I shall try to develop a model that relates many aspects of the negotiation process to outcomes, defined in terms of these criteria. We will be looking for those factors that contribute to or detract from the attainment of agreement, the efficiency of any agreement reached, the stability of the outcome, and the fairness of the result. I shall begin in part 2, however, with a very simple (and not very realistic) model of negotiations between two equal and unitary parties, and I will assume for the sake of simplicity that these two parties are both capable of making rational decisions. I will then examine the problem of interdependent decision making between two such rational individuals to provide a foundation for more complex models of international negotiation.

After creating such a simple, bilateral model, I shall then proceed in part 3 to add additional elements one-by-one, each of which will make the model both more complex and also more realistic. First, I will drop the assumption of equality between the parties, and look at the impact of asymmetries of power and interest. Second, I will modify the assumption that these individuals are perfectly rational, and introduce elements of individual personality and images, political culture, and interpersonal and intercultural communication into the model. Third, I will eliminate the assumption that negotiations are conducted by individuals (or a unitary actor) and focus instead on the role of national bureaucracies and politics on negotiations. Fourth, I will no longer view negotiations in static terms that relate initial conditions to outcomes, but rather I shall look at how the interaction process itself affects the outcomes of negotiations. Fifth, I will dismiss the assumption that the parties are negotiating in a vacuum and introduce the effects of the international environment upon negotiations. Sixth, I will drop the assumption of simple bilateral negotiations and introduce the role of third parties as arbitrators and mediators. Seventh and finally, I will expand the focus to include large, complex, and multilateral negotiations of the kind that occur in regional organizations such as the Organization of American States, global organizations such as the United Nations, and global conferences such as the U.N. Special Conference on the Environment and Development or the Uruguay Round of the General Agreement on Trade and Tariffs (GATT). By adding these elements of complexity one at a time, we can best analyze what special impact each feature has on the overall relationship between the negotiation process and its outcomes. Taken together, these seven explanatory factors will complement the initial axioms about bargaining and will contain the major ingredients necessary to construct a comprehensive framework for the analysis of international negotiations.

The resulting framework, however, should be viewed as more than a simple list of factors that might be used to explain the outcome of negotiations. It is not my intention to set forth a lengthy list of independent variables, presented more or less randomly, from which an analyst or practitioner might pick and choose in order to evaluate a particular negotiation. At the opposite extreme, however, and unlike much of the previous literature on negotiation,[9] I do not provide a single theory, set of concepts, or approach that seeks to explain the outcome of all negotiations or to present general prescriptive advice that claims to be applicable to every negotiation regardless of the parties, settings, issues, or negotiation structures. My objective is to be more open to alternative perspectives than the latter, while also being more systematic than the former.

Perhaps a useful metaphor for describing the approach that I have taken in this book is roughly analogous to a decision tree. In such a process, the analyst begins with some simple binary questions, and the answers to each of those questions lead one down one or another path. At various nodes along each path, additional branching questions are posed, additional choices become available while others may be cut off, and the analysis becomes richer, more specific, and detailed. The analyst begins with the most general explanatory framework possible and, by evaluating the conditions appropriate to any particular negotiation one wishes to analyze, one decides which path to follow. The choice among paths, then, suggests further questions that must be asked and proposes analytical tools that may be helpful in explaining the particular kind of negotiation under consideration.

In other words, the analytical framework presented here is less than a full-blown theory. The state of research in this field is still too primitive to present a single theory that can explain the impact of the negotiation process on outcomes in all classes of international negotiations. Indeed, we are still at an early stage in defining the criteria for selecting among the various kinds of theories that might be applicable to any particular case. Therefore, although some useful advice may be given to practitioners, it must always be presented with appropriate modesty. There is little evidence to support the validity of any single, unique approach to better negotiating techniques. On the other hand, the analysis here seeks to go beyond a simple typology of negotiations or a check list of factors that might account for the behavior of the parties in international negotiations. Rather it seeks to order those factors in a systematic way so as to begin with the most basic choices that an analyst must make—to start with the simplest assumptions that may provide the most general explanation, and then to move along to more refined choices and complex analyses that may offer a more differentiated explanation of the process in particular categories of negotiations.

At the outset, some of the most fundamental questions include: (1) how many parties are involved in the negotiation; (2) are the interests of the parties in direct opposition or are they potentially overlapping and compatible; and (3) what is the structure of the negotiation situation? Once these simple questions have been answered, one may then move on to more complex issues such as the availability of third parties, the decision rules that govern a negotiation, or the changing external environment within which a negotiation is imbedded. The next two sections of this book, therefore, begin with these simple questions and move on to more specific ones. Wherever there is evidence in the literature to elucidate the implications of proceeding down one branch versus another, I shall present those findings. However, it is important to be appropriately modest about the state of theory in this field. While our theoretical conceptualizations and empirical evidence about international negotiations have grown tremendously over the past three decades, we are still far short of a reliable theory to guide us unambiguously through this analysis. Any claim to such theoretical clarity would simply be premature at this stage of research and theoretical development. My task in parts 2 and 3 is to organize the existing knowledge and integrate it wherever possible into a single analytical framework that is hopefully tight enough to provide some useful guidance while remaining flexible enough to respond to the tremendous variations in negotiations taking place around the globe.

In part 4, as already indicated, I shall apply some of these theoretical principles to the case study summarized in the previous chapter. The case study of the negotiations among the United States, the Soviet Union, and the United Kingdom leading to the Partial Nuclear Test Ban Treaty of 1963 will be utilized both as an empirical foundation to validate the framework and as an opportunity to evaluate the utility of the framework in elucidating how the negotiation process affected the outcome reached in one of the most important negotiations of the second half of the twentieth century.

Part 2

Models of Bilateral Bargaining

Chapter 4

A Game Theoretic Foundation

M odern international negotiations are very complex activities in which multifaceted organizations, such as states, interact with one another in very complicated ways. If we want to develop an analytical framework, especially one that will apply to the many different kinds of international negotiations that occur all the time, we must begin by simplifying the process. Sometimes some of the simplest representations of a complex process may reveal the greatest insights about that process. Furthermore, the assumptions with which one starts can serve as a foundation on which to construct a more variegated and sophisticated theory, block-by-block.

Simple models of any process may also give us some deductive or logical power to draw inferences about the fundamental dimensions of a complex topic. As we seek to apply a logical framework to a large number of cases, we may need to modify and enlarge upon this simple formulation. But we can best develop a complex model of negotiations if we derive its essential elements from a simple set of fundamental assumptions or axioms. Different analysts of the negotiation process have started with many alternative assumptions, derived from fields such as human psychology, cultural anthropology, or international relations, to mention just a few. However, the most common foundation for negotiation theory is usually contained in a model of bargaining between two rational, unitary, and equally positioned parties. This model is derived from economic theory and from a special branch of mathematics known as game theory.

At first sight, game theoretic models may seem to have little direct bearing on international negotiations as we normally think of them, and the insights presented by game theory may seem to be extremely abstract. These concepts are developed on the basis of mathematical reasoning rather than upon any observation of actual negotiations in the real world of international diplomacy. While this is a serious limitation to their overall utility in explaining the outcome of any particular international negotiation, such as the test ban negotiations, it may be an advantage in introducing the fundamental axioms underlying a theory of negotiation. Game theory provides the logical underpinnings of any situation of interdependent decision making involving at least some conflicting interests between two or more parties. The very fact that the logical structure is independent from any concrete content helps us visualize the underlying principles without being distracted by the specifics of any particular situation.

Once the underlying principles are understood, they may serve as the foundation for a general theory of negotiation that may be applied to any specific case. In an effort to identify these underlying principles, I will begin with an analysis of the fundamental concepts of game theory. In so doing, I do not mean to suggest that the complexity of any particular negotiation can be fully captured by any such simple or abstract model. But I do assert that some insights may be gained from these models to serve as the foundation upon which a much more complex and sophisticated framework for analyzing international negotiations may be constructed.

Game theoretic models concern the kind of bargaining processes we normally identify with the marketplace, where one party wants to sell an item—a rug, an automobile, or whatever—and the other seeks to buy that product. Obviously the two parties have a common interest in making an exchange, but their interests are in direct conflict over the price of the product: the seller presumably prefers the highest possible price and the buyer prefers to pay the lowest. They must then haggle until they find some middle point at which the value of the money received exceeds the value of the product for the seller, yet the value of the product exceeds that of the money spent by the buyer. At such a point these two parties can reach an agreement.

Bargaining has been defined by Oran Young as "a means by which two or more purposive actors arrive at specific outcomes in situations in which: (1) the choices of the actors will determine the allocation of some value[s], (2) the outcome for each participant is a function of the behavior of the other[s], and (3) the outcome is achieved through negotiations between or among the players."[1]

The study of bargaining is usually based on the theory of mixed motive games, also known as non-zero-sum games, because they were developed to deal with situations of interdependent decision making where elements of both conflict and cooperation coexist. Before I present a game theoretic model of bargaining, however, it is necessary to introduce some basic concepts of the theory of games, especially those found in zero-sum games or games of pure conflict. Obviously these models are not at all appropriate to bargaining situations, since bargaining is possible only when cooperative interests exist, but it is easier to understand the theory of non-zero-sum games by beginning with the simpler theory of two-person, zero-sum games. Game theory was originally developed to analyze simple games of conflict, such as poker, where there are two or more players and where the sum of all the gains and losses of all players equals zero. That is, whatever is won by some players in the game equals the amount lost by other players. After an evening game of poker, a lot of money may have changed hands, but the total amount of money in the room should not have changed; some players have won money while others have lost it, but when all the winnings and losses are added up, the result should equal zero. Since the outcome of a zero-sum game like poker is dependent on the choices made by all of the players, it may provide some interesting insights about processes such as bargaining that involve interdependent decision making.

A game always involves at least six characteristics:

1. There must be at least two players, and games are divided into two broad categories depending on whether there are two players (two-person games) or more than two players (n-person games).

2. Play starts when one player makes a choice or a move from among a fixed number of options.

3. A game may be played only once or it may be extended to a finite or infinite series of plays; in multiple-play games a situation results from the first move that affects the response of the other players.

4. Each play thereafter also produces a certain situation; if the choices are known, as in many situations where the players have complete information, then the situation at each stage of the game affects subsequent plays.

5. In games of successive choices, there are termination rules that determine when the game will come to an end.

6. Every play of the game ends with gains or losses, called payoffs, to all of the players, defined in terms of units of value called utilities.[2]

The values that the players receive from the play of the game, their utilities, reflect the psychological worth to the players of each outcome. A utility is a summary measure of all of the costs and benefits that collectively may be associated with a particular outcome. In international negotiations, for example, it may include a combination of such values as economic wealth, security, freedom from external control, prestige, or anything else that states or other nonstate actors may value.

Game theory basically assumes that the players are rational in that they prefer to receive the highest possible utilities. In other words, players will try to maximize their gains or, if gains cannot be achieved, at least to minimize their losses. These outcomes are usually expressed in probabilistic terms as expected utility, defined as the probability of each outcome times the utility of each possible outcome, summed across all possible outcomes. A rational actor will choose the action that offers the greatest expected utility. In other words, one may prefer a lower valued, but highly likely, outcome to one that may have a higher absolute value, but where the likelihood of obtaining that value is remote.

For example, in trying to decide whether or not to open hostilities against Iraq in the Persian Gulf conflict of 1990–91, the U.S. government had to weigh two choices: (1) extending economic sanctions, which involved low costs, but also seemed to have a low probability of success; or (2) beginning an invasion of Kuwait and Iraq, with higher costs, but also with a higher probability of success. In the debate in the U.S. Congress over authorizing the use of force, different members of Congress expressed different personal assessments of the expected utilities associated with sanctions versus armed combat. In the end, the Bush administration successfully persuaded a majority of the members of Congress of their assessment, namely that the net expected utility of an invasion was more positive (or less negative) than the result expected from a continuation of economic sanctions. Given this assessment, the decision to invade was a rational decision. It is important to note that this does not mean that it was the right decision in a moral sense or even that in retrospect the Bush administration's assessment of the probabilities, benefits, and costs was correct; those all remain open to debate. But, in this sense, a rational decision is simply one in which decision makers choose that strategy which maximizes their subjective expected utilities, as they estimate them at the time they must make their decision.

Games are also classified according to the way in which utilities are distributed. A zero-sum game is one in which the joint utility of all the players equals zero, that is, where the utility of all the players sums to zero; in this case, the gains of some players must be offset by equal losses to others. This is a situation rare in international politics, since there are few situations of pure conflict. However, issues such as territorial disputes can take on elements closely approximating a zero-sum game. For example, in the Camp David negotiations on the Middle East, the Sinai could not belong simultaneously to Israel and Egypt, and the way that would it be divided represented a largely zero-sum conflict between those two states. Conversely, a non-zero-sum game is one in which this constraint does not apply and where the sum of gains and losses may be positive or negative. In such a game, all may win, all may lose, or some may gain while others lose, but the net amount of gains and losses may still be greater or less than zero. For example, in international politics, the basic elements of the cold-war rivalry between the United States and the Soviet Union represented a non-zero-sum game. In terms of security, both could lose from a mutually destructive nuclear war, one could win at the other's expense by achieving military and/or political dominance, or both could win by a cooperative easing of tensions in which both sides felt more secure.

Game theory not only assumes that the players are rational, but it also assumes that they have perfect information. Included in that perfect information is assumed to be knowledge of the utilities of all of the players, including themselves. Later I shall turn to the many situations in international politics where this assumption is not applicable, but for the moment such a simplifying assumption is necessary to present the basic elements of game theory. Given this information about the utilities of all of the players, each player may then adopt a strategy, the set of choices that each player will select in the face of all possible contingencies. In principle, each player should have at the beginning a strategy for responding to all possible contingencies throughout the entire play of an extended game, although we know that in complex games like chess with many choices to be made, such advance planning is impossible for any person to achieve. Nonetheless, there is little doubt that the best chess players are generally those that can adopt a strategy for a series of contingencies well beyond the current choice, as opposed to those beginners that usually develop their strategy one move at a time.

We may also distinguish between two classes of strategies, pure and mixed. A pure strategy applies when one strategy is always the best, whereas the latter involves a random but carefully proportioned combination of choices. The choices and payoffs in game theory are typically depicted in terms of a matrix. In a two-person game, player 1's choices are depicted by the choices along the rows or horizontal dimension (R_1, R_2, R_3 in figure 4.1), whereas player 2's choices are depicted along the columns (C_1, C_2, C_3 in figure 4.1). Traditionally, the payoffs for row are written first and those for column second, separated by a comma. For zero-sum games, only row's payoffs are generally listed, since the payoffs for column are the same with the sign reversed; however, for clarity in the examples presented here, I present both row's and column's payoffs.

Figure 4.1 illustrates the first case of a pure strategy, which applies when both players have a dominant strategy, defined as a situation in which both players have one best choice no matter what the other does. In this case, for row choice 2 is always best: if column chooses C_1, then -1 is preferable to -3 or -2; if column chooses C_2, 5 is preferred to 0 or 2; and if column chooses C_3, 2 is better than 1 or 0. Similarly, for column

Column

		C_1	C_2	C3
	R_1	-3,3	0,0	1,-1
Row	R_2	-1,1	5,-5	2,-2
	R_3	-2,2	2,-2	0,0

Figure 4.1 Pure Strategy—Both Have Dominant Strategy

choice 1 is always best: if row chooses R_1, then 3 is better than 0 or -1; if row chooses R_2, then 1 is better than -5 or -2, and if row chooses R_3, then 2 is preferred to -2 or 0. In this case, even if they did not know one another's utilities, column would always choose 1 and row would always select 2: these are pure strategies. Therefore, there is a determinate payoff in which row always loses 1 and column always gains 1.

The second case of a pure strategy applies when only one player has a dominant strategy, but where there is perfect information, so that the second selects his or her best choice in light of the dominant strategy of the other. This is depicted in figure 4.2, where row has a dominant strategy of R_2. On the other hand, column now prefers C_3 if row chooses R_1, C_1 if row chooses R_2, and C_2 if row chooses R_3. Since column knows, however, that row has a dominant strategy at R_2, then column will always select C_1, producing -1 for row and +1 for column every time this game is played. In both of these cases, neither player's strategy is con-

Column

		C_1	C_2	C3
	R_1	-3,3	0,0	-10,10
Row	R_2	-1,1	5,-5	2,-2
	R_3	-2,2	-4,4	0,0

Figure 4.2 Pure Strategy—One Player Has Dominant Strategy

tingent on the play of the other, as long as the other is assumed to be rational.

The third and most complicated case of a pure strategy applies when neither player has a dominant strategy, but where each players has a saddle point. This point may be found through the key theorem of zero-sum game theory, known as the minimax solution. This represents the point at which the minimum of one player's maxima (the smallest of possible gains) and the maximum of the other player's minima (the smallest of possible losses) coincide. This point of coincidence or the saddle point applies for row when one payoff is the smallest in its row and at the same time the largest in its column; for column it is symmetrical, but the inverse, when a payoff is smallest in its column and largest in its row. In figure 4.3, we can see that -1 is the lowest payoff for row in R_2 and the highest (or least negative) in C_1. For column, 1 is the lowest

Column

		C_1	C_2	C_3
	R_1	-3,3	18,-18	-20,20
Row	R_2	-1,1	5,-5	2,-2
	R_3	-2,2	-4,4	15,-15

Figure 4.3 Pure Strategy—Neither Player Has Dominant Strategy: The Minimax Solution

payoff in C_1 and the highest in R_2. If both players are rational and play their minimax strategies, column can never do better than C_1 with a payoff of +1, whereas row can never do better than R_2 with a result of -1.

A quick examination of figure 4.3 will show that if one player deviates from its minimax strategy while the other continues to play its minimax strategy, the one deviating will only make itself worse off. Suppose, for example, that row is unhappy with the consistent loss of 1 unit of utility from playing R_2, so she shifts to R_1 in the hope of getting a better payoff. However, since column will continue to play its minimax strategy and select C_1, then row's move drops its payoff from -1 to -3, while column benefits from row's irrational move by increasing her payoff from +1 to +3. In other words, the saddle point indicates the best strategy that each player can follow given the structure of the game, and it dictates pure strategies for both players. As Rapoport summarizes this critical minimax principle: "If a two-person zero-sum game has saddle points, the best each player can do (assuming both to be rational) is to choose the strategy (i.e., the row or column of the game matrix) which contains a saddle point."[3]

In games such as these with pure strategies and saddle points no negotiations are required. In these situations the optimal interest of each player is determined by the saddle point, and each will always select her or his pure strategy unilaterally regardless of what the other does. This way each can be assured of maximum gains or minimum losses unilaterally. There is no way that a better outcome can be obtained by negotiating with a rational partner since by definition any payoff that improved one's own position would lead to a reduced payoff for the other. However, we will see later that these unilateral strategies are still relevant to bargaining, because even in non-zero-sum situations in which there are mutually beneficial outcomes, one can also compare outcomes with what one could obtain by playing the game as if it were a zero-sum game in which one plays one's best unilateral strategy. A rational player will never accept a negotiated solution that leaves one worse off than one's best unilateral strategy.

Before developing this argument further, however, it is necessary to introduce one other concept from zero-sum game theory, mixed strategies. A mixed strategy is employed in zero-sum games where there are no saddle points and no pure strategies to follow. A classic illustration of such a game is often called "button-button," in which one player hides a button in her left or right hand and the other attempts to guess which hand it is hidden in. A plausible matrix for payoffs from button-button is presented in figure 4.4.

This game has no saddle point. If hider consistently hides the button in her left hand seeking the maximum gain of +4, then the guesser

| | **Guesser** | |
	G_L	G_R
H_L	-2,2	4,-4
H_R	2,-2	-1,1

Hider

Figure 4.4 Mixed Strategy—"Button-Button"

will figure out the hider's strategy after a very few plays of the game and always guess the left hand; this pure strategy would be costly for the hider because she would now lose 2 regularly rather than winning 4. Similarly, if the guesser follows a pure strategy of always guessing left in an effort to win 2, then hider will figure this out and place the button in her right hand, causing the guesser to lose 2. The solution is, of course, for each player to follow a mixed rather than a pure strategy. The hider should randomize her choices between the two hands, but not in an equal proportion since the payoffs are not equal between the two hands. The best strategy is for the hider to favor her right hand two-thirds of the time and her left hand one-third of the time. Similarly, guesser will make randomized choices between the two hands in a definite proportion. In this case, guesser's best strategy is to select the left hand five-ninths of the time and the right hand four-ninths of the time. The outcome of a game played many times will be for the hider to win an average of two-thirds of a utility each time. Neither can expect to do better over the long run, though each may win or lose different amounts on any single play of the game since the outcome for any one play is not determined.[4]

Thus, we may see that every two-person, zero-sum game has a pair of optimal strategies, either pure or mixed. A rational player will calculate the optimal strategy and play it regardless of what the other player does, and in this way be assured of maximizing gains or minimizing losses compared to any other strategy, which would be suboptimal. The same does not hold true for non-zero-sum games, and it is in part for this reason that these games are more interesting as a foundation for theories of bargaining. In a zero-sum game, no bargaining is required since the structure of the game itself determines the outcomes for rational players. In non-zero-sum games, on the other hand, there are generally no determinate solutions, so that the parties may try to negotiate joint strategies that will improve payoffs for both compared to unilaterally determined strategies. Similarly, in zero-sum games, there are no negotiated solutions that can benefit both parties simultaneously, since their payoffs are always inverse of one another. By contrast, non-zero-sum games may contain outcomes (pairs of strategies) that are preferred by both players to other outcomes, thus introducing an element of co-operation into an otherwise conflictual situation.

One such classic non-zero-sum game, developed by Luce and Raiffa, is known by the title of "the battle of the sexes."[5] Liberally retold, it involves the story of a couple planning to go out every Saturday night through a long winter, but the man prefers to attend the opera and the woman prefers to go to a boxing match. However, because they enjoy one another's company, their preference to go together exceeds their own individual preferences. Yet the question still remains about which activity they will attend each Saturday night. A payoff matrix for such a situation is depicted in figure 4.5. In this matrix there are three different categories of outcomes on any given Saturday: (1) (OP,OP=10,0) or (BOX,BOX=0,10) are the two outcomes in which they agree to go together to one event or the other, so that one gains (the man if they both select OP and the woman if they both select BOX), whereas the other receives 0 satisfaction, but neither loses; (2) (OP,BOX=-3,-3) represents their threat potential, where each one follows his or her own preference and both lose; or (3) (BOX,OP=-2,-2) represents the frustration resulting from what Rapoport calls "misplaced altruism," where both change their minds and do what the other preferred, only to find that the other has changed his or her mind also. Since their disappointment at being alone and at the event that neither one wanted to attend may be partially offset by their knowledge that they both tried to cooperate, their loss may not be as great as in the case where they each went selfishly on their own way.

Woman

		OP	BOX
Man	OP	10,0	-3,-3
	BOX	-2,-2	0,10

Figure 4.5 Mixed Strategy—The Battle of the Sexes

This payoff matrix is depicted graphically in figure 4.6.[6] The polygon depicted in this diagram encloses all of the possible payoffs from any series of mixed strategies that the two could employ over the season. A purely random mixture of strategies could lead to any long-term solution within the boundaries of this polygon. Nevertheless, at any point within this polygon both players can improve their joint payoffs by moving in a northeasterly direction, that is upwards and to the right, except along the line connecting OP,BOX and BOX,OP. Along this northeasterly boundary, usually referred to in economics as the Pareto-Optimal frontier, it is impossible for both players to improve their position simultaneously. If one party improves its position along this line, the other will lose. This line may also be referred to as the negotiation set, and along it the parties find themselves engaged in an essentially zero-

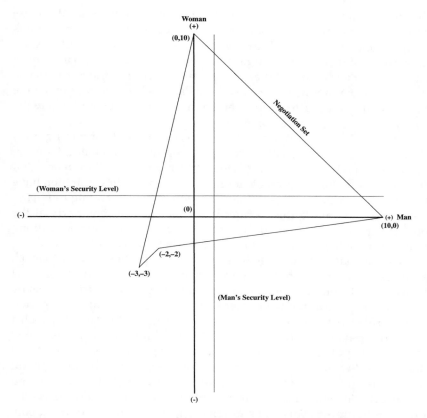

Figure 4.6 The Payoff Polygon—The Battle of the Sexes. Based on Anatol Rapoport, *Two-Person Game Theory: The Essential Ideas* **(Ann Arbor: University of Michigan Press, 1969), pp. 99, 102.**

sum game. In short, the entire polygon depicts a classic non-zero-sum situation. From any given point within this polygon, moves in a northeasterly direction are mutually beneficial and positive-sum, whereas moves in a southwesterly direction are mutually harmful and negative-sum.

Agreement to move toward solutions in the northeast and away from the southwest are essentially cooperative, and this aspect of the bargaining problem has been referred to by Walton and McKersie as integrative bargaining, in which the objectives of one party "are *not* in fundamental conflict with those of the other party."[7] Rational parties will bargain until they have moved as far as possible in the northeasterly direction, that is toward the Pareto-Optimal frontier. Any other solution is suboptimal for them collectively. At the same time, the conflictual elements of bargaining are represented by the possibilities of moves either in a northwesterly direction (where the woman benefits at the expense of the man) or in the southeasterly direction (where the man gains at the woman's expense). Movements in either of these directions are illustrative of distributive bargaining, where one party's goals "are in basic conflict with those of the other party."[8] Of course, the most intense distributive bargaining occurs along the Pareto-Optimal frontier, where the possibility for mutual improvement has disappeared and where the bargaining becomes purely zero-sum.

This model reveals one of the most basic axioms of bargaining theories, namely that actors will strive to reach optimal agreements by moving integratively toward the northeast frontier. Once they reach that frontier, it is no longer possible to make joint gains; they will then have to bargain distributively over the allocation of benefits along that frontier. Bargaining along this frontier involves gains for one party at the other's expense. Therefore, the determination of the specific point along that frontier where agreement is reached is a fairly complex issue.

We may narrow the range within which the parties may try to reach agreement along this frontier, however, by introducing the concept of the security level. Both players may determine their security levels by playing the game as if it were a zero-sum game and by calculating their minimax strategy. This way each player may guarantee him or herself a minimum payoff. In our example, if the minimum is negative, it will intersect the polygon south or west of the origin, in which case it will not intersect with the negotiation set. However, if the minimum payoff for each is positive, then it will intersect north or east of the origin and the security level of each player will intersect the negotiation set as depicted in figure 4.6. This will shorten the negotiation set, so that it consists of that portion of the northeast frontier that exceeds the security level of both players.

This reduced negotiation set may be referred to as bargaining space, the range within which acceptable agreements may be reached. In the example above of the battle of the sexes, if the man goes to the boxing matches two-thirds of the time and the opera one-third of the time, he can guarantee himself a payoff of at least +0.95; conversely, if the woman goes to the opera two-thirds of the time and the boxing matches one-third of the time, then she can guarantee herself an average payoff of +0.95. Neither will accept a solution that produces a lower payoff. Only solutions that fall within this restricted negotiation set or bargaining space may improve their payoffs compared with their best minimax or unilateral strategy.

Therefore, solutions to bargaining problems will fall along the negotiation set between the limits set by the security levels of both parties. These principles, however, suggest only a range of possible solutions to the bargaining problem, not an exact point of solution. Game theorists differ about determining the precise point of agreement, and most recognize that it may depend largely on factors not taken into account by pure bargaining theory. However, several formal attempts have been made to predict the precise point of agreement or contract. Obviously the solution will reflect some mixed strategy, and the balance of the outcomes usually reflects the relative losses to the two parties from the failure to agree. In the absence of agreement, both parties may pursue their own minimax strategies in order to guarantee themselves a certain minimum payoff. Thus, the intersection of the security levels provides a point around which agreement may be fashioned. Of course, the security levels generally intersect well below the northeast frontier. However, if one takes the intersection of the security levels as a starting point and then draws a straight line 45 degrees northeast from that point, the location at which that line intersects with the northeast frontier will constitute the fair or equitable point of agreement, often referred to as the Nash solution.[9] If the utilities of both parties are symmetrical, as in the battle of the sexes example, then they should split the difference between their security levels and arrive at a fifty-percent solution. In this illustration, the two parties should be able to agree to go to the opera together 50 percent of the time and go together to the boxing matches the other 50 percent of the time. In this case, their average payoff would rise to 5 units of utility each, well above their security levels.

On the other hand, if their payoffs were not symmetrical, then this procedure would produce an unequal outcome in favor of the party that had the lower losses associated with nonagreement. For example, if the man lost four units instead of two from solution BOX,OP while woman's remained at two, and if the man lost six units instead of three from solution OP,BOX while woman's losses remained at three, then man's bargaining position would be weakened proportionately and the outcome would tend to favor going together more often to the boxing matches than to the opera as preferred by the woman. This is because the woman's threat potential, the threat to walk out of the negotiations, is greater than the man's because her losses from walking out would be less severe than his. This line of reasoning suggests a third axiom about bargaining that may be derived from game theory.

The game theoretic perspective on negotiations, therefore, suggests three axioms to serve as a foundation for theories of bargaining:

> Axiom 1: In bargaining situations parties will seek optimal solutions, that is, solutions along the frontier beyond which they are no longer able to improve their positions jointly; in other words, all solution should lie along the negotiation set.

> Axiom 2: In bargaining situations parties will not accept agree-

ments that leave them worse off than the results that they could obtain through unilateral actions; that is, they will not accept solutions that fall below their security levels.

> Axiom 3: In a bargaining situation, if the payoffs for the two parties associated with nonagreement are unequal, then the solution will tend to favor the outcome preferred by the party with the lower losses from the failure to agree.

However, all attempts to predict precise points of agreement generally impose more restrictive assumptions than seem plausible with respect to actual international negotiations. As Young has noted, none of the solutions that have been proposed by game theorists "yields good results when treated as 'descriptive' theory rather than 'prescriptive' theory."[10] Therefore, I shall argue in subsequent chapters that, while outcomes from negotiations will generally fall within the rough boundaries defined by bargaining space, the exact results are more likely to reflect other conditions, such as those introduced by psychological, behavioral, structural, and environmental considerations. In short, I do assume that negotiators will be sufficiently rational to avoid solutions that would produce either individual or joint losses. Therefore, they will seek agreements that fall along the negotiation set and within the limits established by their own security levels. Within these bounds, however, the dictates of rationality become ambiguous and a subject of controversy among game theorists, and in fact many variables not accounted for by game theory are more likely to be influential in determining actual outcomes.

The concepts presented in this chapter are highly abstract and have little direct bearing on international negotiations; my primary purpose in this chapter has been to introduce some fundamental concepts that may be applied later as a foundation for analyzing international negotiations. However, I will illustrate some of the major concepts loosely here by reference to the example of trade negotiations between the United States and Japan.

Trade negotiations between the United States and Japan have frequently centered around the very sensitive issue of automobile imports: Japan wants to export more cars to the United States, whereas the latter wishes to limit imports in order to protect the domestic automobile industry. Conversely, the United States would like to export more of its cars to Japan, lowering Japanese barriers to U.S. automobile imports. When the problem is conceived this way, as it often has been in past negotiations, this is largely a zero-sum negotiation: each side wants to decrease the other's imports into its own country while increasing its exports to the other.

This negotiation may be converted to a less zero-sum situation, however, by taking advantage of the economic theory of comparative advantage. Under this theory, trade should be based on each country producing what it can produce cheaper and then trading with the other. In this case, the United States might agree to accept more Japanese automobile imports (making higher quality, lower priced goods available to American consumers, while also benefiting Japanese automobile producers) if Japan reduces barriers to the importation of agricultural products from the United States (allowing less expensive, better produce for Japanese consumers, while benefiting American farmers). There are, of course, upper limits on the mutual profitability of such trade, that is, there is a Pareto-Optimal frontier beyond which such trade may not be expanded in a mutually beneficial way. In addition, the precise terms of trade between Japanese automobiles and American farm produce must still be negotiated, even if the Pareto-Optimal frontier has been reached. Yet such a tradeoff would permit both parties to improve their position jointly compared to the status quo, moving them out toward the northeastern frontier in their terms of trade, rather than leaving them stuck in a fruitless zero-sum negotiation over automobiles treated in isolation. Bargaining theory may not identify the precise solution for the best trading arrangement, but it can certainly assist the negotiators in moving from zero-sum to positive-sum negotiations in which both parties may benefit.[11]

Although game theory provides a useful foundation for models of bargaining, it also has a number of serious limitations that restrict its applicability to the analysis of the bargaining process. Perhaps most important is the fact that game theory is a static model that focuses almost exclusively on the relationship between initial conditions and outcomes, with almost no attention being paid to the process of bargaining. This means that this approach is not very useful in describing more dynamic aspects of the bargaining process. In particular, in real bargaining situations it is almost impossible to identify an optimal strategy for the entire play of the game in advance. Bargaining is a much more interactive process, and strategies may have to adapt accordingly. A second problem stems from some of its simplifying assumptions, especially the assumption of perfect information that is seldom obtainable in the real world where bargaining takes place. Therefore, game theory is incapable of dealing with problems such as uncertainty, the indeterminacy of options, the tactical manipulation of information, or outright deception. Third, game theoretic models tend to assume that utilities are fixed and unchanging, so that a further dynamic element of the process of changing utilities is not captured well within this framework. Utilities may change as a result of a changing environment, as a consequence of manipulation by the other parties, or due to internal changes within any of the parties to a bargaining situation; yet all of these considerations affecting the change of utilities during the course of the bargaining process remain outside the purview of game theory. Finally, in actual bargaining situations the parties will not necessarily obtain solutions prescribed by game theory, that is outcomes that are both Pareto-Optimal and equitable, although game theory may provide a normative guide as to how to approach these standards. The theory may have more normative than predictive power.

As a consequence of all of these limitations, bargaining models of the negotiation process have used a few basic axioms taken from game theory, and then developed a more complex and dynamic theory of bargaining on the basis of those few fundamental axioms. It is to that more complex framework of bargaining that I shall turn to in the next chapter.

Chapter 5

A Traditional Bargaining Model

The kind of game theoretic arguments presented in the last chapter have formed the foundation for many models of bargaining, especially of the bargaining process in international negotiations. As we have seen in the previous chapter, the economist John Nash first applied game theory to the problem of bargaining in general, and this was introduced into the literature of international negotiations by the seminal work of Thomas Schelling, an economist, in his 1960 book, *The Strategy of Conflict*.[1] Schelling argued that "most conflict situations are essentially bargaining situations. They are situations in which the ability of one participant to gain his ends is dependent to an important degree on the choices or decisions that the other participant will make."[2] On the basis of Schelling's work, there emerged in the literature of international negotiations a set of models, all of which took the basic logic of bargaining as the foundation for the study of international negotiation. Indeed, this paradigm or perspective was probably the dominant lens through which scholars of international negotiations viewed their subject throughout most of the decades of the 1960s and 1970s. Therefore, I shall refer to this school of analysts as the traditional bargaining theorists.

This traditional bargaining model found a welcome home within the realist tradition, which dominated the study of international politics in the United States and many other countries for decades. Realists emphasized the role of power in international politics and negotiations. For example, in a classic realist work, Hans Morgenthau argues that there are three primary means of diplomacy: "persuasion, compromise, and threat of force"; the great negotiator was someone who would put the "right emphasis at any particular moment on each of these three means"; and the diplomat "must at the same time use persuasion, hold out the advantages of a compromise, and impress the other side with the military strength of his country."[3] Thus, power was broadly defined in this tradition to include skills of persuasion and artful compromise, but always in the context of military force. This too was quite consistent with

Schelling's definition of bargaining strategy as not being "concerned with the efficient *application* of force but with the *exploitation of potential force.*"[4]

This tradition has been carried on in more recent work in international politics by so-called neorealists such as Kenneth Waltz, whose *Theory of International Politics* became one of the most influential works in the decade of the 1980s. Waltz's thesis is that the structure of the international system is based largely on the distribution of capabilities among actors within the system, and this distribution of power becomes the critical factor in explaining international politics. All interactions among states, including bargaining and negotiation, are highly constrained by the structure of the system. Thus, for Waltz, bargaining is largely viewed as a consequence of the number of major actors in the system—two or more—and of their relative capabilities. In the end, especially in security matters, it is power that is the ultimate deciding factor in international politics, especially the power of large states endowed with extensive capability to control the behavior of others. "To interdict the use of force by the threat of force, to oppose force with force, to influence the policies of states by the threat or use of force: These have been and continue to be the most important means of control in security matters. With a highly unequal distribution of world power, some states, by manipulating the threat of force, are able to moderate others' use of force internationally."[5]

Given the emphasis on power and manipulation within the realist tradition, it is not surprising that realist conceptions of negotiations have tended to emphasize the tactics of manipulation within the bargaining process, such as commitments, threats, and promises. The outcome of the bargaining process is no longer predetermined by the structure of the game, but rather it is directly influenced by the ability to manipulate the positions of other parties with reference to the potential application of force. As we shall see later, much recent work on international negotiation has tried to break with some of these assumptions of the realist tradition. But we shall also see that this break has not been complete, and that almost all theories of negotiation borrow some central concepts and theoretical formulations from these traditional bargaining models. It is in that light that we shall proceed to introduce some of the major elements of this bargaining model, derived largely from the fundamental axioms of game theory presented in the previous chapter.

A basic model of bilateral bargaining is depicted in figure 5.1. In this model we have a single issue, such as the price of an automobile, depicted along the horizontal continuum, referred to as the issue dimension. An agreement may be reached, in theory, at any position along this continuum. This framework focuses on the bargaining process in which the parties stake out positions and then change those positions along an issue dimension. This is roughly analogous to the northwest to

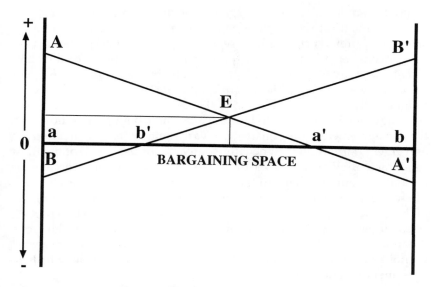

Figure 5.1 A Simple Model of Two-Party Bargaining
1. **Horizontal Axis = Issue Dimension**
2. **Vertical Axis = Gains (+) and Losses (-) Relative to Nonagreement (0)**
3. **A—A' = A's Preference Curve**
4. **B—B' = B's Preference Curve**
5. **a = A's preferred outcome**
   a' = A's minimum acceptable outcome
   b = B's preferred outcome
   b' = B's minimum acceptable outcome
6. **E = point of "equitable" solution, where gains of both parties relative to nonagreement equal.**

southeast dimension of conflict in the game theoretic models presented in the previous chapter.

The value of an agreement (called the payoff by game theorists) at any position along this continuum varies for each of the parties, and this value is expressed on the vertical dimension. Above the midpoint, the value of an agreement is increasingly positive, whereas below this midpoint the value of an agreement is negative and declining in value. At the midpoint, the value of the agreement is zero for each party; at this point, the parties are indifferent between agreement and no agreement. We may then depict the outcomes or payoffs for each of the parties for agreement at all points along the issue dimension. This may be referred to as the preference curves of each of the parties, and they are depicted in figure 5.1 by lines $A-A'$ for actor A and $B-B'$ for actor B. Here we may see that actor A prefers agreements toward the left end of the issue dimension, point a on the horizontal line, where it has substantial positive value from an agreement, and conversely actor B prefers agreements at the far right end of the issue dimension, at point b. Thus, their preferences are inverse, that is A (the buyer) prefers a very low price whereas B (the seller) prefers a very high price for the automobile. We may illustrate this hypothetically by assuming that B opens the bidding at point b, which is a price of $6,000, whereas A responds at point a with an opening offer of $4,000.

The crucial problem is to locate space where both parties, however, find an agreement to be beneficial. Clearly neither party will accept an agreement that produces a negative outcome for itself; one of the most fundamental axioms derived from game theory was that agreements are only acceptable that produce a net positive payoff for each party. Therefore, the range of space within which agreements may occur is set off by the resistance points or points of indifference for the two parties. These resistance points correspond to the security levels in the game theoretic models, in that they indicate the value that a party can get without a negotiated agreement by acting unilaterally, below which an agreement will no longer be advantageous.

These resistance points may be determined in several ways. One may enter into a negotiation with an absolute bottom line set according to some abstract criteria of gains and losses. However, this model suggests that the bottom line should not be set arbitrarily, but rather should be determined by identifying that point at which agreement would no longer be beneficial for the party. In order to determine this point, the party must first ask itself what is the value associated with nonagreement, or in other words, what will happen if the negotiations break off and no agreement is reached. This may be very costly: for example, in the missile crisis in Cuba in 1962, it was evident to many that the failure to reach agreement in the negotiations between the United States and the Soviet Union could lead to a very destructive nuclear war. In this instance, the alternative to a negotiated agreement was extremely unattractive, so that extraordinary measures were taken by both parties to reach agreement.

On the other hand, in buying an automobile, the buyer may always compare the price for the automobile under negotiation with the alternative price that he or she would have to pay for a similar car from another seller. In this case, the buyer may have already located a good car at a reasonable price, and may be interested in agreement only if he or she can get an even better deal from this particular negotiation. However, failure to agree is not necessarily very costly since there is a perfectly satisfactory alternative if the negotiation fails.

A similar situation may be illustrated in international relations, when presidents George Bush and Saddam Hussein (represented in Geneva by U.S. Secretary of State James Baker and Iraqi Foreign Minister Tariq

Aziz) were negotiating over the Iraqi invasion of Kuwait on 9 January 1991. Bush's alternative to a negotiated settlement was not nearly so unattractive as Kennedy's when he was negotiating with Soviet Premier Nikita Khrushchev in 1962. The United States had overwhelming military superiority in the Persian Gulf in place by the beginning of 1991, giving the United States the ability to conduct the conflict with conventional weapons without in any way threatening the territory of the United States. Thus, the alternative to a negotiated agreement, namely conventional war in the Persian Gulf, was not so unattractive for Bush; indeed, many have speculated that he may even have relished the opportunity to "teach Saddam Hussein a lesson." Under these conditions, Bush's resistance point was very high, and he was in a position to demand a great deal from the negotiations before consenting to a negotiated settlement of the conflict. It was for this reason that he sent Baker to Geneva essentially without any mandate to negotiate, since he was under little pressure to achieve a negotiated solution to the conflict.[6]

In the same situation, it is at least plausible that Saddam Hussein perceived that the war option was a dominant strategy: in the unlikely event that Iraq won the war with the U.N. command led by the United States, Hussein would emerge as the undisputed leader of the Arab world. In the more likely case that he lost, he could also portray himself as a martyr for the Arab cause who had at least stood up to the "great Satan." Either alternative seemed preferable to a negotiated settlement that would have almost certainly left Iraq humiliated before the world community. While many Westerners perceived this behavior as irrational, it is clear that the logic of Hussein's calculations had a certain internal rationality that dictated his bargaining behavior and refusal to accept a negotiated settlement in this difficult situation. Aziz came to Geneva with instructions to threaten an Iraqi attack on Israel if the United States began military action after 15 January 1991—the deadline established for Iraqi withdrawal from Kuwait; the Iraqi's would negotiate further only if the United States withdrew that deadline.[7] Stalemate was virtually inevitable, as was the outbreak of open warfare.

This principle through which negotiators determine their resistance points by comparing the value of agreement at any stage with the value of no agreement has been referred to by Roger Fisher and William Ury as the BATNA—the Best Alternative To a Negotiated Agreement. An agreement will be acceptable only if it produces a better result than each party could obtain in the absence of an agreement. As Fisher and Ury note, the BATNA is "the standard against which any proposed agreement should be measured. That is the only standard which can protect you both from accepting terms that are too unfavorable and from rejecting terms it would be in your interest to accept."[8] To pursue our example of bargaining about the sale of an automobile a bit further, the seller may have already received a standing offer of $4,600 for the car; since this alternative is still available, this is the next best alternative to striking a deal with the present potential buyer. At the same time, the buyer may have seen a car that he or she valued about the same at another location for $5,600; as long as the buyer knows that this car has not been sold, this serves as his or her best alternative to agreement. The buyer will not pay more than $5,600 for the car in the present negotiation because he or she knows of a comparable car for $5,600 from another seller.

These resistance points or BATNAs are depicted in figure 5.1 as the point at which the preference curve of each actor crosses the line of neutral or zero payoff, namely point a' for actor A and point b' for actor B. At the point where the preference curve crosses the neutral line, each party has no preference, or in the terminology of economics, is indifferent, between this agreement and the next best alternative. Agreements to the right of a' are unacceptable for A and to the left of b' are unacceptable to B. In our automobile example, a' is $4,600 for the seller, and b' is $5,600 for the buyer. The space between a' and b' is referred to as bargaining space, the range within which agreements must be reached to be acceptable simultaneously to both parties. In our illustration, any agreement between $4,600 and $5,600 is acceptable to both parties in the sense that any agreement within this range would leave both better off than with their next best alternative.

Bargaining theory, just like game theory, does not suggest a clear solution about where agreement will be reached within this range. Of course, just as in the game theoretic formulation, if the two parties' positions are exactly symmetrical in all respects, and if they seek a solution that might be regarded as fair or equitable, then they should agree at about point E, where the preference curves of the two parties intersect. Here, they both are making equal gains, not in absolute terms perhaps, but relative to their own point of neutrality or indifference. This represents the outcome frequently referred to as "splitting the difference" or the fifty-percent solution. In the automobile example, this solution would be to agree at $5,100. This solution is equitable, even though it does not fall midway between the opening offers, because it gives both parties equal gains relative to their next best alternative. In this case, the $5,100 price enables the buyer to purchase the car for $500 less than the alternative, whereas the seller receives $500 more than the next best offer received for the car. The fair solution is midway between the resistance points, a' and b', rather than between the opening offers, a and b.

Of course, in real bargaining the parties seldom reach this precise equitable solution. They may fail to achieve this solution for several reasons. The most important reasons include the fact that they may not necessarily accept the concept of a fair solution, as each one may prefer to obtain a larger share of the distribution than the other. Or alternatively they may not know the true preferences of the other, and they may either misperceive the others' preferences or the others may even intentionally mislead them about their true preferences. That is, while the opening offers, *a* and *b,* are known to both parties, the others' resistance points, *a'* and *b',* are not known. In either case, agreement is more likely to be achieved through a series of incremental steps, beginning with opening proposals at the far ends of the issue dimension and leading through a series of mutual concessions toward convergence somewhere within the bargaining space. This process is generally referred to as concession-convergence bargaining.

Concession-convergence bargaining, however, is very much complicated by the mixed motive nature of negotiations, especially by the simultaneous presence of a common interest in reaching agreement within the available bargaining space and a conflicting interest in achieving an unbalanced agreement within that space that favors one's own position. Thus, in figure 5.1, *A* prefers an agreement as close as possible to the right of point *b',* whereas *B* prefers an agreement just to the left of point *a';* these may be referred to as the targets or aspiration levels of each party, the outcome they would ideally like to realize from the bargaining situation. If the buyer knew the next best offer that had been made to the seller, he would try to buy the car for perhaps $4,700; and if the seller knew the buyer's next best option, he would offer to sell the car for about $5,500.

Walton and McKersie, as noted in the previous chapter, have referred to these two aspects of the bargaining problem by the terms integrative bargaining and distributive bargaining. Distributive bargaining is that aspect of the negotiations concerned with dividing a fixed resource between the parties, where one party's goals are "in basic conflict with those of the other party."[9] In our case, it is the conflict that takes place along the issue dimension, as the seller tries to drive the price higher and the buyer tries to lower the price. By contrast, integrative bargaining refers to "the attainment of objectives which are not in fundamental conflict with those of the other party and which therefore can be integrated to some degree."[10] In the case of the buyer and the seller, it is that aspect of the negotiation characterized by the joint interest in avoiding a stalemate and reaching agreement. As long as a mutually satisfactory agreement is possible, both parties have an interest in avoiding tactics or other mistakes during the bargaining process that will prevent them from achieving an agreement within the bargaining space and provide both with positive results. To use a familiar analogy, integrative bargaining refers to the process of enlarging the pie of benefits, whereas distributive bargaining deals with the problem of dividing the enlarged pie. In a similar vein, Sebenius has referred to this as a distinction between creating value, in which value is added to an agreement, and claiming value, in which the increased value claimed by one party results in less value being available for others.[11]

The fact that elements of integrative and distributive bargaining are present simultaneously in most negotiations creates several dilemmas for the bargaining process, especially for the tactics that a negotiator will employ. It often turns out that tactics which will enhance the probability of an agreement (the integrative aspect) may reduce the individual payoff to the actor who uses those tactics (a relative loss in the distributive aspects of the bargaining). Conversely, if one actor pursues tactics designed to increase his or her own payoffs at the expense of the other (distributive bargaining), then he or she may increase the likelihood of stalemate that will prevent both parties from realizing a mutually beneficial agreement (the integrative bargaining). This dilemma can be illustrated with respect to several aspects of bargaining tactics.

The dilemma flows from what Fred Charles Iklé has referred to as the negotiator's continual threefold choice: "(1) to accept agreement at the terms he expects the opponent would settle for (the 'available' terms), (2) to discontinue negotiations without agreement and with no intention of resuming them, and (3) to try to improve the 'available' terms through further bargaining."[12]

In other words, the negotiator constantly monitors the bargaining situation to determine the current state of the bids, as well as the range of available bargaining space. If there is no bargaining space available, and if there seems to be little or no potential to create bargaining space, the negotiator may elect the second option and break off negotiations. On the other hand, if there is bargaining space, the negotiator still has two choices: accept the present offer of the other party or continue to negotiate in order to try to elicit offers that are preferable. If the third option is selected, the negotiator may try to manipulate the bargaining situation to try to improve the available terms. This is most likely to entail the use of distributive bargaining tactics or tactics intended to claim value rather than to create value. Yet virtually all of these tactics create a dilemma: in trying to obtain better terms than those presently available, option three in Iklé's threefold choice, the negotiator may increase the likelihood of destroying the ability to reach any agreement at all, making option two a more likely outcome. There are a number of tactics that illustrate this dilemma.

The first tactical dilemma concerns the manipulation of opening bids. One party may make an extreme opening bid, for example, party A may open at point a, say \$4,000 in figure 5.1, and B may make a more moderate or reasonable opening, say near point a' or about \$5,600. Then if they make equal concessions to converge at the midpoint between their opening bids (a common outcome in the bargaining process), agreement will normally be reached just to the right of point *b'*, at $4,800 in this illustration. In this case, *B* may be considered to have made a cooperative opening move, while *A* was trying to maximize his or her own gain by an extreme opening. Yet the paradox of this case is that the greedy party may succeed in getting an agreement nearer to the ideal point, well to the left of the available bargaining space and just inside point *b'*, which is $4,600. Such an agreement may be acceptable to *B* if *B* does not know *A*'s preference curve and thinks that this is really a fifty-percent solution. But in reality, it is a very advantageous agreement for *A* because it produces large gains, whereas *B*'s gains from the agreement are marginal. Compared to their next best alternatives, in this illustration *A* would gain $800 whereas *B* would gain only $200. While this is still better for *B* than no agreement at all, it clearly leaves *A* better off.

Of course, if both parties follow *A*'s lead and make extreme opening bids in order to enhance their advantages in the concession-making process, then they may create the mistaken impression that they are so far apart that no agreement is possible. In this case, mutual greediness may create a situation in which both parties lose because they fail to make the necessary concessions to locate the mutually beneficial bargaining space. So it may be advantageous from a distributive point of view to make an extreme opening bid, either to avoid being exploited or to take advantage of the other party, but the effect of both behaving this way is frequently to create a situation in which both may lose by failing to find a mutually acceptable solution to the problem.

A second dilemma inherent in this bargaining model concerns flexibility or the rate at which parties make concessions. In order to reach an equitable solution, the two parties should not only start at about the same distance apart, but they should concede in roughly equal rates, leading to eventual convergence somewhere near point *E*, an integrative outcome. However, each party, fearing that its concessions might appear to the other as a sign of weakness, may be afraid to offer the first concessions. And if *A* does concede first, then *B* may in fact hold firm, waiting for *A* to make still further concessions before reciprocating. Here again the dilemma is that *A*'s flexibility and desire to seek an integrative solution through making concessions may actually enable *B* to exploit *A* by forcing *A* to make most or all of the concessions until *A* has backed up almost to point *a'*. And *B*, through its rigid bargaining behavior, may actually obtain the largest share of the gains in the distributive aspect of the bargaining. In the automobile example, the buyer may raise the offer by $200 in each round while the seller decreases the price only $100, or one may make more frequent concessions, as would be the case if the buyer makes two offers of $100 more for each offer by the seller to reduce the price by $100.

Of course, either party may try to avoid being exploited in this way

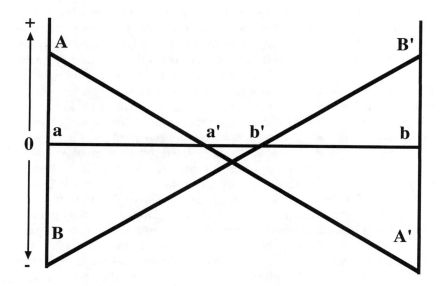

Figure 5.2 Absence of Bargaining Space
1. **Horizontal Axis = Issue Dimension**
2. **Vertical Axis = Gains (+) and Losses (-) Relative to Nonagreement (0)**
3. **A—A' = A's Preference Curve**
4. **B—B' = B's Preference Curve**
5. **a = A's preferred outcome**
   a' = A's minimum acceptable outcome
   b = B's preferred outcome
   b' = B's minimum acceptable outcome
6. **There is no mutually acceptable agreement since the range of acceptable**
   agreements for A (a-a') and for B (b-b') do not overlap at any point.

by behaving rigidly and refusing to make concessions. But if both *A* and *B*, the buyer and the seller, behave this way, each saying that "the ball is in the other's court" and that the other must make the first concession, then neither side concedes at all and the bargaining may end in stalemate. Again in this situation both parties lose by failing to achieve an integrative solution as a result of their individual efforts either to win or avoid being exploited and losing in the distributive bargaining. Even though any settlement between $4,600 and $5,600 was mutually beneficial, the two parties could get hung up at their initial offers of $4,000 and $6,000, with both refusing to make the concessions necessary to find the wide range of available bargaining space.

In recent international relations, this is perhaps roughly analogous to the long-standing stalemate between Israelis and Palestinians. At least prior to late 1993, Israel refused to negotiate directly with Palestinian representatives or discuss any proposal that might lead to the creation of a Palestinian state until Israel's existence and security were fully assured, whereas Palestinians refused to recognize the legitimacy of any Israeli state at least until they had a state of their own. These countries were caught in a set of mutually incompatible opening positions that cut off the potential for further negotiations and made it essentially impossible for either to concede without appearing to give up their most important goal; in this circumstance, neither would concede and a long-enduring impasse was created.

A third dilemma is the use of commitments to misinform the other party about one's resistance point or point of minimum acceptable agreement. A commitment is a firm statement or action intended to signal one's minimum position beyond which one may not concede. The role of commitments has been introduced into the literature on bargaining by Thomas Schelling. In *The Strategy of Conflict* he suggests that a negotiator may use commitments to "squeeze the range of indeterminacy down to the point most favorable to him."[13] Commitments work best when the other party is convinced that one is physically or in some other way clearly prevented from making further concessions. Often a negotiator will reinforce commitments with the threat to walk out of a negotiation rather than to concede.

In integrative bargaining, commitments may be used constructively to communicate the range of available bargaining space. If each party is firm but honest in their use of commitments, then this may actually facilitate bargaining. It prevents efforts to try to force an agreement on a party that is clearly unacceptable. In the case of the automobile, if both parties honestly revealed their alternatives, the range of bargaining space would have become clear and the basis for an equitable solution would have been created. As we shall see below, however, there are incentives against revealing these alternatives honestly, and these incentives might make parties suspicious of anything that the other revealed, even if it were honest.

Commitments may also signal, as indicated in figure 5.2, a situation in which the preference curves of the two parties do not overlap and where there is no bargaining space. If this is the reality of the situation, then it is generally better to accept that fact and either try to redefine the issue in new ways that might promote agreement or even give up and break off negotiations rather than frustrating both parties by trying to reach agreement about a nonnegotiable issue. So when used realistically, commitments may facilitate integrative bargaining or at least head off futile and destructive bargaining. For example, if the potential buyer of the car had seen another equally valued car for $4,800 and the seller had already received an offer of $5,200, there is no bargaining space. The seller will not go below the $5,200 alternative, and the buyer will

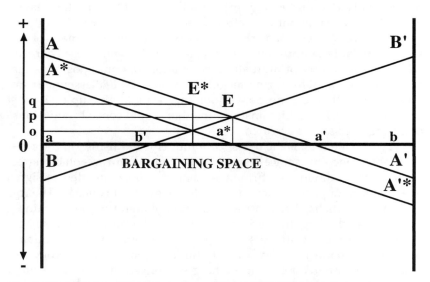

Figure 5.3 A Model of Two-Party Bargaining with Misinformation and Commitments
1. Horizontal Axis = Issue Dimension
2. Vertical Axis = Gains (+) and Losses (-) Relative to Nonagreement (0)
3. A—A' = A's "Real" Preference Curve
4. B—B' = B's Preference Curve
5. a = A's preferred outcome
   a' = A's "real" minimum acceptable outcome
   b = B's preferred outcome
   b' = B's minimum acceptable outcome
6. E = point of "equitable solution, where gains of both parties relative to nonagreement are equal
7. A*—A'* represents A's claimed preference line:
   a) a* represents the commitment of A's minimum position
   b) E* represents the new "fair" settlement point
   c) p represents the original gains for both parties
   d) o represents B's new lower payoff
   e) q represents A's new greater "actual" payoff

never pay that much when he can buy an equally good car for $4,800. In this case, the sooner this information is revealed, the sooner the two parties may realize that they have no basis for agreement. They may then at least break off negotiations amicably rather than engage in a long, drawn out, and tough bargaining process that would inevitably lead to failure anyway, but with all of the animosity created by the tough bargaining detracting from their overall relationship. Hammering away incessantly at intractable problems may be even worse than not negotiating in some circumstances.

A serious dilemma concerning commitments arises, however, when considering the manipulation of commitments to gain a tactical advantage in the distributive aspect of the bargaining. If actor A wants to gain an advantage in the tactical bargaining, A may try to exaggerate the resistance point by committing itself at a more extreme position than its real position. This is illustrated in figure 5.3, in which A commits itself at point a^*, even though its real resistance point was at point a'. This, in effect, creates the illusion for B that A's preference curve looks more like $A^*-A'^*$, rather than the real preference curve of $A-A'$. This then reduces the perceived bargaining space to the range between b' and a^*, and a solution at the fair midpoint between the two resistance points will move from point E to E^*, in a direction favorable to A. Thus, A may profit at B's expense in the distributive bargaining from its deceptive use of the commitment tactic.

For example, the buyer may claim to have seen a comparable car the previous day for $5,200 when it was in fact offered for $5,600. The seller, knowing that his best offer is $4,600, may agree to split the difference and sell the car for $4,900, the new midpoint or E^*. By manipulating the information, the buyer is able to reduce the price by $200, from the former midpoint of $5,100 to the new midpoint of $4,900. The buyer now gains $700 relative to his real next best alternative, whereas the seller only gains $300. Both have still made a profitable deal compared to their next best alternatives, but it is not equitable in the sense that the buyer's profit is considerably greater than the seller's.

Not only can commitments produce inequitable outcomes, commitments can also detract significantly from the ability to reach agreement within bargaining space, thereby undermining the integrative aspects of the negotiation. For example, both parties may commit themselves to immovable positions, which makes the situation look like the one depicted in figure 5.2 where there is no bargaining space. In reality, though, there is bargaining space, as indicated in figure 5.3. While the buyer may claim to have found a comparable car for $5,200, the seller may claim to have received an offer of $5,400 for the car. In this case, both would believe that there was no bargaining space and no basis for continuing to negotiate. Neither would be prepared to accept the other's offer as it stood, and both might perceive that nothing was to be gained by continuing negotiations in search for better terms; this leaves them only the second option in Iklé's threefold choice—breaking off negotiations. They would presumably walk away having squandered an opportunity to reach a mutually acceptable sale. Their desire to win in the competitive negotiation, to claim more value than they really needed, would have prevented them from reaching an integrative agreement in which they both could have created a mutually valuable deal.

Alternatively, party A may misperceive B's resistance point and, being greedy, may commit itself to a position (a*) to the left of b'. Again, if a^* is left of b', then the situation will look like that in figure 5.2 where there is no available bargaining space. For example, the buyer may claim to have found a car offered for sale at $4,500, $100 less than the best offer that the seller has already received, so that the seller will clearly reject this offer and tell the potential buyer that he or she cannot meet that alternative price. Thus, the two may well part company, believing that they have no basis for reaching agreement.

In either of these cases of over-commitment, the over-committed party has two choices. It may hold to its commitment, even if it means a breakdown in negotiations and the loss of a potentially satisfactory agreement. It will usually do this in order to maintain the credibility of its future commitments in the eyes of others, even though this entails a short-run cost. Or it may back down from its commitment, thereby acknowledging that its commitment was a bluff. This may facilitate mutual concessions and an eventual convergence at a point of agreement, but it means that the party backing down will have damaged its bargaining reputation. If the party is shown to use bluffs, then its future commitments may be disregarded, and it may even slide down a slippery slope of concessions that may lead it to concede more than might have been necessary had such excessive commitments not been made. Certainly its reputation in future negotiations is likely to be damaged, and few of its claims will be believed by others. In short, commitments may be useful in seeking disproportionately large gains in the distributive phase of negotiations, but as Schelling observes, "they all run the risk of establishing an immovable position that goes beyond the ability of the other to concede, and thereby provoke the likelihood of stalemate or breakdown."[14]

Within this simple bargaining model, two other related tactics may be employed to try to manipulate the positions that negotiators will take on the issue dimension: threats and promises. Both threats and promises are contingent statements regarding rewards and punishments. Rewards and punishments are elements that one party may add or subtract from the other party's payoff from an agreement. Whether these rewards and punishments are carried out, however, is contingent upon how the other party responds to the demands of the first.

If B threatens A, then B indicates an intention to punish A or to remove a reward from A if A does not comply with B's wishes. B may threaten that if A does not agree to a position preferred by B, then B will punish A by more than the amount that would be lost by A if A capitulated to B's demands. In other words, the threat raises the probable cost to A of nonagreement, so that agreement on B's terms may become more positive relative to the breakup of negotiations when accompanied by punishment. Threats are contingent statements, and the punishments will be implemented only if the other party does not comply. In figure 5.4 this means that B's threat moves A's preference curve to the right by the amount that A expects to lose if the punishment is carried out, multiplied times A's estimate of the probability that the threat will be carried out. Therefore, the benefits to A of an agreement at point E^* go from being very modest (distance r at the left margin) to being much larger (distance p at the left margin). Of course, the absolute benefits do not increase at all; they remain where they were originally. However, since benefits must always be compared with the value associated with nonagreement, and since the costs of nonagreement have gone up due to the threat, then outcomes that were previously only marginally beneficial or perhaps even negative may now become much more positive relative to the more costly condition of nonagreement.

The success of a threat depends upon two major considerations. First, B's capability to implement the punishment directly affects whether or not A will believe that the punishment will produce the threatened loss of utility. Second, A's estimate of the probability that B will actually carry out the threat will affect whether or not A believes that the threat is credible. The expected cost of the punishment to A is a function of the amount of the punishment multiplied times the probability that it will be carried out. This expected cost affects the amount that A's preference curve will move to the right in figure 5.4, and it is also equal to the difference between the relative benefit that A would have received at level r and the amount received at level p. If A believes B's threat and accordingly agrees at the new point of a fair settlement, E^*, then B will benefit from the threat by increasing its gains from level q (that it could have expected to receive before the threat) to level p that it will receive after the threat. In other words, B's threat moved the fair settlement point to the right of the issue dimension in the direction favorable to B. Of course, if the threat succeeds and A complies, then B will never have to carry out the punishment; the execution of the punishment is contingent upon whether or not A complies to B's threat and agrees at B's preferred position.

Promises are logically very similar to threats. In this case B may promise A that if A complies with B's preferences, then B will provide A with a reward (or remove a punishment). Like a threat, a promise is a contingent statement, and its implementation depends upon whether or not A complies; unlike a threat, however, the reward is provided if A does comply. A reward acts to increase the benefits for A from an agreement relative to nonagreement, so A's preference curve shifts to the right just as it did for a threat. The benefits of agreement compared to nonagreement have increased in this case due to an increase in the benefits from agreement rather than from an increase in the costs of nonagreement, which was the case with threats. But the result is logi-

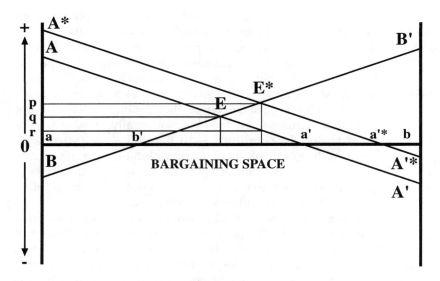

Figure 5.4: Effects of Threats and Promises
1. Horizontal Axis = Issue Dimension
2. Vertical Axis = Gains (+) and Losses (-) Relative to Nonagreement (0)
3. A—A' = A's Preference Curve
4. B—B' = B's Preference Curve
5. a = A's preferred outcome
    a' = A's minimum acceptable outcome
    b = B's preferred outcome
    b' = B's minimum acceptable outcome
6. E = point of "equitable" solution, where gains of both parties relative to
   nonagreement are equal
7. p = B's actual gains after threat or promise
   q = A's and B's gains before threat or promise
   r = A's actual gains after threat or promise

cally exactly the same, as depicted in figure 5.4. *A*'s preference curve
shifts to the right, *A*'s resistance point moves from *a'* to *a**, and the location of a fair agreement moves from position *E* to position *E**, all in the
direction preferred by *B*. In other words, *B* benefits from the promise
just as he or she did from the threat. In a similar fashion, the effectiveness of promises depends on *B*'s capability to provide the promised rewards and on *A*'s perception of the likelihood that *B* will carry out its
promises, and the amount that *A* is influenced to modify its negotiating
position is a function of these two factors multiplied by one another.

Threats and promises are seldom introduced into bargaining over
issues as simple as the sale of an automobile, so that our illustration in
terms of that kind of simple bargaining problem will inevitably be some-

what far-fetched. One fairly common practice in this kind of bargaining is for the seller to make a promise to the buyer. For example, the seller may promise that, if the buyer accepts the proposed price, the seller will also give him a new television set worth $400. That increases the value of the deal by $400 for the buyer, thereby moving the buyer's preference curve to the right. The relative value of the deal compared to the next best alternative, the anchoring point, is now $400 higher. That means that the sale price is also likely to rise in the direction favored by the seller.

Threats are even less common in this kind of situation. But suppose for the sake of illustration that the buyer threatened to come during the night and break the windows of the seller's home, causing $400 worth of damage, if the seller did not agree to sell at the price preferred by the buyer. Without changing the absolute value of the car, this would make the seller's next best alternative a good deal less satisfactory, because not only would he or she have to sell the car for less, but would suffer additional damage to his or her home as well. In other words, the value of the agreement in absolute terms would not have changed, but the costs of nonagreement would have increased, thereby making the relative benefits of agreement compared to nonagreement more attractive at a given point than in the absence of the threat. This would cause the seller's preference curve to move to the left by an amount equivalent to $400, since the resistance point, b', would be $400 lower. This would also move the fair settlement point down in the direction favored by the buyer, making the car less expensive.

Two fairly stark examples from international relations might illustrate these two tactics. In the missile crisis in the Caribbean in 1962, President Kennedy threatened Premier Khrushchev that the failure to withdraw missiles from Cuba would cause the United States to invade Cuba and remove them forcefully. The Soviet Union was clearly not anxious to accept the U.S. offer of a pledge not to invade if the Soviets withdrew, given that withdrawal meant a substantial loss of prestige for the Soviet Union, especially in eyes of the Chinese government and revolutionary movements in the third world. Yet the alternative posed by the threat of an American invasion, possibly setting off a nuclear war that would entail enormous damage to Soviet territory, was clearly even more unattractive. Thus, the Soviets accepted a settlement of the missile crisis with terms that were not very favorable to their interests, but which were certainly preferable to the very costly alternative in the face of American threats. Even a very unsatisfactory option, if it is preferred to the other available alternatives, may be an acceptable basis for reaching agreement.

A more recent example of the use of promises may be found in the negotiation between the Federal Republic of Germany and the Soviet Union over German reunification and the withdrawal of Soviet troops from the former East Germany in 1990. The Soviets were reluctant to accept German reunification because of the intense fear of a united Germany in the USSR, especially after the memories of the two world wars. For similar reasons, the Soviets were very reluctant to withdraw troops from German territory. In order to induce the Soviets to accept their preferred position in these negotiations, however, the West German government offered at least two promises. First, they agreed not to challenge the postwar borders of Poland, especially the Polish-German border; had it been challenged, fears of German expansion would have grown, and a newly assertive Poland might have wanted to reopen the issue of the Polish-Soviet border in territory that had been incorporated into the Ukraine and Belorussia after World War II. Second, they agreed to build housing for Soviet troops in the Western USSR, thereby reducing substantially the economic costs for the USSR of a troop withdrawal. The first move increased the benefits of the agreement for the USSR, while the second reduced its costs. Together they increased the value of an agreement in Soviet eyes relative to their available alternatives. With these promises as inducements, the Soviet Union thus acquiesced in German reunification on the terms proposed by West Germany. An agreement that otherwise probably would have been rejected was thus consummated.

While the logical effects of threats and promises may be identical within this framework of rational bargaining, the psychological effects may be quite different. In general, threats of punishment induce hostile reactions in the recipient, whereas promises of rewards are more likely to induce positive reactions. Of course, even promises may be perceived as tricks or in pejorative terms as bribes, in which case they too may generate hostility and mistrust. For example, in 1965 President Lyndon Johnson tried to persuade the government of North Vietnam to enter into negotiations with the United States to end the war in Southeast Asia on the basis of a formula for agreement proposed by the United States. He offered both a threat and a promise. He threatened to resume U.S. bombing raids against North Vietnam that had been suspended, and hit targets nearer major North Vietnamese cities than in the past, if North Vietnam refused to capitulate. At the same time, he offered North Vietnam one billion U.S. dollars in aid for the reconstruction of their badly destroyed country if they would agree to U.S. terms. Not surprisingly, the North Vietnamese viewed the threat as a blatant attempt at coercion that solidified their will to resist American pressure to negotiate a settlement to the conflict. Perhaps more surprisingly, they saw the aid offer also as a cynical attempt by capitalists to bribe them. Within their ideological framework, an attempt by the United States to get them to sell their national integrity for money was proof of the depravity of capitalism, a system where money was everything and all other values took second place. Thus, both the threat and the promise failed, both because they were not framed in terms that were relevant to the value system of the people the United States was trying to influence and because they were perceived as crude and hostile measures that constituted an insult to their national honor. By contrast, West German promises to the Soviet Union in 1990 were far more clearly intended to promote Soviet national interest, independence, and the ability to withdraw militarily with dignity.

Most psychological studies suggest that people tend to respond much more positively to promises, rewards and other soft behaviors than to threats, punishments and other hard behaviors. Several studies have been conducted by social psychologists to try to identify whether soft or hard bargaining behaviors are more likely to elicit cooperation from a partner. One such classic study was conducted by V. E. Bixenstine and K. V. Wilson, who found that the change in behavior had a greater impact than the level of softness or hardness in the behavior. Their results are roughly reflected in figure 5.5, which suggests that greatest

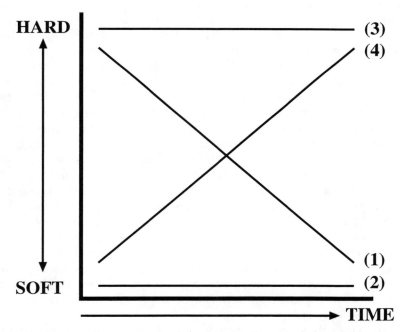

Figure 5.5 Effects of Changes in Hard and Soft Bargaining Styles on Negotiation Outcomes
1) Hard to Soft (most cooperation)
2) Continuous Soft (tied for second-most cooperation)
3) Continuous Hard (tied for second-most cooperation)
4) Soft to Hard (least cooperation)

cooperation is achieved when negotiators change from hard to soft behaviors; there is very little difference between pure hard and pure soft behaviors, and the most conflictual results were obtained when one party started out soft, giving the impression that it could be exploited, and then hardened during the course of bargaining.[15]

Laboratory studies such as this one, of course, are of limited utility when applied to international negotiations because of the simplicity of the conditions under which they were conducted. On the other hand, such studies may at least generate some interesting hypotheses about actual international negotiations. Specifically this study would seem to suggest the following hypothesis: If one seeks cooperation and agreement in negotiations, it may be useful to be clear and firm about one's commitments and fundamental interests at the outset and to then to remain flexible and even soften one's position during the course of negotiations through various concessions.

To summarize thus far, the basic bargaining model is a very simple representation of two-party negotiations. The parties are assumed to be rational in the sense that they will only accept agreements that leave them both better off than they would be in the absence of an agreement. Within the bargaining model, therefore, negotiation should focus on the bargaining space within which mutually acceptable agreements can be realized. In order to identify this range of acceptable agreements, it is rational for the parties to cooperate, since agreement can only be obtained within this space. Locating bargaining space can be facilitated by the judicious use of commitments to signal the other party about one's minimum position below which one cannot concede. Once the bargaining space has been located, the problem is to find a precise point of agreement. This is complicated by the fact that each party may prefer an agreement that gives it a larger share of the profit than the other. Thus, it may be rational for each party to try to move the agreement along the issue dimension toward positions that maximize its interests at the expense of the other. Here strategies such as misleading the other about one's true minimal positions, as well as utilizing threats and promises, may be employed. This aspect of traditional bargaining, therefore, may be characterized by a substantial amount of conflict as each party tries to maneuver about to gain advantages for its own interest. However, overzealous manipulation may backfire and produce stalemates or even the breakdown of negotiations.

Therefore, the dilemma of traditional bargaining is that the contradiction between cooperative and conflictual tactics may make the negotiation process somewhat schizophrenic, alternating between cooperative moves and conflictual ones. Deceit and manipulative behavior may serve one's short-term or individual interest, but it often detracts from the long-run collective interest in reaching agreement. As Sebenius notes, parties caught in this dilemma may tend to reason as follows: "If the other party is open and forthcoming, I can take advantage of it and claim a great deal of value; thus, I should adopt a value-claiming stance. On the other hand, if the other party is tough and adopts a value-claiming stance, I must also adopt such a stance to protect myself. Either way, a strong tendency operating on all parties often results in competitive moves to claim value individually, driving out cooperative moves. The results are poor agreements, deadlocks, and conflict spirals."[16]

The situation depicted by this dilemma may be illustrated by a story known as the Prisoners' Dilemma, which is a classic two-person, non-zero-sum game that models conflict situations of the kind discussed in the previous chapter.

In this somewhat artificial story that takes place in the "old west" of North America, two men work together to rob a bank. After the robbery, they bury their stolen money with the intent of returning after a period of time to dig it up and split the bounty. However, before they return, they are arrested by a sheriff who wants to extract confessions from them, since he has no direct evidence to convict either of the robbers without them. So he places both men in separate jail cells where they cannot communicate with one another. Then this sheriff (who also apparently serves, in effect, as judge and jury) tells the two prisoners that their punishment will depend not only on whether or not they confess, but also on what their partner does. This matrix of choices presented to the two prisoners is depicted in figure 5.6, where the jail sentence of prisoner one is given first in each cell of the matrix, followed by the prison term for the second accused thief.

The choices that the sheriff gives each prisoner are identical for both. They include the following: (1) if neither prisoner confesses, they will both be sentenced for a lesser crime (e.g., possession of an illegal weapon)

Prisoner #2

	Not Confess	Confess
Not Confess	-2, -2	-8, -1
Confess	-1, -8	-5, -5

(rows labeled under **Prisoner #1**)

Figure 5.6 The Prisoners' Dilemma

for two years; (2) if both confess, they will each be sentenced to five years; or (3) if one confesses and the other does not, then the one who confesses will be given a light sentence of one year for "giving state's evidence," whereas the other will be sentenced to the maximum penalty of eight years in jail. A quick look at the matrix of choices in figure 5.6 indicates that the best choice for each prisoner, no matter what the other does, is to confess; this is a dominant strategy for both. For prisoner one, confessing is better if prisoner two does not confess, because one year for confessing is a lesser penalty than two years by not confessing. On the other hand, if prisoner two confesses, then for prisoner one confessing is still better since a five-year term is preferable to an eight-year term. The exact same terms apply in this symmetrical example if we look at the choices from the perspective of prisoner two. Thus, from the point of view of their individual interests, it is rational for both prisoners to confess.

But the dilemma arises if we look at the outcome when both behave rationally. This is found in the lower right-hand cell of the matrix in which both prisoners serve a five-year term. Yet from the collective point of view, this is the worst of all possible outcomes since the combined jail terms equal ten years, greater than in any other cell. Even more curious is the fact that there is another outcome in the upper, left-hand corner where both prisoners are better off by serving only two-year terms each. In the language of economic theory, this outcome is Pareto-Optimal in the sense that both parties can improve their results by moving toward that outcome. So moving to a situation in which neither confesses also seems to be rational.

Here, two different rationalities seem to clash, creating the dilemma. Clearly it is in the interest of the two parties to cooperate and refrain from confessing, but this is rational only if each can trust the other not to defect and seek a superior individual outcome by confessing. The fear that the other might defect and that one might be confronted with the largest sentence, eight years in jail, while the other is free after only one year to dig up the money and live well afterwards, is a powerful one. It is for this reason that the tension between cooperating with the other and defecting is so great. In many ways, this dilemma also captures the essence of what is often referred to as the negotiator's paradox: cooperation to produce optimal agreements may undermine each party's ability to garner a large share of the benefits of an agreement, whereas conflict over the distribution of the benefits may undermine the ability to reach optimal agreements or, at the extreme, any agreement at all.

The Prisoners' Dilemma may be illustrated by the dilemma affecting strategic nuclear disarmament negotiations between the United States and the Soviet Union throughout most of the cold-war period. Each superpower was confronted with two basic choices: (1) agree to disarm; or

(2) continue to build new armaments. In principle, each probably preferred to disarm. On the other hand, if one disarmed while the other cheated on an agreement and did not really disarm, then the cheater might gain a significant strategic advantage that would leave the disarmed party with its least preferred outcome. Therefore, even though the best collective choice was for both to disarm, the fear that the other might cheat made both reluctant to reach agreements for significant disarmament, at least until after 1990. The result was an increasing arms race from the late 1940s through the end of the 1980s that left everyone worse off: the economic costs of the race were high, and the destruction that could occur if nuclear war ever did break out became impossible to imagine. If the two parties could have trusted one another to abide by a negotiated agreement, there was clearly a preferable and jointly beneficial alternative: mutual disarmament. But in the absence of trust, and in an anarchic international system in which there was no external force to enforce an agreement, the worst outcome from the collective perspective appeared to be the rational choice from the perspective of each individual superpower.

Unfortunately, a major limitation of traditional bargaining theory is that it does not suggest a good answer to the Prisoners' Dilemma and to all of the related tensions between simultaneously cooperating to seek integrative solutions and competing to win a larger share of the distributive outcome. Therefore, more recent work on negotiations has tried to emphasize much more the benefits from approaching the negotiation process as a joint problem-solving exercise rather than as an exercise in which each party rationally seeks his or her own individual gain at the other's expense. Such a shift in perspective is essential if our analysis of the negotiation process is to have any hope of escaping from the rather pessimistic predictions of the Prisoners' Dilemma. It is to these expanded notions of negotiation, going beyond simple bargaining, that I shall turn to in the next chapter.

Chapter 6

Problem-solving Models of Bilateral Negotiations

The bargaining approach described in the previous chapter tended to dominate most work on international negotiations from about 1960, when Schelling's *Strategy of Conflict* was published, through the decade of the 1970s. Since about 1980, however, the focus in the field has moved beyond bargaining theory toward an approach that emphasizes the central role of integrative problem solving in international negotiations. This has grown out of a critique of some of the simplest and most artificial assumptions of the bargaining model. First, this model tends to depict issues as falling more or less along a single continuum, with opposed positions at each end. In contemporary international negotiations, however, most issues are certainly much more complex and multidimensional than this.

Second, this emphasis on a continuum also tends to overstate the conflictual or distributive element of negotiations. Even though most bargaining theorists recognize the mixed motive nature of negotiations, the integrative element seldom went beyond the mutual desire to reach an agreement within the available bargaining space. The possibility of expanding or redefining the bargaining space to realize more fundamental or long-term common interests was largely overlooked in this approach.

Third, the bargaining models tend to emphasize the centrality to the negotiation process of taking positions along this continuum, and the dynamics are largely restricted to making initial offers, making concessions and retractions, and eventually either converging toward agreement or becoming lodged in stalemate and then frequently breaking off negotiations. While most negotiations do include these behaviors as important components, these positional bargaining behaviors seem overly stylized and simplistic. Furthermore, from a prescriptive point of view, they tend to emphasize the importance of taking and holding firmly on to fixed positions, which has been found to introduce a great deal of rigidity into most negotiations.

Fourth, this perspective has concentrated on the role of both hard and soft bargaining tactics such as commitments, threats, and promises that may be used to manipulate information and the structure of bargaining. While these tactics have often been employed in real negotiations, their use has also frequently been dysfunctional.

Therefore, the newer approaches to negotiations tend to emphasize both a more subtle, sophisticated model of negotiations and a model that is also more attractive from the prescriptive vantage point as a guide for training negotiators. Metaphorically, this changed focus in the analysis of negotiations has often been referred to as a change in the way negotiators view seating arrangements around the negotiation table. In traditional bargaining, negotiators usually sit across the negotiating table, facing one another from opposite sides as adversaries. In integrative or problem-solving negotiations, the problem itself is the adversary; therefore, the table may be visualized as one in which both negotiating teams sit on the same side and face the problem head on. Thus, rather than confronting one another, they confront together the problem that creates difficulties for both sides.

Many of the foundations of contemporary negotiation theory have been around for a long time. One important work is that of Walton and McKersie on integrative bargaining, previously referred to, in which attitude change took its place along side bargaining tactics in their comprehensive approach to labor-management negotiations. As long ago as 1960, building on a foundation in mathematical models and game theory but extending far beyond these quantitative tools, Anatol Rapoport introduced the concept of debate. Debate, for Rapoport, was not primarily a means of confrontation as we often think of it in everyday usage, but rather it involved a process for discovering underlying commonalities of belief and interest. As he observed: "The model of fruitful debate will be built around that notion . . . that an important task in a debate is to delineate the domain of validity for each of the opposing stands. 'Empathetic understanding' then will emerge as a recognition that practically every conviction has a certain 'domain of validity.'"[1]

The ideas introduced by Rapoport and others of his generation came to dominate much of the theorizing about international negotiations by the decade of the 1980s. Although many theorists adopted this new perspective, two works have been especially seminal: I. William Zartman and Maureen Berman's *The Practical Negotiator* and Roger Fisher and William Ury's *Getting to Yes*. Therefore, the analysis in this chapter will draw significantly from these two works in contemporary negotiation theory.

The work of Zartman and Berman emphasizes the multistage process of negotiation, which they characterize as falling into three phases:

(1) diagnosis; (2) formula construction; and (3) agreement on details.[2] Although these phases do not always occur in a strict temporal order, they do tend to organize themselves in a more or less logical sequence.

Much of the diagnostics may take place in a prenegotiation stage, although the process may continue well into the formal negotiation. The diagnosis is basically the process in which the parties try to evaluate and understand the problem that they are negotiating to decide if it is negotiable, and, if so, what agenda should be followed in conducting the negotiation. An important issue in this phase is one of timing. The same issue may or may not be ripe for solution depending on a wide variety of factors including the state of the problem itself, the domestic situation within the countries affected by the problem, and the international context. Thus, one aspect of diagnosis is to determine if a problem is ripe for solution, and if so to convene formal negotiations rapidly.

Obviously the revolutionary changes that took place in Eastern Europe in 1989 created new conditions that made negotiations on German reunification feasible for the first time since the end of World War II, to say nothing of the salutary impact that these events also had on ongoing negotiations on issues such as conventional arms control in Europe. As Louis Kriesberg has pointed out, issues of timing may refer to the stages in the development of a conflict, only some of which are appropriate for interventions designed to bring a resolution. Timing may also refer to changing events that may cause opportunities for negotiations to be lost if they are not seized upon promptly. As he further notes, "although environmental factors may constrain timing, they need not paralyze negotiators from developing strategies to create conditions which are ripe for conflict resolution: . . . although constituency factors, adversary relations, and the international context constrain de-escalation moves, the variety of possible strategies to initiate de-escalation reveals opportunities for de-escalation over a wide range of times. A long-term strategy may be pursued to help create the conditions so that the time becomes propitious for a short-term strategy."[3]

Diagnosis also involves an attempt to set an agenda for attacking a problem, by which Zartman and Berman mean the development of an informal understanding of the sequence in which issues will be discussed rather than a formal agenda for a conference. Depending on the issue, one may decide to begin with simple and easy issues, trying to tackle more complex or difficult issues later in the agenda. Or one may conclude that the most difficult issue is also so central to the entire problem that it would be pointless to tackle other issues until the underlying major problem had been resolved. Similarly, one may try to take a comprehensive approach to dealing with a problem in its entirety, or one may decide to break a problem down into its constituent elements and deal with these components one at a time. All of these decisions will depend intimately upon how the negotiators evaluate and understand the problem under negotiation, and the entire subsequent negotiation process is likely to be directed and constrained by these initial diagnostic evaluations.

This problem may be illustrated by the dilemma faced by U.S. Secretary of State Henry Kissinger, when he undertook his famous shuttle diplomacy between Israel and its neighbors in the aftermath of the 1973 Arab-Israeli War. It was clear to everyone that the issues of Palestinian statehood and the status of the West Bank, occupied by Israel since the 1967 war, were fundamental causes of tension and conflict in the region; yet the solution to these problems also seemed distant, at best. The more immediate issues facing the parties to the conflict involved establishing a firm cease-fire between Israel and its neighbors and eventually achieving a disengagement of forces between Israel and both Egypt and Syria. Kissinger chose to emphasize the partial solutions that were immediately available rather than to seek a solution to the underlying problems. Since then, analysts have debated, but not resolved, the issue of whether this was a better approach than seeking a solution to the Palestinian issue, trying to open direct negotiations at least with Jordan and probably also with representatives of the Palestinians. Kissinger believed that the essential goal was to begin the process of conflict resolution rather than to seek a resolution of all issues at once, thereby possibly putting in jeopardy even the tenuous cease-fire after the war. His critics have argued that by doing so he may have missed a ripe opportunity to open negotiations focused more directly on the underlying problems.

In short, the diagnostic phase is the one in which the parties make an initial commitment to negotiate with one another in an effort to resolve a jointly recognized conflict of interest. As Zartman and Berman observe: "negotiation is appropriate when the parties see that a problem can only be resolved jointly and when they have the will to end an existing situation that they consider unacceptable, while admitting the other party's or parties' claim to participate in that solution. Perception, will, and equality—of these three, the most important of all is will. Without the will to reach an agreement there will be none, even if the other party's claim to participate in a solution is admitted."[4]

The second phase in this framework is referred to as that of formula construction, the negotiation of a "formula or common definition of the conflict in terms amenable to solution."[5] As Zartman and Berman note, this stage begins when the parties reach a "turning point of seriousness," when each side perceives "that the other is serious about finding a negotiated solution—that is, that the other is willing to 'lose' a little to 'win' a little rather than win or lose all in a non-negotiated approach."[6] The formula they then begin to develop should provide an overarching framework within which a mutually acceptable settlement can be reached: "Formula is best characterized as a shared perception or definition of the conflict that establishes terms of trade, the cognitive structure of referents for a solution, or an applicable criterion of justice."[7]

Formulas may be constructed inductively, from the bottom up, through mutual concessions and compromises; in this case, the process of formula construction is not significantly different from that described in the traditional bargaining model of concessions leading toward a convergence of positions. Therefore, formulas are likely to be developed inductively in those cases where the fundamental assumptions of the bargaining model are met—when the issue is fairly simple and falls more or less along a continuum, where bargaining space can readily be located, and where both parties are willing to make concessions in order to reach a compromise agreement.

On the other hand, formulas are often likely to be constructed deductively, based on some fundamental principles that suggest an integrative solution to the problem that the negotiators confront. These deductive formulas are more likely to be sought when the problem under negotiation is complex and involves multiple dimensions, issues, or parties to the negotiation, or when the issue involves very fundamental interests or beliefs that are not readily amenable to solution by compromise. In this case, a formula may try to upgrade common interests that the parties share or suggest new ways of conceptualizing the issue so that the problem can be resolved integratively. Once such a general formula has emerged, the detailed points of agreement on specific issues will be suggested by the overall framework. Again as Zartman and Berman note, such a "formula or framework of principles helps give structure and coherence to an agreement on details, helps facilitate the search for solutions on component items, and helps create a positive, creative image of negotiation rather than an image of concession and compromise."[8]

As noted above, the search for formulas begins most often when the issues under negotiation are not defined in such as way as to suggest the presence of bargaining space along a well-defined dimension. This may result from a situation like that depicted in figure 5.2 in the previous chapter where there is no apparent overlapping bargaining space, or it may result from a complex set of interlocking issues that make bargaining space extremely difficult to identify. When faced with this situation, negotiators may try one of two broad techniques in order to create formulas: (1) they may try to redefine the issues under negotiation, either by disaggregating them into subissues or aggregating them into interlocking issues; or (2) they may engage in creative problem solving or brainstorming, in which they try to create new solutions through a process of trying to work the issue through together.

One common approach to issue redefinition may be referred to as issue disaggregation, a process also referred to by Roger Fisher as one in which the parties fractionate the issues in conflict.[9] This kind of procedure may be most useful when comprehensive agreement seems to be blocked by some important component, in which case the negotiators may decide to disaggregate the issue and seek agreement only on those components of the problem that are not hopelessly blocked. As Fisher notes: "Dividing up a problem makes it possible for countries to agree on issues on which they have common interests, limiting disagreement to those issues on which they truly disagree."[10] These issues of disagreement may be set aside in the hope that the positive results of a partial agreement may eventually facilitate settlement of the more comprehensive problem. On the other hand, this approach runs the risk that the parties may become content with a partial solution, thereby losing an opportunity to seek a more comprehensive or optimal agreement.

As already noted, this may have been the case with regard to Henry Kissinger's shuttle diplomacy in the Middle East. Kissinger tried to break the issues down into manageable pieces and focus immediately only on those issues that seemed readily amenable to solution, namely a cease-fire between combatants and a disengagement of their military forces.[11] But he was more concerned with personal success and enhancing the power of the United States in the region, and this led him to avoid negotiations with Jordan over the issue of the status of the West Bank, and thereby to avoid the whole issue of the status of the Palestinian people. Kissinger's need for success led him to seek fractionated solutions that were guaranteed to be successful, while diverting his attention from "the heart" of the problem.[12] Rather than seeking more comprehensive, but less certain agreements, he chose the less risky route of seeking partial agreements on the immediate problems while forgoing more basic solutions to the underlying problems within the Middle East.

A second approach might be called issue aggregation in which subissues are linked together to create package agreements out of components that would be nonnegotiable if treated separately. One such approach is the creation of tradeoffs, in which issues are linked together to create a mutually beneficial combination of issues as a formula for agreement. This process is illustrated in figure 6.1, where two issues are linked. As this figure suggests, there is no overlapping bargaining space for the two parties on either issue, since their preference curves intersect below the line of neutrality or indifference. At first sight this would seem to create stalemate on both issues. However, in this case, the issues are not perfectly symmetrical for the two parties, as each one has more intense feelings (and therefore a steeper preference curve) for different issues. A seems to have strong feelings about issue one, since A receives high benefits from agreements at the left end of the spectrum that A prefers and very negative outcomes from agreements at the far right end. On the other hand, B's preferences on issue one are quite flat, and B is largely indifferent to any agreement, with only modest gains and losses associated with either end. Conversely, on issue two, B has intense feelings because of high rewards at the right end of the continuum and large losses at the left end, whereas A is more neutral about all solutions. It is precisely this asymmetry of intensity or importance of the two issues that provides the basis for creating a formula through a tradeoff.

A solution to this problem can be found by agreeing to a solution in which A wins on the issue that is more important to it, issue one, whereas B wins on the issue about which it feels more intensely, namely issue two. If A's gains on issue one exceed its losses on issue two (the net of $o - p$, where the negative amount of $o - p$ on issue two is subtracted from the positive value of $o - p$ on issue one), then A will still find the overall agreement beneficial. Of course, the same applies to B, whose gains on issue two must exceed its losses on issue one (the net value of $o - r$ summed across the two issues) in order for the package agreement to be beneficial. This approach is built on one of the fundamental axioms of human exchange developed by George Homans, which may be simply stated as follows: "The open secret of human exchange is to give to the other man [sic] behavior that is more valuable to him than it is costly to you and to get from him behavior that is more valuable to you than it is costly to him."[13] In such cases, two apparently nonnegotiable issues may be aggregated into one package that is mutually beneficial for both parties. This is the kind of formula that may be created through linking or aggregating issues.

This process may be illustrated by the negotiations between the United States and the Soviet Union from 1972 through 1979 on the second Strategic Arms Limitations Treaty (or SALT II). In these negotiations, a major American priority was to reduce or eliminate 308 Soviet heavyweight, multiple warhead missiles, the so-called SS-18s. At the same time, this was the most sophisticated weapon in the Soviet arsenal, which their military staff sought to protect at all cost. Thus, an impasse was created. Initially it appeared that the issue might be resolved primarily through a concession-convergence process, in which the number of SS-18s would be cut in half, a classic fifty-percent solution. On the other hand, this solution did not really please the military in either country. Another issue of significant impasse in the negotiations, however, arose about 1975 when the United States began deploying a new missile, the Air-Launched Cruise Missile (ALCM) on its strategic bombers. The Soviets argued that each new missile should be counted against the overall limit on missiles to be set by SALT II. The United States countered that these were still strategic bombers carrying the missiles and that the missiles themselves were too short-range to qualify as strategic missiles under the definitions already agreed to in previous negotia-

Issue #1

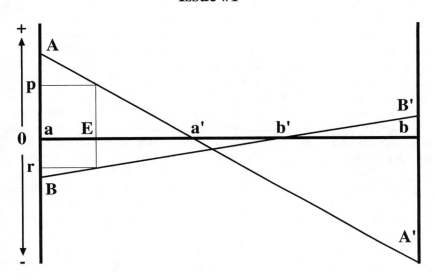

Issue #2

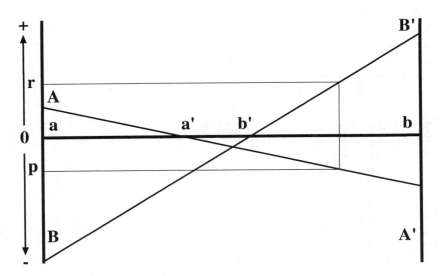

Figure 6.1 Tradeoffs—"Issue Aggregation"

tions. Therefore, the United States wanted to have each bomber count under the limits on the number of strategic bombers, just as they had when they were only equipped with classic gravity bombs.

At first these two issues seemed largely unrelated in the negotiations, and the only thing that they really had in common was that they had become two of the most important obstacles to agreement by late 1978. However, it had also become apparent that the Soviet military assigned a higher priority to retaining its SS-18 missiles than it did to limiting U.S. ALCMs. Similarly, the Pentagon seemed to believe that acquiring ALCMs to modernize its aging bomber fleet, especially after President Jimmy Carter had canceled the program for the development of the new B-1 strategic bomber was a higher priority than reducing the threat from Soviet heavyweight missiles. Thus, the two issues became linked in the negotiations, and a formula was created that permitted the Soviets to retain their SS-18s, with limitations on their modernization, while the United States was allowed to deploy a specified number of ALCMs on each bomber and still have the bomber count as only one delivery vehicle.

One may, of course, argue from an arms control point of view that this tradeoff was clearly suboptimal. Indeed, many of the critics of the treaty in the United States on both sides of the political spectrum seized upon this compromise as a major point of criticism, causing some to argue that the Soviet right to retain a large number of SS-18s made the treaty fatally flawed. But from the point of view of the military establishments in both countries, which had a great deal of influence over the negotiations, it was a mutually beneficial tradeoff. That at least enabled the countries to break two important impasses in the negotiations. Thus, an arms control agreement was consummated that also limited many other systems where agreement had already essentially been achieved, but where the fruits of that agreement could not be realized until all important issues in contention had been resolved. Therefore, by aggregating these issues and trading them off against one another, the United States and the Soviet Union were finally able to reach an agreement on SALT II in 1979.

A final approach for creating formulas, perhaps best described as creative problem solving, is most appropriate when the issues are even more complex than those discussed already—when any recombination is unlikely to produce agreement or where fundamental values like national integrity, honor, and survival are at stake. This is most likely to occur through a process of joint brainstorming, in which previous conceptualizations of the problem are discarded and when the parties actually work together to define the problem in a new light. The essence of this approach is to try to persuade the parties to discard their zero-sum, conflictual perceptions of the conflict, and reconceptualize it anew so that both parties perceive that they can benefit. It is this aspect of negotiation that has been most amplified by Fisher and Ury, and I will return to this issue after discussing the third phase in Zartman's approach to negotiations.

Zartman and Berman's third phase refers to the negotiation of "details to implement the formula on precise points of dispute."[14] A formula only provides a general guideline or framework for an agreement, so once a formula is created the negotiators must turn their attention to working out all of the necessary details required for implementing the agreement. Negotiations on details often focus on specific and piecemeal parts of the problem, but if they are undertaken with the guidance of a formula, that formula usually provides a set of criteria by which the detailed agreements may be evaluated. But the negotiation of details also provides a test of the formula's viability.

As Zartman and Berman note, the settlement of details "can be accomplished only on a trial and error basis. There are times when speedy agreement on a formula is followed by a long and arduous search for agreement on details."[15] Many of the behaviors already described that are found in the traditional bargaining model may also be evident in this phase of negotiations—especially concessions, reciprocity, and exchanges of positions. This phase normally comes to an end when, "through concessions or through joint discovery of implementing details," both parties "have moved to a point which they feel is the best they can do under the circumstances."[16]

Of course, sometimes negotiations on details may reveal problems that cannot be solved within the framework of the agreed formula, in which case the parties may have to return to the second phase in order to adjust or improve the formula so that it can cover all necessary details. In still other cases, the formula may actually emerge from the process of negotiating about details. Often when negotiations are stalemated on the broad issues, negotiators may turn their attention to details, if for no other reason than to occupy time until the domestic or international context changes and becomes ripe for more serious negotiations. However, occasionally in the process of discussing details, a formula may emerge inductively.

An illustration of this issue may be found in the case of the negotiations on Mutual and Balanced Force Reductions (MBFR) in which NATO and the Warsaw Pact sought to reduce conventional forces in Europe. These negotiations began in 1973, and were superseded by the much more fruitful Conventional Forces in Europe (CFE) negotiations in 1989. In the early years of MBFR, however, the effort to find a formula for agreement was frustrated because the two alliances had quite different conceptions of what would constitute such a formula. For example, NATO wanted to achieve numerical parity between the conventional forces of the two alliances, whereas the Warsaw Pact wanted to maintain the existing balance of forces at a lower level by requiring equal percentage reductions in the forces of both sides. Another issue around which the two sides produced different formulas consisted of a debate about whether force ceilings should apply to each alliance member individually or to the alliances collectively. The Warsaw Pact argued that the limitations should apply to individual countries, because they wanted a result that would limit forces of the former West Germany, their historic enemy and the country with the most sophisticated conventional army in Europe. NATO's proposal giving each alliance freedom to decide within itself how forces would be distributed was disadvantageous to the Soviet Union because it enabled the United States to withdraw from Europe under domestic political pressure, while it permitted U.S. forces to be replaced by an increase in the size of the West German Bundeswehr. By contrast, NATO wanted this flexibility to determine the national composition of alliance forces both to avoid singling out Germany as the "bad guy" in Europe and also to forestall any eventuality in which domestically motivated decisions by individual NATO countries to reduce forces might produce a significant decrease in NATO's overall defense capability if other countries were prohibited from making up the shortfall.

The inability to resolve these impasses caused MBFR to shift toward a negotiation on details by late 1977, especially on trying to define precisely how to count military forces and verify personnel limitations. While this approach proved ultimately fruitless until the political climate changed dramatically in Europe in the late 1980s, it did help to produce formulas to overcome at least some of the sources of stalemate. One such inventive formula, also retained in the eventual CFE agreement signed in 1990, was often dubbed the sufficiency rule. This idea was introduced formally into MBFR in the early 1980s as an attempt to bridge the gap between NATO and Warsaw Pact positions on national versus alliance-wide ceilings. The formula was a simple one: no one country could possess more than a fixed percentage, typically 50 percent in the original formulation, of the collective ceiling for forces allotted to either alliance under an agreement. Under this formula, NATO could retain the basic concept of a collective ceiling for the entire alliance, and West Germany was not singled out by name; furthermore, the same rule would constrain the percentage of Soviet forces stationed in Eastern Europe as part of the Warsaw Pact. For the Warsaw Pact, it achieved their major objective of creating a de facto limitation on West German forces, even though they were not identified individually, but it was obvious that only West Germany was likely to hold anywhere near 50 percent of NATO forces in Europe. Thus, an integrative formula was developed, neither from disaggregation nor from aggregation of issues, but rather through creative problem solving emerging from the intense discussion of minute details.

Perhaps the most important finding of recent theory and research about international negotiations is the importance of approaching the negotiations from a problem solving rather than a confrontational perspective. This is evident in all three phases of Zartman and Berman's approach, especially in the construction of formulas. This is the essential theme of an important and influential work on negotiations by Roger Fisher and William Ury, *Getting to Yes*.[17] They argue that parties to a negotiation should not view one another as adversaries bargaining against one another, but rather they should view the situation as one in which they have a common problem that needs to be overcome by taking joint decisions. Therefore, the adversary in the negotiation is the common problem, not the other party. In this way, negotiators may avoid personalizing their conflicts with other countries, and they may be able to distinguish between the people who represent other countries (who are presumed to be well intentioned) and the problems that need to be solved. If the people on the other side are treated as persons of good will, then one may work with them to solve the problem, rather than working against them to try to win at their expense. In short, they recommend an alternative to the use of either hard or soft bargaining tactics: "Be soft on the people, hard on the problem."[18]

Fisher and Ury build upon some of the fundamental assumptions of the traditional bargaining model, despite their critique of its overall utility. Perhaps the most important of these is the assumption that each party to a negotiation has a bottom line—a resistance point or a position beyond which they may not concede further. As noted in the last chapter, Fisher and Ury suggest a critically important way for each negotiator to identify his or her own point of minimally acceptable agreement, which they term the best alternative to a negotiated agreement (BATNA). Each negotiator should ask him or herself what alternatives they have available if negotiations fail, and they should then seek to identify the best possible outcome from these other options. This in effect gives them the value of nonagreement, which may be compared with the value of any possible agreement; agreements will be acceptable only if they have positive value or value that exceeds that of their next best alternative. The BATNA then provides a standard against which all possible agreements may be evaluated.

Yet in identifying BATNAs, Fisher and Ury emphasize the importance of focusing not on the superficial positions taken by the parties, as is most often the case in traditional bargaining, but rather on the interests underlying those positions. Unlike traditional bargaining models, where parties may stake out positions on an issue continuum for any tactical reason, Fisher and Ury stress the importance of identifying the inherent interests that may underlie those positions. The BATNAs should then reflect those underlying interests, and the goal of a negotiation is to fashion an agreement that serves those basic interests. Positions may simply reflect bluffs or other attempts by one party to mislead the other or gain advantages in distributive bargaining. But interests of states are generally consistent and enduring over time, and they may help each country determine its own BATNA, as well as helping each side to estimate the BATNAs of the other by studying their long-term interests. Because interests do not change frequently and may be deduced in part from a careful analysis of another country's history, political system, culture, and economic condition, it is easier to judge the basic interests of another country than it is to guess about the validity of specific positions they may take on issues under negotiation. At the same time one must be cautious and accept the fact that one may misperceive or at least not fully understand the interests and needs of others. It is difficult for a representative of one country to stand in the shoes of a diplomat from another country and perceive that country's interests in the same way. But since interests reach deeper than the attitudes and opinions of any particular representative, they at least offer a way to depersonalize conflicts and seek more enduring values that seem to motivate representatives of states as they negotiate.

Thus, if one focuses on the enduring interests of the other party, it is frequently possible to differentiate rhetorical positions that are bluffs from those that represent real commitments. It is easier to identify the range of bargaining space and look for mutually beneficial solutions that may provide relatively equitable benefits to both parties if one can estimate accurately those interests that influence the choice of the BATNA of the other party and of oneself. In this case, it may be possible to estimate relatively accurately where those BATNAs lie, so that one does not have to rely on opening positions as an indicator of each party's position, especially given the ways discussed previously in which such opening positions may be manipulated to seek tactical advantages in bargaining. It is less difficult to find fair or equitable solutions that fall midway between the resistance points of the two parties rather than halfway between their opening positions. Since these kinds of fifty-percent solutions represent approximately equal benefits for both parties relative to their next best alternative, this would also seem to offer a normatively superior criterion for a fair outcome than is the case when one splits the difference between potentially exaggerated opening offers and demands.

Once one has identified the interests of the parties, then one may proceed to creative problem solving, in which the parties individually, or together, try to invent options that will produce mutual benefits. In this effort, the parties should not restrict their search to the options that are often neatly defined for every problem, or to ways in which the problem has been defined in the past. Rather, the parties must seek ways to invent creative options. This requires the parties: "(1) to separate the act of inventing options from the act of judging them; (2) to broaden the options on the table rather than look for a single answer; (3) to search for mutual gains; and (4) to invent ways of making their decision easy."[19]

The emphasis in this approach is for each party to try to view the problem from the perspective of the other and try to find solutions that meet the other's concerns. In this sense, they try to find the valid points in the positions of the other party, develop empathy, and then seek solutions that seem to incorporate the interests of the other. Fisher and Ury particularly note the value of phrasing proposals in terms of "yesable propositions," that is "a proposal to which their responding with the single word 'yes' would be sufficient, realistic, and operational."[20]

The essence of this approach is one of converting the negotiation from a zero-sum to a non-zero-sum game. This may be illustrated by a little parable about two women who are arguing over the same orange that both want to use. They first consider dividing the orange in half, but that way both lose; neither will have enough orange to meet their needs. They begin to discuss their reasons for wanting the orange: one wants to make orange juice and the other wants to make orange marmalade. This discussion of their basic interests reveals an obvious mutually beneficial solution. Instead of cutting the orange in half, they peel it; the entire peel goes to the woman who wants to make marmalade, whereas the entire interior goes to the woman who wants to make orange juice. With this division, they are both satisfied; indeed, each one got as much as if she had obtained the entire orange for herself.

In international diplomacy, this parable resembles roughly the situation at Camp David in 1978 when U.S. President Jimmy Carter sought to mediate the conflict between Israel, represented by Prime Minister Menachem Begin, and Egypt, under President Anwar Sadat. After Kissinger's shuttle diplomacy of 1974–75, the Sinai, the territory lying between Egypt and Israel, was divided down the middle by a line of disengagement. Throughout modern history the Sinai had been part of Egypt. However, Israel had captured the Sinai in the 1967 war, although small sections of it were recaptured by Egypt in the 1973 war. Kissinger's shuttle diplomacy had approached the problem essentially as a zero-sum negotiation, and the Sinai was temporarily divided more or less in half between the two claimants by a disengagement zone. When Sadat and Begin came to Camp David, they also approached the issue in essentially zero-sum terms; both lay claim to the entire Sinai territory. However, President Carter clearly realized that every kilometer the boundary moved from the disengagement line toward Egypt was a victory for Israel and a loss for Egypt, and every kilometer it moved in the opposite direction represented a gain for Egypt and a loss for Israel. As long as the issue was defined this way, neither side was prepared to budge.

In his mediating role, however, President Carter encouraged the two adversaries to seek a mutually beneficial, positive-sum solution rather than to continue dividing the Sinai. There was no way this issue could be disaggregated, however, and there were no other issues of comparable importance to the two that could be linked to it as a mutually beneficial tradeoff. Therefore, a solution could only be found through creative problem solving. A prerequisite for this, however, was a diagnosis of the fundamental interests that lay behind their positions in which each claimed all of the Sinai for itself. After discussing the issue, it became clear that Egypt's interest in regaining control of the Sinai was to restore its national integrity, to regain territory that it perceived to have been unjustly stolen from it by force in 1967. Thus, the fundamental Egyptian interest was one of restoring its own sovereignty over the Sinai. On the other hand, Israel's interests in the Sinai basically boiled down to security. The 1967 war broke out when Egypt had demanded that U.N. Peacekeeping Forces in the Sinai be sent home, leaving Egyptian armies equipped with heavy battle tanks on Israel's borders. As a small and vulnerable country, Israel felt threatened by a powerful neighbor with large quantities of hostile troops on its borders and within a few hours of its capital. Thus, Israel's interest in retaining control of part if not all of the Sinai was not based so much on a claim to legitimate sovereignty as it was based on the need for self-defense in the face of a hostile neighbor.

The formula that was discovered, and became the foundation for the 1978 Camp David accords, was one in which the entire territory of the Sinai was returned to Egypt, but the entire territory was also demilitarized. Thus, like the parable of the two women and the orange, both countries achieved their essential objectives. Egypt regained complete sovereignty over the territory, and Israel assured itself that Egyptian troops, tanks, and artillery would be removed far back from the border. Neither had to concede to the other; instead, both could accept the agreement as one in which they gained. Fisher and Ury have described the outcome of this agreement as follows: "Reconciling interests rather than positions works for two reasons. First, for every interest there usually exist several possible positions that could satisfy it. All too often people simply adopt the most obvious position, as Israel did, for example, in announcing that they intended to keep part of the Sinai. When you do look behind opposed positions for the motivating interests, you can often find an alternative position which meets not only your interests but theirs as well. In the Sinai, demilitarization was one such alternative."[21]

Identifying options for mutual benefit may also be facilitated by trying to find objective criteria as a basis for a formula, some universal principles that seem to be above the narrow interests of either party. These criteria may be suggested by legal norms, ethical principles, custom, market conditions, expert opinion or technical analysis, or other similar criteria that are somehow independent of the parties to the conflict. If the parties can agree upon a set of objective criteria that would be acceptable to both, then these criteria may frame a formula that both can accept. Fisher and Ury note: "By discussing such criteria rather than what the parties are willing or unwilling to do, neither party need give in to the other; both can defer to a fair solution."[22] It is generally easier to save face by conceding to a universally recognized principle than by appearing to give in to a long-time enemy.

It is not even necessary that these objective criteria be lofty principles; they may simply represent solutions that are unique, conspicuous, or salient, and have substantial prominence. In a discussion of tacit bargaining in the absence of communication, Schelling has argued that people may coordinate their behavior to find common, salient solutions even without communicating. For example, given a map of a territory, two individuals who have been separated may both decide to try to find one another at a bridge across a prominent river; if two individuals are asked separately to divide $100 into two piles, they usually agree tacitly to divide it into two equal piles of $50 each.[23] In international negotiations, for example, when trying to negotiate a date at which control over the Panama Canal would be fully turned over to Panama, given a range of possibilities between 1998 and 2028, the United States and Panama agreed in their 1978 treaty to effect the changeover at midnight 31 December 1999–1 January 2000. There is nothing that makes the turn of the century an intrinsically appropriate date, but it certainly was a conspicuous solution on which the two parties could agree.

These problem-solving approaches to negotiation then suggest an approach which does not lead to the appearance of Prisoners' Dilemma conflicts as readily as traditional bargaining. Where each seeks its own individual, short-term interest, the two parties generally end up being worse off. By contrast, when the two parties seek to cooperate to achieve mutually beneficial solutions, this usually tends to reinforce the long-term self-interests of each of the parties as well. It does so in part because this approach prevents optimal solutions from being undermined by mistrust and conflict, as in the Prisoners' Dilemma. It also serves long-term interests because agreements based on mutual interests also tend to endure, while agreements that may undermine the fundamental interests of at least one of the parties are likely to be violated and eventually to dissolve.

This approach also argues for different tactics to produce agreement. In the bargaining perspective, agreement generally depends on the flexibility of the parties to make concessions to one another that will provide convergence. In situations in which bargaining space exists, as Schelling notes: "There is some range of alternative outcomes in which any point is better for both sides than no agreement at all. To insist on any such point is pure bargaining, since one always would take less rather than reach no agreement at all, and since one always *can* recede if retreat proves necessary to agreement. Yet if both parties are aware of the limits to this range, *any* outcome is a point from which at least one party would have been willing to retreat and the other knows it! There is no resting place. There is, however, an outcome; and if we cannot find it in the logic of the situation we may find it in the tactics employed."[24]

In short, finding agreement in bargaining is a tactical issue, and greater flexibility in the use of these tactics may facilitate agreement. Too much rigidity in tactics may create stalemates, even though both parties know that flexibility could produce agreement. Yet too much flexibility may induce exploitative tactics from the other party. Hence the Prisoners' Dilemma reappears. Pruitt and Lewis have tried to overcome this dilemma by introducing the notion of flexible rigidity. They recommend a combination of tactics: "While remaining relatively rigid with respect to ends (i.e., goals or aspirations)—holding fast to them over a period of time—they must be flexible with respect to means, trying out various options in search of one that satisfies both sides."[25]

A similar notion has been captured by Pruitt and Rubin, who urge negotiators to pursue a strategy of firm flexibility. In this approach one is firm about one's basic interests, while being tactically flexible "about how one's own interests are achieved in order to be open to new ideas about how to reconcile them with Other's interests."[26] While the concept of firm flexibility or flexible rigidity offers an advance over most tactical prescriptions derived from traditional bargaining models, it does not solve altogether at least two problems. On the one hand, in negotiations where there are fundamental conflicts of interest, rigidity about the goals might block progress altogether, no matter how flexible one is about means. On the other hand, too much tactical flexibility may be perceived by the other as a sign of weakness the other party may exploit to its own benefit. Thus, the negotiator's dilemma cannot be completely resolved within the traditional bargaining perspective.

Conversely, within the creative problem-solving perspective, tactics are defined more in terms of process than in terms of behaviors designed to affect movement on the issues. Flexibility entails a willingness to engage in a search process through trial and error to try to identify a formula. It may involve the use of techniques necessary to develop empathy with the other side and recognize at least the partial validity of the partner's position, and thereby begin to develop a shared image of the problem. It may entail identifying underlying needs, aspirations, and interests of the parties and then working together to invent mutually beneficial solutions to their joint problems, often with the aid of a third-party facilitator or mediator. John Burton has summarized the procedures of the problem-solving method of conflict resolution as follows: "First there must be a careful analysis of parties and issues. Second it is necessary to bring those two parties whose relationships are most affected into a facilitated interaction situation in which relationships are analyzed in depth. Other parties and issues are dealt with in due course in the same way. At this stage no proposals are entertained, nor is there any bargaining or negotiation. When there is an agreed definition of the problem, and a full assessment of the costs of existing policies based on a knowledge of responses to the denial of human needs, there can be exploration of positive options."[27] In short, the conflict resolution process within this framework requires a very different kind of flexibility from the willingness to make accommodations and seek compromise solutions that is so characteristic of traditional bargaining.

Can these two broad perspectives, one based on traditional concession-convergence bargaining models and the other based on creative joint problem solving, be reconciled? For all of the reasons mentioned above, the two perspectives have been viewed by most theorists as antagonistic, and the proponents of each perspective have frequently criticized those taking the opposing point of view. However, these two approaches may both capture certain key aspects of negotiations, but each may be treating only a part of the process. In the classic parable about three blind men feeling an elephant, each man perceived something different: one found the tail and believed that he was touching a rope, the second felt the trunk and believed he had found a hose, and the third thought that the leg was a tree. None perceived the entire elephant. So it may be that there is no single paradigm that explains all aspects of negotiating behavior, and proponents of each of the two perspectives may be examining only one aspect of the negotiation process or one particular type or class of negotiations.

In addition, part of the difference between these two perspectives represents a difference in the analysts' goals. Often proponents of problem solving take a normative or prescriptive approach: they recommend problem solving as a method not only for reaching agreement, but also for achieving efficient, optimal, or fair results. On the other hand, most advocates of the bargaining approach tend to support their work with empirical evidence that suggests bargaining models provide a useful framework for describing how states actually negotiate or for explaining the outcomes of specific international negotiations. Therefore, to some extent at least, the two perspectives have talked right past one another, because their fundamental purposes have usually been quite different.

Without attempting to develop a full reconciliation of these two perspectives here, it is useful to identify some of the characteristics of the negotiation process or classes of negotiations that may be best treated by one perspective versus the other. Furthermore, the dichotomy between prescription, on the one hand, and description and explanation, on the other, may also be overdrawn: both perspectives may provide valid descriptions and explanations of behavior in different kinds of negotiations, and both may provide useful prescriptive tools for dealing with different kinds of problems.

It may be possible to identify the scope conditions for the applicability of each perspective primarily on theoretical grounds. Many negotiable issues resemble the classic bargaining problem of a buyer and seller haggling over the price of any good, such as a used car. In such a situation, each party has an opening bid and an undisclosed point of minimal acceptable agreement (the BATNA or resistance point). As long as the resistance points of the parties are not mutually exclusive, there exists between them a range of acceptable agreements—the bargaining space. In these kinds of situations, the primary problems for the negotiators are twofold: (1) to identify the approximate range of bargaining space within which agreement may be reached; and (2) to engage in concession-making until the positions of the parties converge somewhere within that space.

In these kinds of situations, where bargaining space is known to exist on an issue that is more or less linear, the process of reaching agreement may be fully explained by bargaining models. Prescriptive advice may be useful in assisting the parties to reach agreement by encouraging negotiators to remain flexible in making new offers, accepting offers of the other party, and making concessions to the other, while avoiding impasses based on rigid commitments and retractions of previous offers. The major dilemma in these bargaining situations, as noted previously, derives from the fact that bargaining tactics designed to win a larger share of the good for one party may create a stalemate and thus detract from the ability of the parties even to reach agreement. Tactics designed to facilitate rapid and efficient consummation of agreements may cause the party using such tactics to be exploited and receive a smaller share of the gains than might have otherwise been possible. Thus, bargaining theory still has an important explanatory and prescriptive role to play: namely, giving advice about how to juggle these competing demands of the bargaining situation in such a way as not only to reach agreement, but also to reach agreements that the parties will consider fair or equitable in terms of some common standards of distributive justice.

On the other hand, many negotiating problems are not readily susceptible to solution by this kind of bargaining. These kinds of problems tend to have several features that differentiate them from issues more amenable to solution through concession-convergence bargaining:

1. There appears to be an absence of bargaining space, which can either reflect a real conflict of interest or misperception of the situation by one or more parties.

2. There are multiple and complex issues, which are linked in such a way that they cannot readily be negotiated one by one; that is, the negotiation situation is characterized by a condition referred to by Robert Keohane and Joseph Nye as "complex interdependence."[28]

3. There are multiple parties whose preferences are quite different and crosscutting rather than reinforcing, so that there is no clearly defined and mutually agreed issue dimension along which bargaining may occur.

4. There is intense emotional involvement by the parties, mutual misperceptions are common, tensions are high, the most fundamental needs and interests are threatened, and the parties' cognitive framing of the problem prevents the identification of a clear issue dimension or bargaining space.

If any or all of these conditions pertain, then traditional bargaining behaviors are not likely to produce an efficient or fair solution. There is no room for flexibility if it is defined in terms of soft rather than hard bargaining tactics. What is needed in these situations is a problem-solving orientation that includes such features as issue redefinition (aggregating issues or packaging tradeoffs, disaggregating issues or fractionating, and reframing issues through role reversal or other perspective-taking techniques); basing the outcome on widely recognized principles that suggest mutually beneficial solutions rather than on the result of power-oriented tactics; utilizing actors in various third-party or mediating roles—ranging from fairly passive "good offices" to quite active exertion of influence by third parties on the main parties in conflict—to assist them in reaching agreement; and task-oriented group behaviors, including the emergence of efficient leadership and the effective "management of complexity" by the group. All of these many techniques for problem solving will be taken up in greater detail in subsequent chapters.

In summary, a comprehensive model of the negotiation process cannot rely either on a simple bargaining or problem-solving paradigm alone, but instead we must evaluate each and every negotiation to determine whether or not one approach or the other, or some combination of the two, is likely to be most appropriate to facilitate agreement. Thus, the appropriate negotiating processes must be determined situationally rather than abstractly, and in one situation a flexible, successful negotiating process may require a willingness to engage in soft rather than hard bargaining tactics, making reciprocal concessions, and seeking a convergence of positions; in other situations the attainment of agreement may require a willingness to explore alternative definitions of the problem; work with other countries in a task-oriented, problem-solving approach; and seek solutions based on interests and principles rather than on power or bargaining skill.

Therefore, these two perspectives taken together suggest a fundamental approach to negotiations in which two rational parties may try to maximize their joint interests by seeking solutions to problems together through the process of negotiation. They may bargain, try to problem solve, or employ some combination of the two methods. In spite of their simplifications, both perspectives offer a basic foundation for virtually all systematic approaches to the analysis of international negotiations; the axioms and assumptions of bargaining theory and of the problem-solving perspective together provide a starting point for further analysis. Even in its more sophisticated versions, these approaches to negotiation also simplify or neglect altogether many aspects of the process that may have an important impact on the outcome of negotiations.

Thus far in this analysis, I have assumed that we are dealing only with two parties trying to negotiate rather than with multiparty negotiations. I have assumed that their interests and power are approximately symmetrical rather than unequally distributed. I have treated the parties as if they were unitary actors rather than as complex political systems with multiple interests in the issues under negotiation. I have examined the negotiations as if they were taking place in a vacuum rather than in a complex and interdependent international system, And I have treated the negotiators as if they were rational actors, trying to achieve optimal and mutually beneficial outcomes, thereby neglecting many of the human characteristics of negotiations, especially the fact that the participants in international negotiations often come from multiple cultures with very different value systems and ways of framing issues. Therefore, I will turn in part 3 to these many additional factors that will introduce greater complexity, but also hopefully greater realism, into the framework for the analysis of international negotiations.

Part 3

Complexity in International Negotiations: Toward a Comprehensive Framework

Chapter 7

The Impact of Power and Influence: Symmetry and Asymmetry

In part 2, I developed a model of international negotiations that was based largely on two rational, unitary actors— alike in all respects and bargaining with one another in order to achieve an optimal result. I viewed this issue both from the perspective of the benefits to each individual party and from the point of view of maximizing joint benefits, and I examined some of the contradictory pressures exerted upon negotiators when the search for individual gains seems to come into conflict with a search for mutual benefits. In this analysis I relied fairly heavily upon formal models of bargaining. With the aid of these models, we can analyze the initial conditions that affect the actors and then hazard some predictions about the kinds of outcomes they are likely to reach. Even when we depart from the formal bargaining models to consider problem solving, there is still an assumption that two well-intentioned individuals could behave rationally and work together cooperatively to achieve an optimal solution that enhances their joint benefits.

Yet the conditions assumed by such formal models seldom pertain in the real world of international negotiations. Often more than two parties are involved, and seldom are they internally unified. The utilities of the actors are often complex and shifting over time, so that each party may be uncertain even about its own utilities, to say nothing of the preferences of the other party. These are likely to be unknown as a result of factors such as imperfect information, faulty communications, or even deliberate concealment or deceit. The issues too are complex, often containing many dimensions so that an actor's preferences may be inconsistent or even contradictory from one issue to the next. Actors have power that they can exercise to influence the outcome of the bargaining process, and these resources are not often distributed equally between the parties. Finally, negotiations are conducted by individuals who represent their states, and, while they may try to serve as detached servants of the national interest, their own personality, cognitive structure, and culture affect their behavior when they negotiate. Therefore, very few international problems are solvable in the analytical sense implied by formal models of bargaining.

Models of bilateral bargaining and problem solving have certainly introduced some very useful concepts for negotiation theory as presented in the previous chapters, including the concepts of security levels,[1] targets and resistance points,[2] and the "best alternative to a negotiated agreement" (BATNA),[3] all of which tend to suggest that rational negotiators will seek to reach agreement within some specified range that I have called bargaining space. These concepts may be formalized as axioms that will help to set the basic parameters of bargaining situations. Yet attempts to derive deductively valid solutions to bargaining problems have largely failed to produce satisfactory results when applied to real international negotiations. Furthermore, many bargaining problems are unable to be solved by traditional bargaining techniques. This requires the introduction of concepts of creative problem solving, including debate, learning processes, persuasion, and brainstorming in the search for valid solutions. Yet the very creativity required by these approaches also defies attempts by social scientists to identify specific outcomes that they will be likely to generate. The outcomes of most negotiations in international relations will usually be determined through the process of negotiation itself, rather than being derived analytically from some clearly defined set of initial conditions and axioms.

One way in which many analysts have responded to this lack of realism is to throw out formal bargaining models altogether, rejecting them as totally irrelevant to international negotiations. Obviously that has not been the tack that I have taken in this book, because I believe that the axioms of these bargaining and problem-solving approaches are an essential foundation to any negotiation theory. But they are just a foundation and not the fully constructed edifice, so they alone are insufficient as a basis for negotiation theory in the international arena. Indeed, they teach us as much by what they leave out as by what they provide in the way of fundamental axioms. Anatol Rapoport's observations about the limits of game theory may be equally applicable to the negotiation problem as a whole: "game theory leads to some genuine impasses, that is, to situations where its axiomatic base is shown to be insufficient for dealing even theoretically with certain types of conflict situations. These impasses set up tensions in the minds of people who care. They must therefore look around for other frameworks into which conflict situations can be cast."[4]

My task in this section will be to look around for other frameworks that will help us understand the negotiation process in international relations better. I shall do this by first examining each of the simplifying assumptions upon which the basic bilateral framework was constructed and then relaxing those assumptions one by one. This process involves a clear tradeoff that must be made explicit. Ideally there are two important criteria that should guide the process of theory construction: (1) a useful theory should be parsimonious, in that we would like to explain as much as possible about the negotiation process with as few key variables as possible; and (2) a useful theory should be sufficiently rich so that it can be applied to a wide variety of problems and contexts in a very complex international setting.

Unfortunately, these two criteria often compete with one another. Each time that we relax an assumption, we sacrifice deductive power and parsimony of explanation. These are no small losses, since both are valuable in the process of theory construction. Yet when put up against the loss of the ability to explain complex international negotiations adequately on the basis of these simple assumptions alone, these are necessary sacrifices. The result should be a theoretical framework that is more subtle, complex, and capable of explaining important variations in many different types of international negotiations. In the end a theoretical framework that appears to be irrelevant to practitioners of international negotiations, or that cannot explain in any nuanced way some of the complex interactions that occur in international negotiations, will ultimately be of little value.

Therefore, in part 3 of this book I shall proceed to relax the assumptions of the initial model one at a time. Each time, I shall present the major new explanatory factors that may be introduced when these assumptions are relaxed, and I shall evaluate the gains in explanatory power that are achieved as a result. This may also be viewed as a process in which new components may be added to the basic model one at a time, each one of which introduces additional elements of complexity and richness into the attempt to explain the outcomes of international negotiations. At the end I hope to be able to achieve a theoretical framework for the analysis of the international negotiation process that is sufficiently rich and flexible to be applied to a wide range of international issues in multiple and different contexts.

ASYMMETRY OF POWER AND CAPABILITIES

I will begin in the present chapter by relaxing the assumption that the two parties in the negotiation model are alike in all respects. This assumption of equality and symmetry between the parties made it possible to make the parties completely interchangeable, and reach conclusions that ignored any difference of power. Power here refers to both resources that the parties to the negotiation may hold and their ability to exert influence on one another through the process of negotiation. Yet parties to international negotiations often vary a great deal in terms of these attributes, and these differences may have a significant impact on the outcomes of international negotiations. Thus, the consequences of these differences must be taken into account by any valid theory of international negotiation.

Most considerations of the impact of power and influence on international negotiations are presented within the context of the realist tradition of international politics. The key concept in the realist tradition is power. Yet power is defined by the realists in many different ways, ranging from absolute capabilities that an individual country may possess, through relative or comparative capabilities distributed across two or more countries, to much more vague concepts like power over the minds of individual persons. For example, Claude defines power very narrowly as "military capability—the elements which contribute directly or indirectly to the capacity to coerce, kill, and destroy."[5] Obviously, this definition is too narrow for an analysis of power in negotiations. While the ability to coerce, kill, and destroy may be used as a threat, or as a means to bypass negotiations so that states can achieve their objectives by direct action, power within the negotiation process obviously must mean something broader than brute military force. At the other end of a continuum, however, falls Morgenthau's classic definition: "When we speak of power, we mean man's [sic] control over the minds and actions of other men. By political power we refer to the mutual relations of control among the holders of public authority."[6]

This definition is so broad that power can be just about anything that affects human behavior. When used in this way as an explanation for behavior and outcomes in negotiations, it risks creating a tautology since just about anything can be explained at this high level of generality. At the same time, important distinctions risk being overlooked by the abstractness of this notion of power. In short, power may be defined so broadly that its usefulness in explaining international negotiations is limited. Rather than defining power so broadly, it may be preferable to break the concept of power down into its many components and then to utilize the most relevant of those components in constructing a theory of international negotiations.

The first element of power that I shall consider is the raw capabilities of states. Capabilities here are defined as the resources that states may utilize in various ways in the negotiation process. These resources may be potential or actual, but they are relevant to negotiations either when states explicitly utilize them to try to manipulate the negotiation process or sometimes when they operate as background factors that implicitly affect the behavior of states as they negotiate, even though they may not be mentioned explicitly.

There are, of course many elements that make up both the potential and the actual capabilities of states, as well as their comparative or relative positions in a global hierarchy of state capabilities. Realist writings on international politics tend to emphasize military capabilities almost exclusively, although more recently a much greater emphasis has been placed by so-called neorealists on economic capabilities. Certainly there are states like the Soviet Union that, until it disintegrated in 1991, was strong militarily but relatively weak economically, whereas other states like Japan have substantial economic power with few military capabilities. The relevance of these differences may depend in large part on the issue under negotiation. For example, the USSR had a relative advantage over Japan concerning the dispute over the Kurile Islands, which the Russian Federation retained even after the dissolution of the Soviet Union. Russia occupies the islands, and Japan lacks the military capacity to threaten credibly to dislodge them.

On the other hand, there can be little doubt that Japan wields considerably greater influence in global economic negotiations. For example, Japan is a major actor in the so-called G-7 summit negotiations of the world's major economic powers, whereas the Soviet Union and later Russia have been forced to come to these negotiations as a nonparticipant pleading almost desperately for economic assistance. There can be little doubt that Japan's superior economic might give it an ability to affect the outcomes of these negotiations, whereas Russia remains totally dependent on the decisions of others when it comes to making decisions about Western economic assistance to the countries of Eastern Europe. Whether Japan can use its economic capabilities to influence the Russian Federation to yield its military position in noneconomic negotiations on issues such as control over the Kurile Islands remains to be seen.

The global hierarchy of relative capabilities may be most heavily influenced by a combination of military and economic resources. If the United States has power in the present international system greater than that of any other country, it is because of its combination of capabilities in both the traditional military domain and in economic resources. As Joseph Nye concludes in a recent assessment of the U.S. relative capabilities on the world scene: "The United States today retains more traditional hard power resources than any other country. It also has the soft ideological and institutional resources to retain its leading place in the new domains of transnational interdependence."[7]

Any analysis of capabilities, however, must also define these more broadly than in just military and economic terms. Among the additional components of capability which ought not to be neglected is the political cohesion and effectiveness of a state's government, which may be especially influential in affecting the outcome of international negotiations. For example, in the negotiations leading up to the Paris Peace

Treaty of 1973, the Vietnamese negotiators had far fewer military or economic capabilities than did the United States, but they represented a united country whose leaders believed that they were defending their homeland against a foreign invader. Furthermore, any dissent that may have been present at home about these negotiations could effectively be repressed by an authoritarian government. By contrast, the United States was deeply divided at home about the fundamental issue of U.S. involvement in Vietnam, a division that seemed to deepen with each passing year and the expansion of U.S. military operations deeper into Cambodia, Laos, and North Vietnam. In this context, Vietnam had greater political capabilities than did the United States to support their negotiating position in Paris.

This fact seemed to contribute to a decision by the United States to make early unilateral concessions in the negotiations in the hope of getting the North Vietnamese to reciprocate. Therefore, a tremendous inequality of military and economic resources was largely canceled out by the political cohesion of the North Vietnamese government in support of their objectives, both at the negotiating table in Paris and on the ground in Southeast Asia. Indeed, in the final stages of negotiations in 1972 the United States broke off a cease-fire and resorted to the controversial December bombings of Hanoi and Haiphong, the principal cities of North Vietnam, in order to try to redress the balance and gain support for the agreement from their erstwhile South Vietnamese allies.[8] Despite this desperate attempt to reverse the trend of the negotiations and at least to create the impression of tilting the process toward the results that the United States preferred, it is hardly surprising that the results of the 1973 Vietnam Peace Accords would have been quite favorable to the North Vietnamese position, so favorable in fact that they were able to consolidate control over all of Vietnam within two years after the accords went into effect.

Education and the skills of one's population are likewise an important factor in negotiations. Some countries have large numbers of skilled, well-trained diplomats, and this gives them certain bargaining advantages over others whose diplomatic services may be dominated by nonprofessionals, such as those who acquired their positions through political patronage. The ability to call upon expert advice from an extensive government bureaucracy and a large number of research institutes may also enhance a country's position, especially in negotiations involving highly technical issues where expertise and command of information may provide important advantages. This is especially important as international transactions become ever more dominated by highly technical issues, such as arms control, economics, and the environment. On issues such as these, the role of subject-matter experts becomes critical to the negotiation process. As Peter Haas has noted, a critical role is played by the "networks of knowledge-based experts—epistemic communities— . . . in articulating the cause-and-effect relationships of complex problems, helping states identify their interests, framing the issues for collective debate, proposing specific policies, and identifying salient points for negotiation."[9] Those states that have access to this knowledge and to the support of these so-called epistemic communities of experts thereby have access to a special form of capability in the conduct of negotiations.

There is no doubt that this factor gives a substantial advantage to large and relatively wealthy countries, with highly educated and technically sophisticated specialists. For example, at negotiations in Vienna in 1992 on an "Open Skies" treaty permitting military overflights for reconnaissance and to establish confidence that other countries were not preparing threatening military actions, there was a substantial asymmetry among the many participating delegations. At one extreme was the United States, with a large delegation sent to Vienna solely for purposes of negotiating that specific treaty; the ambassador was supported by a staff of military and intelligence experts, who were familiar with all aspects of the technology of aircraft and photo-reconnaissance equipment to be utilized in conducting open skies inspections, and by other advisors who were acquainted with the political and legal issues entailed in the negotiations. By contrast, many of the smaller countries such as Belgium or Bulgaria had only two or three individuals on their delegations, perhaps each one with some expertise on legal, political, or military issues, but without any large supporting or highly specialized staffs. Furthermore, these same individuals were representing their countries simultaneously, in some cases, in the U.N. agencies located in Vienna; in the International Atomic Energy Agency, which regulates nuclear proliferation and that was dealing at the same time with sensitive issues concerning the Iraqi nuclear program; in the negotiations on Confidence and Security-Building in Europe, which produced a new agreement known as the 1992 Vienna CSBMs document at about the same time; in negotiations on Conventional Forces in Europe to seek an agreement on the reduction of military personnel throughout Europe; in the Conflict Prevention Center of the Conference on Security and Cooperation (CSCE) in Europe, which was trying to mediate or help in other ways to resolve the open conflict between Armenia and Azerbaijan in the disputed province of Nagorno-Karabakh; and in the Conference on Security and Cooperation in Europe, which was drafting a mandate for the future architecture of European security to be adopted at a summit in Helsinki later that year. When two or three people must divide their attention among so many important negotiations, each requiring specialized knowledge, obviously their capabilities to affect any agreement are very limited. This put them at a relative disadvantage in comparison with other countries, such as the United States, which had separate delegations at the vast majority of these negotiations, each staffed with a wide range of substantive experts on the topics under negotiation.

Finally, volition or willpower is an important attribute in negotiations. Countries that care deeply about issues may be willing to negotiate with greater care, stay at a negotiation longer, and have higher levels of aspirations than those who are less committed to an issue. All of these factors may enhance a state's ability to hold out against rapid or extensive concessions, even when put under pressure from countries with greater military or economic resources. For example, in the negotiations between the United States and Panama that produced the Panama Canal Treaty in 1978, the government of Panama was strongly committed to a successful outcome of their negotiation with the United States because it involved the most essential values concerning their national identity. Obtaining sovereignty over the Panama Canal Zone had become the major symbol of the national integrity of the country, and the failure to obtain such an outcome would have almost certainly brought down the government of President Omar Torrijos. Indeed, Torrijos' domestic weakness became a paradoxical source of strength, in part because the United States did not want his government to fall and be replaced by a more radical and leftist regime that would be even harder to negotiate with.[10]

By contrast, for the United States the Panama Canal, though important, was of less significance than, for example, the concurrent negotiations with the Soviet Union on the SALT II Treaty on limiting strategic nuclear weapons or the Camp David negotiations between Israel and Egypt that sought a peaceful resolution to important components of the Arab-Israeli conflict in the Middle East. While certain domestic interest groups, especially the "zonians," U.S. citizens who lived and worked in the Canal Zone, lobbied with the strong support of the ideological right-wing in the U.S. Congress against turning over the Canal Zone to Panamanian jurisdiction, the overwhelming majority of individuals and interest groups were far more concerned about the cold war and the threat to U.S. security from the Soviet Union or about the continuing tension and conflict in the Middle East. Reducing those threats through arms control agreements or through an Israeli-Egyptian accord was also a higher priority for the Carter administration than the agreement on the Panama Canal Zone, though a successful agreement there was also seen as important for improving U.S. relations with all of Latin America. On balance, however, the will power and commitment of the government of Panama provided it with capabilities that offset its obvious weaknesses relative to the United States in military power and economic resources. The result was an agreement that seemed to balance the interests of both the United States and Panama far more than one might have predicted if one assumed that the agreement would be a simple reflection of the vast difference in the military and economic capabilities of the two countries.

Therefore, it is important to keep in mind that capabilities are multidimensional, so that states that are powerful on some dimensions may be weaker on others; a state's net capabilities will be some combination of its capabilities on all of these dimensions, and its capabilities may also vary from issue to issue depending on which capabilities may be most relevant for affecting the outcome of negotiations on any specific issue. It is essential to look not only at overall capabilities of individual states, but also to look at their relative capabilities on those dimensions that are most relevant to the particular issue under negotiation.

Furthermore, one must pay attention not only to the absolute capabilities of states or even to the relative distribution of capabilities, but also to the specific processes through which differences in capabilities are introduced into the negotiations. Too often realists have jumped directly from an assessment of the capabilities of states in a particular negotiation to conclusions about the outcomes of the negotiations, without examining the negotiation process that intervenes. Of course, there may be some circumstances in which resource considerations lie in the background and exert only an indirect effect on the negotiations. For example, in negotiations between the United States and Guatemala, or between the Soviet Union and Bulgaria, it was seldom necessary to make explicit reference to differences of capabilities between the two countries or to link the application of these capabilities directly with issues under negotiation. Dramatic differences in resources have a pervasive effect on such negotiations even if they are not brought specifically into the discussions. However, in most cases capability differences affect negotiations largely through the role they play in supporting influence by one actor relative to another within negotiations. It is through the use of capabilities to influence behavior that capabilities become converted from static absolute or relative attributes of states into dynamic instruments that affect interactions in all of international politics, including negotiations.

In a classic treatment of influence in international politics, J. David Singer notes that an influence attempt consists of the following elements: "(a) A's *prediction* as to how B will behave in a given situation in the absence of the influence attempt; (b) A's *preference* regarding B's behavior; and (c) the techniques and resources A utilizes to make (a) and (b) coincide as nearly as possible."[11]

In this way, we may differentiate between influence attempts intended to change behavior and those that seek to reinforce behavior. That is, if actor *A*'s goal is to get *B* to do what *A* prefers rather than what *A* predicts that *B* would do otherwise, then *A* must first determine what she prefers for B to do and what she predicts that B would do in the absence of any influence being exerted upon it. If A prefers that B continue his present behavior but believes that he prefers to change to something less liked by A, then A will attempt to reinforce B's present behavior and deter B from changing his behavior in ways that A believes to be undesirable. Conversely, if A prefers for B to change to a new behavior while B prefers to continue the status quo, then A must use influence to induce B to change his behavior. Of course, A's assessment of what B would prefer to do otherwise and A's prediction about what B is likely to do otherwise are always subjective, and A may guess wrong and therefore fail to exert the appropriate influence. However, once A has determined whether she wants to reinforce or change B's behavior, she must then examine possible techniques.

It is at this point that the theory of influence brings us back to the discussion of bargaining found in chapter 5, a clear illustration of the role of basic bargaining theory as the foundation for much of the elaboration that needs to be made upon it. The primary influence techniques identified by Singer are, of course, threats and promises. To recapitulate briefly, a threat is a conditional statement by A that if B behaves the way she prefers rather than according to A's preferences, then A will carry out a punishment or remove a reward from B. Conversely, a promise is a conditional statement by A that if B's behavior conforms with A's preferences rather than his own, A will provide a reward or remove a punishment. The effectiveness of threats and promises further depends on two primary factors: (1) whether or not B perceives that A will actually carry out the threats or promises; and (2) the magnitude of value lost or gained if they are carried out in comparison with the increment of value that B would obtain by doing what he prefers otherwise rather than complying with A's preferences. The first of these factors in turn depends upon two additional considerations, namely (1) B's perception of A's will or determination to carry out these rewards and punishments; and (2) B's perception of A's capabilities to carry out these rewards and punishments. Thus, possessing adequate capabilities or resources to implement threats and promises through providing rewards and punishments is a necessary, but not a sufficient, condition to exert influence. And it is through the application of these potential capabilities to exercise influence that states convert raw resources into a usable instrument for the conduct of international relations.

As Singer points out, influence is always two-directional, in the sense that, "while A is planning or attempting to influence B, B is itself exercising some impact on A's behavior. The very classification of B by A as a potential target of influence immediately leads to some degree of influence by B upon A, even when B makes no conscious influence attempt."[12] Nevertheless, for analytical purposes we may classify influence attempts as falling along a continuum ranging from primarily symmetrical (equal and two-directional) influence to asymmetrical (primarily one-directional). Influence is symmetrical when B can use counterthreats or counterpromises to cancel or to in some other way substantially negate A's attempt to influence B. Conversely, influence is asymmetrical when B has little or no such ability to exert influence in reply to A. While the difference between these two conditions may reflect a difference in the will power between A and B, most often it will reflect a difference in the capability to make credible threats and promises and implement them through providing rewards and punishments. Thus, inequalities in capabilities are important primarily because they translate into a difference in the ability of the two parties to exert influence on one another. If the ability to influence in a bilateral relationship is held primarily by one party and not by the other, this will create a significant asymmetry in their ability to affect the outcome of negotiations.

Not surprisingly, this approach was very influential on much of the writing about international negotiations in the early 1960s, such as that of Schelling and Iklé, who emphasized the role of commitments, warnings, threats, and promises in negotiations. As conditional statements, these behaviors depend heavily upon their credibility and the extent to which the object of influence believes that the rewards and punishments will actually be implemented. Credibility, in turn, depends on both the perceived will power of the other party to carry out these tactics and on its perceived capability to implement rewards and punishments. The unequal distribution of power or capabilities across the states in the international system translates into a differential ability to employ these negotiating tactics successfully. Therefore, *ceteris paribus*, states with greater capabilities have an advantage in negotiations.

A second way in which inequalities of resources may affect negotiations is through the ability of states to go beyond influence to the actual use of coercion to bring about their preferred outcome if negotiations fail. As the models of negotiation presented in chapter 6 emphasized, negotiators are often influenced by their alternatives if negotiations break down. While coercion has recently become a less ubiquitous feature of international relations than it has been in some past eras, it still remains a possibility available to many states in the international system. The use of force by Serbia against Bosnia's Muslim population beginning in 1991 certainly dramatically illustrates that the end of the cold war has not necessarily ushered in an era of peace and stability. And when the possibility to employ force does exist, states with lesser capabilities to coerce others may be forced to continue negotiations or accept terms of agreement, even if the terms are unfavorable, rather than risk becoming a victim of overt coercion. Alternatively, states with the capability to get what they want through brute force rather than negotiation may be quite willing to see negotiations break down if they have an advantageous alternative in these circumstances. Of course, they may utilize the threat to break off negotiations and employ coercive punishments as a tactic within the negotiations, but these may serve as implicit threats even when they are not explicitly introduced into the negotiations.

Thus, for example, when U.S. Secretary of State James Baker met with Iraqi Foreign Minister Tariq Aziz in early January of 1991 in Geneva to try to persuade the Iraqi government to cease their occupation of Kuwait, there was a great deal of asymmetry in the situation. Indeed, Baker declared that this was not a negotiation, merely a meeting for purposes of communication. He could hold out for complete and total capitulation by Aziz, because the failure of their talks could provide the pretext for the United States to abandon the diplomatic chambers in favor of the battlefield to try to resolve the dispute on their terms. In other words, the best alternative to a negotiated agreement for the U.S. administration was in all likelihood a politically beneficial military victory. The foreign minister of Iraq, on the other hand, appeared to have no negotiating options short of outright capitulation, since his country was vulnerable to the application of military force by the United States. Indeed, aside from an ability to inflict some punishment on U.S. allies such as Israel with its Scud missiles, Iraq had little or no capability to coerce the United States. While this weak BATNA on the part of Iraq might at first sight have been an argument in favor of their acquiescence, this appeared to be an even more unfavorable outcome than a military defeat, so long as Saddam Hussein had at least some hope of surviving the war and emerging from it in political control.[13] The result was that any efforts to reach a negotiated settlement were likely to fail, so that the issue would be decided by brute force rather than through diplomacy.

Of course, the use by the United States of coercive military force was possible in this instance largely due to a unique configuration of the international political system, in which the cold war had come to an end and the Soviet Union joined in support of the coalition led by the United States in the United Nations. This was a rare circumstance in the recent history of international relations where resorting to blatant coercion was seldom a plausible option. In this exceptional instance the ability to utilize coercive force led to the rapid breakdown of an international negotiation and the continuation of diplomacy through the application of military power. Certainly in the recent past, and probably in the vast majority of situations that are likely to appear in the present international system, coercion was simply not an available option. Therefore, inequalities of capabilities are most likely to influence the negotiation process itself through their role in reinforcing threats and promises issued either implicitly or explicitly within the negotiating chambers rather than by causing the negotiation process to break down.

Finally, it is important to note that it requires negotiating skill to translate raw capabilities into an ability to exert influence at the negotiating table. Military capabilities, though obviously relevant, should not be overemphasized, especially in an international system where the application of military force is increasingly dangerous and less likely to be used as frequently as in the past. As long as one can negotiate rather than use brute force, military power differences may not usually exert a determining influence on the outcome of negotiations. Rather it is the balance of capabilities that are directly relevant to the issue under negotiation, and the ability to use those capabilities effectively to gain influence and support one's bargaining tactics, that may be most relevant to the outcome of negotiations.

ASYMMETRY OF ALTERNATIVES TO A NEGOTIATED AGREEMENT

Most of the preceding analysis of capabilities and influence, however, assumes that negotiations are taking place within the context of traditional win-lose, distributive bargaining. If one allows oneself to engage in distributive bargaining, then it is clearly the case that differences in capabilities will exert an important effect on the outcome of negotiations. Furthermore, it will generally be the powerful who will win and the weak who will lose. As Roger Fisher and others have pointed out, this makes it especially important for those who are weaker on these traditional dimensions of power to seek an alternative, more principled approach to negotiations. In such situations, the task of the weaker party is defined by Fisher and Ury as follows: "In any negotiation there exist realities that are hard to change. In response to power, the most any method of negotiation can do is to meet two objectives: *first,* to protect you against making an agreement you should reject and *second,* to help you make the most of the assets you do have so that any agreement you reach will satisfy your interests as well as possible."[14]

In bargaining, the BATNA or resistance point (points a' and b' in figure 5.1 from chapter 5) represents the point of minimum acceptable agreement. As Fisher and Ury have suggested, this minimum acceptable agreement is determined largely by each party's best alternative to a negotiated agreement. A negotiator must always be conscious of what benefits or harm she would receive in the absence of an agreement, and should never be pressured or coerced into an agreement that will leave her worse off than would be the case if she walked out of the negotiations and pursued the next best alternative to the negotiated agreement. Knowledge and firmness about these alternatives should give the negotiator confidence that he or she cannot be forced into accepting a totally unacceptable agreement. It also should enable a negotiator to identify and even accept a beneficial agreement, even if the other party seems to

111

be gaining even more because of a power advantage. The standard for an acceptable agreement within this framework should be coming out ahead compared to one's own alternatives, not compared to the other party. As Fisher and Ury note, the BATNA "is the only standard which can protect you both from accepting terms that are too unfavorable and from rejecting terms it would be in your interest to accept."[15]

The effects of the BATNA in influencing asymmetrical outcomes in negotiations can be further explicated by returning to the axiomatic base in the game theoretic models presented in chapter 4, especially to the concept of the security level. To illustrate this point, I present a slightly revised version of figure 4.5 from that chapter here as figure 7.1. As noted in chapter 4, there is no clear consensus among game theorists about how to locate the single point of expected agreement along the Pareto-Optimal frontier, that is within the restricted negotiation set or bargain-

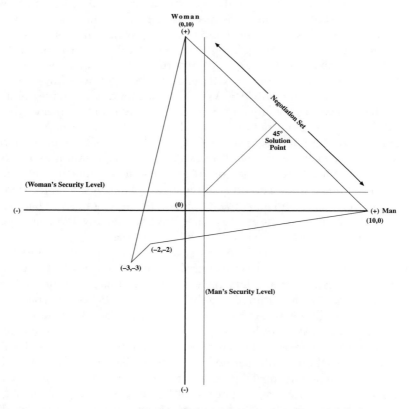

Figure 7.1 The Battle of the Sexes: A Symmetrical Solution. Based on Anatol Rapoport, *Two-Person Game Theory: The Essential Ideas* **(Ann Arbor: University of Michigan Press, 1969), pp. 99, 102.**

ing space. However, one approach introduced by Shapely is particularly relevant to the issue of asymmetrical outcomes.[16]

The main issue here is to estimate what is often referred to as the status quo point, that is the outcome that both parties would receive if there is no agreement. Obviously, the status quo point also corresponds to the best alternative to a negotiated agreement, because the status quo result will presumably lead each party to pursue its next best available option. From the discussion in chapter 4, I showed that every non-zero-sum game may be played by each party as if it were a zero-sum game. The zero-sum outcome for each player is equivalent to what she or he could achieve if there were no cooperation to reach a better solution. The task here is to play one's own minimax strategy and to assure oneself of a result at least as good as one's own security level. The actual outcome may be better, depending on how B responds, but in no case can A be made worse off than the result from the minimax strategy. And in virtually all cases, A's decision to play a minimax strategy will leave B worse off than if he had cooperated. Of course, if B also plays his minimax strategy, then the outcome will be at the intersection of the security levels of both players in figure 7.1.

The calculation of the minimax strategy, however, requires consideration of the values of all possible payoffs, including the values in the lower left quadrant of the matrix in figure 7.1. The status quo point is then calculated on the basis in part of the amount of losses that each player will suffer from noncooperative outcomes. Of course, if both players have equal losses from nonagreement (in figure 7.1 when both lose either -2 or -3), then the outcome will be to split the difference between the preferences of the two parties, the equivalent of the fifty-percent solution. The solution point on the Pareto-Optimal frontier, which may be located by drawing a forty-five-degree line from the intersection of the security levels in a northeasterly direction until it intersects with the Pareto-Optimal frontier, is halfway between each party's preferred outcome, so that they each win 5 by going to the opera and the boxing matches together 50 percent of the time. The result is a symmetrical outcome, as both receive equal gains relative to their minimax strategy. On the other hand, if the woman's losses from the failure to agree are greater than the man's, for example, if she receives -6 when they each go their own way while he receives -3, or if she receives -4 and he gets -2 when each follows the preference of the other, then the status quo point will shift downward as in figure 7.2. The point at which the forty-five-degree line from the intersection of the security levels reaches the northeast frontier will move in a southeasterly direction and produce more favorable results for the man.

The axiom that results from this analysis, then, may be stated as follows: If the losses associated with nonagreement in a bargaining situ-

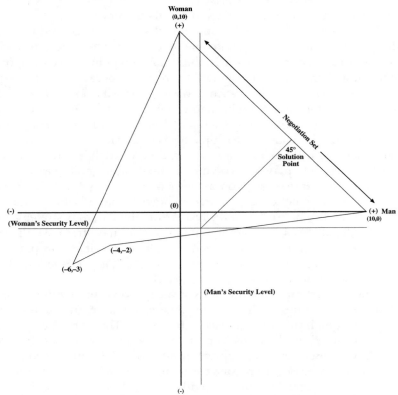

Figure 7.2 The Battle of the Sexes: An Asymmetrical Solution. Based on Anatol Rapoport, *Two-Person Game Theory: The Essential Ideas* (Ann Arbor: University of Michigan Press, 1969), pp. 99, 102.

ation are unequal, the player who stands to lose the most from the failure to agree will stand to gain a smaller share of the outcome if an agreement is reached.

In other words, inequality in losses from noncooperation can produce asymmetric outcomes even in the case where Pareto-Optimal agreements are reached along the negotiation set. This is because the party that can threaten the other with an outcome of nonagreement more credibly, because it stands to lose less from the failure to agree, is in a better position to demand a greater share of the gain from a cooperative outcome. And an outcome that is unequal, but still leaves the party with lesser gains better off than its next best alternative, is still an acceptable agreement to that party so long as it behaves rationally. Shapely refers to this form of influence as the threat potential. The lower the costs of noncooperation, the greater the potential to threaten the other party with noncooperative outcomes in an effort to extract a greater share of any potential gains.

John Nash, who first developed the classic bargaining game, has also suggested a similar but slightly different conclusion in what he described as the extended solution to the bargaining game.[17] In this case, instead of *A* threatening *B* to go to *A*'s security level, as in Shapely's proposed solution, *A* may threaten to take *B* to *B*'s own security level. In this case, the party that suffers greater losses by being left at his or her own security level can less credibly threaten to walk out of the negotiation, and thereby is placed in a weaker bargaining position. Both solutions effectively amount to the same thing in terms of their practical implications. In other words, the game theoretic model suggests that the party that receives the greater costs from nonagreement, and therefore suffers greater loss from the breakdown of negotiations, is likely to be able to obtain a proportionately smaller share of the outcome; conversely, the party that will lose less from nonagreement has a greater threat potential to walk out of the negotiations and is able to obtain a proportionately greater share of the outcome of an agreement.

This form of asymmetry is largely independent of power, defined as capabilities and ability to exercise influence. In some cases, of course, the two may reinforce one another. In the Panama Canal negotiations, for example, the United States stood to lose less from the breakdown of negotiations, because the status quo favored the U.S. position. The United States had controlled the Panama Canal Zone since 1903, and it was Panama that was demanding a change in the status quo through negotiations. However, since the status quo outcome generally favored the United States, also the actor with greater resources, the U.S. threat to walk out was more credible than the Panamanian threat to do likewise, and this was an important element of advantage for the United States in this negotiation.

However, in other situations the potential threat to walk away from negotiations may offset asymmetries introduced in the negotiations by differences in capabilities. For example, in the Vietnam Peace Talks, the United States stood to lose more than North Vietnam from the continuation of the war. Short of an all-out invasion of North Vietnam by the United States or the use of nuclear weapons against Vietnam, there was little that the United States could do to North Vietnam that had not already been tried. And the North Vietnamese knew full well that a combination of domestic political opinion and world opposition restrained the United States from undertaking either of these more drastic options. On the other hand, the continued loss of human life and economic resources in the Vietnam War had become an intolerable political strain in the United States, and the Nixon administration came to realize that its political survival—first in the 1972 elections, and then subsequently in the Watergate scandal—depended in part on extricating the United States militarily from Southeast Asia. Thus, the North Vietnamese possessed a very powerful threat potential of walking out of negotiations, and this undoubtedly contributed a great deal to their ability to negotiate successfully with a country that had far more capabilities and other resources to exert influence.

This analysis suggests that countries that are lacking in traditional capabilities such as military and economic resources may compensate for this in part by seeking to identify attractive alternatives to negotiated agreements. Not only will this give such a country a better option if negotiations fail, but that very possibility also is likely to improve its relative position in influencing the outcome of the negotiations in a direction favorable to its preferences. Improving one's alternatives not only assures one of getting a certain level of benefit if negotiations fail, but it also may enable negotiators to raise the minimum and thereby improve their outcome from the negotiation itself. As figure 5.1 indicated in chapter 5, if party A wants to improve its negotiating position, it may seek new and better alternatives to a negotiated agreement. If its alternatives improve, then the point of minimum agreement, a', moves also to the left to reflect this fact. As the preference curve $(A-A')$ shifts leftward as a result, then so does the point of a fair agreement, E, move to the left in the direction favored by A. In short, without any improvement in its capabilities or influence potential, A is able to enhance its position just by improving its alternatives. This works largely because the credibility of A's threat to break off negotiations has increased, since the costs of discontinuing negotiations are not as great when the alternatives to a negotiated agreement are more favorable. As Fisher and Ury summarize this conclusion: "The more easily and happily you can walk away from a negotiation, the greater your capacity to affect its outcome."[18]

One domain in which both forms of asymmetry, those resulting from inequalities of capabilities and ability to exercise influence as well as those emanating from the lack of acceptable alternatives, are felt is in global North-South negotiations, such as those within the U.N. Conference on Trade and Development (UNCTAD) on the New International Economic Order through the 1970s and early 1980s. In these negotiations, the poorest states found themselves at a bargaining disadvantage in virtually all respects. Obviously, they were at a significant disadvantage in terms of economic resources compared to developed countries or regions like North America, Western Europe, or Japan. Military power, even if they had possessed it, was largely irrelevant to these negotiations. Even Soviet rhetorical support for the position of the southern countries within UNCTAD was of little or no value in the negotiations, since the military capabilities possessed by the USSR were irrelevant to bargaining on this issue, and the USSR was far weaker in all other elements of capabilities.

But even more significant was the problem of alternatives. For example, in bargaining about the terms of trade in primary products, the South had little alternative but to sell much of their produce to the North. For countries that produce one or a few products, there is a limit to domestic consumption, especially of goods such as coffee, bananas, sugar, or palm oil. Therefore, in most instances the failure of negotiations means that the products will simply rot in the fields or in the storage facilities of the developing countries. By contrast, the countries of the North could generally seek alternative sources, alternative products, or simply do without most of the products produced in the South if it came to that. For example, coffee can be purchased from many sources in Latin America, Asia, and Africa; alternatively, tea may substitute for coffee if it becomes too expensive. Thus, the consumer states have a wide range of options, and, although they suffer from the failure of negotiations, they stand to lose far less than their bargaining partners to the South. As a consequence, they are able to drive a harder bargain and generally negotiate terms that are more favorable to their interests than to those of the countries of the South.

There are several strategies that weaker countries can pursue to try to offset this bargaining advantage based on alternatives. First, they can try to reduce the alternatives available to the other side. For example, they may form a producer cartel to control the worldwide export of a single commodity, thereby cutting off alternative sources of supply in the North. This strategy was successfully pursued for a time by the countries belonging to the Organization of Petroleum Exporting Countries (OPEC) that were able to work together to control the supply of petroleum on the world market long enough so that they were in a position to bargain much more effectively about the price. On the other hand, petroleum is a unique product, because of its limited availability in some parts of the world, because of the very high dependence on it by all developed countries, and because of the high cost of converting to alternative energy sources. Attempts to form cartels to bargain about export prices of other commodities such as sugar and coffee have all failed to hold together or achieve more favorable results from negotiations, because none of these products have the same unique characteristics as petroleum. And even in the case of petroleum, one major defector from the cartel was sufficient to undermine its effectiveness in negotiating petroleum prices on the world market. Thus, for example, when Nigeria cut its export prices in early 1983, it effectively undermined the effort of OPEC hard liners, such as Iran, to maintain the cartel's stranglehold on the world price of oil, so that in a London meeting in March 1983 OPEC finally decided to cut the price of crude oil and impose internal production quotas on its members.[19]

A second strategy is for the countries of the South to seek to expand their own alternatives, rather than reducing the alternatives of their negotiating counterparts in the North. One way this might be done is to diversify their own production, so that they are less dependent on the export of single commodities and have greater domestic needs for products that cannot be sold on favorable terms on the global market. For example, during the 1980s Chile shifted from very heavy dependence on the export of one commodity, copper, to the production and export of large quantities of fruits and vegetables consumed widely in the North; the fact that the growing season in Chile was inverse to that of North America, Japan, and Western Europe, and their climate was otherwise suited for the cultivation of products widely consumed in these countries, enabled them to provide a wide range of products to many buyers during the winter season in the northern hemisphere.

Another variant on this strategy is to increase trade arrangements within the South, so that these countries have broader export markets within their own region. So, for example, the effort to create an economic market called Mercosur within the southern cone of South America reflects a desire not only to increase trade within that region, but also to produce greater alternatives to selling their products to the North. The very presence of these expanded alternatives, however, does not mean that they will always have to exercise this option; the most important implication is that these expanded alternatives should enhance their ability to bargain more effectively with the North and receive higher prices for their exports. From the point of view of affecting the negotiation process the goal of improving alternatives to agreement is not only valuable in itself, but also because it is itself an element of bargaining power that can assist states in striking agreements on more favorable terms to the states possessing these options.

In conclusion, insofar as negotiations include a distributive element and thus constitute more than an exercise in identifying a joint optimal solution, that distribution is likely to reflect the differences in many forms of bargaining power that the parties to the negotiations may possess. In ethical terms, one may argue that it is best to seek equitable solutions where the gains of both parties from an agreement relative to their next best alternatives are equal. And it would be inappropriate to dismiss altogether the value of trying to identify fair solutions, even when negotiations involve extensive elements that are primarily distributive in nature. But it would also be incorrect to assume that states will always seek the fairest possible agreement in negotiations, especially when they may exploit advantages in bargaining power to seek outcomes that benefit their individual interest rather than a collective interest. In this chapter, I have shown how these distributions may be affected by several forms of bargaining power.

First, I considered the impact of traditional elements of power as defined by realist scholars of international relations. These included the absolute and comparative capabilities that states possess, along dimensions such as military force, economic viability, national unity, education, access to expertise and information, volition, and negotiating skill. They also included the ability to utilize these capabilities to execute punishments and provide rewards in order to carry out threats and promises in an effort to try to influence the behavior of one another within negotiations. Second, I examined the impact on bargaining power of the alternatives that states have to accepting a negotiated agreement. By affecting the value of the status quo, of the outcome if negotiations break down, these comparative alternatives to negotiated agreement have a significant impact on a state's ability to influence the outcome of distributive negotiations in directions that it may prefer. Those states with more attractive alternatives, and consequently with lower losses associated with the failure of negotiations, are more likely to be influential in claiming a larger share of the value being distributed within negotiations, whereas those states that will suffer more from walking out of negotiations are placed at a bargaining disadvantage and are likely to end up with a smaller share of the benefits from any agreement that may be reached. Thus, in international negotiations the outcomes may be highly asymmetrical, and this asymmetry is likely to be a consequence of the many inequalities in capabilities, influence, and alternatives that states possess when they come to the negotiating table.

Chapter 8

The Individual Negotiator:
The Human Dimension

In part 2, the parties to negotiations were treated as unitary, rational actors who were interested in maximizing interests or utility over the long run. Negotiation was a means by which they sought to advance their national interests and goals in an anarchic world. In that model I assumed that the actors had access to more or less perfect information and sought to select the best means to optimize their ends or goals. Of course, in spite of our tendency to reify the state and treat it as if it were an actor in its own right, we also realize that states as such never act. Rather actions are taken by individuals who are empowered to act on behalf of states in international relations. In negotiations, these are the individual diplomats or other negotiators who fill these roles. As human beings, of course, while they are capable of a certain degree of knowledge and rationality, they are also limited in both capacities; there may even be different interpretations of what constitutes rationality or knowledge. Their information is at best incomplete and imperfect, their beliefs may be less than completely logical and consistent, and their behavior may reflect less than fully rational calculations of interest. In most cases they have quite imperfect information even about their own preferences and utilities, to say nothing of those of other parties in a negotiation. Furthermore, they are seldom capable of making purely rational decisions or selecting the optimal means to achieve their desired ends.

Limits on rationality attributable to individual behavior may be examined from three perspectives: (1) cognitive psychology that looks at the dynamics of image formation and change; (2) individual personality attributes; and (3) the development of group norms and behaviors within a specific cultural context. All of these perspectives are most likely to influence negotiations through their impact on the communications process, which is an integral part of any negotiation.

THE NEGOTIATOR'S COGNITION: IMAGE AND REALITY

Instead of possessing perfect information about their environment, individuals generally hold images of that reality; an analysis of how these images are formed and maintained provides the core of the cognitive approach to the analysis of negotiating behavior. The fundamental assumption of this perspective is that perceptions of reality, not objective reality itself, largely determine human behavior. Images refer to the structure and content of human cognition, that is, of the belief system of any individual. Different individuals and groups of individuals clearly perceive the world differently, and no one can ever be sure of what constitutes reality. All human beings are capable of misperception, that is, seeing the world differently from the way all available evidence suggests it should be seen, but individuals also differ in the degree to which they are prone to misperceive people and events in their surroundings.

The work in this area is often called social cognition theory, which analyzes the ways in which people use past experience to organize their knowledge into systematic structures that help them understand and react to the world about them. Since the world of experience is clearly too complex for any human being to grasp fully, all individuals must simplify that reality to make it understandable to them. It is the process through which this simplification occurs and through which a person's understanding of the world is structured in his or her mind that is of interest to us in our analysis of negotiators' images. As Bazerman and Carroll have noted, "social cognition research studies the nature, origins, and use of these knowledge structures, including stereotypes, categories, norms, roles, implicit theories, schemas, prototypes, scripts, heuristics, and attributions."[1] This approach views negotiators as individuals who try to understand their situation by constructing a cognitive image about the reality of the negotiation situation, and then they use that to make projections and predictions about the future. Social psychologists have looked at the process of how these images are formed and how they are maintained or changed, although the theoretical concepts that they have used to explain these processes have also been modified somewhat over the past several decades. I shall now look at several different perspectives in image formation and change.

In the decade of the 1960s and 1970s the major emphasis of the social psychologists was on the ways in which individuals maintained consistency or balance in their attitudes and beliefs, and sought to avoid stress or cognitive dissonance resulting from inconsistency among components of the belief system or between beliefs and actions.[2] Although there are many different strains in the development of consistency or balance theory, the major ideas that are relevant to an analysis of negotiator cognition may be synthesized around a few simple concepts.

Psychologists in this tradition have frequently noted that human images are composed of three basic components: (1) evaluative images, which are beliefs about good and bad; (2) affective images, which are feelings of likes and dislikes; and (3) cognitive images, which are beliefs about the facts of the world, as well as the causal relationships among those facts.

The evaluative and affective aspects of most people's images tend to form at early ages. They may be based on values inculcated by the family, by the individual's religious or philosophical upbringing, by the process of acculturation within a particular collectivity of persons, or by one's formal socialization or education. Furthermore, most of these beliefs are well formed by the time one reaches adulthood, even though they usually remain poorly articulated and often largely implicit. These aspects of the image usually become so much a part of an individual's beliefs about the world that he or she is not really even aware of their existence. Therefore, in most cases these components of the image or belief system remain largely unexamined and unquestioned.

By contrast, the cognitive component of the image continues to grow and expand as the person encounters new information and experiences. New facts and new assumptions about causal relations are added to the image constantly. Indeed, the human mind is bombarded daily with an almost infinite number of new pieces of information, so many in fact that no single person can possibly attend to all of that information. Therefore, information must enter the image selectively, and that process of selection is not purely random. Indeed, a set of filters are set up by the human mind at each of several stages including: (1) selective attention, which means that people will only pay attention to a relatively small portion of all of the information potentially available to them; (2) selective retention, which means that only a limited portion of the information to which one pays attention will be retained in the memory; and (3) selective recall, which implies that most people will only be able to recover from their memories a limited portion of the information stored away in the past.

Some cognitive information, therefore, will pass through each of these filters while others will not. Which information is attended to, retained, and available for recall is also largely a function of its compatibility with the other components of one's image, the evaluative and affective elements. Most people strive for consistency between their fundamental, implicit, and underlying beliefs and their cognitive maps that help them to explain how the world works. Information that is inconsistent with or challenges the fundamental assumptions of one's belief system—one's beliefs about good and bad, right and wrong, desirable and undesirable, joy and pain—tends to be filtered out in one way or another. The information may be ignored in the first place; few people

122

seek out information that they know in advance is likely to challenge their basic beliefs. The information may not be remembered, or it may be forgotten quickly; most people remember better those things that are pleasurable or that one believes to be good rather than the painful or the evil. Finally, facts may be rationalized, a process in which information is reinterpreted to try to make it consistent with preexisting beliefs and values. Through these various filtering processes most people unknowingly and subconsciously build up perceptions about the world around them that reinforce their underlying values and beliefs and that avoid the stress, dissonance, and pain of having to confront a reality that challenges those beliefs. Through processes like this, virtually all human beings misperceive reality, at least in part, and tend to interpret reality in ways that are consistent with their underlying, and usually implicit, belief system.

The famous Swiss psychologist Jean Piaget treated the process by which basic images are reinforced or modified as one develops cognitively as characterized by assimilation and accommodation. These mechanisms affect how the external environment interacts with the existing belief system: assimilation refers to the process by which the external factors are incorporated into the existing conceptual framework, and accommodation refers to how that framework is modified as a result of the incorporation of new information. In Piaget's words: "thought organizes itself in adapting to objects, and thought structures objects in organizing itself."[3]

As a result of these processes the belief system comes to be organized in systematic ways. One such organizing principle is captured in what is known as cognitive balance theory. One version of this, developed by Fritz Heider, looks at the relationship between a person (P), another person (O), and an external object (X). He examines the relationships among these three entities in a triangle, in which the objects are linked by positive or negative bonds. The relationship among these three components may be balanced, if all three relations are positive or if one is positive and the other two are negative, as depicted in figure 8.1; all other configurations are unbalanced. Heider defines a balanced state as "a situation in which relations among the entities fit together harmoniously; there is no stress towards change."[4] By contrast, unbalanced states create cognitive stress for P, so there is a tendency to move away from unbalanced states to reduce stress. These configurations will generally mean that individuals (P's) will develop positive sentiments toward other persons (O's) with whom they share common relationships (either positive or negative) with third parties or external objects (X), and they will feel more negative sentiments toward others when they have divergent attitudes toward those external objects. Thus, attitudes are affected not only by the direct relationship with other parties,

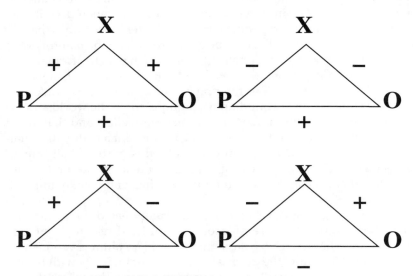

Figure 8.1 Four Balanced P-O-X Triangles

but also by the degree of co-orientation toward third parties or objects. As Heider concludes: "we tend to like people who have the same beliefs and attitudes we have, and when we like people, we want them to have the same attitudes we have."[5]

Charles Osgood adds to the *P-O-X* model by assigning values to each of the objects in the model in addition to the relationships among them. Every side of the triangle may be treated as what he refers to as an evaluative assertion, that is with affective and evaluative characteristics being assigned to each. Affective components are treated on a continuum from liking to disliking, and the evaluative components may be considered as ranging from positive to negative. Thus, looking at the relationship between *P* and *O*, Osgood has the person assigning an evaluation to *P* and *O*, as well as to the relationship between them. Again, balance exists only when there are an even number of negative signs, two or zero. Assuming that *P* evaluates itself as positive, then it will tend to express positive attitudes toward *O* if the relationship between them is positive (zero negative elements) and negative attitudes toward *O* if the relationship is hostile (two negative elements). This same logic of balance may then be extended to all three sides of the *P-O-X* triangle.

These pressures toward balance may create various forms of misperception in the complex interactions among individuals that occur in international negotiations. If, for example, another negotiator (*O*) is perceived negatively by *P* and then behaves in a conciliatory fashion, this creates an unbalanced situation (P is positive, the relationship is positive, and O is negative). This perception is unstable for P, and there is pressure to change one of these elements. Since P is unlikely to abandon the positive evaluation of self, this change must occur either in the relationship or in the other party. There are two possible changes to restore balance. P may recognize the positive nature of the new relationship and thereby change his or her attitude toward O in a positive direction. Thus, O's behavior may change P's attitude to create a fully positive relationship. Alternatively, P may perceive that the action is a trick since O is viewed negatively, so the relationship needs to be reinterpreted as negative in order to create a balanced relationship.

In short, either the perception of the relationship itself or the attitude toward the other party must change to preserve balance. Which element changes depends primarily on which of the components is felt most intensely. In the context of negative interactions, a positive action by another purportedly hostile party is not likely to be acknowledged as a positive behavior. The strong hostility toward the other may outweigh the short-term appearance of a more positive relationship as P attempts to preserve consistency in attitude. This may be one of several reasons why attempts to send conciliatory signals in negotiations may be missed altogether or misperceived as tricks or having some other malevolent motive lying behind them.

For example, throughout much of the history of the cold war, Soviet conciliatory gestures in arms control negotiations were often perceived by many in the United States as tricks designed to lure the West into complacency. Those who perceived the Soviets as implacable enemies could not conceive that they might be capable of making any positive offers in negotiations. Thus, some opportunities to overcome differences and reach agreement may well have been lost because of this tendency of individual negotiators to try to maintain balance and consistency in their attitudinal structures.

Individual human beings differ, however, in the extent to which they are subject to these kinds of distorting cognitive effects. Indeed, psychologists such as Rokeach have suggested that human beings tend to fall at various points along a continuum from open-minded to closed-minded.[6] Open-minded individuals tend to be less cognitively rigid, more tolerant of ambiguity, and more receptive to inconsistent information that challenges their fundamental beliefs. At the extreme, of course, they may be "wishy-washy," unable to decide about almost anything because of their extreme openness to all points of view. Short of this extreme, however, they also tend to have more flexible images that are able to adapt to new information and changing conditions so that their images usually remain fairly close in touch with reality.

Closed-minded individuals, on the other hand, are more cognitively rigid, more intolerant of ambiguity, and more resistant to information that is inconsistent with their basic values and beliefs. They tend to filter out a substantial amount of information about reality in order to protect their images from dissonance and preserve a kind of internal consistency and orderliness in their beliefs. Their concepts "tend to be more bifurcated, absolutistic and black-white," and they tend "to be closed to events that imply multiple alternatives and alternate evaluations of the situation."[7] For these individuals, of course, perceptions and reality may diverge widely, and those misperceptions may frequently cause them problems in dealing with other people whose images of reality are different from their own.

As with most continua, presumably most people do not fall at either end of this dichotomy but somewhere in the middle. Furthermore, since this is an individual characteristic, it is probably also the case that individuals are fairly evenly spread around the globe across this continuum; certainly there has been no systematic evidence collected to suggest that one country or one culture is more or less open- or closed-minded than others. But since this is a fairly universal phenomenon, it is also likely that diplomats are about as likely as any other group of people to be distributed across this continuum, some being more open-minded and others more cognitively rigid.

Another way to look at this difference in the propensity to simplify complex realities in balanced images may be found in the concept of integrative complexity. Initially this approach sought to explain individual differences in the complexity of cognitive rules through which people process and structure incoming information. Specifically, individuals may proceed through stages going from the concrete to the abstract, in which "the ambiguous or undifferentiated is broken or differentiated into parts and then integrated or interrelated into a conceptual pattern."[8] The concept of integrative complexity has, however, been expanded into an interaction framework that looks at cognitive functioning as a joint consequence of long-term dispositions based on early learning and socialization, and more immediate situational factors such as environment, time pressure, information, and role requirements.[9] Integratively complex individuals have a high "awareness of multiple perspectives on problems and of interrelations among perspectives," whereas the other end of the continuum is characterized by "lack of awareness of alternative ways of viewing problems" and "rigid rules for making decisions."[10] In negotiations, we may then hypothesize that "low integrative complexity will be associated with competitive behavior, and high integrative complexity with coordinative behavior."[11]

Tetlock's research has revealed that there is a tendency, as conflicts escalate, for arguments utilized by diplomats to become less cognitively complex, and more simplified and stereotyped. This tendency in turns creates obstacles to the kind of sophisticated, problem-solving negotiations that may be required to resolve such conflicts before they escalate out of control. As the ability of negotiators to reason in complex, integrative terms declines, they are more likely to resort to power-oriented pressure tactics rather than to seek integrative and innovative solutions. A vicious spiral may ensue in which escalating conflict reduces people's ability to think in complex and nuanced ways, which in turn contributes to the further escalation of conflict. Such a spiral may cause conflicts to grow rapidly out of control and lead to violence rather than to negotiated solutions.

Furthermore, these cognitive factors may often be exacerbated by international conflicts, thereby causing them to have a more severe impact on international conflict resolution than in many other contexts. Negotiations frequently occur in the presence of fairly intense conflict, where the other party may be viewed as an opponent or even as an enemy. As Ralph White has pointed out, this often produces black and white mirror images.[12] Each party to a conflict tends to perceive the other as active, aggressive, and even diabolical, whereas it sees itself as a passive victim, virile, and moral. Selective perception sustains these images, and there is an absence of empathy, the ability of each to see the conflict from the other's point of view. Each party tends to blame the other as the initiator and cause of the conflict, whereas it views itself as making a justified response to the provocations of the other. Any information that contradicts the diabolical enemy image or the moral self-image is systematically excluded, so that both parties go on deluding themselves about their mutual responsibility for the conflict. And since each believes, in the mirror image, that the other is the cause of the conflict, each also believes that the other is responsible for taking the initiative to end it. Each believes that the other should be the first to make a concession, to propose a compromise, or to invent a novel solution. But since this image is shared by both parties, each waits for the other to move; neither takes the initiative to move negotiations forward. The common result then of this form of mutual misperception in conflict situations is that negotiations become stalemated, not due to the structure of the problem, but due to the rigid perceptions that each party holds about the other in the midst of conflict.

These problems may be especially serious for negotiations that occur in the midst of intense international crises. In these situations, diplomats almost by definition must operate under intense stress. While psychologists find that some stress tends to improve human performance, the majority of psychologists conclude that high stress generally impairs cognitive performance seriously. This impairment reduces a person's span of attention to a few specific tasks rather than to the broader picture of events, increases their cognitive rigidity thereby closing their minds further to new information, and shortens their time perspective to a focus only on immediate events and consequences. Holsti summarizes these findings succinctly as follows:

> the casualties of crises and the accompanying high stress may include the very abilities that are most vital for coping effectively with such situations: establishing logical links between present actions and future goals; searching effectively for relevant policy options; creating appropriate responses to unexpected events; communicating complex ideas; dealing effectively with abstractions; perceiving not only black and white, but also distinguishing them from the many subtle shades of gray that fall in between; distinguishing valid analogies from false ones, and sense from nonsense; and, perhaps most important of all, entering into others' frames of reference. With respect to these vital cognitive abilities, the law of supply and demand may sometimes operate in a perverse manner; as crisis increases the need for them, it may also diminish the supply.[13]

In short, the context within which many international negotiations occur, characterized by varying levels of conflict and sometimes even by intense crisis, plays havoc with the cognitive abilities of the individual diplomats who must conduct those negotiations. The worst problem is that these situations make it very difficult for an individual to empathize with the other, to see the problem from their point of view. There is, of course, no easy solution to this problem, stemming as it does from an inherent characteristic of the person who must engage in the activity of negotiation. Perhaps the best mechanism for coping with this problem, however, is simply awareness of the problem itself, of the tricks that conflicts may play on even the most open-minded individuals. Such an awareness of this difficulty may inspire negotiators to take special care to keep an open mind in all conflicts and seek ways of understanding the conflict better from each other's point of view.

In contrast to the approach that emphasizes the drive for balance and consistency as a source of misperception in negotiations, more recent psychological theories have emphasized the ways in which individuals tend to perceive certain cause and effect relations—often called attribution theory.[14] As summarized by Jönsson, this change in focus somewhat shifts the explanation given for the distortion of information and misperception in human cognitions: "Whereas cognitive consistency theorists assume that people see what they expect to see by assimilating incoming information to preexisting images and interpreting new information in such a way as to maintain or increase balance, attribution theorists have been concerned with the individual's attempts to comprehend the causes of behavior and assume that spontaneous thought follows a systematic course that is roughly congruent with scientific inquiry."[15]

Like consistency and balance theories, attribution theories both seek to establish the logical underpinnings by which human beings make causal inferences and to identify and explain "the sources of imperfection, bias, or error that distort these judgments."[16] It sees individual lay persons as behaving very much like intuitive scientists, making "causal inferences using criteria analogous to those used by the trained social scientist."[17] However, research on how people make causal inferences has also revealed a substantial set of attribution errors, which "deviate from normative standards of logical and scientific inference."[18]

Much of this work has been reflected in international relations research in the approach known as cognitive mapping. This perspective presumes that individuals engage in a kind of quasi-causal reasoning underlying their thought processes. The analyst then attempts to extract the individual's perception about antecedent causes and possible consequences of various international events. This may not only reveal the underlying logical basis of a negotiator's positions, but it may also uncover logical inconsistencies in these thought processes and in the ordering of preferences that impede a purely rational decision making in the course of negotiating. This analytical procedure has been used by Axelrod to analyze the cognitive maps of the members of the British Eastern Committee of the Imperial War Cabinet in 1918, which was responsible for policy toward Persia in the immediate aftermath of World War I. He found that the decision makers were guided by large and complex cognitive maps, and they used these causal arguments as a basis for argumentation within the committee. Furthermore, he found a high degree of consistency and deductive linkages within their reasoning process.[19] Similarly, Bonham and his colleagues used the technique of cognitive mapping to compare two negotiations, one in 1905 between Sweden and Norway over the dissolution of their political union and the other in 1919 at the Versailles Peace Conference over the future of the Saar Basin.[20]

Additional implications for negotiations flowing from the kinds of judgmental errors typically found in negotiator's cognitive structures have been analyzed by Bazerman and Carroll.[21] They note that negotiators may strive for rationality, but that the kind of behavior predicted by rational actor models derived from economic theory is usually limited by a wide range of cognitive simplifications and biases that distort their perceptions and communications. In their view, "a great deal of the suboptimality that can be observed in negotiation is the result of deviations from rationality in the judgmental processes of negotiators."[22] Specifically, they identify a number of such judgmental errors on the part of negotiators:

1. Negotiators are frequently overconfident in their negotiating skills and their ability to reach a successful result, often causing them to make excessive opening bids, refrain from making concessions, and believe that they can persuade third parties of the justness of their position.

2. Negotiators frequently escalate their commitment to previous positions and behaviors in order to justify their present performance and avoid admitting past mistakes.

3. Certain highly salient information may be brought disproportionately to bear in analyzing a problem because it is more easily remembered.

4. Prospect theory holds that individuals will frame negotiation problems in terms of gains and losses, and that they will be willing to run considerable risk when it comes to avoiding loss, but will be very risk averse when it comes to achieving gains.[23]

5. Negotiators tend to exaggerate the zero-sum nature of negotiations, believing that a "fixed pie" is to be divided when negotiating with someone who is believed to be an opponent or enemy.

Similarly, negotiators may tend to misperceive or misunderstand the decision processes of the other participants. As Bazerman and Carroll summarize this hypothesis, *"individuals in competitive situations make simplifying assumptions that deviate from normative logic about the decision patterns of opponents in order to make the task cognitively more manageable."*[24] Of course, negotiators differ substantially in their perspective taking ability, that is in their capability to view a conflict from the point of view of the other party. And these capabilities may have a direct impact on whether or not the individuals are fully capable of engaging in problem-solving negotiations as opposed to competitive bargaining.

The fundamental attribution error, which has been identified by attribution theorists, is "assuming that other people's actions reflect their inner dispositions, giving too little attention to the power of situations to call forth behavior."[25] Cognitive failings of individuals are sometimes erroneously attributed to motivational purposes. As described by Jeffrey Rubin, this kind of attributional distortion causes negotiators to misperceive both themselves and their negotiating partners: "Kind acts by one's adversary are attributed to manipulative intent, while uncharitable acts are attributed to an undesirable, untrustworthy disposition.

One's own kind acts, in turn, are attributed to one's being a truly nice, kind person, while one's less wonderful behavior is attributed to circumstances or to behavior by the other person that has necessitated an unkind response."[26]

In negotiations, one party may fail to understand the extent to which the other's position is dictated by either domestic or international conditions beyond that party's control, so that these behaviors will be attributed instead to the malevolent intent of the opponent. When U.S. officials have criticized the Japanese for failing to negotiate on the basis of a level playing field about trade in agricultural commodities, for example, they have often attributed this to a kind of perverse nationalism and a superiority complex on the part of Japanese trade negotiators; this may, in fact, simply reflect domestic political constraints imposed by Japanese farmers over which the Japanese negotiator has little or no influence. This false attribution may cause U.S. negotiators to try to bring the Japanese counterpart around to the U.S. view of reality through various pressure tactics rather than trying to deal with the situation that is the real cause of the deadlock. As Bazerman and Carroll note: "One false attribution can cause the unraveling of what would otherwise have been a successful negotiation for both sides. Effective negotiators are likely to be those who can most accurately assess the true causes of their opponent's behavior and also manage the attributions that the other party will make of their own behavior."[27]

When taken together, all cognitive theories pose some very serious problems for negotiation theory. The rational model suggests that actors should freely make concessions and reach compromise solutions in order to achieve results that are mutually acceptable, and in many cases they must even work cooperatively with the other party to solve problems together to realize collective gains. The rational theories tend to assume that the prospect of achieving such gains is sufficient motivation for parties to make the concessions or to engage in problem-solving activities in order to obtain these benefits. But the dilemma arises when we realize that most international negotiations take place in situations characterized by a history of conflict, so that the parties often hold negative images about one another at the outset. Both cognitive consistency theories and attribution theories predict that, in these situations, the individuals will tend to selectively perceive information that reinforces these hostile images and then attribute that to the underlying untrustworthiness or insincerity of the other party. They are also largely oblivious to their own shared responsibility for the conflict or their own contributions to the negative images and hostile behavior of the other party. Thus, negotiations may become locked into a vicious cycle of interactions in which both parties hold hostile images of one another and behave accordingly within the negotiations; these negative interactions are then taken by each party as confirming evidence of the aggressiveness and hostility of the other. Unless some way can be found to break this cycle, the spiral of hostile perceptions and threatening behavior will increase until negotiations break off, often leaving the parties in a more intense conflict than when negotiations opened. In crisis situations, this spiral of cognition and behavior may even lead to violent conflict and war.

A key question that then confronts social cognition theorists in the study of negotiation is how to break this vicious cycle. How can these hostile attitudes be changed and what kind of conciliatory behavior is likely to induce a re-evaluation of these perceptions? A number of different techniques have been suggested, and I will consider a wide range of these for overcoming the problems of individual psychology later in this chapter. At this point, it suffices to underline the importance of trying to initiate behavior that will demonstrate clearly and unambiguously the inconsistency between the opponent's perceptions and one's actual intentions. Jönsson has suggested several factors that may enhance this discrepancy and help one of the parties confront the inconsistency rather than trying to reinterpret behavior in order to preserve the original balanced structure.

1. Surprise will tend to get the attention of the other party to the inconsistency between its perception and the reality.

2. The behavior should be clearly seen as being voluntary and relatively costly for the party trying to change the others' images; conversely, an action that probably would have been done anyway and in no way seems to contradict one's interests is not likely to be perceived as sincere.

3. The behavior should be repeated for some period of time, even if it is not initially reciprocated. As Jönsson notes: "A series of moderately risky concessions, not easily dismissed as the product of self-interest or hostility, would finally succeed in persuading the adversary to reciprocate and thus set into motion a spiral of tension reduction."[28]

THE NEGOTIATOR'S PERSONALITY

Thus far in this chapter I have looked at cognitive factors that affect how individuals behave in negotiations. The cognitive perspective looks at how people structure their attitudes and beliefs about the way the world works and then how these images affect the way people behave. Yet another individual dimension that may affect negotiating behavior is the personality of the negotiator. Individual personality may exert more or less influence on the negotiation process depending, in part, on the latitude given to individual negotiators by their home governments. Highly constrained individuals may have little personal impact on negotiations, following instructions from home closely, so that their own personality has little effect on the process. Obviously most negotiators do not operate in international settings on their own volition, but rather they are instructed carefully to follow guidance from the home capital. Conversely, negotiators who have been given considerable freedom by the home government may be able to influence the process a great deal through the force of their own personality. The impact that personality has depends, of course, on the individual traits of any particular negotiator. Several personality dimensions may be relevant.

First, individuals may be either task-oriented or affect-oriented, sometimes referred to as instrumental or expressive.[29] The former individuals tend to be very business-like and precise, prefer to work quietly and efficiently, focus on the details of the negotiation, focus on the future rather than the past, and appear to have little at stake personally in the outcome. These people tend to concentrate on instrumental, goal-directed tasks and seek solutions to the problem at hand. By contrast, affect-oriented individuals tend to be more emotional, inject themselves and their personality into the negotiations, focus more on the big picture rather than on details, are more concerned about the past than the future, and tend to make emotional and rhetorical displays to express their strong personal feelings about the issues. Affective behaviors within negotiations are those that are intended to maintain the structure of the group and create a certain tone for the interactions among the group's members.[30]

Effective negotiations generally require some balance of these two personality types: task-oriented people are especially necessary for the detail phase of negotiations, as well as for problem solving in a calm and quiet way. On the other hand, more affective negotiators may be needed to overcome impasses and inspire the negotiators to work hard and think creatively when negotiations have become bogged down. Yet there is also a dilemma that often hinders the ability of these two factors to work in tandem, especially when it pertains to the impact of these two personality traits on group leadership. Attempts to lead any group such as a set of negotiators toward instrumental solutions to common problems may disturb the group's equilibrium and cause tensions in the expressive area of the group's activities. Thus, individuals who attempt to lead in a group's instrumental activities lower their chances of being highly valued by their colleagues according to affective criteria.[31]

Second, personalities may be distinguished according to whether or not an individual is a leader or a follower. Followers are those who take orders, who do routine work effectively, but who seldom take initiatives. They may be necessary for the routine work involved in most complex negotiations, but they are unlikely to play a major role in creative problem solving. Leaders are those individuals who enjoy taking charge. They tend to influence the group dynamics by their leadership skills, may direct the course of a negotiation, and are essential, in most cases, for identifying and creating formulas to solve disputes. On the other hand, if there are too many leaders additional conflicts may be created, not by differences over the substantive issues, but rather from a competition to assume leadership roles. Effective negotiations will often generate a natural internal hierarchy, resembling a pyramid, with one or a few leaders on top, and an increasing proportion of followers below. In negotiations where the group dynamics are operating effectively, the leaders may take the initiative in developing formulas, while the followers will be charged with most of the tasks necessary for the negotiation of details.

Third, individuals may be classified into those who tend to be more concerned with absolute versus relative gains.[32] The former tend to be cooperative problem solvers, concerned with producing large benefits for everyone, whereas the latter behave competitively in order to seek victory over the other even if it means that both are somehow made worse off. To some individuals the major criterion for success in a negotiation is the absolute benefit that they can derive from an agreement, regardless of the effect on the other; if the other benefits from the agreement as well, so much the better from the point of view of the problem solver. For example, in economic terms some people may be happy if all countries are getting richer, even if the richer countries are gaining more rapidly than the poorer ones. Yet to other individuals the criterion for success is not absolute gains, but relative gains, that is the margin of advantage that they have over the other party. What counts for the winner is victory and leaving the other party worse off, regardless of the size of the spoils. In terms of the economic example used above, it is the relative gains in wealth that are important; such a person might prefer an outcome in which no one gains rather than a result in which both groups gain, but where the opponent gains more than he does. It follows, therefore, that the winner personality tends to do better at the distributive aspects of traditional bargaining, although he or she may often create stalemates in the effort to gain an advantage. By contrast, the problem solver tends to be more effective in the integrative aspects of negotiations, especially where creativity and inventiveness are essential. This individual is more adept at seeking mutual benefits from a negotiation, although at times she or he may be taken advantage of in more conflictual or distributive bargaining situations.

On the other hand, on the basis of prospect theory referred to earlier, Janice Gross Stein has argued that a decision to cooperate "does not depend principally on whether the problem is one of absolute or relative gains . . ., but on the prior question of how leaders frame the problem."[33] Prospect theory suggests that individuals will consider gains and losses relative to some reference point such as the status quo, an aspiration level, or, as suggested in chapter 4, in terms of the best alternative available to a negotiator if negotiations fail (the BATNA or resistance point). Whether an outcome is framed as a gain or a loss relative to this reference point is likely to have a great effect on one's behavior due to the psychological propensity of individuals to be "more willing to take risks to avoid losses than to make gains, in large part because losses loom far larger than gains."[34] Furthermore, individuals tend to give greater significance to certain rather than to uncertain or probabilistic outcomes. As Stein concludes: "The certainty effect magnifies the impact of risk aversion with respect to gains and risk seeking with respect to losses. Prospect theory predicts that people will choose a sure gain rather than take a chance on a larger gain that is probable, even if the latter promises higher expected utility. They will also choose to take a chance on a larger loss that is merely probable rather than face a smaller loss that is certain, even when the certain option would minimize expected loss. Both these predictions contradict the expectations of standard models of rational choice."[35]

This tendency has several consequences for negotiation behavior. Especially if the status quo rather than the BATNA is taken as the anchoring point, it may cause one to magnify one's own concessions (perceived as losses) and undervalue the concessions of the other party (that are perceived as gains). On the other hand, if issues under negotiation can be reframed to focus on the certain joint losses from the failure to cooperate, the risks associated with an agreement may appear more acceptable and so cooperation may be easier to achieve.[36] Thus, a situation that seems to be deteriorating into an almost certain and costly war may make even a costly agreement to cooperate (viewed as a gain relative to the almost certain alternative of all out war) seem acceptable. This seems to be consistent with the kinds of behavior exhibited by President Kennedy and Premier Khrushchev as war appeared to be imminent in the missile crisis in the Caribbean in October 1962.

A fourth personality factor affecting negotiating behavior is authoritarianism. The classic authoritarian personality tends to be conservative, emotionally cold, to seek power, and be hostile to "out groups" including minorities and foreigners.[37] This kind of personality rigidly classifies others into "in groups" and "out groups," exhibiting strong solidarity with the former and intense hostility toward the latter. Such an individual may tend to have a certain latitude of acceptance, within which the similar views of others are perceived as essentially identical to one's own views, and a latitude of rejection, beyond which the views of others are perceived to be sufficiently alien that individuals holding them are cast into the "out group." [38] He or she also tends to orient toward others with strong awareness of authority relationships, exhibiting submissiveness toward those who are higher up the hierarchy of authority and striving to exercise power over those who are lower on the scale. This kind of authoritarian personality has also been found to be correlated with nationalistic and ethnocentric thinking rather than an international outlook.[39] Thus, an authoritarian personality is likely to distrust negotiators from other countries and exhibit hostile or even xenophobic attitudes toward them. His or her orientation is likely to be extremely competitive with little room for compromise or cooperation.

Fifth, the negotiating styles that individuals exhibit may also reflect different personality traits. For example, Casse and Deol have noted that negotiators tend to reflect some combination of four rather distinct ideal types of negotiating styles.[40]

The first of these is the factual style, which reflects the essential assumption that "the facts speak for themselves." Negotiators employing this style are likely to be historically or past-oriented, emphasizing factual details relevant to the negotiations. Their reasoning style is likely to be largely inductive, going from the specific to the general. They place a great emphasis on tracking the details of negotiations, clarifying specific issues, and seeking concrete empirical evidence to back up assertions. During the course of negotiations, this kind of person is likely to point to past statements of the other side, perhaps calling attention to inconsistencies between present statements and prior ones. This kind of negotiator tends to be most effective at the detail stage of negotiations, while being considerably less effective in problem solving and inventing creative formulas to solve intractable issues. They are likely to be perceived by others as lacking in imagination, being unable to see the big picture, relying too heavily on past experiences, and having difficulty comprehending conceptual arguments and possible solutions to problems.

By contrast, the second negotiation style involves intuitive individuals that tend to believe that "imagination can solve any problem." These individuals generally focus on the broad issues and seek creative and imaginative solutions to problems. They tend to be future-oriented, often believing that the historical roots of problems are irrelevant or even a hindrance to problem solving. They tend to be warm and enthusiastic in their interpersonal relations, while being primarily deductive in their reasoning processes, emphasizing the general rather than the specific dimensions of issues. They tend to seek the essential issues and dismiss the details as trivial and unimportant. They may also switch topics frequently in the search for creative ideas, rather than dwelling too long on approaches that seem to be leading to deadends. Intuitive individuals are likely to be most useful in the phase of negotiations where formulas must be created and where inventive problem solving is called for rather than bargaining. They may be perceived by others as imprecise and unrealistic, not very practical, and willing to proceed on the basis of incomplete or inaccurate information. Therefore, however creative they may be, they risk having their ideas rejected as impractical and unrealistic by more factually oriented individuals.

Normative individuals, the third style, tend to view negotiations as bargaining. These individuals have a clear sense of personal values—right and wrong, good and bad, likes and dislikes—through which issues may be evaluated. They may view negotiations as a contest between these values and are likely to try to steer the outcome toward normatively correct solutions. Agreement for its own sake has little value to these individuals, since the only good agreement is one that embodies the correct normative principles. Of course, these will be articulated as fair solutions, but fairness must be defined by some external, normative criteria and not just as a splitting of the difference between initial positions or some such result that emerges inductively from the negotiation process. Their reasoning processes tend to be very value-oriented and judgmental. Their behavior within the negotiations is likely to be dominated by the use of influence and power-oriented bargaining tactics such as using threats and promises, commitments and concessions, and rewards and punishments to try to direct the outcome of the bargaining in directions that favor their normative principles. They are likely to rely heavily on the power of authority and status in identifying correct solutions to issues. Needless to say, these kinds of individuals are likely to be most effective in negotiations that entail concession-convergence, power-oriented bargaining rather than problem solving. On the other hand, they are likely to be perceived by other negotiators as highly subjective, as lacking a logical or empirical basis for their proposed solutions, and as being overly critical of others.

Conversely, analytical individuals, the final style, tend to believe fundamentally that "logic leads to the right conclusions." These kinds of individuals tend to break issues down into their parts and then search for ways to recombine them that will produce breakthroughs in negotiations. They tend to use an instrumental, linear reasoning process that emphasizes the analysis of cause and effect, and the relationships between parts and wholes. They like to dissect the positions of the participants in negotiations to identify underlying interests and the logical structure of their argument, while criticizing logical errors on the part of other participants. These individuals tend to be especially effective in several roles. In the diagnostic phase, they are typically adept at unveiling underlying sources of conflicts and problems and suggesting new ways to look at issues. And in problem-solving negotiations, they tend to be especially skillful at issue disaggregation and aggregation, identifying ways to fractionate issues and recombine them to create novel tradeoffs across issues; thus, they may be especially valuable in the creation of formulas that emerge from a recombination of the issues under negotiation. On the other hand, they may be perceived by others as cold and analytical, lacking any sense of values, and being ineffective in relating to others as individuals.

As Casse and Deol suggest, the ideal negotiator will in some way combine all of these styles in the conduct of negotiations, and they prescribe flexibility across all four styles as optimal for an effective negotiator: "No style is good or bad, effective or ineffective. It depends on the situation in which we are placed. By and large, our negotiating effectiveness is a function of our ability to switch from one style to another. A critical factor in negotiation is to know what styles we feel more comfortable with and to learn how to identify other people's styles. The more able we are to use various styles, the more efficient we become."[41]

Of course, as I have suggested above, these styles are likely to reflect the personality traits of various individuals, and any given negotiator is likely to feel more comfortable with some of these styles than others. In addition, I have noted that some styles are more likely to be effective in certain kinds of negotiations or in different stages of the same negotiation. The demands of each phase and each type of negotiation seem to require different negotiating skills and therefore individuals who tend to emphasize one or the other of these personality traits. While personality traits have probably seldom, if ever, been a major criterion for determining the makeup of diplomatic delegations, there is at least some evidence to suggest that this factor might be looked at more seriously than has been the case historically.

CULTURE AND NEGOTIATING BEHAVIOR

An additional set of human factors that affect negotiating behavior stem from group and social norms that may be common to a particular culture. Until now we have looked at variations among individual negotiators, and most of the cognitive characteristics and personality traits can be found in varying degrees everywhere in the world. In other words, individuals vary considerably on some of these dimensions, but these variations are not strongly associated with the social context in which one was raised. By contrast, cultural values are those that are shared by a group of people who, as a result of a common heritage, acquire certain common values, outlooks on the world, systems of reasoning, and other cognitive attributes; furthermore, these outlooks and values are generally not shared with members of other groups.[42] Raymond Cohen has defined culture as "the outward expression of a unifying and consistent vision brought by a particular community to its confrontation with such core issues as the origins of the cosmos, the harsh unpredictability of the natural environment, the nature of society, and humankind's place in the order of things."[43]

Although these factors affect how individual negotiators may behave in diplomacy, these factors are exhibited by most or all individuals coming from particular countries or cultural groups with relatively minor individual variations within the cultural group on these dimensions. While the rapid spread of communication and information around the globe in the past few decades has tended to homogenize some of the different characteristics of various world cultures, there can be little doubt that each social group retains certain basic views and expectations about the world that are shared within the cultural group and set it apart from other groups. Indeed, the same symbols and behaviors may mean different things within different cultural contexts as a result of these critical differences. Although there is disagreement among scholars who study international negotiations about the significance of these cultural variations, there is widespread agreement that these factors exert at least some significant impact on how individuals perceive the world and how they behave in situations where they are brought face-to-face with representatives of different cultural groups. As Glen Fisher has pointed out, these differences may range from "contrasting sets of values that determine the hierarchy of negotiating objectives themselves" to contrasts "as trivial as behavior mannerisms that subtly block confidence and trust."[44] Although much attention has been devoted in some of the popular media to the latter dimension, certainly the aspect of culture that is most relevant to international negotiations is that which Cohen has described as entailing "the confrontation of profoundly incompatible, culturally grounded assumptions about the nature of the world, verbal and nonverbal communication, and key aspects of behavior."[45]

The concept of culture has usually been stressed by anthropologists, and it serves for them as the way of accounting for beliefs, practices, and forms of social organization displayed in the communal life of different branches of the human race. Culture is transmitted through the processes of acculturation and socialization, in which individuals are brought up in a social context and inculcated with the values based on the historical traditions and beliefs of the group with which they are raised. Out of these beliefs and traditions arises a sense of identity as belonging to a unique group. This group may range, at the small end of the scale, from the extended family or a tribe to, at the larger end of the scale, membership in a large national community or to a religious or ethnic community. Thus, one may find one's cultural roots in a tribal association (the Ibo in Nigeria), in a country (being Japanese), in an ethnic group (being an Arab), in a linguistic group (francophone Belgians), or in a religion (Islam). This cultural association is then seen as molding an individual's full image of the world in which he or she lives.

Glen Fisher has suggested that culture may influence the negotiation process in several ways. First, culture affects the ways in which diplomats view the negotiation process itself. For example, he points out that Americans are more inclined to see negotiations as pragmatic efforts to solve problems, whereas French diplomats are more inclined to see them as deriving logically valid solutions. There also may be variations in the public versus private aspects of negotiations. For example, Japanese negotiators do not like to expose disagreements in public; therefore, for them differences are to be resolved in private negotiations, and public diplomacy serves only to formalize those relationships once agreement has been reached behind closed doors. Still other countries tend to emphasize the fact that negotiations are public fora for open displays of general and often emotionally charged rhetoric, whereas individuals from some other cultures prefer to "get down to business" as rapidly as possible and view rhetorical displays as a complete waste of time. Mexican diplomats are frequently associated with the former behavior, whereas Swiss or German diplomats typically tend to be of the latter type.

Second, the style of decision making also tends to vary along cultural lines. Some countries tend to be highly bureaucratized, and the negotiating culture may consequently downplay the significance of any particular incumbent in the negotiating role; this tends to characterize the approach to negotiations by the United States according to Fisher. American delegations are often composed of competing bureaucratic agencies, and the tenuous relationship between negotiators and Congress tends to make the process both uncertain and impersonal. By contrast, in other cases, the personality of a distinguished leader is predominant in a negotiation, especially in countries such as Mexico according to Fisher; once the person in charge, whose identity may not be obvious, has made a decision, the negotiation may move forward with few other interferences. Similarly, the Japanese need for consensus means that arriving at a negotiating position can be a lengthy process and, once completed, the degree of flexibility is extremely limited. This again contrasts with the style in the United States where positions can change as bureaucratic coalitions gain and lose in influence over the process and as elections and other political pressures bring new preferences and priorities to the negotiation table.

Third, national character also seems to exert some effect on negotiations. These national character traits are seen by some as influencing how different cultures approach negotiations. For example, the American impatience to achieve results quickly and efficiently has often been contrasted with the patience and willingness to maintain an inflexible position over time in order to achieve long-term national objectives, often associated with countries such as the Soviet Union or Japan. While noting these differences, it is important not to slip into a stereotyped or rigid notion of national character in which, for example, some cultures may be thought of as lazy, always tardy, highly emotional, or being unconcerned about results, whereas others are thought of as industrious, efficient and on time, pragmatic and serious, and focusing on concrete results from beginning to end. Too often stereotypes that negotiators hold about the national character of their counterparts from other countries interfere with their ability to deal with their partners as unique individuals or to seek to identify the real interests which they represent.

Fourth, cross-cultural noise refers to the small behavioral characteristics that can affect the perceptions and attitudes of others with whom one is negotiating. These factors can include gestures, the distance at which one stands from one's interlocutor, how greetings are exchanged, how one sits, the formality or informality of how one dresses, how one addresses one's counterpart, to mention just a few of the typical small factors that collectively can convey the wrong impression in a negotiation. While the significance of these rather superficial considerations can certainly be exaggerated, Fisher concludes that "ignoring the 'noise' that might complicate an already delicate balance of negotiating factors is at the least shortsighted, and tuning in on what might appear to be superficial cultural manifestations can often lead to more profound insights into the counterpart's psychological environment."[46]

Fifth, interpretation and translation may introduce cultural bias into the negotiation. There are several specific problems here. First, some words may not find direct translations in other languages, and this may have an impact even on how the underlying concept is understood (or not understood) in the other culture; it may have an impact on the precision with which certain specific ideas may be conveyed between one language and another. Second, some false friends between two related languages may create misunderstandings when interpretations are overly literal or do not appreciate the different meanings of cognates in the different language groups. Third, substantive jargon associated with the issue under negotiation may create difficulties for translators who are not fully conversant with the substance of the issues under negotiation and with the special use that may be made of everyday terms in the context of specific, technical issues. Fourth, individuals may negotiate in foreign languages beyond their ability, pretending to understand more than they do; rather than accept the embarrassment of admitting that they did not understand, some negotiators may agree to what has been said without fully understanding it. Needless to say, this can lead to substantial embarrassment and misunderstanding at later stages in the negotiations or when the time comes to implement an agreement that was not fully understood by at least one of its parties.

Although there are many dimensions of culture, one that has received a great deal of attention in recent research is that which distinguishes between individualistic and collectivist world outlooks.[47] Individualism, which is characteristic of many European and North American cultures, emphasizes such values as individual legal rights, suspicion of centralized authority, and an emphasis on freedom to assert individual behavior. As Cohen notes, they "hold freedom, the development of the individual personality, self-expression, and personal enterprise and achievement as supreme values."[48] These societies also place a great deal of emphasis on the mobility of the individual to overcome social hierarchies, and status within society is attained by one's accomplishments rather than inherited. Conflicts within these societies are frequently adjudicated within a legal framework where individual rights are predominant.

The collectivist culture, on the other hand, is frequently more characteristic of non-Western societies, both in the former socialist countries and in many parts of the third world. Here authority is highly respected, whether it be the family, the church, and/or political leadership. The welfare of the group often takes precedence over the welfare of any individual members, and individuals generally achieve their self-identity more through group membership than through their own individual personality. As Cohen emphasizes: "The collectivist ethic has the welfare of the group and cooperative endeavor as its guiding themes, and it subordinates individual wishes and desires to that leitmotiv. Indeed, the individual is identified on the basis of group affiliation and individual needs in terms of communal interests."[49]

This ethos tends to be more accepting of rigid social hierarchy, and authority is ascribed or inherited rather than achieved through one's own efforts. Conflicts in collectivist culture are frequently dealt with through conciliation, according to the need to maintain group harmony rather than individual rights.

Obviously, these two are very broad cultural categories, and they do not distinguish between the more particular cultural characteristics that, for example, may be shared by all Latin Americans, or only by Mexicans, or only by people from certain regions or social groups within Mexico, etc. Each of these different levels of social division present opportunities for cultural differences to arise and be perpetuated from generation to generation through the processes of raising and educating children within a culture, as children learn to adapt to the norms of the group within which they must live.

The impact of culture has led analysts such as Cohen to suggest a model for conducting negotiations where intercultural differences are significant, which he refers to as "Model C," the "culturally sensitive" model. This contrasts with both the traditional bargaining model and the problem-solving model, since both of these imply some universal human characteristics that transcend cultural differences. By contrast, the culturally sensitive model does not share the assumption that "underneath we are all pretty much the same." Instead, the culturally sensitive negotiator is aware of the significance of religious and cultural beliefs held by other parties to the negotiations, is conscious of the fact that the Western conception of "rationality" is itself a culture-bound value, and does not necessarily assume that techniques that work in one culture can be transferred readily to interactions with other cultures.[50]

The impact of these culturally sensitive factors in many negotiations has been challenged by others who observe that a fairly universal culture of international negotiation has emerged in the international system in recent decades. As Zartman and Berman have noted, "by now the world has established an international diplomatic culture that soon socializes its members into similar behavior."[51] Certainly any one who has observed an international conference cannot help but remark upon the many similar habits and styles of behavior of the diplomatic representatives from around the world. No matter what their national origins, most come from the upper socioeconomic classes in their home country; many attended the same universities in the United States, Western Europe, or in Moscow, where they read the same standard works in history and international relations; most dress alike, eat at the same restaurants, and attend the same cultural and social events; and perhaps most importantly, the vast majority share a self-image of being part of an international diplomatic community descendent from the traditions of British or French diplomacy of the nineteenth century. Furthermore, as Winfried Lang, an Austrian diplomat, has pointed out, there are many shared values that form the underpinnings of this "negotiation culture," which include "(a) a sense of accommodation (at least somewhat stronger than the sense of confrontation), (b) awareness of the need for efficient and reliable communication, (c) the importance attached to flexibility and creativity, (d) willingness to go beyond traditional constraints of a national character, and (e) readiness to give higher priority to dispute prevention than to dispute settlement. This negotiation culture is constrained, however, by national interests imposed by the respective government on its negotiators by means of more or less stringent instructions."[52]

Another factor that reduces the impact of culture derives from the highly specialized nature of many international negotiations on complex issues such as disarmament, the environment, or international trade. This means that national delegations often are no longer composed exclusively of professional diplomats or politicians, but rather include scientists, economists, medical professionals, military officers, intelligence specialists, and so forth. Each of these professions has its own professional concepts, jargon, and ways of defining problems that are shared across national, ethnic, and religious boundaries. As Lang notes, these experts "represent their professional culture at least as much as they represent their national culture."[53]

It is not surprising that in negotiations such as the Strategic Arms Reduction Talks (START) between the United States and the former Soviet Union, some of the most productive meetings took place across the table between expert groups of military officers or even intelligence officers of the two countries; often these individuals seemed to understand one another better than their counterparts from other branches and professions within their own country. Although cultural differences did not wash out completely, they were often overwhelmed by the professional interest and curiosity that the groups of professional advisors from the two countries held in common with one another and did not share with some other delegates from their own countries.

In summary, the impact of culture seems to depend a great deal on the nature of the issue under negotiation and the kind of negotiation that is taking place. In some cases, the national interests of countries are so wrapped up in culturally derived values and beliefs that culture influences all aspects of a negotiator's approach to the issue; the way in which they order their preferences and make tradeoffs, the kinds of negotiating tactics that they employ, and the way they conceive of the conflict resolution process itself all reflect their cultural heritage. These kinds of factors are likely to be especially salient in highly political negotiations, where cultural conflicts are themselves very much a source of the problem; certainly the conflict between Israelis and Palestinians or between the United States and Cuba are very much influenced by these kinds of deep and pervasive cultural factors. By contrast, to the extent that many negotiations in contemporary international relations are highly technical or reflect bureaucratic interests, the cultural factors are likely to be subordinated to other interests or partly washed out by the existence of a transnational professional culture.

INTERCULTURAL COMMUNICATION AND THE NEGOTIATION PROCESS

All of the factors mentioned above—whether individual cognitive frames, individual personality, or cultural norms—affect negotiations primarily through their impact on the communication process within negotiations. Therefore, in applying these psychological and anthropological factors to our understanding of international negotiation, we must examine briefly a fundamental model of interpersonal communication.

Basically, a simple model of communication may be considered to consist of seven stages, as follows:

1. A sender has a message in his or her mind to convey to another person or persons.

2. The sender must encode that message by converting it into verbal (spoken or written) or nonverbal (action) symbols to be transmitted.

3. These symbols are then transmitted as a message through a communications channel; this may be written messages sent through diplomatic channels or spoken messages at a meeting, or any other form of transmitting messages, but the message always consists of some nonrandom signal (for example, words) that are presumed to convey meaning from one individual to another.

4. These messages may be affected by noise, which is random or extraneous signals that interfere with the transmission of the nonrandom content of the message.

5. Once these messages are transmitted, they are then decoded by a receiver, which is the process through which those signals are interpreted by the recipient.

6. The receiver then acts on the basis of the message as he or she has interpreted it.

7. Feedback is information that is returned to the sender about the way in which the message has been received; positive feedback should indicate that the message has been received and interpreted accurately, whereas negative feedback suggests that the message has been misinterpreted or misunderstood by the receiver.[54]

The central hypothesis in this model is that communications across cultures requires that all elements of this model be in harmony, and that no distortions interrupt the free flow of information across this model. However, in reality there are frequently a number of sources of distortion that may enter into the process of crosscultural communication. The first originates from different images held by the sender and the receiver of the message, that may cause them to encode and decode the same signals differently. In other words, the images held by each party to the communication reflect their basic worldview, resulting from all of

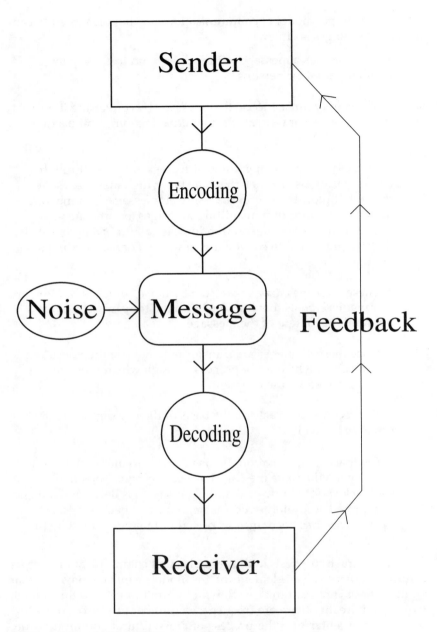

Figure 8.2 Simple Model of Communication

the factors of individual cognitive style, personality, and culture noted previously. Insofar as these images are congruent, one would expect the two parties to encode and decode the same messages more or less identically, so that the message would be understood in roughly the same way. On the other hand, if the two parties have very different images, the receiver may decode the message in different terms from those used by the sender to encode it, so that the sender and the receiver may interpret the same message very differently. As Cohen notes, "for there to be real understanding—true communication in the normative sense of the term—the parties engaged must be able to draw upon matching semantic assumptions."[55] The absence of such congruity, often due to cultural differences, may create a great deal of difference in the way in which the identical message is understood by the two different parties. The result is a failure to communicate the same meaning between the two parties; what may look like an objective message will be interpreted differently within the contrasting subjective images of the two parties.

A second problem may be with the message itself. A message must contain sufficiently unambiguous and nonrandom information so that it can be received clearly. Insufficient or conflicting information in the message may create confusion. Furthermore, language differences may create special problems for international communications, since messages are often encoded in one language and then translated to another before being decoded. The translation process can be another source of distortion within the message itself.

A third source of faulty communication may arise from noise, especially when a large quantity of extraneous or random information is received so that the receiver cannot distinguish between the message and the noise. Voice communications across electronic media such as the telephone often have static or background noise that affects the clarity of communication. By analogy, the use of excessive information, much of which may be irrelevant to the message, may also create noise. And, as noted above, cultural noise may intervene due to culture-specific habits that may be misunderstood or confuse persons coming from different cultures.

A fourth source of difficulty is distinguishing between positive and negative feedback. In order for the sender to learn that a message has not been received or that it has been misunderstood, she or he must receive some negative feedback. Yet individuals generally look for and assume positive feedback in the absence of any clear evidence to the contrary. Psychological consistency theory suggests that individuals will strive to make the feedback they receive fit in with their preexisting images, and attribution theories further suggest that individuals will attribute inconsistencies or negative feedback to malevolent intent on the part of the other party rather than to misunderstanding, which may frequently be more appropriate. Furthermore, individual or cultural differences may in some circumstances even cause negative feedback on the part of the receiver to be interpreted as positive feedback; frequently, indications of misunderstanding are not seen or may be interpreted as tactical manipulations of the communication process rather than as genuine indicators of a failed communication.

All of these factors may exert a substantial impact on international negotiations. Since most international negotiations usually take place across different cultures and since they always involve different individuals, the very different frames of reference of the negotiating parties may cause frequent miscommunication and misunderstanding. The fact that language differences frequently arise in international negotiations can also be a source of error in the communication of messages. The distances over which many international communications must travel may also introduce various forms of noise, although technology is presently reducing some of these problems. Yet technology has also created the possibility of transmitting such vast quantities of information, thereby creating an information overload, that it becomes increasingly difficult to distinguish between the relevant and the irrelevant, the message and the noise. Therefore, the very process of negotiation, which requires above all clear communications of goals and interests in order for the parties to identify bargaining space, BATNAs, and possible formulas for agreement, may be disrupted by inadequate communication due to any of these human factors in negotiations.

The cognitive balance models discussed above also have significant implications for communications. Theodore Newcomb has transformed Heider's P-O-X model into a basic model of communications between two persons (A and B) about something (X), calling the resulting triangle an A-B-X model.[56] He notes then that A and B may be considered to be jointly oriented toward this X, and that the linkages among the three elements tend to preserve the requirements of balance: they possess either zero or two negative bonds. Therefore, the extent of A's and B's co-orientation toward X will affect, and be affected by, the communications between A and B. Insofar as there is consensus about salient X's (either positive or negative), there will tend to be positive communications; conversely, disagreement about X is likely to be associated with hostile communications. Experimental evidence tends to supports the hypothesis that an imbalanced A-B-X situations lead "to feelings of negative affect," whereas "situations defined as balanced result in feelings of positive affect."[57]

Balance theory, on the other hand, does not prescribe a single causal direction; that is, imbalance may either lead to a change in the symmetry of co-orientation or a change in communications. What is clearly suggested by this model is the likelihood of mutually reinforcing cycles:

the development of consensus about important external factors may contribute to more positive communications, and more positive communication facilitates the development of consensus about critical issues; conversely, hostile communications and dissensus about critical issues or events are mutually reinforcing. Once negotiators find themselves caught in a vicious spiral, the dynamics of maintaining cognitive balance may make it difficult to escape. On the more positive side, however, the development of shared evaluations and positive communications may create a mutually reinforcing cycle, and breaking this pattern is likely to be a source of psychological strain or dissonance for the actor who interrupts the cycle.

Communications problems frequently present serious obstacles to the successful conduct of international negotiations. There are, on the other hand, some techniques that negotiators can use to try to overcome these problems. First, in order to create greater congruence of images, so that encoding and decoding overlap, it may often be useful to develop empathy, the ability of one party to see the issues and problems as the other party sees them. As Ralph White points out, in international relations as in many other interpersonal relations, empathy is often very difficult: "Empathy normally has the disturbing effect of requiring us to see double—to hold in suspension two interpretations of the same facts, the other fellow's and one's own. Complexity and uncertainty are introduced. The human mind, seeking simplicity and certainty, rebels. And empathy is choked off."[58]

Therefore, developing empathy requires overcoming the natural tendency of the human mind to avoid ambiguity and the psychological tension that results from seeing double. Negotiators need to develop an ability to take the perspective of other parties, without necessarily accepting the positions of the other as absolutely legitimate or true. One technique for building empathy and reducing the perception of threat has been suggested by Anatol Rapoport as an important component of debate, based on permissive therapy;[59] this approach has frequently been called role reversal. The process of role reversal involves three steps:

> 1. Each party must be able and willing to exchange roles with the other and state the other's position to their satisfaction; that is, each must repeat the other's position until the other has confirmed that it has in fact been stated fully and correctly to his or her satisfaction.

> 2. Then each party must be able and willing to state the conditions under which the other's position is valid or has merit. Rapoport refers to this as "delineating the region of validity of the opponent's stand."

3. Finally, each party must be able and willing to assume that in many ways the opponent is like him or herself, called by Rapoport "inducing the assumption of similarity." The goal here is to show that a common ground exists where the parties share common values, and their awareness of the common ground helps them understand the circumstances that have led the other to hold their positions. Only after all three stages, Rapoport argues, may the parties truly be considered to have empathized with one another.[60] Once this stage has been reached, however, they may proceed to negotiate on the basis of a clearer under-standing of both their real differences of interest and their common interests.

Research on role reversal has generally suggested that it is most ef-fective in overcoming conflicts that are characterized by high levels of misperception and misunderstanding; by contrast, in some cases where there are deep differences of values and interests, it may actually clarify those differences and even intensify conflict. Role reversal has generally been viewed skeptically by policy makers and diplomats because it nec-essarily accords a certain legitimacy to the beliefs and positions of the other party; thus, many negotiators fear that it will weaken their posi-tion in the distributive component of negotiations. As a result, there is little evidence from actual international negotiations of the use of role reversal, but it seems to be a promising approach that may help to over-come communications problems, especially in negotiations that are clouded by a history of intense emotional conflict and related misun-derstandings between the parties.

A variant to this approach to try to reduce the divergence between the ways parties encode and decode the same communications is the technique of conducting communications-oriented, problem-solving workshops.[61] The purpose of this approach has been "to provide parties to a conflict an opportunity to meet each other on an unofficial basis to discuss their relative concerns and to provide them with some skills and knowledge that will enable them to resolve their conflict peacefully."[62] The primary emphasis of these workshops is to induce subjective changes of attitudes and perceptions in the parties, especially to encourage them to conceptualize issues in positive-sum rather than zero-sum terms. The fundamental assumptions are that misperceptions can be overcome through interaction and that knowledge about one another can be learned in ways that will affect future behavior. Sometimes these workshops function as opportunities for the parties to communicate with one an-other under conditions strictly controlled by a third party; in other cases, these sessions resemble sensitivity training groups to try to sensitize participants to the underlying needs and concerns of the other parties.

The idea is then to induce learning on the part of the participants about one another and about new opportunities for creative solutions to existing problems. Sill other workshops focus on promoting informal problem solving; as suggested by Kelman and Cohen, "they are intended to give participants the freedom, opportunity, and impetus to move away from the rigid reiteration of official positions and from efforts to justify their own side and score points against the other side, and, instead, to absorb new information, explore new ideas, revise their perceptions, reassess their attitudes, and engage in a process of creative problem solving."[63]

No negotiations actually occur with any of these techniques; instead, these informal meetings will ideally provide the basis for making suggestions to government officials as a foundation for reconceptualizing negotiations at an official level, including the prenegotiation phase, the negotiations themselves, and post-negotiation implementation of agreements. Unfortunately, however, there have been few, if any, documented attempts to do this reported in the research on this technique to date.

A second category of techniques for improving communications in negotiation is to use redundancy, repeating a message in as many different ways as possible and through as many different channels of communication as possible in order to overcome noise. Just as a telephone operator may use redundant information such as "B as in boy" and "P as in Paul" in order to overcome noise on the telephone line that makes it difficult to distinguish between letters such as b and p, so a negotiator may repeat the same messages in different ways in order to reinforce them. Different channels of communication may be especially useful. For example, actions or other nonverbal behavior may be used to reinforce messages transmitted verbally. In negotiations, back channel communications between senior governmental officials may reinforce those messages transmitted over the negotiation table by diplomatic representatives. Of course, it is also essential that the different forms and channels of communication present consistent messages that reinforce rather than contradict one another. The more different ways in which a particular message can be transmitted, in general, the more likely it is to be received correctly.

Finally, negotiators can make better use of feedback. One must first be aware of the natural human tendency to want to receive positive or supportive feedback. Therefore, positive feedback, especially when delivered by others, should always be regarded with some suspicion. One should also seek some clear repetition of feedback in order to confirm its content. Finally, one should observe closely the behavior of the receiver to see if it does reflect the fact that the receiver has actually received the message fully and accurately.

In conclusion, I cannot overemphasize the importance of clear and effective communication to the success of international negotiations. All negotiations depend on communication, and this is one area in which the human element cannot be discounted. Such effective communication, especially across national, cultural, and linguistic barriers, requires constant attention to make sure that messages are sent clearly and interpreted similarly by both parties. It also requires an awareness of the individual and group sources of potential misinterpretation so that conscious efforts must be made in negotiations to communicate in spite of these differences. And finally, it requires a willingness to acknowledge misunderstandings when they occur, learn from them, and adapt one's behavior to compensate for these misperceptions. Greater sensitivity to these individual and cultural factors that impede communication will not guarantee success in overcoming conflicts of interest in international negotiations, but it can enhance the possibility that negotiations will actually focus on those differences of interest rather than being complicated or disrupted unnecessarily by extraneous conflicts based on misperception and misunderstanding.

Chapter 9

Negotiations and Foreign Policy:
The Impact of Bureaucratic Politics

U ntil this point I have treated the state as a unified actor or party to negotiations, almost as if the state behaved like a single individual. Yet in reality we also know that states are composed of groups and individuals, and that these various components of the state may often be divided among themselves. Not only is the state a pluralistic set of groups and institutions, but also negotiations are affected by a particularly critical division of roles within the state, between policy makers in the home government (often referred to as principals) and the diplomats who serve as their representatives (or agents). This section will consider the dynamics of these various elements of the state as they affect the negotiation process.

Most rational theories of negotiations have assumed that states are autonomous actors in international relations that have clearly defined national interests, a neatly ordered set of preferences about goals to be sought and values to be maximized. The national interest must be "related to general objectives, not to the preferences or needs of any particular group or class, or to the private power drives of officeholders," and it entails an ordering of preferences that "must persist over time."[1]

On the other hand, critics of this approach argue that there is no such thing as a generally shared set of objectives or preferences. Rather, the state operates within the context of competition among branches of government, among agencies of the executive branch, and in the midst of political and class conflicts that divide the larger society. Agencies and organizations within the governmental bureaucracy vie with one another to determine policy. Each of these groups develop their own rationality, often based on specific interests of the group rather than the general interest of the state. As a result, the state as a whole operates at best on the basis of *"the principle of bounded rationality,"*[2] In this case, its preferences reflect the net outcome of a process of bargaining and compromise within the government to arrive at policy decisions, often without explicit agreement upon goals, but rather on the basis of a lowest common denominator of agreement about specific decisions.

Furthermore, this phenomenon occurs to some degree or another in virtually all states and organizations, in spite of differences among the structures of states. There is, of course, some degree of truth to the proposition advanced by Lall that the "forms and conventions of the constitutional structures of states have a direct bearing on the maneuverability of governments in the course of a negotiation."[3] On the other hand, sometimes the importance of these structural differences may also be exaggerated. Some political scientists have discussed hierarchical decision making in authoritarian or so-called totalitarian states as if a single individual somehow made all of the decisions and as if all other individuals were simply subservient agents to that single dictator. Such states are often contrasted with democratic or pluralistic states and organizations, within which decision-making powers are assumed to be widely distributed throughout the organization. This, however, is a false and immensely oversimplified dichotomy. Obviously, some states are more pluralistic and others are more centralized in their structure, but the bureaucratic politics perspective on negotiations emphasizes that all states to some degree try to reconcile conflicting interests and needs on the parts of constituent groups and individuals, and thus all states are affected to a greater or lesser degree by this kind of bureaucratic and political pluralism.

When it comes to the conduct of negotiations, certainly the perfectly centralized authoritarian model was always very much of an oversimplification, despite the frequent popular assertion that centralized authority gave authoritarian states an advantage in negotiations since they were assumed not to be hindered by internal divisions. According to some analysts, this gives authoritarian states an ability to act rationally and even ruthlessly in pursuit of an overriding national interest or dominant ideology. Certainly there has been a great deal of ideological homogeneity found at the highest levels in authoritarian regimes such as Germany under Hitler or the Soviet Union under Stalin. Yet even in these extreme cases, ideology did not always produce consensus about how to deal with specific issues under negotiation, with the possible exception of a few highly visible negotiations such as those at Yalta and Potsdam that were conducted personally by Stalin, the dominant political figure. But even for such states in more ordinary negotiations, there were certainly conflicts of interest between military and domestic economic priorities or between the ideas of different officials about how to deal with adversaries such as Great Britain or the United States.

There are, of course, wide variations in the latitude for choice given to negotiators by governmental authorities, but this varies not only from one political system to another or from one country to another, but also from one issue to another. For example, in the mid-1980s negotiations involving the two nuclear superpowers were characterized by very different degrees of flexibility provided to the negotiators by the White House and the National Security Council. In the negotiations in 1986–87 on the reduction of Intermediate-range Nuclear Forces (INF) in Europe, Ambassador Maynard Glitman was held on a very tight rein by Washington, and every change in the negotiating position of the United States had to be approved at the highest levels in Washington. At the same time, Ambassador Robert Barry, who was negotiating in Stockholm in a multilateral effort to develop new confidence and security-building measures for Europe, was given almost complete discretion to negotiate within a broad framework. Since few vital interests of the United States would be directly affected by the outcome of this latter negotiation, Barry was fairly free to advance his own ideas (and those of his delegation) and respond as he thought best to proposals put forward by other countries.

In short, while all states are guided in their negotiating behavior by some overriding notion of the national interest, all are also divided internally to a greater or lesser degree by different interpretations of the national interest or other ideological guide posts, different political interests on the domestic scene, and conflicts of bureaucratic interest among the agents who must formulate specific negotiating positions and carry out the actual task of negotiating with other countries.

Furthermore, the national interest does not necessarily persist with continuity over time. Interests may shift as a result of changes in the domestic political balance or governments may change due to electoral defeat or revolution. As a result, the negotiator must seek objectives that are frequently shifting during the very course of negotiations. Perhaps nothing illustrates this more dramatically than the rapid shifts in the Soviet national interest during the tumultuous period from 1986 through the breakup of the Soviet Union itself in 1991. Among these principles of the Soviet national interest that were thought to be more or less immutable, the following basic assumptions were modified or cast aside altogether by the new Soviet leadership under Gorbachev: (1) the notion that the preexisting balance of conventional forces in Europe, with a numerical superiority for the Warsaw Pact countries, guaranteed stable security; (2) the belief that the presence of a series of buffer states between the USSR and their potential Western enemies was an essential element of Soviet security; (3) the assumption that a divided and relatively weak Germany was necessary to prevent any renewed military threat to Soviet security; and (4) the concept that only a centrally planned, command economy could provide the economic foundations for the Soviet military establishment. Obviously these major modifications in the way in which Soviet leaders perceived and defined their national interest led to a whole series of changes in their negotiating positions on a wide range of specific issues.

Clearly such a rapid and comprehensive modification of the national interest is the exception rather than the rule in international politics, but this is a dramatic illustration of the kinds of changes that affect the way in which the national interest is conceived by the leaders of most states as the individual decision makers change, as the structure of their government is modified, or as changes within either their domestic or international environment permit or produce changes in their foreign policy outlook.

Since negotiation is perhaps the most ubiquitous tool of diplomacy, it follows that its conduct is dependent on the foreign policy decision-making process of the states or organizations that are interacting diplomatically. As I shall discuss in the next chapter, that interaction itself affects the process and outcome of negotiations, and the result of the negotiation process may often produce more than the sum of its parts, in the sense that the result may be more than a simple midpoint among the positions and interests of the parties. However, it cannot escape being shaped in large measure by those fundamental, if shifting and at times divided, interests. The focus of the bureaucratic process model of negotiations is therefore on how the negotiating positions of the parties are formed and modified throughout the course of a negotiation, and how decisions are reached by each party regarding Iklé's classic three-fold choice: accept possible agreements, continue to negotiate and seek better terms, or break off negotiations.[4]

This is not the place to develop a full-blown framework for the analysis of foreign policy decision making in order to examine its impact on the formulation of negotiating positions. However, some of the basic elements of such a framework may be summarized briefly. Ever since the pathbreaking work of Snyder, Bruck, and Sapin, scholars have focused their analyses of foreign policy upon a set of individuals usually referred to as decision makers.[5] Decision makers are those individuals who are empowered by virtue of their position to act on behalf of the state in its foreign relations. These decision makers are usually organized hierarchically. Those at the very top typically define the national interest as it relates to specific policy issues, determine overall policy goals, and make decisions about those issues that most affect the fundamental national interest. As one descends the hierarchy, individuals assume increasingly specialized roles along functional lines, with individuals at each successively lower layer of the hierarchy being responsible for an increasingly specialized area of concern or sphere of competence. Moving down the hierarchy also reduces the latitude for independent choice.

Decision making may be viewed in a cybernetic model as consisting of a series of inputs from an environment, of decisions to be made about how to respond to those inputs, of a series of policy outputs through which those decisions are implemented, and finally of feedback that returns to the decision makers to inform them about the consequences of their decisions within their environment.

In the input phase of the process, individuals are at least formally responsible for collecting and passing on information to assist higher level officials in making their decisions. After the decisions have been made, these same individuals or others may be charged with implementing those decisions and passing back to higher level officials feedback about the success or failure of their goals. Even in the input phase, decisions must still be made about questions such as what information should be passed on to higher levels, what priority should be given to it, and what channels and media of communication should be used to relay that information. In the output stages the persons charged with implementation often find that they are informed of general decisions about policy made at a higher level, but they are often left considerable latitude to determine how to apply those general and sometimes vague policy guidelines in the concrete circumstances in which they are working. Finally, they must decide what information to relay back to decision makers about the impact of their decisions on the environment. Although many of these may seem like small decisions as opposed to grand policy choices, the cumulative effect of a long series of incremental decisions at each phase may actually have a greater impact on policy than the broad decisions made by national leaders.

In spite of this consideration, the decision makers upon whom foreign policy analysts tend to focus most of their attention are usually the executive branch officials, especially heads of state, foreign ministers, defense ministers, national security advisors, and the like. However, the decision-making circle on some issues may be broadened to include the legislative branch or even the judiciary. These decision makers are usually viewed as operating within two somewhat different environments, which create the events that require decision makers to act, which provide the information to aid them in deciding how to act in particular circumstances, and which constrain their choices by setting limits on what can be decided and what decisions can be carried out. The domestic environment includes the prevailing political differences, economic conditions, and cultural and social factors within the country that affect its interests, preferences, and positions in negotiations. The international environment provides the challenges requiring a response and sets the limits on what is possible.

As noted above, this framework for decision making is based primarily on an information-processing model in which information may be depicted as flowing to these decision makers from both the domestic and international environments. The central decision makers then process this information within the context of their definition of their interests, they set goals and determine which goals will be given highest priority, and they decide upon specific policies to achieve those goals. Those decisions are then communicated to those who must implement them in the field; the defining characteristic of foreign as opposed to domestic policy is that those decisions are intended to have their primary impact in the international rather than the domestic environment, although there clearly may be secondary effects (often very important ones) in the internal environment as well. Finally, information is returned to the decision makers as feedback about the impact of those decisions in both environments: positive feedback suggests that the decision makers' goals are essentially being realized, whereas negative feedback indicates that the goals are either not being achieved or some other negative consequences have been felt that were not intended or expected by the decision makers. In theory, then, the decision makers should act on this feedback and adjust their decisions as necessary to move them closer to their objectives in an ever improving succession of small steps.

Of course, real foreign policy decisions seldom correspond in their specifics to this fairly neat and coherent model, but the model nonetheless provides a benchmark against which decision making may be studied. When this model is applied to international negotiations, the process of conducting such negotiations may be viewed simply as one part of the larger process of making and implementing foreign policy. Negotiations provide one important source of information to decision makers about the international environment, by helping to inform them about the needs, interests, goals, and priorities of other countries with which they are interacting. As noted above, negotiators must make decisions about what positions to take in a negotiation, about what does and does not constitute an acceptable agreement, about when to accept or reject an agreement, and about whether to continue or break off a negotiation. Presumably negotiations will be one of the many instruments, and often a very important instrument, for the conduct of their foreign policy, although it must also take its place alongside other instruments of foreign policy, including economic instruments (revaluing currency, applying economic sanctions, providing loans and economic aid, etc.), military instruments (acquiring new arms or disarming, shows of force, employment of coercive force, etc.), and psychological elements (use of propaganda, cultural and educational exchanges, terrorism, etc.). Most of these other instruments, of course, may be used in conjunction with negotiations: they may either be used as instruments to reinforce negotiating positions or the negotiations may be employed as means to utilize one of these other elements. Negotiations are one of the most important levers used by states to achieve their foreign policy objectives. Thus, an analysis of the bureaucratic politics approach to negotiations is inseparable from the bureaucratic politics framework for the analysis of foreign policy decision making in general.

This brings us back to an issue that was introduced at the beginning of this chapter—the relationship between the negotiator and the decision maker. From one perspective, all negotiators may be viewed as decision makers. At a minimum negotiators must decide what information to send back to other government officials about what is transpiring in the negotiations, and they must decide how to implement whatever negotiating instructions they have been given by their governments. These decisions, however small they may appear at the time, can have a huge cumulative effect both upon the conduct of negotiations and upon the ability to achieve larger foreign policy goals. For example, a negotiator's failure to communicate to the home government a concession or new proposal from their counterpart may result in a significant lost opportunity to reach agreement and solve important problems. Or a negotiator's failure to carry out new instructions effectively may cause embarrassment to his or her country if these mistakes are rectified or may misdirect the course of negotiations if they are not corrected.

While these examples illustrate the minimum decision-making activity assumed by negotiators, in most cases negotiators also exert a more significant and direct impact on foreign policy decision making. Many negotiators have the latitude to make decisions throughout the process of negotiating that will affect their country's foreign policy. This may include decisions about introducing new proposals, making concessions, retracting previous offers, making threats or promises or any other tactical moves, accepting or rejecting offers and proposals of other parties, as well as the tactical decisions concerning the timing and sequencing of each of these negotiating moves. While some negotiators must receive permission from home prior to making such moves, it is often their initiatives and suggestions that motivate governments to make appropriate adjustments in their negotiating behavior. And, at the extreme, some negotiators may have complete latitude to make major decisions about their negotiating positions on their own. This is particularly true for negotiations among heads of state, such as in so-called summit conferences, or when other high level government officials act themselves in a capacity as a negotiator.

We may then depict the latitude of a negotiator as falling along a continuum from complete constraint, where the negotiator is totally bound by instructions, to complete latitude, where the negotiator may act entirely on her or his own initiative. However, in all but the latter extreme case, the international negotiation process is affected by a secondary negotiating process between the negotiator, acting as an agent, and the home government or principal decision makers who provide guidance and instructions for the negotiator. I shall examine the dynamics of this particular negotiation process below.

The bureaucratic politics model of negotiations tends to view the negotiator in quite different terms, however, from that of the individual or psychological model that we considered in the previous chapter. In the individual model, the negotiator's behavior is affected primarily by her or his images and beliefs, personality, and self-concept as an individual. In the bureaucratic politics model, on the other hand, the negotiator's behavior is largely determined by the role that she or he plays, which may be defined "by a set of complementary expectations."[6] A role refers first to a set of expectations that are assigned to an individual by virtue of her or his place in some organizational hierarchy, referring to both the vertical structure of the hierarchy (superior-subordinate relationships) and the horizontal (functional division of labor) structure of the organization. These role expectations are collectively determined, and an individual is usually rewarded and receives approval when she or he fulfills the role expectations and is faced with disapproval or perhaps even punished when she or he deviates from those expectations. Because role expectations represent group norms, they can be powerful influences on individual behavior. The role secondarily refers to the expectations held about that role by the role incumbents, whose perceptions of the expectations attached to their role by others inevitably influence their own expectations about how they should behave in that role.

Obviously, individual and role factors interact in affecting the behavior of an individual negotiator. One way of looking at this tension is to suggest that role expectations form constraints or limits within which individuals may vary according to their belief systems and personality but beyond which they may not stray. Alternatively, one may also note that some personality types may be more likely to conform to role expectations, whereas others may be inclined to strike out beyond the limits normally set by role expectations. But in all organizations there exists some limits outside of which an individual cannot normally stray without risking losing a place in the organization altogether, either because she or he is replaced in that position or because others find a way of working around and cutting her or him out of all important decisions. Furthermore, the interaction between these two factors may be an important function of the individual's position in the vertical hierarchy. Kahn notes: "as one ascends the organizational hierarchy, the enactment of the role increasingly reflects attributes of the individual as well as the formalized requirements of the position. Generals have more discretion in their role behavior than do foot soldiers. But even at the highest levels, the demands of the role tend to overwhelm individual values and preferences."[7]

Role expectations do not only reflect an individual's position in a vertical hierarchy, but also in a horizontal or functional one. Foreign policy decisions are typically made by large and complex governmental bureaucracies, composed of many agencies. Frequently, many of those bureaucratic agencies are represented in the negotiation process, sometimes at the negotiation site itself, but virtually always in the home government offices in which decisions are made to guide and instruct the negotiators. Each organization or agency tends to have its own private goals. These include for all organizations the absolute necessity of perpetuating itself, of finding tasks for it to perform even if they may not at first appear evident.

This is illustrated by what might be referred to as the "March of Dimes" phenomenon. The March of Dimes is a charitable organization in the United States that was created for the sole purpose of eliminating polio as a health threat. And, indeed, with the invention of the polio vaccine and the virtual elimination of that once dreaded disease, the March of Dimes could have been considered to have been successful beyond its highest hopes. Yet once it achieved its goal, logic might say that it could then cease to exist. But it turned out that the March of Dimes as an organization had its own private goals, like all organizations, in addition to its purported public health objectives, and thus it sought to perpetuate itself even after its function seemed to have disappeared. The ready solution was to seize upon birth defects as another public health problem to which the organization could devote itself in the future. In international politics, a similar problem confronted NATO and other institutions born of the cold war that needed to redefine their functions in order to preserve their organizations in the aftermath of the fall of communism and the disintegration of the Soviet Union.

Not only do most organizations want to survive, but they usually also want to prosper. Prosperity for organizations may be measured in many different ways, but it may include increasing its budget or personnel strength or the influence of its leaders (the latter also tending to grow in proportion to the size and budget of the organization). Within one country, therefore, organizations may all formally be pursuing the same goals as defined by the national interest, but they may simultaneously be competing with one another to advance their own institutional goals. Conflicts among ministries of foreign affairs, defense, and economics are classic in affecting the negotiating behavior of states, as each of these and many other agencies of the executive branch may have different priorities or even conflicting preferences about the outcome of a particular negotiation.

Finally, organizations may pursue goals based on the interests of the special constituencies that they represent rather than upon the national interest. Ministries may develop close relationships with private groups outside of government with which they interact frequently, such as the commonly shared interest between ministries of defense and defense industries, between ministries of labor and trade unions, or between ministries of agriculture and farmers' organizations. Legislative institutions may reflect the broader interests of the domestic political groups that they represent, including political parties or even public opinion in the home districts of their members.

The result of all of these organizational considerations is that foreign policy is guided not only (if at all) by some abstract and coherent notion of a national interest, but also by a more chaotic set of bureaucratic forces, each with its own private interests that it may seek to advance along with or even over the national interest. Negotiating positions are typically determined through some complex internal negotiations among the different agencies and interest groups that are likely to be affected by a particular negotiation, and the final negotiating position will inevitably be some negotiated position that may reflect a lowest common denominator of agreement among these groups or, in some cases, the preferences of the most influential groups with the best access to the top decision makers.

This interaction between intrastate and interstate negotiations has frequently been conceived as a two-level game, an approach that has been formalized by Robert Putnam.[8] The basic bargaining model presented in chapter 5 may be expanded to include three linked sets of bilateral bargaining: one between the two states and the other two between each set of principals in the home government and their respective representatives or agents in the negotiation. Agreement requires that all three sets of bargaining space (called win sets by Putnam) overlap. Putnam refers to the interstate bargaining as a Level I negotiation, and then he adds that a Level II negotiation takes place within the constituents about whether or not to ratify the agreement. He notes that ratification may be conceived of more broadly than the formal process of legislative action to endorse an agreement, as it may also include "any decision-making process at Level II that is required to endorse or implement a Level I agreement, whether formally or informally."[9] The anticipated effect of these Level II constraints has the effect of reducing the bargaining space (or win-set) of the negotiators in the international arena. The size of the bargaining space, in Putnam's analysis, depends upon three primary factors: Level II preferences and coalitions; Level II institutions; and Level I negotiators' strategies.[10]

Rather than conceiving of the impact of the bureaucratic constraints primarily as the anticipated effects of a ratification debate (largely though not exclusively in the legislative arena after an agreement has been negotiated, as Putnam does), I would argue that there is an even more fundamental impact of the domestic arena beginning with the prenegotiation stage and continuing through the implementation phase of a negotiation. For example, in the early phase of U.S.-Soviet negotiations on Intermediate-range Nuclear Forces (INF) in Europe in 1981–83, the position of the United States was highly constrained by bureaucratic elements within the Reagan administration, especially by civilian officials in the Department of Defense, rather than by a concern that the Senate would reject an agreement. A substantial range of proposals that might have been acceptable to the Senate in a ratification debate were not acceptable to the most hard-line members of the Reagan administration, and the domestic constraints on the negotiators originated from the outset within the bureaucratic struggles of his administration rather than from any concern that an eventual agreement might fail to be ratified. Thus, throughout this first phase of the negotiations, there was no apparent bargaining space between the nuclear superpowers due to the tough position forced on the U.S. negotiators by their own bureaucratic constituencies.[11]

Dean Pruitt has suggested a model of the impact of bureaucratic politics on negotiations that views the interaction in terms of a highly interconnected communications network rather than in terms of the two-level game. In this analysis, the bureaucratic arena may be conceived as consisting of a set of stakeholders, those individuals and groups that will be affected by the negotiation, each of which has a set of essential objectives that they want to realize. In order to be accepted, then, a position that a country takes in a negotiation (whether a decision to open negotiations; an initial proposal to present within the negotiations; any modification of that position during negotiations; an eventual decision to accept or reject an agreement, or a decision to break off negotiations; or the extent to which an agreement is willingly and eagerly implemented) must meet with the approval of all critical stakeholders.[12] This obviously tends to drive the negotiating positions of states toward a lowest common denominator of agreement among its principal domestic actors.

In theory, once a consensus has been reached about a negotiating position, the negotiators should be instructed to seek an outcome in the interstate negotiation that achieves the objectives that were determined through the intrastate negotiations. Indeed, in classical diplomacy the foreign ministry was often conceived as an agency that was more or less neutral with respect to policy preferences, but whose task was to try to negotiate the results preferred by stakeholding groups within the home government. As a result, in classical diplomacy the foreign ministry generally had a primary, and often an exclusive, role in negotiating agreements with foreign governments. All of this has very much changed, however, in modern negotiations for several reasons. First, foreign ministries themselves have frequently become more politicized than in the past, and various agencies within most foreign ministries have strong preferences concerning the outcome of negotiations. Second, the complex issues that are negotiated in the contemporary international system are often beyond the substantive competence of foreign ministry officials.

Therefore, contemporary negotiating teams often include representatives from a wide variety of agencies. While this improves the competence of the negotiating team to deal with complicated substantive issues, it also carries the intrastate conflicts about policy over into the negotiating arena itself, blurring the distinction between Level I and Level II negotiations. Conflicts often develop within a negotiating team over differences in how to implement negotiating instructions, and often deals that were struck at home prior to the negotiations may be broken during the course of negotiations, when the conflicting priorities of different agencies are reintroduced by the representatives on the negotiating team. These differences may be further exacerbated the more broadly a negotiating team represents various domestic constituencies. For example, although it is still rare, some countries such as the United States now often include parliamentary representatives on negotiating teams to assure a smooth process for ratifying any agreements that may be reached. The United States also occasionally has included so-called public representatives on its negotiating teams. For example, at the meeting of the Conference on Security and Cooperation in Europe in Helsinki in 1992, representatives of various human rights groups were frequently attached to the U.S. delegation, and were occasionally permitted to speak in plenary sessions as members of that delegation. However, these public groups seldom have much direct influence over policy decisions.

To summarize the argument presented thus far about the bureaucratic politics model in negotiations, the negotiation process must often be considered as one in which two separate negotiating processes overlay one another, an intrastate and an interstate negotiation. In the former, domestic actors try to tug and pull the negotiation outcome in different directions that reflect their various preferences and priorities, at the same time that the delegations from the various states are trying to reach agreement among themselves. The fact that these two separate negotiations are often occurring simultaneously, and that they tend to feed off of one another, frequently makes the negotiation process an extremely complex one to manage. It also tends, as organizational theorists like Simon would suggest, to encourage negotiators to try to reach satisfactory agreements that all stakeholders can accept, rather than optimal ones that might enhance to the fullest extent possible the joint national interests of all of the participating states.[13]

Viewed from a communications perspective, the negotiation process may be seen as representing the very center of a complex communications net, such as that depicted in figure 9.1. Each party can be considered to contain a number of different principals who communicate among themselves and, to some degree through a single channel, to the negotiators in the field. Although there may be back channel communications directed between principals in different countries, the major communications links between countries take place through the negotiators. The negotiators serve as transmission links between the principals in the different countries. In addition, persuasion, bargaining, and problem solving occur between each pair of nodes in the diagram, not just among those at the negotiating table.

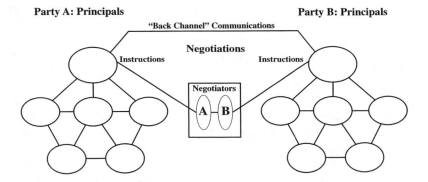

Figure 9.1 A Communications Net Model of International Negotiations

On the basis of this kind of analysis, Pruitt has suggested three criteria for effective negotiations:

(1) Accurate information about the positions, interests, priorities and assumptions of the stake-holders must flow through subsidiary arenas into (and often beyond) the negotiation arena. . . .

(2) Potential agreements must be presented to powerful stake-holders in a persuasive manner. . . .

(3) Problem solving usually takes place in a number of arenas, not simply in the negotiation arena. . . . [T]he most crucial problem solving may well take place in an arena that is inside one of the organizations.[14]

This is accomplished, according to Pruitt, largely through a branching chain of intermediaries, each of whom serves as a link between the principal stakeholders and the representatives in the field. Each individual in the chain performs a "Janus-faced" role of presenting the views of each party in the chain on each side to those on the other side, relaying information along lengthy communications channels. The effectiveness of the negotiation team, therefore, depends upon the ability of the various links in this chain to bridge gaps and provide effective interpretation of the perspective of each party to every other party in the chain. His model "assumes that organizations consist of suborganizations, which negotiate with each other in the same way that the parent organizations negotiate. Hence, no clear distinction is drawn between negotiation and preparation for negotiation."[15]

In the midst of these crosscutting negotiations stand the diplomats, frequently caught in the middle between these competing negotiations. On the one hand, they are members of their national decision-making organization, though any individual diplomat may only represent one subgroup within the larger foreign policy bureaucracy. On the other hand, they represent their state in its dealings with other states, also composed of bureaucratic organizations. Organization theorists say these individuals occupy boundary roles. Robert Kahn observes: "People in such roles are more distant from members of their own organization—often more distant physically as well as psychologically—and they are necessarily closer to people in the external environment. Second, people in boundary roles must represent their organization to those outside it. Third, and more difficult, they must attempt somehow to influence people outside in ways that serve the organizational interest. Finally, they bring information about the external environment into their own organization, and not infrequently they attempt to bring their own organization to a more realistic understanding of that environment and its demands."[16]

People who occupy these boundary roles frequently find themselves caught in a conflict between the different role expectations of the two groups. This has been referred to by Walton and McKersie as the boundary role conflict, or the conflict that results when a negotiator is caught between the different expectations of the home constituency and the other parties to the negotiation.[17] The negotiator is trapped between the requirements of being an agent who must represent the interests and demands of his principal, and being a party to an interaction with other agents that have different sets of responsibilities to their own principals, but who also seek to accommodate those different expectations in a single agreement all parties can subscribe to.

This problem occurs in part because of the fact that the negotiator is first and foremost a representative of the home government to the negotiation. Therefore, his or her primary goal is to carry out the instructions of the home government, pursuing the national interest as defined by that government. Therefore, one role of the negotiator is to represent the government's position to the other party. On the other hand, the negotiator is often far removed from the home government, relying on cables, telephones, fax messages, diplomatic couriers, and other limited means of communication. This means that the negotiator must perform dual functions, which have been defined by Druckman as primarily "monitoring the other side for evidence of *movement* and monitoring one's own side for evidence of *preferences*."[18] At the same time, the negotiator must try to persuade the other to accept the preferences of her or his own side and persuade her or his own side to respond to the movements of the other party.

The negotiator is likely to be granted flexibility to initiate new proposals and respond to the other side in part to the degree that she or he is trusted by the principals at home. Ironically, this trust is likely to be greater for those negotiators who have played their role in the past as defined by the principals and have been perceived as carrying out their instructions. By contrast, a negotiator who tries to be too innovative may discover that her or his flexibility is reigned in altogether by the government at home.

Furthermore, the negotiator deals with the other party directly, usually on a face-to-face basis. It is often easier for the negotiator to develop empathy with the other party as a result of this direct communication than it is for the home government, which views the other party often as a group of faceless individuals. This personal contact usually enables the negotiator to develop a better understanding of the other party's position than is the case for most people back home, and often the negotiator may recognize merit or validity in the other's position that may not be seen by those who view the conflict from a greater physical and psychological distance. There may, of course, be exceptions, and occasionally "familiarity may breed contempt," but generally the personal experience of interacting with the other party as a concrete individual will enhance empathy rather than enmity. In these cases, the negotiator may find him or herself in a situation where it is necessary to explain the other's position to the home government, and may at times even advocate that the government accept parts of that position he or she believes to be valid.

Certainly one of the paradigmatic illustrations of this tension is found in the early phases of the negotiations between the United States and the Soviet Union over Intermediate-range Nuclear Forces (INF) deployed in Europe. This case has become so identified with the issue of the boundary role conflict that it became the basis for a fictional play, *A Walk in the Woods*, that ran successfully on the London and New York stage for some time. The actual event upon which this drama was based occurred in the summer of 1982. The United States was represented by Ambassador Paul Nitze, a long-time diplomat and defense official, who had resigned from the SALT II delegation during the Carter years in the White House to help form the Committee on the Present Danger, a group of conservative critics of Carter's arms control policies. With the Reagan administration, Nitze became ambassador to the INF negotiations, serving under one of his partners in the Committee on the Present Danger, Eugene Rostow, who was named by President Reagan to head the Arms Control and Disarmament Agency (ACDA). His partner on the Soviet side was Yuli Kvitsinsky, who also had a history of engaging in informal, back channel negotiations to break logjams in previous negotiations (most notably the Four Power negotiations on the status of Berlin in 1970).[19]

Nitze's instructions had been quite rigid from the moment the negotiations opened. He was supposed to seek a so-called zero-option, in which the deployment by the United States of 572 INFs in Europe scheduled to begin in late 1983 would be canceled only if the Soviets agreed to eliminate all of their older intermediate-range missiles (SS-4s and SS-5s) and their new generation missile (the SS-20). In the early negotiations it appeared extremely unlikely that the Soviets were prepared to compromise and accept the zero-option. Therefore, Nitze began to search for partial agreements that might be mutually acceptable. One popular idea was to break apart the new systems scheduled to be deployed by the United States: 464 Cruise missiles and 108 Pershing II missiles. The latter were sufficiently accurate, fast, and long-range to pose a serious threat to targets well inside the Soviet Union and were perceived as highly provocative by Soviet leaders, although they also were perhaps less well suited to their strategic task than long-range missiles based in the United States. Therefore, by offering to cancel their deployment, the United States might relieve Soviet fears of a provocative U.S. first strike without any significant loss in the ability of the United States to retaliate against Soviet hard targets in the event that war broke. Thus, Nitze believed, this weapon might be abandoned altogether, and then the two sides might agree on a much lower number of Cruise missiles and SS-20s to be deployed by both sides than was planned at the time, although greater than the target of zero advocated by the United States.

Nitze and Kvitsinsky then began a series of private meetings for dinner and walks through the botanical gardens below the Palais des Nations in Geneva. This culminated in a rendezvous in the Jura Mountains outside Geneva on 16 July 1982 when the two diplomats strolled together through the woods and down the mountain, from a pass near the French border back toward the outskirts of Geneva. There, sitting on a log in a light drizzle, the two men worked out "a joint exploratory package for the consideration of both governments."[20] When the deal was presented to the two capitals, however, the response on both sides was negative. At first Washington showed some interest, but the primary proponent of the zero-option proposal, Assistant Secretary of Defense Richard Perle, opposed the informal agreement vigorously. Despite a great deal of debate in Washington, President Reagan in the end supported the opponents of the agreement and, according to Talbott's account, told Nitze to tell the Soviets that he was "working for one tough son-of-a-bitch."[21] When Nitze returned to Geneva in September, he again took a "walk in the woods" with Kvitsinsky, who informed him that the deal had been resoundingly rejected in Moscow as well and that he had been attacked by members of the Politburo for engaging in his private, back channel negotiations. Indeed, Nitze's boss, Eugene Rostow, was dismissed by President Reagan in January 1983, although it is unclear whether or not this was directly related to the flexibility that he granted Nitze to try to work out an informal INF agreement. What was clear, however, was that the mutual understanding and empathy that had been developed between the two sets of agents was not shared by either's principals in Washington or Moscow, so that an important opportunity to reach agreement was lost, at least until there was a major change in the principals in Moscow after 1986.

This boundary role conflict may be further intensified by the different reward structures that apply for the home government and the negotiator. The home government cares primarily about the content of the agreement, about whether or not it serves their national and/or bureaucratic interests, and less about whether the agreement is fair and just. Agreement for its own sake certainly has no value to the home government and will usually be rejected out of hand. For the people back home, agreement is simply a means to achieve some other broader national or organizational ends. By contrast, for the negotiator agreement itself is often interpreted as a sign of professional success, so that agreement may become an end in itself rather than a means to another end. Advancement within their profession along with national and international recognition are among the rewards granted to successful negotiators. Therefore, the negotiator generally has a greater incentive to reach agreement than do the people back home.

The conflict then arises because of the desire of the negotiator to reach agreement on terms that reflect joint interests that may be shared with the other party, whereas the government may be more reluctant to accept the other side's positions as valid and may drag their feet before agreeing. In other words, the negotiators may be quicker to recognize joint, absolute gains that can be shared mutually, while the home governments may be more inclined to focus on relative gains from an agreement between the parties in which each government fears that the other party may gain relatively more than themselves. A negotiator may be torn, therefore, by the necessity to conduct two simultaneous negotiations. The first is the direct formal negotiation with the other side, where the negotiator represents the government position. The second is an informal negotiation with the home government to try to persuade them to accept legitimate positions advanced by the other side, especially those that may advance joint, absolute gains. In each role, the negotiator may be arguing for directly opposing positions, and this obviously creates a certain psychological stress on any human being. Yet an effective negotiator must be able to balance these boundary role conflicts successfully in order to fulfill the simultaneous expectations of two different and often conflicting roles.

Still another boundary role conflict may emerge if the negotiator finds himself "aligned with one of two or more conflicting factions within his own organization."[22] At this point, the negotiator becomes a participant in the bureaucratic conflict at home, and his flexibility to negotiate may depend on whether or not the faction that he supports in fact emerges relatively well off within the bureaucratic struggle. And if this internal conflict becomes public, the negotiator's credibility with the other party may be undermined, if he is no longer viewed as having the undivided confidence and support of his government back home. This kind of bureaucratic conflict, therefore, differs from the more general form of the boundary role conflict. In the former case, "the opponent becomes an ally of sorts,"[23] whereas in the latter case, the role conflict is largely internal to one's own country and has little to do with interactions with the other party.

This kind of conflict was also present in the U.S. government during the early phases of the INF negotiations. Ambassador Nitze's "walk in the woods" was more or less sanctioned by ACDA, and the resulting proposal even gained some considerable support from the Joint Chiefs of Staff. On the other hand, it was strongly opposed by the civilian leadership of the Defense Department, especially Secretary Caspar Weinburger and his deputy, Richard Perle, who were also able to gain support from the staff of the president's special assistant for national security affairs, William Clark. Indeed, Clark's deputy, Robert McFarlane, is reported by Talbott to have remarked that Nitze had "wandered off the reservation," and that they needed to restore "discipline to the process."[24] When the disagreement in Washington became known to the Soviets, Nitze was informed that any future back channel negotiations would have to take place with the clear understanding that Nitze was speaking for Secretary of State George Shultz, not just for himself.[25]

Management of these simultaneous and multifaceted aspects of even a fairly simple bilateral negotiation can be a very demanding task for a diplomat. The organizational theory about negotiation does, however, suggest some basic advice about ways in which the process can be managed to produce positive results. Successful management of these roles depends above all else on frequent and extensive communication back and forth between the negotiators and the government. Since one of the purposes of negotiation is to gain information about the other party, including their interests, preferences, and if possible their bottom lines, negotiators should communicate information about the other party and about the general progress of the negotiations to the home government. They should also present arguments of the other party that they believe reflect their real interests or deep needs, so that the government can be brought along with position changes that the negotiators might propose in an effort to accommodate those interests. The negotiators should indicate which aspects of the other's positions reflect real interests as opposed to largely rhetorical positions.

Negotiators who adopt a problem-solving orientation need to identify mutual interests held in common with the other party. Thus, they should inform the home government about new ideas for redefining the issues under discussion. They should also try to gain as much flexibility as possible from the government to explore multiple options for agreements. This way, if they engage in brainstorming or other techniques for inventing new ways to solve the problem, they will not be confronted with such serious opposition from back home. This effective communication must occur within each linkage in the communications network that makes up the negotiation process, within the negotiation itself, between negotiators and home governments, and among the various agencies within the home government with a stake in the outcome of the negotiations. Pruitt notes: "The key to flexibility is for there to be good information transmission, persuasion and problem solving *in as many arenas as possible*, so that as many stake-holders as possible become part of the process. Otherwise some of the stake-holders are likely to block the progress of the negotiation."[26]

While seeking to gain flexibility to be creative in negotiating, negotiators should seek maximum clarity about the limits of that flexibility. They should establish clearly with the home government their BATNAs and the resultant minimum level of acceptable agreement, and they should not deviate from that without clear permission from back home. The negotiators must be careful not to force the government into a position where it must either accept an agreement that is less attractive than its other options or where it must veto an agreement and thereby jeopardize the entire negotiation. Especially before making concessions and proposals that break new ground, one must seek full guidance from the principals in the government. As noted previously in chapter 5, a negotiator who appears soft and then hardens his or her position can create such a bad atmosphere that negotiations may be placed in jeopardy. It is generally better not to make any initiatives or concessions than it is to modify one's position in ways that will later have to be retracted. There can be little worse for the general atmosphere of negotiations than a negotiator who appears flexible, but who appears also to be constantly overruled by an intransigent government back home. Therefore, the negotiator must make the special effort to persuade the home government of the value that can be gained from making new proposals or concessions so that these will have the full support of the government as the negotiations unfold.

Finally, negotiators may often seek the reinforcement of the government when necessary to break an impasse or seal the final stages of an agreement. This may often take the form of back channel negotiations between senior officials, reinforcing the moves made by the negotiators. At other times, this may take the form of highly visible negotiations, such as summit conferences between heads of state, designed to overcome stalemate or complete the final stages of a difficult negotiation. For example, throughout the negotiations on both SALT I and SALT II Henry Kissinger had engaged in frequent back channel negotiations with Anatoly Dobrynin, the Soviet ambassador in Washington, or Soviet Foreign Minister Andrei Gromyko, which had frequently helped to break log jams in the formal negotiations in Geneva.[27] Similarly, much progress was eventually made in breaking the stalemate in the INF negotiations at the Reykjavik, Iceland, Summit Meeting between President Reagan and General Secretary Gorbachev in October 1986; negotiations that had been dragging on for years without any progress suddenly gained new vigor, and agreement was reached in just over one year's time after the heads of state had overcome some of the major differences that had previously divided the two countries.[28]

Even though there may often be conflict between officials and negotiators, the skillful negotiator must minimize this in the presence of other parties. Of course, there may be times when seeking instructions from home may be used tactically to buy time in negotiations, or when the presence of so-called intransigent political forces back home may be used to enable a negotiator to reinforce or toughen a negotiating position. But like all distributive bargaining tactics, these must be used with care and sensitivity so that they do not disrupt the negotiations. And in the final analysis, the negotiator will generally be more effective if the other party believes that the negotiating team enjoys the full support of senior officials in the home government. This will only occur, however, if in fact there is frequent and extensive communication between the negotiating agents and their governmental principals.

At the same time, a negotiating team may try to appeal over the heads of an intransigent set of negotiators across the table directly to the principals in the other side's home country. A great deal of diplomatic activity, as Putnam notes, may involve efforts to expand the bargaining space by such activities as "wooing opinion leaders, establishing contact with opposition parties, offering foreign aid to a friendly, but unstable government."[29] By trying to influence the domestic political and bureaucratic structure in the other country, they may hope to induce modifications in the negotiating position in ways that are conducive to achieving a more favorable agreement.

The interorganizational and intraorganizational negotiation processes dovetail in an effort to find solutions to problems that can meet not only the interests of two parties in a bilateral negotiation, but also all of the major internal actors or stakeholders on both sides of the negotiating table. This in effect becomes what Kahn has described as a problem in the "management of interdependence."[30] In contrast to the realist emphasis upon negotiations between states as unitary actors pursuing a single, unchanging national interest, this emphasis on the interaction between the domestic and international dimensions of diplomatic activity presents a much more complex model of negotiations that is more consistent with liberal conceptions of a global system characterized by complex interdependence. In this case, the negotiation process may be utilized in order to create regimes that provide joint rules of thumb for collective behavior in place of individually determined, self-interest motivated behavior.[31] The goal of the negotiation process in this context is to meet the essential needs and preferences of the major interest groups influencing the process within both of the interacting parties rather than being restricted by the narrow interests of specific groups within one or more of the parties to a negotiation.

Chapter 10

The Interaction Process in International Negotiations

In the two previous chapters I examined how individual states establish their negotiating behavior, both in terms of the influence of individuals and of bureaucratic organizations within their foreign policy-making institutions. In this chapter, I turn to an examination of the bilateral interaction process. The basic thesis of this chapter is that the negotiating process is influenced by the dynamics of that process itself. States may respond initially to internal influences on their behavior, but once they become involved in a relationship with another party, they become part of a system of interaction. And that system of interaction in turn affects the behavior of each of the parties in that system and influences the eventual joint consequences of their collective behavior. In this chapter I shall first examine the interaction process in the prenegotiation phase, and then I shall turn to the negotiation phase itself later in the chapter.

THE PRENEGOTIATION PHASE

Before formal negotiations can actually get underway, decisions must be made about whether or not to open formal proceedings. These decisions often take place through a series of formal and informal encounters that seek to lay the groundwork for deciding whether or not to open formal negotiations, decide on the timing for opening negotiations, and begin to establish an agenda to guide them. Sometimes this process may be quite formal and actually constitute a negotiation in itself, as is the case when formal meetings are held to adopt a mandate or agenda for the actual negotiations. Thus, the Uruguay Round of the negotiations on the General Agreement on Trade and Tariffs (GATT) was opened by a ministerial conference in Punte del Este, Uruguay, in September 1986. At this meeting, a formal mandate was adopted to guide the negotiators through a long and complex formal negotiation that would stretch out over many years, meeting mostly in Geneva. Equally, if not more often, even these formal prenegotiations are preceded by informal explorations that lay the foundation for negotiations.

These informal negotiations may often begin as a part of the general activity of day-to-day diplomatic interactions. They may identify a problem that needs to be solved. This may be followed by further exploration to determine whether or not the time is ripe to open formal negotiations about that problem, and to refine the joint definition of the problem to be solved. These kinds of activities that occur prior to a negotiation present a special problem for analysts of the process. While they are not part of the negotiation process per se, they play a large role in the shaping of that process. Some analysts have suggested that these activities should be treated as part of the actual negotiation process,[1] whereas others have called for a separate model of prenegotiations, distinguishing it from the negotiation process itself.[2] These contending positions suggest fundamental differences about the status of prenegotiation phases.

The first of these positions tends to view negotiations as part of the foreign policy process in general, so that decisions made in the larger realm of diplomatic interactions are themselves directly linked to the negotiations. Saunders has proposed examining a four-stage process that consists of defining the problem, committing oneself to negotiate, arranging the negotiation, and negotiating.[3] This scheme emphasizes those activities involved in setting the stage for a negotiation, and the first three stages all in some sense constitute prenegotiation. The stage is set when all parties agree on a common definition of the problem, that is when they reach understandings about interests and objectives as well as about what they might expect to achieve through negotiation. These understandings are most difficult to achieve among states where value differences are the primary obstacle to negotiation. This is clearly the case in Middle East diplomacy, the region from which Saunders draws his examples. It is less problematic when basic value differences are either not at issue (between allies) or are subservient to common interests likely to be served by an agreement (superpower arms reductions). The understandings reached are often formalized in documents such as a declaration of principles or a mandate for negotiations. They symbolize a commitment to negotiate and enable the parties to work on preparations including the choosing of a site and setting the agenda.

By contrast, Janice Gross Stein looks at prenegotiation more as a separate process in itself, which in turn structures the actual negotiation process. On the basis of a series of comparative case studies of prenegotiation, she concludes that "the process of prenegotiation was generally characterized by important structuring activity. It set broad boundaries, identified the participants, and, in at least half the cases, specified the agenda for negotiation. Even in those cases where it produced only a rough outline of the agenda, it nevertheless reduced uncertainty and complexity by establishing what would be kept off the table. In every case, prenegotiation framed the problem and set the limits of the negotiation to follow."[4]

Brian Tomlin has suggested a five-stage model of prenegotiation, moving along a continuum from the decision of whether or not to negotiate toward making decisions about what to negotiate: (1) problem identification refers to the stage at which conditions or events change so as to create a problem that is recognized by several parties; (2) a search for options to deal with the problem then commences (in which negotiation may be considered among the possibilities) and then a shift toward consideration of what to negotiate and generally to a more formal process; (3) the commitment to negotiate represents the stage at which the parties jointly recognize the desirability of pursuing a negotiation route to solve their problem; (4) a formal agreement to negotiate is then reached; and (5) finally, the parties set the parameters for the negotiation, in effect adopting an agenda that specifies the range of issues that will and will not be included in the negotiation. This stage then may overlap with the formal opening of the negotiation process itself.[5]

Unresolved issues concerning the nature of the relationship between the parties frequently hamper efforts to initiate serious negotiating. The parties may be stuck in a prenegotiation phase, as was the case regarding negotiations between Israel and the Palestinians over the status of the West Bank territory after the signing of the Camp David accords. For at least fifteen years prior to 1993 negotiations on this emotional issue never got past the prenegotiation stage. Similar problems may occur in the area of arms control, as Husbands makes evident in her analysis of the Conventional Arms Transfer (CAT) talks. These talks never got beyond the prenegotiation stage, a result that was due in part to domestic opposition to these talks from defense industries in many participating states.[6] The issue of restraints on arms transfers was complex, and the negotiators were constrained throughout by both political and economic considerations. These pressures were further complicated by a large number of potential countries whose behavior would have to be coordinated to produce meaningful restraint, including the United States, Japan, the Soviet Union, most countries of both Western and Eastern Europe, and even some newly industrializing nations of the third world such as Brazil. All of these parties had to be brought together around the same agenda, and their ability to reach a consensus about that agenda was complicated by many and varied sources of domestic opposition. Thus, it was never possible to get these talks past the prenegotiation phase despite several years of effort in the late 1970s.

In their classic study of the negotiation process, I. William Zartman and Maureen Berman roughly equate the prenegotiation stage with what they call the diagnostic phase of negotiations.[7] States are generally not willing to participate in formal negotiations unless they perceive that they have something to gain from negotiating an agreement in comparison with acting unilaterally toward a particular problem. A number of factors may change a state's perceptions of when it might benefit from negotiating agreed solutions to problems. First, an event in the international environment may change their perceptions of the costs and benefits of various solutions. For example, Iraq's substantial military defeat in the Persian Gulf War of 1991, by undercutting the perceived strength of one of the major backers of the Palestinians, may have enhanced the willingness of the latter to enter into prenegotiations and eventually into direct talks in Norway with Israel over the issue of Gaza and the West Bank.[8] Second, a domestic change in one of the parties may also create a new opportunity for opening negotiations. For example, the victory of Prime Minister Yitzhak Rabin in the Israeli elections in June 1992 signaled a potential significant change in Israel's negotiating stance with the Palestinians over Gaza and the West Bank compared with the previous policies of the Likud government.[9] Third, the parties may find themselves locked in what Touval and Zartman have called a hurting stalemate; this is "a situation that is very uncomfortable to both sides, and that appears likely to become very costly."[10] In these situations, they may find that the costs of not negotiating have grown so high that the potential benefits of negotiations now appear relatively more advantageous. This seemed to characterize the decisions by Israel and Egypt to open negotiations at Camp David in 1978 to settle the increasingly costly stalemate that had ensued after the 1973 war in the Middle East. Finally, the parties may recognize opportunities that either had not existed before or had not been perceived, including opportunities to make new decisions; create new political, economic, or social orders; or seize opportunities to change for the better. Certainly this was the case between the former Soviet Union and the Federal Republic of Germany in the months following the breakdown of the Berlin Wall and the disappearance of the former communist regime in East Germany.

The actual use of the prenegotiation phase by the parties continues to be influenced by the tension between integrative and distributive negotiations referred to at length in previous chapters. If parties approach the prenegotiation phase as a prelude to a largely distributive negotiation, they will undoubtedly try to use it to their advantage in structuring the ensuing formal negotiation. Of greatest importance here is control over the agenda-setting elements in this stage. They will try to see that the negotiation agenda contains those items in which they have the greatest interests at stake, over which they believe that they can exercise the greatest tactical control during the negotiations, and where they believe their partner to be the most vulnerable. On the other hand, they will try to exclude from the agenda items over which they stand to lose a great deal and from which they can gain little, items where their resources for exerting influence are weak, and issues where they may be most vulnerable to attack. Since structuring the negotiation here can have a determining effect over the outcomes, parties approaching a negotiation from a distributive vantage point are probably correct in believing that conflictual bargaining can be won or lost by the way in which the agenda is structured. Thus, for example, in the series of negotiations between Israel and Egypt after the 1973 Middle East war, Israel sought to exclude the status of the West Bank from the agenda to the greatest extent possible, focusing the negotiations on issues such as the cease-fire, disengagement, and eventually conflict settlement between Israel and Egypt on their common border. At the same time they tried to avoid discussion of the most complex issues where they stood to lose the most, such as sovereignty for the West Bank and Gaza, self-determination for Palestinians, and the status of Jerusalem.[11]

On the other hand, if they approach the prenegotiation phase from a more integrative perspective, the parties are likely to use it extensively for diagnostic purposes. The emphasis here is to utilize this phase to come to understand more about one's own needs and interests, the needs and interests of the other party, and ways in which those needs and interests do or do not coincide. From the latter knowledge, one may be in a better position to utilize the negotiations to try to bring a greater coincidence of those needs and interests, or by "upgrading the common interests" as suggested by Ernst Haas,[12] to realize mutually beneficial results. Zartman and Berman suggest a checklist of seven precepts that should be followed in the prenegotiation phase:

1. Review and be well briefed in the facts of the problem, its cause, history, its changes and evolution.

2. Look into precedents and referents governing similar situations.

3. Know the contexts and perceptions that give meaning to the situation and its components.

4. Try to list and understand the stakes and interests of each side.

5. Be aware of the affective elements in both parties' viewpoints of the situation, and of the emotional components of the other party.

6. Think of alternate solutions on these bases.

7. While such studies are going on at home and contacts are

being made to persuade the other party about the negotiability of the problem, talks can also begin in order to hear the other party's point of view.[13]

In summary, the prenegotiation phase can be utilized most effectively as a learning opportunity, through which the parties may come to understand themselves and one another better as their needs and interests relate to the problem to be negotiated. It has a significant function in reducing uncertainty prior to entering into formal negotiations. In an ideal situation in which this phase is utilized effectively, the parties should be able to enter into a negotiation with a clear and more shared understanding of the issues and their interests. This understanding may not always facilitate convergence in the negotiation phase, especially if it clarifies the differences that may exist between the parties, but it at least increases the chances that the subsequent negotiations will be based on a realistic assessment of the problem rather than on mutual misperceptions and misunderstandings of one another and of the fundamental issues being negotiated. In this way the negotiation may at least address the essence of the problem rather than peripheral or unrelated issues. It may also help the parties separate out issues that are potentially negotiable from those that are not, so that progress can be made during the actual negotiations on solvable problems, while time is not wasted and emotional tensions are not exacerbated by trying to negotiate problems that are largely incapable of being solved at a particular time or in a specific negotiating context.

These conclusions have received some support from research done by social psychologists in laboratory or experimental settings. These studies have focused on the impact of prenegotiation communication on subsequent negotiations. The most general conclusion of much of this research is that bargaining was facilitated to the extent that parties avoid intensive unilateral strategy preparation (focusing on distributive bargaining tactics) and focus instead on the issues per se during prenegotiation caucuses. Moreover, it made little difference whether the caucuses were unilateral, involving only separate meetings of negotiating team members from each side, or bilateral, in which members of opposing teams met together. In either case, the experimenters found that informal, issue-oriented discussion was more effective than either tactical preparation or no prenegotiation communication.[14]

In addition to these substantive considerations largely concerning the setting of an agenda, a wide range of prenegotiation activities may improve the atmospherics of the subsequent bargaining process. For example, attention may be devoted to the quality of the physical setting for negotiations and to the provision of adequate logistical support. Opportunities may be created in this stage for opening up informal channels of communication, issuing trial balloons, and widening the range of options for the negotiators to meet in diverse settings. Effective use of prenegotiation preparations may significantly differentiate successful from unsuccessful negotiations. They form part of the larger diplomatic context for negotiation.

From an academic, if not so much from a practical, point of view one may debate whether to consider the prenegotiation phase as part of the context for negotiations or as an essential part of the process itself. Viewed as context, the prenegotiation process may affect decisions about when and where to negotiate and the atmosphere of negotiations; viewed as an integral part of the negotiation process, it frames the agenda and substance of a negotiation at the beginning, just as an implementation phase frames it at the end. Theorists who conceive of negotiation primarily as a subfield of international politics are likely to emphasize the prenegotiation phase as an essential aspect of the context, whereas theorists who seek to develop negotiation theory are likely to view this as just an initial stage in the process itself. Whichever perspective one takes, however, the prenegotiation phase is primarily of interest because of the impact that it has on the bargaining process itself.

THE NEGOTIATION PHASE

Reciprocity and Bargaining

Chapter 5 presented some of the many tactics available to negotiators to influence the process of bargaining: offers, demands, concessions, retractions, threats, and promises. In that chapter I looked at two actors who entered into a bargaining relationship with divergent opening positions and then went through a series of tactical moves to converge toward some point of agreement between those initial conditions. I referred to this as a concession-convergence model of the bargaining process. Since this represented a model of bargaining, my focus at that time was on unilateral manipulation of tactics by each party individually, while recognizing that the joint set of unilateral decisions by the two actors largely determines the outcome. From this unilateral perspective, however, I largely overlooked the dynamics that might occur in the interactions between these two actors. It is these interactive dynamics, and the extent to which they facilitate or impede agreement in negotiations, that form the central focus in this section. My working assumption here is that it is the interaction of these tactics and modifications of positions, not their unilateral pursuit, that determines the outcomes of negotiations.

The simplest, and in some ways the most pervasive, models of the interaction process is that of mutual responsiveness. This is an incremental process where equivalent and responsive behaviors by both sides lead either toward or away from agreement. This is a dynamic in which the two parties more or less repeat the behavior of the other in a mechanistic fashion. From a prescriptive point of view, this dynamic forms the essence of the golden rule: "do unto others what you would have them do unto you." From an analytical perspective, this is usually referred to as tit-for-tat behavior. This dynamic has been investigated thoroughly in a recent work by Robert Axelrod, in which he makes a strong case for the value of this tit-for-tat dynamic, namely cooperating when the other cooperates and behaving conflictually when the other fails to cooperate in Prisoners' Dilemma situations.[15] Basically this dynamic consists of each party reacting in subsequent rounds by producing the same behavior as the opponent in the previous round. Thus, concessions lead to concessions, retractions to the other's pulling back, threats are reciprocated by threats, and promises by promises. When aggregated, all of these behaviors may be referred to as using soft, or cooperative actions to respond to like behaviors by the other party, and hard, or conflictual responses to similar actions by the opponent.

Axelrod's argument is based on certain qualities of this strategy: (1) it avoids "unnecessary conflict by cooperating as long as the other player does"; (2) it is easily provoked "in the face of an uncalled for defection by the other"; (3) it is forgiving, quickly providing a reward after responding to a provocation when the other returns to cooperation; and (4) it is clear and easily recognized "so that the other player can adapt to your pattern of action."[16] Results of a series of computerized contests run by Axelrod showed that tit-for-tat was the most effective among a number of strategies for eliciting cooperation from an opponent: it encouraged cooperative behavior by programmed players using a wide range of opposing strategies, ending up with the most points overall across Axelrod's simulated contests.[17]

Laboratory studies with human subjects are somewhat more mixed. For example, Rapoport and Chammah reported that tit-for-tat generated 46 percent to 72 percent cooperation over three hundred trials of a Prisoners' Dilemma game.[18] Wilson, however, has shown that a tit-for-tat strategy produces higher levels of cooperation than several variants, including both a more conciliatory and a more retaliatory strategy, as well as a natural variant. In this study, three different strategies were attempted: (1) a conciliation strategy, in which one actor tried to initiate some unilateral cooperative initiatives in order to induce the other to cooperate; (2) a retaliation strategy, in which one actor retaliated for conflictual behaviors on the part of the other with a series of conflictual responses; and (3) a reciprocation or tit-for-tat strategy, in which the one party responded in each round exactly as their partner had behaved in the previous round: cooperation was replied to with a cooperative response and conflict was met with conflictual behavior.

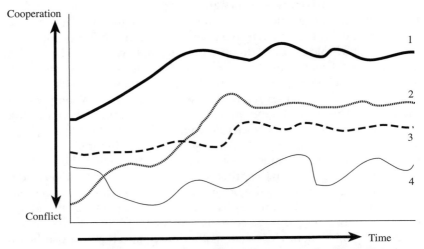

Figure 10.1 Effects of Different Models of Reciprocation on Conflict in Prisoner Dilemma Games
1) **Tit-for-Tat reciprocity**
2) **Retaliation for conflict**
3) **Conciliation for cooperation**
4) **Natural Play (not programmed).**
Adapted from Warner Wilson, "Reciprocation and Other Techniques for Inducing Cooperation in Prisoner's Dilemma Game," *Journal of Conflict Resolution*, **Vol. XV, No. 2, p. 172, copyright © 1971 by the University of Michigan Press. Printed by permission of Sage Publications, Inc.**

These strategies were tested in a game that was played for one hundred rounds, and a fourth or control group was used in which no systematic strategy was employed but the play of the game was more or less natural. The results are summarized in figure 10.1. The highest level of cooperation over the long-run was generated by tit-for-tat reciprocity, as expected on the basis of Axelrod's findings in the computerized contests. The other two programmed strategies, on the other hand, did about equally well in eliciting cooperation, but less well than the tit-for-tat approach. In the early rounds the other two strategies produced substantial increases in cooperation, but this did not endure as well as in the tit-for-tat case, so that cooperation tended to tail off in the late rounds. However, all programmed strategies were successful in inducing more cooperation than the control group.[19]

A number of experimental studies provide insights into the conditions under which tit-for-tat is likely to be effective. The target of influence is likely to respond cooperatively if she sees herself gaining more from mutual cooperation than from mutual noncooperation and is concerned primarily with her own gains (individualistically motivated).[20]

The strategist may elicit cooperation to the extent that the negotiator carefully monitors the other's behavior and does not over- or undermatch the other's level of noncooperation (makes the "punishment fit the crime").[21] It is also likely to be more effective when the parties move sequentially than when they move simultaneously.[22] Variants on the tit-for-tat theme may enhance its effectiveness. Bixenstine and Gaebelein found that a strategist who was slow to retaliate but also slow to forgive was more effective than immediate tit-for-tat; they advise "to induce maximum cooperation in another be suspicious and enter into trusting behavior gradually, but at the same time, be tolerant of and slow to retaliate to his acts of untrustworthiness."[23] Komorita and Mechling showed that the effects of tit-for-tat are enhanced by an earlier period of unconditional cooperative behavior, and the more cooperation then the better the responsiveness.[24]

The tit-for-tat strategy has several shortcomings that require that it be supplemented on occasion by other approaches. One of these is that the responses that one party desires to elicit from the other may not be obvious. This is particularly evident in many of the experimental studies where the participants are not permitted to communicate except through the play of the game. However, in negotiations there is usually the possibility to communicate verbally, so that this problem may be partially overcome by calling the target's attention to the desired response. The former may try to make clear the link between the desired response and the cooperative behavior or reinforcement with which one will reciprocate; indeed, the credibility of this linkage may be built up over time when one party demonstrates consistency in reciprocating as promised. Another problem is that tit-for-tat may be viewed as being unnecessarily escalatory: the other party is immediately punished if one lapses even once into noncooperation. One solution is Axelrod's "tit-for-two-tats"—retaliate only after the other's second lapse.[25] Another is to combine the delayed retaliation with a verbal warning to the effect that one will not keep on giving the other "one last chance to reform."

Even more serious, however, is the problem of getting locked into a cycle of mutual conflict escalation, when both parties behave conflictually and reciprocate this noncooperation in a seemingly endless spiral. Tit-for-tat is hopeless for this situation since it refuses to cooperate until the other party cooperates; in the jargon frequently employed by diplomats, this implies that at all times "the ball is in the other side's court." Put another way, it lacks a way to break the cycle of noncooperation; it needs a starting mechanism. As Fisher has remarked concerning the U.S.-Soviet relationship during the cold war, if "we behave no better than we think they are behaving, the relationship is likely to get steadily worse."[26] This problem is especially severe in situations of low trust or when both parties have become rigidly committed to a set of mutually incompatible positions, and both are afraid for whatever reason to make the first move to break the deadlock.

There are a number of possible mechanisms for trying to break through this kind of stalemate, all of which typically entail various forms of signaling and covert problem solving. One technique is to engage in back channel negotiations, in which the parties attempt to engage in informal discussions behind the scenes to find ways to begin a process of mutual cooperative responsiveness rather than repetitive conflict. Similarly the parties may engage intermediaries to relay signals about a desire to reverse the competitive spiral. One special form of back channel negotiation is often referred to as track two diplomacy or citizen diplomacy.[27] This approach is based on the assumption that government-to-government diplomacy is rigid, formal, and overly constrained by official instructions. By contrast, track two diplomacy is informal, flexible, and unofficial. It is generally undertaken by private citizens or nongovernmental organizations that take the personal initiative to resolve conflicts and promote agreements. The Pugwash meetings between Soviet and American scientists might serve as one example of this kind of process, as would the role played by groups such as Amnesty International. On occasion even individual private citizens have served as go-betweens in a negotiation and have helped to break an impasse through their personal intervention. As John McDonald notes: "Persons involved in Track Two efforts have as their objective the reduction or de-escalation, of conflict within a country or between countries by lowering the anger, tension, or fear that exists, by facilitating improved communication, and by helping to bring about a better understanding of each party's point of view."[28]

Even when verbal linkages are not available, one may send various nonverbal conciliatory signals, often referred to as tacit communications or the use of sign language.[29] In international negotiations this may frequently take the form of conciliatory actions taken outside of the formal negotiations. Thus, for example, Soviet President Gorbachev announced his intention to withdraw unilaterally 240,000 Soviet troops, 10,000 tanks, and other heavy military hardware from Eastern Europe in December 1988 in order to break a stalemate in conventional arms control negotiations in Europe. The mechanism designed to signal a desire to cooperate that has received the most attention in the literature on negotiations, especially under conditions of high mutual suspicion and the absence of trust, is the use of unilateral initiatives.

Unilateral initiatives violate the basic rules of tit-for-tat since they are cooperative responses to the other's noncooperative behavior. But they are intended to be introduced in a situation where tit-for-tat behavior has caused the parties to be caught in a stalemate of mutual conflict. The goal is to encourage a positive, cooperative response from the other party, usually reciprocity. The best known theory about unilateral initiatives, developed by Charles Osgood, is the Graduated Reciprocal Initiatives in Tension-reduction or GRIT strategy.[30] The basic idea behind the GRIT strategy is for one party to a conflict to announce a series of unilateral, trust-building initiatives. These initiatives must be sufficiently significant so that they signal a clear desire to de-escalate the conflict and break the stalemate. At the same time, they must not go so far as to risk excessive exploitation. In terms of the bargaining theory presented in chapter 5, they should not risk reducing one's own position beyond one's security level or BATNA.

According to Osgood, the initiator should observe a series of rules: an announced time table should be presented for a series of moves, the other party should explicitly be invited to reciprocate, and the party should follow the time table for some time even if the initiatives are not reciprocated at first. The initiator should also retain a capability to retaliate if the other party tries to exploit these initiatives, and should be prepared to carry out that retaliation and punish a hostile response. On the other hand, cooperative behavior by the other party should be rewarded immediately by further initiatives. In short, this method is an application of psychological theories of behavior modification to the realm of international relations.

For example, Osgood proposed that the United States should have initiated a series of unilateral moves toward disarmament as a clear signal to the Soviet Union of their will to end the cold war. These measures of disarmament would have to be sufficiently deep so that they could not be dismissed by the Soviets as mere tokenism, or even worse as a trick. On the other hand, they could not be so deep as to eliminate unilaterally the U.S. second-strike retaliatory capacity, thereby possibly leaving them vulnerable to a disarming first strike by the Soviets. Osgood then argued that the United States should invite the Soviets to respond with a series of unilateral disarmament moves of their own, responding in kind to American unilateral reductions. If the Soviets did not respond immediately, the United States would need to continue its reductions gradually for a limited period of time, allowing an opportunity for trust to build and suspicions to be reduced. However, unless there were eventually significant responses by the Soviets, the United States would have to stop well short of dismantling its retaliatory capability. However, Osgood argued that these measures would likely induce a Soviet response, which would then enable both sides to continue to reduce their nuclear forces. This could occur either through a series of tit-for-tat measures decided more or less unilaterally, or, after some tentative trust was established, through formal negotiations calling for mutual and reciprocal force reductions. Osgood has also suggested that this approach could have been utilized to end the war in Vietnam and stimulate negotiations on "mutual and balanced force reductions" in Europe.[31]

In actual negotiations, GRIT has not been employed explicitly very often. Some have contended that U.S. President John Kennedy engaged in a series of GRIT-like measures after the Cuban Missile Crisis in 1962 to pave the way for the Partial Nuclear Test Ban Treaty negotiations in 1963, a case which we shall return to in part 4. Pruitt and Rubin have suggested that Egyptian President Anwar Sadat's dramatic flight in 1977 to Jerusalem was a similar unilateral initiative intended to pave the way for new negotiations on the Middle East conflict. While this was only one move and not a series of measures, Sadat did announce the move in advance and called explicitly for reciprocation by Israeli leaders.[32] On the basis of this example, Pruitt and Rubin conclude that "GRIT is more likely to work—to elicit problem solving behavior from Other—when it is part of a firm but conciliatory package. In addition to demonstrating trustworthiness, Party should demonstrate strength and a dedication to his or her own basic interests. This enhances the likelihood that Other will be motivated to reciprocate Party's conciliatory initiatives."[33]

Extensive research on international negotiations using the strategy of unilateral initiatives is limited. One exception is a study of unilateral initiatives in arms control negotiations by William Rose. He used five cases to explore some hypothesized conditions for the successful execution of unilateral initiatives in Soviet-American relations: U.S. initiatives taken in 1962–63 (moratorium on putting weapons into orbit), 1963 (postponement of underground nuclear tests; moratorium on atmospheric nuclear weapons tests), 1964–65 (phase-out plans for the B-47 bomber), 1967–68 (conditional restraint on ABM production), and 1978 (deferral of the production of the neutron bomb). He found that the unilateral initiatives were immediately successful only in the case of the partial test ban negotiations, although there were also some delayed successes regarding orbiting nuclear weapons and the antiballistic missiles. He concluded that unilateral initiatives are most likely to be successful when the signals are clear, complete, and consistent. These demands should not lead to a net decline in the security for the other, and they should affirm the principle of equality and reciprocity. They should be seen as part of an overall effort to reduce perceptions of international tensions.[34]

Additional research on the GRIT strategy has been done by social psychologists working with laboratory experiments. For example, Lindskold, Betz, and Walters have provided laboratory tests of GRIT, concluding that there is a "readiness on the part of subjects to follow an adversary's lead in changing the climate of a relationship from competitive to cooperative." They conclude somewhat optimistically that it is possible to disrupt conflictual cycles "with honesty, conciliation, and responsiveness—all unambiguously communicated."[35] Conditions under which initiatives are likely to be effective are when the other party feels dependent on the initiator, when she or he feels that the initiator cannot be exploited, and when she or he decides that the benefits of cooperation outweigh those of competition.

Based on the experimental evidence, it would appear that the strongest case can be made for a combination of reciprocity (tit-for-tat) and unilateral conciliatory initiatives. This would consist of responding in kind equally to conciliatory and coercive moves made by an adversary, while retaining the option to initiate unilateral moves if the interaction becomes locked into a cycle of mutual competition. This tactic is intended to convey the message of being firm, but fair. Patchen summarizes the experimental research on eliciting cooperation as follows: "A policy of unconditional cooperation tends to bring exploitation by an adversary whereas a policy of consistent coerciveness tends to lead to a fight. However, a strategy that begins with firmness—including the threat or use of coercion—in the early stages of a dispute and then switches to conciliation appears generally to be effective in securing cooperation from an opponent."[36]

Patchen has further noted that experiments, computer simulations, and field studies of actual interactions among countries show a remarkable convergence of findings: "a strategy that combines unilateral conciliatory initiatives with a general policy of reciprocity is desirable." An exception noted by Patchen is the case of an adversary that is more powerful than one's own side and has exploitative aims. However, in most situations where the parties are interested in enhancing their own security without achieving domination over others, "a basic strategy of reciprocating both rewarding behavior and punishing behavior by the other, combined with using conciliatory initiatives to break out of competitive spirals, seems to be effective."[37]

One reason why states invariably hesitate to employ unilateral initiatives, however, is fear of having one's cooperativeness being exploited by the other party. This propensity to engage in exploitation can be evaluated by considering models of interaction known as Richardson Process models. Richardson Process models were originally developed to explore the dynamics of arms races.[38] A change in a state's annual expenditures on armaments is considered to be related to the changes in three variables: (1) a positive function of the other state's expenditures on arms; (2) a negative function of its own armaments expenditures, referred to as exhaustion; and (3) a positive functions of its permanent grievances toward the other party. The interaction between the two parties is then treated as a pair of simultaneous, differential equations for the two parties combined.[39] When translated into the language of negotiations, however, the first two variables may be considered to constitute demands while the last may be considered as perceived threat or hostility. In this way, a change in one negotiator's demands is a function of the other negotiator's demands along with his or her own prior demands and perceived grievances.[40]

Otomar Bartos has noted that the relationships between demands may be reciprocal or exploitative. In the former case, "the negotiator responds to his opponent's initiatives by emulating them: the more the opponent lowers his demand, the more the negotiator lowers his; the more the opponent raises his demand, the more the negotiator raises his." By contrast, a negative relationship indicates exploitation; the more the opponent lowers his demand, "the more the negotiator raises his, thus taking advantage of opponent's cooperative attitude."[41] Bartos' experimental research generally supported the presence of reciprocal rather than exploitative behaviors. He found, "Richardson's assumption that negotiators tend to reciprocate to be more correct than the assumption that they exploit each others' concessions."[42] In addition, he found that a modified Richardson model has a mathematical "equilibrium in concessions rather than in demands," giving further support to the conclusion that negotiations usually involve a reciprocal trading of concessions in order to reach agreement.[43] A test of these models in the Partial Nuclear Test Ban negotiations by Hopmann and Smith revealed again that the strongest single explanation of the behavior of the two nuclear superpowers in these negotiations was the behavior of the other, so that tit-for-tat reciprocity was highly evident. However, when they looked at measures of perceptions rather than behaviors, they also found a weak tendency for some exploitative behavior in these negotiations. The United States "tended to toughen their negotiating stands when they perceived the Soviets in more positive terms, while relaxing their stands when they perceived the Soviets as tougher."[44] I shall discuss this study more fully in chapter 14.

The experimental and quantitative empirical studies of reciprocity suggest two interesting hypotheses about international negotiations. First, if one seeks cooperation and agreement in negotiations, it may be useful to be clear and firm about one's commitments and fundamental interests at the outset, and then to remain flexible and even soften one's position during the course of negotiations through various concessions. Second, concessions are most effective if they are reciprocated immediately, producing a sequence of mutual concessions that tends to converge toward the middle of the available bargaining space between the resistance points of the two parties.

Findings such as these may be explained more adequately if we conceptualize interactions within negotiations as a learning process. In this kind of model, each negotiator is gauging the other's behavior in order to try to locate an expected point of agreement. By estimating one's own and the opponent's BATNAs, or points of minimum agreement, one may begin to get some idea of the range of possible solutions. Within this range, one then develops an expectation of where the other party may agree to settle, and this expected solution forms a kind of aspiration level, a goal to be attained. The negotiator then monitors the interaction process for clues about the bottom line and aspiration levels of the other party, and adjusts one's own aspiration levels accordingly. These expectations, of course, may be subject to manipulation and misperception. Exaggerated demands and inflexible behavior by the other may cause the first to lower one's aspirations, and therefore concede more than might have been necessary to reach agreement; this is itself a form of exploitative behavior. Alternatively, flexibility in the form of behaviors such as unilateral initiatives and frequent concessions may cause one to raise one's aspirations and seek to exploit the apparent weakness of the other. If these expectations were excessive, this may cause frustration and hostility as the negotiator eventually has to lower her or his sights when faced with an opponent who becomes rigid after initially appearing flexible.

These changing behaviors may induce learning if they follow a consistent pattern that becomes known by the other party. When this occurs for both parties, they may eventually adjust their expectations and find a point of mutually acceptable settlement. Alternatively, as Cross points out, the kinds of tactical manipulations that are commonly found in distributive bargaining situations may enhance uncertainty rather than positive learning, with the following two consequences: "First, . . . strategy choices are affected by uncertainty: large amounts of uncertainty may, for example, encourage very large, initial payoff demands as a kind of insurance against making an unnecessarily generous offer. Thus, bluffing may induce counter-bluffing. Second, by reducing the confidence which one party may place in his own estimate of his competitor's behavior, large values of V_A and V_B [uncertainty] will slow the learning process and increase the persistence of initial expectations."[45]

Another variation of this model views negotiations in terms of a stochastic learning process. In such a model, behavior at each stage by one party is a probabilistic function of its own and the other's behavior at prior points in the interaction. Using these kinds of models, analysts may compute the probability that cooperative behavior will be reciprocated by a positive response. In these reactive models, cooperation must be based on "*symmetrical* relations, where each member has (or perceives he has) an equal share of social control over the further development of the relationship, and where the partners have mutual influence on one another."[46] Still another learning model suggested by Coddington incorporates the process of forming expectations, making evaluations of those expectations in terms of new information, and then making adjustments in those expectations in order to identify junctures where strategy changes will occur. In this framework, bargaining consists of a reiterated set of cycles in which party one announces a demand, party two uses that demand to evaluate expectations about party one, and party two then makes a demand based on adjusted expectations, which in turn causes party one to revise expectations about two's behavior, and so forth in a continuous cycle of decisions, expectations, and adjustments.[47] Coddington's model goes beyond the mechanical assumptions of most other models of responsiveness. Bargaining is not construed simply as actions and reactions; it is characterized by staged sequences of information processing by the participants. Each party monitors the trends in the other's behavior over time and may make delayed responses to those changes at a later point in time. These elements are present particularly in long and complex interactions such as those that occur in international negotiations. Druckman has identified a pattern of responsiveness similar to that presented in Coddington's model, which he calls threshold-adjustment in his study of negotiations between the United States and Spain to extend American rights to base Strategic Air Command forces in Spain.[48]

Joint Problem Solving

All of the approaches discussed above seem to be most relevant for bargaining situations that combine the usual tension between distributive and integrative negotiations described in chapters 4 and 5. However, it may also be important to consider the role of the dynamics of the interaction process in negotiations characterized more by problem solving, although this is a topic about which much less research has been conducted (that cries out for a great deal of additional study). Obviously, reciprocity may be as important in problem solving as it is in bargaining, although it may take more variegated and subtle forms. It no longer consists primarily of responding to offers with counteroffers, concessions with counterconcessions, or threats with counterthreats. Rather, it seeks to establish a process of collective give-and-take in which both parties try to participate equally in the joint search for mutually beneficial solutions. It no longer emphasizes a process of mutual yielding that leads to some convergence at a midpoint, but instead emphasizes a process of mutual exploration and invention that uncovers new ways of analyzing the issue and discovers new solutions to the problem.

I have already discussed in chapter 6 the general principles of the problem-solving style of negotiations. In this chapter, therefore, it suffices to point out some of the interactive activities that can occur between the parties that are likely to facilitate creative problem solving. Amabile has described the essential components of creative problem solving as consisting of five stages: fact finding, or the gathering of information about a problem; problem finding, or the clear formulation of a specific problem to be solved; idea finding, or the generation of possible solutions; solution finding, or the evaluation of the generated solutions; and acceptance finding, or the selling of the final solution to others.[49]

Similarly, Pruitt and Rubin have suggested four steps for utilizing problem solving to break stalemates:

1. The parties should try to determine if there really is a conflict of interest, or if the conflict is primarily illusory and the result of misunderstandings and misperceptions. If it turns out to be the latter, then the conflict may simply disappear. In some ways, this may account for much of what happened at the end of the cold war. Once most countries realized that the Soviet Union had neither the capability nor the intention of extending their empire over the rest of the world following the collapse of the Berlin Wall in November 1989, the major schism on the international scene since 1945 virtually disappeared within a matter of months.

2. Each party should analyze its own self-interest and should set high, but reasonable aspirations for what it hopes to achieve from the negotiation. If parties are not clear about their interests, they may give off signs that indicate weakness to the other, thereby setting off a cycle of exploitation and returning the process to more conflictual bargaining. If they do not have reasonably high aspirations, they may be willing to settle for lowest common denominator compromises rather than seeking more optimal and mutually beneficial results. At the same time, the aspirations must remain realistic so that they do not cut off the potential to reach integrative agreements.

3. When each party is clear about its own interests and aspirations, then it should attempt to persuade the other to accept at least its most important goals as valid. This means, of course, that each party will have to be prepared to reveal its underlying interests and needs to the other, at the possible risk that the other might use these to its own advantage. Yet unless both parties are willing to run the necessary risks of revealing information reciprocally, they will never be able to identify potential integrative solutions to their problem. The two parties should then jointly seek ways of reconciling their different aspirations with one another.

4. If at first they fail to identify appropriate integrative solutions,

they should simultaneously and reciprocally lower both sets of aspirations and continue to search for integrative solutions that may bridge or embrace jointly these lowered aspiration levels. They should continue this process of search and adjustment until either agreement is eventually found or until they agree between themselves that no agreement is possible and they decide to withdraw from negotiations.[50]

In the final analysis, just as in distributive bargaining, Pruitt and Rubin have concluded that the key to problem solving is also for each party to be "firm but conciliatory" in a pattern of mutual responsiveness: "Party is advised to be firm about his or her own basic interests—yielding only when it is clear that they cannot be attained—but conciliatory toward Other in the sense of being responsive to Other's basic interests also. An important aspect of being conciliatory is to be flexible about how one's own interests are achieved in order to be open to new ideas about how to reconcile them with Others' interests. Hence, this policy can also be described as involving *firm flexibility*."[51]

Still another process that parties may utilize together in an effort to invent creative solutions is referred to as brainstorming. The main goal of brainstorming is for a group of people to work together cooperatively to identify new ideas. The key principle required for this process to work effectively is that all group members must defer judgment about ideas and about the individuals who suggest ideas; ideas should not be criticized at the outset of the process, and individuals should feel free to suggest any ideas, no matter how crazy they may at first appear, without fearing that either they or their ideas will be criticized. In addition, brainstorming seeks to generate as many ideas as possible, again regardless of their initial apparent implausibility. An idea is valued less for its intrinsic validity than for its ability to generate still more new ideas. Once a large number of ideas have been advanced, the parties may search through them for possible solutions to their problems by looking for interesting combinations among the many ideas generated during the brainstorming session and searching for ways to improve upon the quality of those ideas.[52] Such a brainstorming session may most often be held during a time when negotiations are in recess or informal sessions; the whole purpose is to generate unique ideas that may be discussed in more formal negotiations and may provide new approaches to dealing with the issues under negotiation.

Finally, one may focus not just on the immediate interactions that have created the conflict or problem to be solved or just on the interactions within the negotiations themselves, but upon the entire interactive relationship between the parties over the long term. Fisher, for example, suggests that negotiations are a means to build long-term relationships, and that they will also be affected by the nature of those long-term relationships (unlike most of the studies reviewed thus far in this chapter that have focused far more extensively on immediate interactions). In building enduring relationships, he suggests, reciprocal tactics such as tit-for-tat may do more harm than good: "But the fact that reciprocity is good on substantive matters, and the fact that we would like to achieve a process that it [sic] reciprocal, does not mean that the strategy needed to build such a relationship can be based on the principle of reciprocity. In fact, to base a strategy for dealing with people on the principle of reciprocity is likely to doom that strategy to failure."[53]

Fisher explicitly rejects the tit-for-tat approach to negotiations, both because of the dangers of its locking in a cycle of mutual hostility and because it may reinforce the tendency of individuals to misrepresent their relationship with the other in such a way that each party perceives itself to be good, while the other is perceived as evil. While Fisher acknowledges that tit-for-tat may be the least bad of all options in situations in which verbal communications are impossible, he suggests that this does not make it an appropriate model for international negotiations, where verbal interactions are at the very center of the process. Therefore, Fisher argues, contrary to the notion of firm flexibility favored by analysts such as Pruitt and Rubin, the best approach to the negotiation process is to be unconditionally constructive. Instead of responding in kind, he maintains that negotiators should meet emotional action with rational response, misunderstanding with an effort to understand, the other's failure to listen with an effort to consult them whenever possible, deception with reliability, coercion with persuasion, and rejection with caring and openness to learning from the other. In other words, constructive responses are always to be preferred over reciprocating noncooperative behaviors. For example, he suggested that the best strategy for the United States to build a constructive relationship in the latter years of the cold war with the Soviet Union was to "do those things, and only those things, that are good for the relationship and good for us whether or not they are reciprocated."[54] This is especially important for the long term. That is, international negotiations are usually not only about solving some specific problem, but also about changing fundamental relationships in international politics over the long haul.

While Fisher's critique of reciprocity makes many valid arguments, especially when long-term interactions are affected by an important negotiation, it does not completely resolve the original tension with which I began this book: between cooperating to seek mutually beneficial solutions and playing tough to avoid being exploited. No matter how hard one tries, there can be no assurances that an unconditionally constructive strategy will not be perceived as a sign of weakness by the other party, tempting it to respond with conflictual behaviors intended to exploit the perceived softness. While seeking to initiate constructive relationships whenever and wherever possible, there probably can be no substitute for the sense of the experienced diplomat who may estimate subjectively when these unconditionally constructive actions will most likely yield cooperation from the other party versus those conditions where flexibility will have to be supplemented by a good measure of firmness about one's fundamental interests in order to avoid being taken advantage of.

While negotiating theory may help us identify this fundamental dilemma and even explore many of its implications, it has not yet identified any clear and unambiguous criteria for determining precisely when flexibility or firmness, reciprocity or unconditional constructive behavior, are likely to be more appropriate in producing mutually beneficial and relatively optimal outcomes in international negotiations. This is undoubtedly an important topic that may require a great deal more study before any satisfactory set of systematic criteria can be developed to replace the often vague intuitions of the experienced negotiator.

Chapter 11

The Impact of the International Environment

This chapter begins by relaxing the assumption that international negotiations take place in a political vacuum. Rather it starts from the premise that international negotiations constitute a subsystem of the larger international system, and that the employment of the negotiation process to resolve international conflicts depends very much on the state of relations among parties in the international environment. Depending on the state of this environment, especially on the state of international relations among the parties to a dispute, conditions may or may not be ripe to open negotiations, for negotiations to break out of stalemate and advance, to become stalemated, for agreement to be achieved, or for negotiations to be broken off. In addition, there may be an element of circularity in this process: success in negotiations may in turn affect the changing state of political relations in the international environment, and vice versa.

THE IMPACT OF THE STRUCTURE OF THE INTERNATIONAL SYSTEM

Initially I shall look at a more or less static element of the international environment that usually changes very slowly, namely the structure of the international system. At the risk of some oversimplification, the structure of the international system may be said to consist of two major factors: (1) the distribution of resources or capabilities across actors within the system (or the balance of power in classical realist terms) that establishes a hierarchy of influence relationships among the actors in the system (or patterns of dominance and subordination that affect the pecking order of international politics); and (2) the patterns of conflicting and cooperative interests that link the actors in the system, which often affect the formation of blocs, coalitions, alliances, regimes, or integrated communities among units with common interests, and conversely confrontations and even wars.

The first set of structural factors largely determines whether negotiations take place between parties that are roughly equal in resources
and in the capability to exert influence, versus situations where those
relations are primarily asymmetrical. The significance of the latter set of
relationships for negotiations was already discussed at length in chapter 7. Of course, these structural relationships are not firmly locked into
place and fixed over time. Thus, the negotiating context may be very
much influenced by changes in the relative position of the actors at the
time of negotiations. States may enter or leave the ranks of the great
powers, and the relative position of major actors may change over time.
For example, theorists of the power transition have suggested that the
relationships between states that are rapidly gaining in power and over-
taking more powerful countries and the states whose dominant position is being challenged may be very different from that which transpires
between two states whose position of approximate parity has been established over some period of time.[1]

Even immediate and relatively minor changes in the hierarchical
relationships may have significant effects on negotiations. For example,
following the disastrous defeat suffered by Egypt in the 1967 war with
Israel, Egypt feared negotiating with the Israelis because of Egypt's clear
position of military inferiority; they simply did not want to negotiate
from a position of distinct weakness. Even though the 1973 war between
these two countries ended more or less in a deadlock at about the status
quo ante, initial successes by the Egyptian military had enhanced their
confidence in their military capabilities, and the Egyptian army had at
least shown that it could hold its own militarily against the Israelis. Under
these conditions, it was easier for Egypt to participate constructively in
a series of negotiations that led to the cease-fire and disengagement agreements of 1974 and 1975 and the Camp David accords of 1978 on the
Sinai. Shifts in the balance of power between parties may exert significant influence on a decision to open negotiations, on the process of negotiations, and on the frequency and substance of agreements reached.

Another dimension, less often treated by structural realists, is the
pattern of conflicting and cooperative interests that exist among actors
in the international system. At the extreme, neorealists tend to treat states
as undifferentiated actors in an anarchic system. In this situation, as
Kenneth Waltz notes: "To achieve their objectives and maintain their
security, units in a condition of anarchy—be they people, corporations,
states, or whatever—must rely on the means they can generate and the
arrangements they can make for themselves. Self-help is necessarily the
principle of action in an anarchic world."[2]

It does not necessarily follow from this, however, that all states act
completely alone, nor that they are in some sort of Hobbesian "war of
all against all." Some states have very few overlapping interests and

very infrequent interactions, so that they remain largely irrelevant to one another. Thus, the relationships between Bolivia and Burma have little impact, if any, on the overall structure of the international system. Other countries have more or less compatible interests, such as the United States and Canada, while others have intensely conflictual interests, such as Israel and Syria throughout most of the period after 1948.

These patterns of conflict and cooperation may also change over time, as they move along a continuum from incompatible interests to overlapping interests and from open warfare to complete political integration. The broad extent of this continuum of international relationships may be illustrated by indicating some of the major kinds of relationships likely to be found at various points along this continuum.

The conflictual end of the continuum is characterized mostly by open warfare where states are engaged in direct conflict with one another and where the very survival of one or more as independent states is at stake. While there still may be some common interests that affect the conduct of that warfare, the basic relationship is one of intense hostility and almost complete opposition of interests. A special case here occurs when conflict becomes sufficiently intense that it threatens to break out into violence or warfare, or threatens in other ways the vital interests of states; this situation, usually defined as a crisis, will be considered in greater detail later in this chapter.

Short of open warfare, relationships may be characterized by the use of coercive diplomacy, through which states try to influence the behavior of others by threats of the use of force, sometimes complemented by shows of force to demonstrate their commitment. Moving toward the center, states may have significant, but nonviolent conflicts of interest, which nonetheless may be managed by nonviolent, noncoercive means. Negotiation is a common tool in these kinds of conflictual relationships, where cooperative interests may still exist in limiting or resolving the fundamental issues in conflict.

As relations among states become more cooperative, the relationship may be characterized by détente, a French word meaning a relaxation of tensions; cooperative elements may be enhanced in the presence of a pattern of interaction that is still basically characterized by opposing interests.

As cooperation expands, this may lead to a rapprochement, in which agreements are reached between previously hostile states, and then to entente, in which previously opposed parties recognize a similarity of outlooks and interests that may lead to the development of common understandings about how to deal with some of the major issues that affect their relationship.[3]

Still further at the cooperative end of the continuum are relationships characterized by extensive policy coordination. This may occur more or less informally through what are often called regimes, which may be defined as "norms, procedures, and institutionalized arrangements worked out by interested states to regulate relations in a particular issue area such as trade, environmental and health problems, or atomic energy."[4] Or this may be characterized by participation in formal organizations intended to realize common goals, such as an alliance like the North Atlantic Treaty Organization (NATO) or a global organization such as the World Health Organization.

Finally, at the most cooperative end of the continuum, lies integration. In this situation, states may begin to place important functions previously handled by individual states into the hands of a common, unified authority. Certainly the best example of this in recent international relations is the development of the European Union, in which the functions of a single market have been applied to fifteen countries in Western Europe as of the end of 1995. At some time this integration may reach the point where a completely federal structure emerges, in which a supranational institution takes over the major functions previously performed by separate states, including the adoption of a common defense and foreign policy. At that point, however, a new and integrated single actor will have been created within the international system, and the relations among the parts will no longer appropriately be treated as a subject of international relations, having in effect become domestic relations among components of a single entity on the world stage. This was the case, for example, with regard to the United States after the adoption of the Articles of Confederation. From that time on, the separate states of the United States no longer acted as independent entities in the global arena, but as one integrated actor within a federalist system.

These patterns of conflict and cooperation tend to affect the creation of various coalitions of states within most international negotiations at any given time in history. Thus, for example within the U.N. system throughout the cold-war period, it was traditional at least in the 1970s and 1980s to refer to four (sometimes three) groups of states: group A usually refers to the developing countries of Asia and Africa; group B consisted of the developed, industrialized countries of North America, Western Europe, and Japan (essentially the members of the Organization for Economic Cooperation and Development—the OECD); group C consists of the developing countries from Latin America, although it was often lumped together with group A to form the so-called Group of 77, which actually had approximately 125 members by the late 1980s); and group D, which included the former socialist countries of the Soviet Union and Eastern Europe. Similarly, the Conference on Security and Cooperation in Europe (CSCE) tended to coalesce prior to 1990 into three groups, including the members of NATO, members of the Warsaw Pact, and a third group of neutral and nonaligned states.

However one conceives of the structure of the international system, it is clear that negotiations occur frequently between both members of the same coalition and between members of different or sometimes opposing coalitions. Yet the nature and style of the negotiation process is likely to be completely different. Although there were some tough issues to be resolved in the negotiations between the United States and Canada to create a free trade zone between these two countries, the negotiations were conducted between two highly interdependent countries with a long history of cooperation. While there was undoubtedly occasional resort to hard bargaining, by and large these kinds of negotiations are more likely to be conducted in a problem-solving mode with explicit search for mutually beneficial solutions; where bargaining does occur, on the whole one would generally expect to find that relatively soft bargaining tactics tend to prevail: promises are used more often than threats, frequent new offers are advanced, and concessions tend to be made in a reciprocal and mutually responsive fashion.

This contrasts significantly with negotiations between traditional adversaries. In these cases, psychological barriers to communication and understanding are likely to be great. Most issues are approached initially from a bargaining paradigm, and it can often be very difficult to shift the negotiations to a more problem-solving orientation. Negotiators tend to see the negotiation in win-lose rather than win-win terms, and each party seeks to win a larger share of whatever benefits may be derived from the negotiation through manipulation of the bargaining process to serve their individual interests. This manipulation is likely to make extensive use of hard bargaining tactics such as commitments, threats, stonewalling, rejection of new ideas, and even retraction of previous offers and concessions. Thus, stalemate and breakdown may be more frequent, and whatever agreements are reached are more likely to be suboptimal and relatively inefficient. This is not to suggest that it is impossible to achieve more constructive negotiation processes between traditional enemies, just that it normally takes a great deal more effort, imagination, and even risk on the part of the contending parties to move toward a negotiation process that is more likely to yield satisfactory, if not always optimal, results.

Finally, relations among states may be influenced by changes in the relationships of one or both with third parties. For example, when open conflict appeared between the two major communist bloc allies, the Soviet Union and the Peoples' Republic of China in the early 1960s, relations between the Soviet Union and the United States began to improve, facilitating the negotiation process between the two superpowers on such important issues as arms control from 1963 onward.

IMPACT OF INTERNATIONAL TENSIONS AND DÉTENTE ON NEGOTIATIONS

As noted above, these structural considerations tend to be rather static in the sense that they change slowly. Although the international system underwent a substantial restructuring after World War I, after World War II, and again after 1989, the fact remains that throughout very long periods of time the fundamental patterns of hierarchy and cooperation/conflict have remained more or less unchanged. Nonetheless, even within these basic structural relationships, temporary adjustments may occur. As noted already in chapter 7, even relatively weak states may achieve temporarily special capabilities that assist them in negotiating on a more or less equal footing with their stronger counterparts on specific issues under particular conditions. From the point of view of this chapter, it is also important to note that even basic patterns of conflictual or cooperative interests may also be subject to short-term changes in emphasis. Even fundamentally cooperative relationships may be interrupted by periods of tension, such as that which occurred between the United States and Great Britain after the Suez crisis in 1956, when the United States opposed British and French military involvement in Egypt and called upon the United Nations to request that its two allies withdraw from the Suez Canal. Similarly, fundamentally conflictual relationships may be characterized by thaws or periods of détente, in which at least the atmosphere of the relationship between the parties improves. This was the case in the relationship between the two primary cold-war antagonists—the United States and the Soviet Union—for a brief period after Stalin's death in 1953, following the signing of the Partial Nuclear Test Ban Treaty in 1963, and again after the SALT I Treaty in 1972. The cycle of coercive diplomacy, nonviolent conflicts of interest, and détente was an important environmental influence on negotiations throughout the entire period of the cold-war system, and variations in this cycle may have been closely linked to short-term changes in the negotiations occurring on various international issues throughout this entire period, even though the basic system structure remained fundamentally unchanged.

A number of empirical studies of negotiation have suggested that the negotiation process directly mirrors what is occurring in the overall political relationships among the parties, so that breakthroughs in negotiations may depend on a general improvement in the political relationships among adversaries.

With respect to arms control negotiations, this approach has been characterized by Singer as the tensions-first hypothesis, which asserts that political differences among adversaries must be resolved prior to negotiating on disarmament. The armaments are seen by proponents of this view as being largely symptoms of the underlying political conflict, and the arms may not be removed as long as the basic differences remain unresolved.[5] On this basis, many argued that disarmament negotiations between the United States and the Soviet Union were unlikely to produce any meaningful results as long as the cold war continued between these two superpowers. There were fundamental conflicts over political ideology (democracy versus authoritarianism), over economic systems (market capitalism versus centrally planned economies), and over specific issues (such as the division of Germany and Korea, in particular) that explained why these two states armed against one another. As long as these disputes existed, according to proponents of this view, each side had a motive to engage in violent behavior against the other to preserve and advance its own ideological positions and specific interests. As long as these motivations for violent action remained, then military armaments to defend against such threats were also appropriate. Therefore, while arms control might have helped to stabilize this tenuous balance of terror and make accidental or preemptive wars based on miscalculation or misunderstanding less likely, it really accomplished little to eliminate nuclear weapons or the threat of nuclear war from the planet. That process required a prior settlement of the deeper issues of the East-West conflict.

Similarly, any dispute may be seen as the outward manifestation of deeper underlying conflicts, and some may argue that steps need to be taken to resolve those conflicts before meaningful negotiations can take place. For example, hostilities in the Middle East between Israelis and Palestinians (Jews and Arabs) run so deep and have been built up over so many centuries that negotiations to resolve these conflicts had to await some breakthrough in the larger relationship, according to the tensions first hypothesis. Thus, proponents of this perspective suggest that negotiations on peripheral issues such as a cease-fire and disengagement after the 1973 war between Egypt and Israel might have been possible without any settlement of underlying disputes, whereas negotiations on issues such as the status of the West Bank, because they touched on these core differences between Israelis and Palestinians, could not take place in any meaningful sense without some significant changes in the international environment. Arab recognition of Israel, discussion of the status of the Palestinians and of Jerusalem, and ultimately resolution of the issue of sovereignty over the West Bank all seemed to hinge on a larger political settlement. These core issues could not be handled by the kind of bilateral shuttle diplomacy that Secretary of State Kissinger employed between Israel and both Egypt and Syria between 1973 and 1975, which remained restricted to issues where only more peripheral values were at stake.[6] Indeed, breakthroughs in negotiations on these deeper issues seem to have been mostly a consequence of changes in the overall nature of global and regional international politics. In 1978, Soviet-American détente and a changing relationship between Egypt and the other Arab states facilitated one step forward at the Camp David negotiations. And in 1994 the end of the cold war, especially the end of Soviet backing for states such as Syria and Iraq and for nonstate actors such as the Palestine Liberation Organization (PLO), facilitated breakthroughs in negotiations between Israel and both the PLO and Jordan.

An alternative view about arms control negotiations, sometimes called the armaments first approach, holds that armaments may be in part a consequence of preexisting political conflicts, but that they also reinforce those conflicts in a vicious cycle. This position suggests that, even though armaments may initially be obtained in response to other sources of conflict, they become themselves an integral part of the problem between two countries locked in an arms race. Armaments create fears, tensions, and perceptions of mortal threat between states. It is often difficult for national leaders to negotiate constructively with an opponent who has the capacity to destroy their own country completely, as in the case of nuclear weaponry; with a state that has attacked civilian populations with chemical weapons, as in the war between Iran and Iraq in the decade of the 1980s; or when an opponent has the capacity to drive one's country "into the sea," as Israel's opponents threatened to do on numerous occasions. Thus, to wait to open negotiations until conditions in the external environment are perfect may be to condemn conflict resolution to a never-ending stalemate. A conflict may continue or even be reinforced without any effort made to negotiate even the easiest and most superficial issues in dispute. Conversely, negotiations on some of the preliminary or surface issues may help to create an atmosphere more conducive to tackling the deeper issues in dispute at a later stage.

In the case of the cold war, it is evident that the dramatic changes that occurred in the Soviet Union during the Gorbachev period made a whole new range of negotiations possible and enabled long-standing negotiations that had been stalemated—such as the negotiations on Strategic Arms Reduction Talks (START); Intermediate-range Nuclear Forces (INF); and Mutual and Balanced Forces Reductions (MBFR), renamed the talks on Conventional Forces in Europe (CFE) in 1989—to achieve agreements calling for deep reductions in nuclear and conventional weaponry on both sides of the cold-war divisions. On the other hand, it is unlikely that the fundamental political changes in East-West relations would have come about had it not been for previously negotiated agreements, such as the Strategic Arms Limitation Treaties (SALT) of 1972 and 1979 (the latter was never ratified) and the Helsinki Accords adopted by the Conference on Security and Cooperation in Europe (CSCE) in 1975. Thus, the negotiations may themselves be seen as having promoted dramatic and long-term political changes in the international environment of the cold war by moving superpower relations toward détente and rapprochement, which in turn enabled further and more significant negotiations to take place on specific disputes.

The international environment and specific negotiating fora may be seen as mutually reinforcing arenas, where it is impossible to determine which came first—progress in negotiations or political changes in the long-term international relationships. As Inis Claude has observed: "The truth is that this is a circular problem, in which causes and effects, policies and instruments of policy, revolve in a cycle of interaction and are blurred into indistinguishability."[7] Therefore, the negotiation process and the external international environment may change more or less in tandem.

There are several plausible political explanations for this relationship. Many negotiators have observed that the atmospherics of negotiations are influenced by the state of external tensions among the parties. In conditions of relative détente or even more cooperative interactions, when the negotiators are more relaxed and open with one another, the situation is much more likely to permit a problem-solving rather than a confrontational bargaining style, and agreement may be viewed as a part of a developing process. In other words, under conditions of relaxed tensions it is generally much easier to move to a problem-solving orientation than when hostilities are intense. This is not to suggest that problem solving is impossible during periods of intense conflict, but it is essential to recognize that it is far more difficult to engage in such a process and utilize it constructively when tensions are high. When there are high levels of tensions, negotiators tend to be cautious, unwilling to explore novel options or risk being taken advantage of if they initiate new proposals or make concessions. They may be more likely to hold hostile mirror images of one another, with each assigning blame to the other for the conflict and expecting the other to take the initiative to resolve it. They are more likely to adopt a zero-sum, confrontational bargaining style in the negotiations, and pursue hard bargaining tactics such as making commitments, making warnings and threats, and even retracting previous offers and concessions.

Similarly, the state of the international relationship may significantly influence the constraints under which negotiators operate, especially from their counterparts in their own government. The more relaxed the state of relations with their negotiating partner, the more support they may see for reaching agreement from within their own government and even from the public at large. When the officials back home have less to fear from a bad agreement or when they feel less restrained by an active public opinion, they may give the negotiators a great deal more flexibility to explore multiple options and respond rapidly to the dynamics of the ongoing negotiation process. Conversely, at times of high tension, they risk being accused of seeking agreement at any price with an untrustworthy enemy. In an effort to avoid these charges from public opinion or political officials, their ability to negotiate freely and constructively with the other parties may be undermined. Under such conditions, they are likely to keep a tight reign on negotiators, giving them little latitude to act flexibly on their own and possibly forcing them to shun agreement, even if it were attainable.

In addition, international tensions may actually be manipulated by policy makers to try to influence the course of negotiations. In some cases, decision makers may try to increase tensions in order to put pressure on negotiators to make concessions or otherwise approach agreement. For example, in the practice of arms control negotiations, a frequent tactic is to buy so-called bargaining chips. These are typically weapons that one country procures not because they enhance their security, but rather because they may serve as relatively useless weapons to offer to eliminate in exchange for the elimination by the adversary of some of its weapons perceived as threatening to the security of the first. If used successfully, therefore, they may enable a country to gain concessions from its opponent without having to give up anything of real value. However, there are also several potential problems with the utilization of these kinds of threatening weapons deployments. First, they may intensify hostilities between the parties, since the deployment of new weapons during negotiations may be viewed as a sign that the other is not negotiating in good faith. Second, once obtained, bargaining chips may be much harder to give up for domestic bureaucratic and political reasons than originally foreseen.

Thus, for example, the Nixon administration agreed to proceed with the development and deployment of so-called Cruise missiles, largely as a bargaining chip to give up in the second round of SALT negotiations in exchange for reductions of Soviet heavyweight, multiple warhead missiles. Cruise missiles fly at slow speeds but with highly accurate guidance systems that enable them to fly low, change course frequently, and hone in precisely on a predetermined target. The first problem was that these weapons' accuracy made the Soviets fear that they might be used by the United States as part of an attempted disarming first-strike against Soviet missile bases, especially against liquid fueled missiles that required many hours to launch. These weapons enhanced Soviet fears about overall American strategic policy, especially the fear that their deployment might indicate a shift in strategy from a reliance primarily on a deterrent, second-strike approach to a disarming first-strike strategy—a fear that was reinforced by public statements of Nixon's secretary of defense, James Schlesinger, who spoke on several occasions about a new strategy of utilizing limited nuclear options. The second problem was that, after the Soviets essentially agreed to the planned exchange of reductions in the SALT negotiations, the U.S. military services had be-come enamored with these new weapons and were extremely reluctant to agree to significant constraints on their deployment. The deadlock resulting from this misuse of bargaining chips was a major factor in post-poning a SALT II agreement from about 1975, when agreement might have been achieved had it not been for the Cruise missile dispute, until agreement was finally reached in 1979. By that time the international and domestic environments had deteriorated to the point that it was no longer possible to get the two-thirds positive vote in the U.S. Senate required to proceed with ratification of the treaty.

Similarly, parties other than participants in the negotiations may try to affect the international environment in ways intended to influence the negotiations. Thus, for example, radical Arab groups have engaged in various tactics to try to disrupt Middle East peace negotiations. Their frequent fear that more moderate Arab groups might make excessive concessions to Israel in order to achieve peace often prompted these groups to increase hostilities whenever these negotiations seemed to be about to get under way, or when agreement appeared likely, in order to disrupt them. Hostages may be taken, armed assaults may occur, and airplanes or ships may be hijacked in order to derail potentially fruitful negotiations. Thus, for example, soon after the United States unveiled the so-called Rogers Initiative, proposed by Secretary of State William Rogers on 19 June 1970 to promote a cease-fire in the war of attrition between Israel and both Egypt and Jordan, and after its acceptance by Egypt on 23 July a group of radical Arab terrorists hijacked two airlin-ers, one American and the other Swiss, and eventually destroyed them with explosives in the desert. This was a largely unsuccessful attempt to threaten moderate Arab leaders, especially Egypt's new President Anwar Sadat, and dissuade them from reaching agreement with Israel.

Up to this point I have discussed theoretical arguments and evi-dence from empirical research to support two basic hypotheses about the relationship between the international environment and the negoti-ating process. The first hypothesis may be summarized as follows: In-creases in international tensions and external conflict frequently hinder the process of international negotiations or create stalemates, both through their political effects on the governments and publics of partici-pating states and through their psychological effects on the negotiators themselves.

Before proceeding, at least two exceptions and qualifications to this hypothesis must be noted. First, there may be some situations of ex-treme conflict or tension that are so severe that they produce an over-whelming incentive to resolve a conflict. This may have been the case with regard to the impact of the Cuban missile crisis on the partial nuclear test ban negotiations. Many analysts of that crisis have noted that it dramatically affected both Kennedy and Khrushchev's perceptions of the dangers of a nuclear war, thereby encouraging them to make the necessary concessions to reach agreement in the long-stalemated negotiations.[8] I shall treat the issue of crisis negotiations later in this chapter, and I shall discuss the partial nuclear test ban case further in chapter 14.

Second, Touval and Zartman have identified another aspect of external tensions that may turn out to be functional for making breakthroughs in negotiations, namely the "hurting stalemate."[9] In this instance they suggest that long periods of pain and suffering may finally lead parties locked in a dispute to realize that neither can benefit from continuation of the conflict and that both have no choice but to reach a negotiated accommodation. Up to a point, of course, mutual suffering usually just makes the parties to a dispute dig in their heels more firmly; however, beyond some point the parties may become so desperate that they are prepared to negotiate seriously in spite of the risk of having to give up on important and long-defended interests. Such may have been the case between Israel and Egypt prior to the Camp David accords. Similarly in Nicaragua, six years of long war without any apparent victory in sight, plus a deepening economic crisis, may have led the Contras and Sandinistas into a cease-fire in March 1988, achieved more out of the desperation and suffering of both parties rather than out of any belief in an external improvement in mutual relations. Each party was prepared to gamble that it could win through the ballot box what it had been unable to win through years of armed struggle—unambiguous political authority to control the government of Nicaragua.

Both of these exceptions to the first hypothesis have one common element, namely that they both suggest a curvilinear relationship between external tensions and ripeness for dispute resolution. Up to a point, external tension detracts from the ability to negotiate a resolution to the conflict; but once the conflict itself becomes so intense or so enduring that it clearly has become more costly than any plausible negotiated agreement, then the external conflict may actually turn out to make a positive contribution to conflict resolution. Of course, the threshold beyond which the relationship changes will differ in every case, and some parties to conflicts have demonstrated what seems like an endless ability to endure suffering with little or no prospect of gain; certainly this was the case for most of the conflict on the "Western front" during World War I, and it also appeared to apply to the hard-fought war between Iran and Iraq from 1980–88. In other words, the threshold for a hurting stalemate clearly depends upon the relative ability of state leaders and populations to withstand pain. But, as Blainey has suggested, peace becomes possible when all parties to a conflict believe that they will "gain more by negotiating than by fighting."[10]

The second hypothesis about the relationship between parties to a dispute outside negotiations and their behavior within negotiations may be summarized as follows: Relaxation of international tensions and increased international cooperation, though not a sufficient condition for an improved negotiation process, frequently facilitates the negotiation process and enhances the ripeness of international disputes for negotiated settlement.

This hypothesis also needs to be qualified. It clearly states that improved external relationships merely facilitate rather than necessitate a set of ripe conditions for achieving agreement. In some cases, of course, there may be a substantive connection between the changing external events and the issues under negotiation. In this way, the external events may remove substantive obstacles that were previously hindering agreement. On the other hand, the hypothesis does not necessarily assume a direct connection between issues; it suggests that external events will be mirrored in negotiating processes, even if the relationship is largely coincidental, due to improved atmospherics and political receptivity to agreement. In this instance, however, a mere improvement in coincidental relationships does not necessarily imply that substantive differences will somehow automatically be overcome. Insofar as negotiations were blocked due to tensions, mistrust, and misperceptions, the improved international environment may break down some of those obstacles to agreement. But it will not necessarily solve the substantive problems themselves; the most that can be expected is for improved external relations to facilitate agreement by making the process more open, more task-oriented, aimed at problem solving rather than victory, and potentially more creative.

This distinction may be illustrated by reference to relations between the United States and the Soviet Union. The détente between the two nuclear superpowers that followed the Cuban missile crisis of 1962 illustrates a situation in which the political changes affected primarily the negotiating atmosphere, especially by making it clear that the two adversaries shared an overriding common interest in avoiding nuclear holocaust. This facilitated negotiation of several major arms control agreements, especially the Partial Nuclear Test Ban Treaty of 1963, the Nuclear Non-Proliferation Treaty of 1968, and the SALT I Treaty on Anti-Ballistic Missiles in 1972. However, in no case did the détente lead directly to agreement on these complex issues. Long and difficult negotiations were required, in part because the issues were technically complex, but more importantly because each side still feared that the other might exploit an advantage in the agreements to achieve unilateral military advantages. Détente thus referred, as its definition implies, to a relaxation of tensions that facilitated a more constructive process of negotiation, but it did not in itself remove specific obstacles to agreement on arms control issues.

This contrasts markedly with the rapid progress made in the Strategic Arms Reduction Treaties (START) and the Conventional Forces in Europe Treaty (CFE) between 1990 and 1993. In these instances, extremely complex issues were resolved with great haste, and major reductions were agreed upon in a short period of time, whereas the most minor limitations in previous years had required extensive and detailed negotiations. The difference, of course, was largely due to the disappearance of the cold war itself; the structure of the international system had undergone a fundamental transformation, as opposed to a movement along the conflict-cooperation continuum within the same system structure. Once the Warsaw Pact disintegrated and communism ceased to be the guiding ideology of the Soviet Union, and once it became evident that the Soviet Union and subsequently its successor states (especially the Russian Federation) had to give priority to economic concerns over military ones, the need for large military arsenals simply disappeared. By the end of 1990 there simply was no longer a fear of a massive Warsaw Pact conventional assault upon Western Europe, so that the need to maintain large NATO conventional armies disappeared. And in the nuclear realm, once all countries reverted to a posture essentially of minimum deterrence, the need for large strategic forces was also eliminated. In these circumstances, subtle issues and technical concerns were surpassed by the overriding political reality in which the massive armaments of the cold war had simply become obsolete.

Therefore, the negotiations were changed fundamentally by the radical differences in the environment, and the changed political circumstances had a direct bearing on the issues under negotiations. Weapons that, a few years before, had seemed essential to national security were no longer needed. The negotiations after 1989 struggled consistently and often unsuccessfully just to keep up with the changing political environment, and the changes in that environment itself made substantive changes in negotiating positions not only possible but often mandatory. In this case, the significance of the changed international environment was so important overall in affecting the negotiations that the process variables we have examined in previous chapters became almost irrelevant by comparison. The outcome of these negotiations was affected only marginally by the actual conduct of the negotiations, and for the most part the results were almost preordained due to the fundamental changes in the international system. Such dramatic changes in the international environment are, of course, rare in history, and in most negotiations in more normal times the other process variables invariably interact on a more equal basis with the international environment to affect the outcome of negotiations. However, the system transformation following the end of the cold war illustrates quite clearly the dramatic changes that may occur in negotiations as a result of major alterations of the international environment within which negotiations are embedded.

One final consideration involves the deliberate manipulation of the external environment by the decision makers in one state in order to affect the negotiation process, commonly referred to as linkage. In this case, one state's negotiators may make their acceptance of an agreement contingent upon some change in the behavior of the other parties with regard to issues having no direct bearing on the negotiations. Thus, for example, Henry Kissinger tried to make use of linkage diplomacy—especially of the trilateral relationship among the United States, the Soviet Union, and the Peoples' Republic of China—to influence the negotiations seeking to end the Vietnam War. He tried to use the rapprochement between the United States and China, culminating in President Nixon's visit to Beijing in February 1972, to induce the Chinese government to put pressure on Hanoi to negotiate more flexibly. Shortly after Kissinger visited Beijing in July 1971 the Chinese invited Prime Minister Pham Van Dong of North Vietnam to visit Beijing; when he finally came in November, the Chinese encouraged him to stop short of demanding complete political control of South Vietnam.[11] After Nixon's visit in February 1972 Chinese support for North Vietnam appeared to decline considerably. Similarly, Kissinger flew to Moscow in April 1972 to pave the way for a summit meeting between President Nixon and General Secretary Brezhnev scheduled for the following month, at which time the SALT I negotiations were expected to be concluded. At this meeting, Kissinger told Brezhnev forcefully that progress on détente depended significantly upon a halt to North Vietnamese offensive military actions in Vietnam, in which Soviet arms were being employed to kill U.S. soldiers.[12] Although there appeared to be little direct and immediate impact on North Vietnamese negotiating positions in the Paris peace talks, these efforts at linkage seemed to reduce significantly support for the North Vietnamese from the two major communist states—the Soviet Union and China—whose rivalry had included competition to support and influence the Vietnamese struggle for national liberation.

These efforts illustrate Kissinger's strong belief in the wisdom of manipulating international events, including not only direct relations between the parties to a conflict, but also third parties that have close relations with the disputing parties, in order to enhance the prospects for negotiating solutions to various disputes. At the same time, they also illustrate the limits to such linkage diplomacy in situations where the third parties may have limited influence over one's negotiating partner; indeed, in both matters of the conduct of the war in Vietnam and the use of diplomatic negotiations to end that war, U.S. officials seem to have overestimated the influence of both China and the Soviet Union over the policy of their ally in Hanoi. In the end the United States had to resort to massive bombings of North Vietnam in December 1972, both to convince the North Vietnamese to accept a final settlement and even more importantly to convince the reluctant U.S. ally in South Vietnam that a peace accord did not mean a complete abandonment of the government in Saigon to their communist opponents.

In order to be effective it is necessary for a deliberate policy of linkage to facilitate agreement by changing the relative costs and benefits for the parties associated with agreement versus their BATNA, their next best alternative to a negotiated agreement. Insofar as Kissinger's linkage policy on Vietnam achieved some limited success, it was largely because it reduced Hanoi's ability to rely on sustained military, economic, and political support from Moscow and Beijing to pursue the war effort as an alternative to a political settlement if negotiations failed. Such deliberate linkage may also create fears of being manipulated that may engender resentment and a desire to avoid being pressured. If the linkage process produces this kind of psychological response by the other parties, then it may turn out to be quite dysfunctional with respect to overcoming impasses. Throughout the negotiations on peace in Vietnam, the U.S. delegates were frequently insensitive to the need by their North Vietnamese counterparts to avoid feeling pressured and manipulated by the superior power position of the United States; when faced with such pressure, their negotiating positions often became more intransigent rather than more flexible. For example, following Kissinger's visit to Moscow in April 1972, Kissinger met with North Vietnamese negotiator Le Duc Tho in Paris on 2 May only to find that the North Vietnamese seemed to feel no pressure to negotiate; according to Kissinger, this turned out to be one of the most fruitless negotiations that he had with his North Vietnamese counterparts.[13]

Due to the ambiguous and possibly even contradictory effects that deliberate linkage policies may exert on negotiations, the general hypotheses presented above would not seem to apply. Deliberate linkage may have very different effects than those predicted by these hypotheses, depending upon the subtlety with which it is presented and the way in which it is perceived by its intended target.

NEGOTIATION DURING INTERNATIONAL CRISES

Before leaving the topic of the international environment, it is important to note that the negotiation process may be substantially different when one reaches at least one extreme end of the conflict-cooperation continuum, namely when the conflict becomes so intense as to constitute an international crisis. Crisis bargaining has been a subject of study all to itself, yet in many ways it is just a special case of the strong impact of a particular set of environmental conditions on negotiations.

I have already discussed the impact of increased international tensions on negotiations, but the concept of crisis introduces a set of environmental conditions that are usually qualitatively different from the normal ebb and flow of tensions between nation-states. At the most general level, Charles Hermann has defined a crisis as "a situation which disrupts the system or some part of the system (i.e., a subsystem such as an alliance or an individual actor). More specifically, a crisis is a situation that creates an abrupt or sudden change in one or more of the basic systemic variables."[14] Some analysts have suggested that the definition should go somewhat further and also incorporate an increase in the likelihood of violence or war. For example, Oran Young asserts that an international crisis "is a set of rapidly unfolding events which raises the impact of destabilizing forces in the general international system or any of its subsystems substantially above 'normal' (i.e., average) levels and increases the likelihood of violence occurring in the system."[15] The problem with the inclusion of an increase in the probability of violence or war in the definition is that it restricts crises primarily to those disputes that are likely to set off violence. It ignores the kinds of crises that may occur in negotiations in which threats of physical violence are not present and are usually totally inappropriate, such as most economic negotiations. In the case of trade negotiations such as those in the context of the General Agreement on Tariffs and Trade (GATT), for example, the failure of negotiations might set off a trade war, a round of reciprocal protectionist measures, but it is extremely unlikely to produce overt violence. Yet such instances probably should be included within the definition for the purpose of analyzing crisis as opposed to normal negotiations. Charles Hermann has further specified the definition of crisis as including three components: "Specifically, a crisis is a situation that (1) threatens high-priority goals of the decision-making unit, (2) restricts the amount of time available for response before the decision is transformed, and (3) surprises the members of the decision-making unit by its occurrence."[16]

Of these three components of crisis, the first two would appear to be necessary conditions and the third would seem to enhance the intensity of a crisis, although it is certainly conceivable to have a crisis that was foreseen by all of the relevant participants, but is a high threat situation with little time for decision making. Therefore, in analyzing negotiations under crisis conditions, I shall concentrate primarily on the effects of high threat and time pressure.

As I already noted in chapter 8, one of the first and clearest casualties of negotiation under crisis conditions is frequently the rationality of the participants. The primary intervening variable here is stress, created largely by the threatening nature of the situation. Stress dramatically affects the performance of individual negotiators and the decision makers to whom they are responsible. A large experimental literature on stress-related effects suggests a number of hypotheses about the relationship between stress and negotiating behavior. Stress in this context affects the way individuals interpret a situation, especially situations where they perceive that they have little control over events. Typical effects of stress reported in the experimental research include oversimplified perceptions, reduced tolerance for ambiguity, cognitive rigidity, less efficient problem solving, and increased hostility or aggressive behavior.[17] The psychological literature indicates that the major factors that tend to produce stress are a lack of information about the future leading to feelings of uncertainty.[18] While some moderate levels of stress may enhance human performance, as Ole Holsti notes, the results of experimental research by psychologists draw quite different conclusions about the effects of the kind of high stress that is likely to be produced in an intense international crisis: "The preponderance of experimental evidence indicates that intense and protracted stress, although it may improve simple psychomotor output, impairs cognitive performance. The relationship between cognitive performance and stress is often described as an 'inverted U.' Low to moderate stress may facilitate better performance but, according to most of the experimental evidence, protracted high stress degrades it."[19]

Holsti goes on to suggest three primary domains in which crisis-induced stress may cause cognitive functioning to deteriorate. First, there is likely to be a reduced attention span and important issues may be neglected while trivia may take on excessive importance. As Holsti observes: "As a consequence, important dimensions of the situation may escape scrutiny, conflict of values may be overlooked or suppressed, and the range of perceived alternatives is likely to narrow, but not necessarily to the best ones."[20] Second, there is likely to be an increase in cognitive rigidity, in which individuals frame issues within a simplistic framework and seek to reduce all complex issues to fit that framework. Frequently these frames will also take on moralistic tones, and actors and actions are likely to be perceived dichotomously in terms of good and bad, just and unjust. Typically in negotiations, each of the parties may see itself as the defender of absolute good against an enemy that represents absolute evil. This may result in mirror images, in which a dichotomy arises between one's own nation-state (perceived as a passive, innocent victim and defender of a just cause) facing an active, aggressive opponent representing evil.[21] As Holsti adds, the individual decision maker "is likely to establish a dominant percept through which he or she interprets information and to maintain it even in the face of information that might seem to call for a reappraisal."[22] The third consequence of heightened stress is an altered time perspective, especially one in which time seems to be speeding up and deadlines seem to be approaching rapidly. As a consequence, search for information about options may also be sped up, but also it may become less systematic and less productive. As a result, as Holsti concludes, "other actors and their motives are likely to be stereotyped, and the situation itself may be defined in overly simple, one-dimensional terms, for example, that it is a zero-sum situation, or that everything is related to everything else. The ability to invent non-obvious solutions to complex problems may be impaired."[23]

These cognitive changes induced by the stress of a crisis may have several obvious effects on negotiations. First and foremost, negotiations are likely to be framed almost exclusively within the bargaining paradigm, and opportunities for problem solving are likely to be overlooked or abandoned. In a situation of intense crisis, where mirror images of mutual hostility prevail, it is very unlikely that negotiators will be able to adopt a problem-solving orientation. Even if the parties are confronted with an overwhelming common problem—perhaps the outbreak of a major war—it is asking a lot to expect them to be able to perceive the war as a joint threat to their common security and join together to solve the problem. They are rather likely to see each other as the cause of the problem and consequently to see the negotiation in strongly adversarial terms. This is not to suggest that a constructive solution could not be easier to achieve if the parties were able to rise above these rivalries, as to some degree both President John F. Kennedy and General Secretary Nikita S. Khrushchev did in 1962 in resolving the missile crisis in the Caribbean. Obviously, these two leaders were able to grasp at least intuitively some of the fundamental concepts suggested in the approach to negotiations advocated by Fisher and Ury, as the common interest in survival exerted considerable restraint on their actions.[24] But this case was probably more the exception than the rule, and resort to competitive bargaining is the most likely negotiation process to be adopted in the presence of intense crises.

Second, negotiators and the decision makers they represent are likely to become cognitively more simple and rigid, with reduced attention span, and an inability to consider multiple options to solve the problem. Viewing the other party as an adversary in a struggle of good against evil, they are likely to attribute evil intent to even the most benign behaviors, both verbal and nonverbal, of the opponent. They are more likely to reciprocate conflictual behavior regardless of the behavior of the other. Their bargaining tactics are likely to emphasize firm commitments rather than flexibility, threats rather than promises, and retractions of previous offers rather than advancing new initiatives or concessions. Each is likely to perceive that "the ball is in the other's court," to use a tennis analogy frequently invoked by diplomats. But when both parties perceive that the ball is "in the other's court," neither sees the need to play the ball or to serve. The result is typically stalemate. Even within the bargaining paradigm, agreement is likely to become more desired, but more difficult to reach than it was before the appearance of the crisis. The parties are likely to become deadlocked in a stalemate in which each waits for the other to blink first, to make the first move to de-escalate the crisis. But if both wait for the other and neither takes the initiative to reach agreement, the negotiations are likely to remain stuck in impasse. Communications between the two sides are likely to become increasingly difficult and perhaps even break down altogether. Cultural stereotypes may replace a nuanced understanding of the impact of cultural factors as they affect communications and negotiations.

Third, the psychological distance separating the negotiators from the diplomats back home is likely to increase, and the boundary role problem is likely to become even more severe than in normal negotiations. In this situation, there is at least some hope that negotiators involved in face-to-face interactions may still recognize the humanness of their opponents, even empathizing with the difficult and complex situation in which their opponents may find themselves trapped, while decision makers in national capitals may dehumanize the opponents and attribute all blame for the crisis to their actions. Thus, not only may communications break down between the two parties, but they also may be degraded even among the members of each party to the negotiation.

Not only is crisis-induced stress likely to affect the individual participants in negotiations, but it is also likely to have an impact on the organizational and bureaucratic components of the negotiation process. The hypotheses about the impact of stress on bureaucratic behavior, however, tend to be less one-directional than is the case when dealing with individual behavior. For example, Graham Allison and others have noted several salutary effects that crises may have on bureaucratic behavior. For example, the decision-making locus is likely to move to the top of organizations where parochial bureaucratic distortions are less likely to prevail. Furthermore, the distorting effects that are frequently introduced as information moves up a bureaucratic hierarchy from the field where it is gathered, through many layers of bureaucratic organizations each of which synthesizes and combines it with other information, may be reduced because the highest level decision makers may take charge of gathering information themselves. Furthermore, the national interest is more likely to be clearly defined in crisis situations, so that disputes among parochial bureaucratic interests may be shunted aside. All of these enhance the likelihood that decisions may be made and negotiations conducted under the control of a unitary, rational actor rather than a plethora of feuding bureaucratic agencies.[25]

By contrast to this fairly optimistic appraisal, several psychologists have called attention to the possible deleterious effects of stress on organizational behavior. For example, stress may tend to call forth well learned or dominant responses rather than flexible and innovative ones.[26] Translated into the language of bureaucratic politics, this means that routine bureaucratic behavior and standard operating procedures are employed more frequently than are novel responses to the crisis situation. Furthermore, stress is likely to cause alternatives to be narrowed rather than expanded, a tendency to rely on worst case scenarios as a basis for decision making, and an enhancement of the ideological component of the problem as opposed to pragmatic bargaining within the bureaucratic organization.[27] Finally, crises may tend to enhance "group think" within the decision-making and negotiation teams, a process of conformity within working groups that is characterized by a deterioration of mental efficiency, moral judgment, and the ability to test and evaluate reality against external standards. Bureaucrats may become increasingly isolated from the outside world as they work long hours to reach difficult decisions. And the goal of maintaining group solidarity and cohesion to deal with the high threat situation may take precedence over searching for creative responses to the threat. As Holsti concludes: "As a consequence, groups may be afflicted by unwarranted feelings of optimism and invulnerability, stereotyped images of adversaries, inattention to warnings, and powerful, if sometimes subtle, pressures against dissent."[28]

All of these factors are likely to translate into an approach to bargaining that resists the exploration of multiple options, brainstorming, and other techniques that may be necessary for successful problem solving within negotiations. They may make it harder for the negotiators, who have direct and personal contact with the other party, from having much of an impact on the decision, either because their input may be largely disregarded or because they may feel themselves under subtle pressures to tell their superiors back home what they believe their superiors want to hear. Once again, the quality of decision making and of the process of conducting negotiations may be significantly degraded by the occurrence of an international crisis.

Thus far I have looked primarily at the effects of stress induced by high threat to central values on the negotiation process. Another characteristic of crises, the presence of short decision time, may also have a significant impact on negotiations. As suggested by the metaphor of a crisis as used in medical language, it is a situation that is approaching a turning point after which time either a resolution will be achieved or the situation may break out of control. Typically this occurs in situations where the participants have little or no control over the timing of this turning point, and usually it seems to be looming just over the horizon. This puts negotiations under considerable pressure to reach agreement before the "point of no return" is reached, at an uncertain but nonetheless definite point in the near future.

The effects of this kind of absolute deadline, which lies largely outside the control of the negotiating parties, on the negotiation process may be mixed. The most basic and common conclusion is that deadlines, especially those imposed from outside the parties, are likely to facilitate the reaching of agreement, but those agreements are more likely to be suboptimal than agreements arrived at without such serious time pressures. The pressure of time, as already noted, significantly reduces the possibility for negotiators to engage in an exploratory search process in the hopes of discovering innovative and mutually beneficial outcomes to the conflict that may make both parties significantly better off. Alternatives to agreement tend to fade away for both parties as the crisis pressure mounts, so that the best alternative to a negotiated agreement becomes increasingly less attractive. Resistance points move further apart and bargaining space may widen. In this light, agreement—any agreement—begins to seem better than the alternatives for both parties. There is a tendency to seize whatever agreement may be available at the last moment before the crisis explodes, even if options that would have been better for both parties were also available, though as of yet undiscovered, or even if the agreement leaves one party a good deal less well off than the other.

The tendency to reach agreements under time pressure is partially explained by experimental findings that suggest there is a significant decrease in demands and increase in concessions as the end of a negotiation approaches. For example, Bartos concludes that his "data suggest the existence of an *end game:* the very last concession of the negotiation is exceptionally large."[29] This may be preceded, however, either by a long series of smaller concessions or sometimes by a period of toughening demands and reduced concessions, in apparent preparation for last-minute, breakthrough concessions as the deadline approaches. Indeed, there may even be retractions shortly prior to the deadline, as each side hopes to induce even greater concessions from the other side. Obviously, in a competitive bargaining situation characterized by high threat, each party knows that the deadline weighs on the opponent as well as on itself, and each may hope that the opponent will be forced into making the bigger concession as the crisis approaches its critical point. This admittedly risky strategy worked for President Kennedy in the Cuban missile crisis, as the Soviets agreed to pack and return all of their missiles in Cuba in a public and dramatic concession in exchange for private assurances by the United States not to invade Cuba and agreement to remove intermediate-range missiles from bases in Turkey. Of course, if both parties persisted in playing the game of chicken up to the final moment, the result might not have been nearly as fortuitous as it was in the fall of 1962.

The outcome of crisis negotiations may not only be suboptimal in terms of sacrificing greater possible mutual benefits that might have been uncovered if the parties had more time to explore innovative options, but it may also produce highly inequitable outcomes as one party caves in at the last moment to achieve agreement and avoid impending disaster. This aspect of time pressure is summarized in a useful metaphor by Zartman and Berman: "Deadlines tend to facilitate agreement, lower expectations, call bluffs, and produce final proposals, but also lead negotiators to adopt a tough position that will make them look good if—and therefore when—negotiations fail. They often have a sort of 'musical chairs' effect (since musical chairs is a game that hangs on surprise deadlines): Parties tend to come to an agreement wherever they are when the deadline hits, but, this being the case, they try to maneuver to be in the best position when the music stops, whether there is an agreement or not."[30]

In conclusion, despite some possible salutary contributions of crises to effective international negotiations, overall crises tend to degrade the quality of negotiations along several dimensions. First, and foremost, they tend to encourage the adoption of a negotiation process characterized by hard bargaining that utilizes a concession and convergence model of moving toward agreement. Bargaining typically takes precedence over problem-solving. Instead of using diagnostics to clarify the nature of the problem and constructing mutually beneficial formulas based on principles, considerations of pure power and interest frequently prevail. Second, these crises tend to cloud the thinking of negotiators and make them more cognitively rigid, and to interfere with communication and mutual learning through the negotiation process. Third, they tend to make the bureaucratic constraints on negotiations more rigid through enhancing reliance on routine responses, increasing pressures for group conformity, and rigidifying communications between agents and principals—negotiators and decision makers at home. Fourth, they tend to reinforce the tendency for negotiations to remain locked into stalemates of reciprocally hard behavior, making it more difficult to generate the kinds of initiatives that may be necessary to break out of the vicious spiral of escalating conflict. In spite of a few mitigating factors noted above, most of the pressures created by crises are likely to make negotiations even more difficult than under more normal conditions and make conflict resolution harder than ever to achieve.

Given the nature of many of these constraints introduced into the negotiation process by crises, many of which are an almost unavoidable part of the nature of crisis itself, it is difficult to come up with constructive lessons for crisis bargaining. The first obvious lesson, of course, is to underline the importance of avoiding crisis situations whenever possible. Conflicts of interest are an inherent part of international politics, but crises are not inevitable. Negotiators must strive as part of the negotiation process to avoid crises or any form of deadline pressure and stress that leaves them out of control. The second set of lessons involves what has become known as crisis management, of which bargaining in crises is an important component. This literature has stressed the importance of coordinating negotiating behavior and actions taken elsewhere in the international environment in such a way as to try to minimize the dangerous components of crisis decision making and crisis bargaining.

Perhaps the most important conclusion here is the necessity for participants in crisis bargaining to be aware of what is occurring around them, especially of the tricks that crisis-induced stress may play on both their cognitive functioning and the dynamics of their group behavior as national decision makers and international negotiators. A participant in a crisis who is reflective and conscious of what is transpiring has a better chance of responding creatively in crisis bargaining than one who is unaware of these constraints and proceeds as if this were a perfectly rational contest of wills and national interests. As Ole Holsti has noted, President Kennedy's handling of the Cuban missile crisis of 1962 was very much influenced by the fact that shortly before the missiles were discovered on Cuba in October of 1962, he had read Barbara Tuchman's book, *The Guns of August,* about the outbreak of World War I in the summer of 1914. Thus, he was especially determined to avoid some of the pitfalls of crisis diplomacy that had, according to Tuchman's account, been largely responsible for a minor crisis in the Balkans in the summer of 1914 escalating into the first major global war of the twentieth century. Several weeks after the conclusion of the Cuban missile crisis, Kennedy revealed his awareness of the effects of misperceptions and miscalculations on the world's leaders in 1914 and how it had affected his behavior during the missile crisis: "Well now, if you look at the history of this century where World War I really came through a series of misjudgments of the intentions of others . . . it's very difficult to always make judgments here about what the effect will be of our decisions on other countries."[31]

While this kind of self-awareness of the limitations of human and organizational rationality is a necessary prerequisite for effective crisis bargaining, it alone does not provide a sufficient guarantee that future international crises will be resolved through the same kind of bargaining process that ultimately led to the resolution of the Cuban missile crisis. Even after the end of the cold war, when the very survival of the planet is less likely to be at risk in international crises, the number of these international crises may mount even as the severity of their consequences declines. There is then a need for more effective negotiation processes that can overcome the natural tendency for crises of all sorts to produce ineffective negotiation processes. Negotiations under crisis conditions typically lead at best to suboptimal and unequal outcomes, or at worst to unproductive impasses as the crisis passes beyond a point of no return. The end of the cold war has not necessarily brought an end to crises of this sort, so that the need for a better understanding of negotiation under crisis conditions is likely to be as great in the post-cold-war international system as ever.

CONCLUSION

This chapter has examined the impact of the international environment on negotiations. I looked first at the impact of system structure, that is the distribution of capabilities across actors within the system, and I emphasized that this structural factor affected primarily the issues of symmetry and asymmetry among the parties to a negotiation, which was discussed previously in chapter 7.

Of greater centrality in this chapter was a second set of systemic factors, namely the patterns of interactions among units within the international system along a conflict-cooperation continuum. Here I distinguished between two broad categories of change, both of which may exert a significant impact on negotiations. First, interaction patterns may change fundamentally when the international system undergoes complete transformation such as that which occurred after the end of World War II or again since 1989. Enemies may become allies and vice versa; intractable conflicts may become negotiable; and highly distributive bargaining may be converted into integrative problem solving and even into a process of policy coordination. Second, interactions among units within any international system may change their character over time, moving back and forth along the conflict-cooperation continuum. Periods of coercive diplomacy and intense conflicts of interest may alternate with periods of détente or even rapprochement and entente; ententes may deepen and move toward the formation of regimes, alliances, or even integrated political communities. Conversely, cooperative relationships may deteriorate and even threaten to move toward violence. The special case of an international crisis may appear at a point where a conflictual relationship reaches a crucial turning point, where it is likely either to turn violent or turn toward greater cooperation.

The primary argument of this chapter has been that the nature of any particular negotiation depends very much on the international context within which it is set. The general nature of the relationships between the parties to the dispute, and to third parties with close relations to the disputants, may color the kinds of negotiating processes that are likely to be employed or that may even be appropriate within any set of circumstances. Intensely distributive bargaining is rare among parties enjoying a relatively cooperative relationship, and integrative problem solving may be very difficult, though perhaps not impossible, to achieve among parties to intense, deep, and enduring conflicts or in times of crisis.

Furthermore, ongoing negotiations may be influenced by variations along the conflict-cooperation continuum over time, or by the sudden appearance of a crisis in a fluid and changing situation. And at those rare moments in history when the international system undergoes fundamental transformation, the negotiations that are in progress at the time may themselves be completely transformed. Possibilities for agreement may be opened or closed by such changes in overall relationships among units within the international system, and the character of the negotiation process may be transformed completely.

Finally, it is important to note that negotiations may also exert a reciprocal effect back into the system of relationships among units within which they are imbedded. Certain key negotiating breakthroughs, such as the Partial Nuclear Test Ban Treaty of 1963 or the Camp David Accords between Egypt and Israel in 1978, may significantly transform the broader range of political relationships among the parties to those agreements, which may in turn facilitate further agreements in the future. Conversely, the failure of negotiations, such as those between the United States and Japan in 1941, may lead to war. In turn, this may make further negotiations impossible until a new fundamental relationship has been established as a result of the outcome on the battlefield. Negotiations are by no means the totality of interactions that take place among units in international politics, but they are an important component of those interactions that are affected by and reciprocally affect the totality of those relationships.

Chapter 12

The Role of Third Parties:
Arbitration and Mediation

In previous chapters, we have been dealing only with bilateral negotiations, in which two parties face one another in direct negotiations.
The two parties in dispute may be more or less successful in arriving at
an agreement, but in the previous analyses the outcomes depended primarily on their own interests and negotiating skill in overcoming differences. In this chapter, I will introduce third parties that are not direct
participants in the negotiations, but whose role is to assist the conflicting parties to reach agreement in what otherwise basically remains a
bilateral negotiation.

Third parties are usually individuals, occasionally individuals of
high regard in the international community acting alone, who play third-
party roles because they represent another important actor in international relations such as a state, an international organization, or a
nongovernmental organization. Usually these individuals are selected
both because the actor they represent has some relevant power, authority, or legitimacy in the eyes of the parties to the dispute and because of
their own personal skills as go-betweens. In some cases, actors may continue to serve third-party roles, even though the specific individuals
change. For example, the United States has played a third-party role
between Israel and its Arab neighbors at least since 1970, although the
individuals performing that function have changed over time, including Secretaries of State William Rogers and Henry Kissinger during the
Nixon years, President Jimmy Carter during his administration, Ambassador Philip Habib on numerous occasions especially during the
Reagan years, and Secretary of State Warren Christopher and President
Bill Clinton after 1993. Although each of these individuals has brought
his own personal style and third-party techniques to the process, all have
acted as representatives of a powerful state, the United States, with important interests in the Middle East region. In other instances, the per-

sonal characteristics of the individual may take priority over his status as an institutional representative. An example of this was when former U.S. President Jimmy Carter mediated between the U.S. government and the military rulers of Haiti under General Raoul Cedras in September 1994 to seek a peaceful route to return the democratically elected president of Haiti, Jean-Bertrand Aristide, to power.

In some respects, third-party roles are completely consistent with the basic structure of bilateral negotiations in the sense that they seek to help the parties to a dispute find cooperative interests that take priority over their conflicting interests. As Rubin has noted: "Like bargaining, third party intervention also emerges at the interface of cooperative and competitive interests, although in a rather different way. Here the parties' competitive inclinations are presumed to dominate to such an extent that the disputants are unable or unwilling to reach agreement of their own accord; each wants so much and/or is willing to concede so little that a conflictual impasse tends to result. Given this impasse, however, the disputants are sufficiently cooperative that they are willing to invite or accept the intrusion of one or more external (third) parties who may be able to break the conflictual stalemate."[1]

This analysis suggests that third-party roles are most relevant when a stalemate has been reached and the parties need outside help to resolve their remaining differences. In most cases, the parties to a dispute prefer to settle their differences on their own without outside intervention. However, often the dispute turns out to be so bitter, and novel solutions so difficult to discover, that they must turn to a third party to help them resolve their differences.

Indeed, Touval and Zartman have suggested that third-party intervention is most likely to be successful when the parties have encountered what they call a "hurting stalemate."[2] This is a situation in which the parties feel uncomfortable and where events may be on the threshold of worsening, perhaps through an escalation of the conflict, or getting better through the resolution of the conflict. Like a medical crisis, these may be situations in which the conflict is approaching a critical turning point: either it will get worse and perhaps degenerate into violent conflict, or new efforts will be made to find a resolution. Alternatively, these opportunities may arise after a long period of unsuccessful negotiation where the burdens of the conflict no longer seem bearable to either party. On the verge of exhaustion, they may turn to a third party to try to break a long-standing stalemate. This may be particularly true if the parties both want to bring an end to their conflict, but seek face-saving ways to do so. In these situations parties to a conflict may both realize the need to make concessions, but neither may be willing to make the first concession for fear that this will make them look weak and damage their future reputation as a negotiator. Each party, as

Zartman and Touval note, "may feel that making concessions through a mediator is less harmful to its reputation and future bargaining position than conceding to the adversary in direct negotiations."[3]

Identifying these turning points, when third-party roles may be useful, is an important aspect of utilizing third-party interventions successfully. Most often such situations will cause the parties themselves to request the assistance of a third party to help them resolve their differences. However, the two disputants may not necessarily share the desire to accept mediation with equal enthusiasm. As Lall has pointed out, in disputes where the issues confront a country with status-quo-oriented goals against a revisionist state that seeks to change the status quo, the latter is more likely to favor the use of third parties than the former: "parties in possession are less receptive of third-party efforts than are parties who feel that such efforts are likely to result in a solution or adjustment more favorable to them than the continuation of the status quo."[4] At other times, however, a third party may intervene without being invited, either because it has some legal obligations to do so (such as when the United Nations enters into some disputes among its members at the request of the Security Council, as was the case when the Security Council tried to intervene to bring an end to years of heavy fighting between Iran and Iraq in 1988) or because it sees its own interests threatened by the conflict and seeks to head off escalation that might spread and put its own goals at risk (as when the United States assumed a mediating role after the 1973 war in the Middle East).

Once a conflict reaches the point where the parties wish to seek the assistance of a third party, there arise two logical questions: (1) who should be selected to perform the third-party role; and (2) what kind of role should that third party play in order to assist the parties to reach an agreement? The first question that arises about mediation is "who should be selected as a third party?" Traditionally, the answer to this question is that the third party should be neutral, someone acceptable to both disputing parties. As Fisher has noted, traditional thinking about negotiation goes so far as to believe that an "ideal mediator is seen as a kind of eunuch from Mars who happens to be temporarily available."[5] Clearly such individuals are very hard or impossible to find. Nevertheless, a neutral third party has many advantages in that he or she is believed by both parties to be fair and impartial. For example, Oran Young has noted that, "impartiality . . . would seem to be at the heart of successful intervention in many situations."[6] Young also observes: "a meaningful role for a third party will depend on the party's being perceived as an impartial participant [in the sense of having nothing to gain from aiding either protagonist and in the sense of being able to control any feelings of favoritism] in the eyes of the principal protagonists."[7]

In international negotiations, relatively impartial third parties may come from international organizations where a person's status or role, such as that of the U.N. secretary general, gives him or her a kind of neutrality. The influence of the leader of an international organization may be enhanced by the fact that his mediation is normally reinforced by the support of a substantial majority of the membership of the organization, and therefore of the relevant international community. Thus a mediator chosen by the U.N. Security Council or by a substantial majority of the General Assembly may be seen as not only operating on the basis of his or her personal prestige, but also as representing the will of a substantial majority of the states in the international community. For example, U.N. Secretary General Perez de Cuellar was able to persuade Iran and Iraq to accept U.N. Security Council Resolution 598 as a basis for ending their lengthy war in 1988.[8] Based on his experience in mediation undertaken within the framework of the United Nations, former Indian Ambassador Arthur Lall has concluded: "The influence or effectiveness of third parties in negotiation tends to increase when a plurality of states (and the Secretary-General of the United Nations and/or other [sic] designated person) constitute the third party, or have made explicit their support for the efforts of the third party."[9]

Alternatively, the third party may come from a country that is perceived as being neutral with respect to a particular dispute. Thus, Sweden has frequently been a source of mediators, especially in the Arab-Israeli disputes. In 1948 Count Folke Bernadotte was appointed by the United Nations to mediate following the end of the British mandate in Palestine and the proclamation of Israeli independence. Bernadotte was selected by the five permanent members of the U.N. Security Council on the recommendation of Secretary General Trygve Lie. He was the nephew of the Swedish king, head of the Swedish Red Cross, and well known internationally for his humanitarian work during and immediately after World War II.[10] These impressive credentials from a citizen of a neutral country made him appear to be an ideal mediator. Unfortunately, his efforts at mediation came to a tragic end when he was assassinated in Jerusalem on 17 September 1948 some four months after he took up his difficult assignment. Almost twenty years later another senior Swedish diplomat, Gunnar Jarring, was accepted by both Israel and its Arab neighbors as a mediator in the aftermath of the 1967 Six Day War in the Middle East. Jarring both represented a country that was not identified with either party in the Middle East and that also was formally neutral in the cold-war conflicts that partially lay behind the Middle East dispute. He also had considerable diplomatic experience both in the Middle East and in other U.N. missions, having served as an intermediary between India and Pakistan in the Kashmir dispute.[11]

Finally, the third party may be an individual whose personal background or whose role makes him or her above reproach in the eyes of the parties. For instance, Pope John Paul II was selected as a mediator between Argentina and Chile in their dispute over conflicting claims to territoriality over islands located in the Beagle Channel at the southern tip of South America. In both of these predominantly Catholic countries, the pope was seen as someone completely impartial to the partisan disputes between the two conflicting countries.[12]

Other analysts have not insisted so much on the absolute necessity of complete impartiality, but rather have stressed that a third party must be trusted by both of the parties to a dispute not to disregard their fundamental interests.[13] This view recognizes the reality that completely objective, dispassionate third parties are seldom or never available, and furthermore may not always be needed. Often the best that one can hope for is a third party that is not biased in the sense that she or he will not be willing to sacrifice the interests of one of the parties in favor of those of the other. Again as Fisher has noted: "Third parties can be judged on their respective merits, which include their ability, their interest in promoting a peaceful accommodation of the conflict, and their acceptability to the parties."[14]

Thus, it is often results that count more than form, and a third party may be acceptable to both parties to a dispute if she or he is believed to be able to assist the parties in finding a mutually beneficial solution to their conflict. There may even be times when a partisan third party can be advantageous, especially when the interests held by the third party can be beneficial to a negotiation. Third parties may have several different kinds of stakes in the outcome of an agreement. On the one hand, their primary stake may be just in reaching a settlement, since the potential escalation of the conflict undermines the interests of the third party. For example, the United States has long promoted a solution to the Arab-Israeli conflict because that conflict places a continuing strain on U.S. relations with Arab countries, with which the United States generally seeks a constructive relationship and on which it partially depends for its supply of oil. That particular interest does not so much push the United States to favor one side over the other, as much as it is a factor in encouraging it to promote a peaceful settlement of the dispute; reaching an agreement is generally more important for the United States than the specific terms of that agreement.

Yet even a partisan interest in the dispute does not necessarily disqualify someone from serving as a third party to try to aid the parties in conflict to resolve their dispute. For example, if one disputant may be required to make especially significant concessions in order to reach agreement, it may be useful to have a third party whom that party especially trusts (even if the third party might be thought to favor that party) simply because such a partisan third party may be in a better position than a perfectly neutral party to obtain those meaningful concessions.

Thus, U.S. Secretary of State Henry Kissinger was found to be an acceptable mediator between Israel and both Egypt and Syria after the 1973 war in the Middle East, even though he was widely perceived to be very pro-Israeli. But this fact alone made it possible for him to extract concessions from Israel that no one else could have obtained. And he could do so without ever running the risk that Israel would believe that he would sell out their most fundamental interests. The realization that he played this special role made him an acceptable mediator to the governments of both Egypt and Syria.[15]

Similarly, Algeria, though a Muslim country apparently closely tied to Iran, became acceptable to the United States in 1980 as a mediator between the United States and Iran over the Tehran embassy hostage crisis. In early November 1980 the Algerian ambassador in Washington approached the U.S. State Department to transmit an Iranian proposal to resolve the hostage crisis. Shortly thereafter, a U.S. team led by Under Secretary of State Warren Christopher went to Algiers to discuss these proposals and explain fully the U.S. position. For the next several months, the Algerian government acted as an intermediary to transmit messages between the two parties. The Algerians served simultaneously as constructive critics of the U.S. counterproposals and acted as an "honest broker" that could extract Iranian concessions without appearing to sacrifice the interests of the Islamic fundamentalist state. There can be little doubt that the skillful Algerian intermediaries, taking advantage of their initial position of trust in Tehran, were able to advise the United States on how to formulate an acceptable proposal, advocate acceptance of the main points of that proposal to the Iranian leaders, and assist in fashioning an acceptable compromise and persuading both parties to accept it.[16] As Gary Sick, advisor to the U.S. National Security Council on Iran during the Carter administration, concludes: "The Algerian team was everything one could hope mediators to be: discreet, intelligent, perceptive, persistent, skeptical, and inexhaustible. Their careful questioning of the successive U.S. position papers consistently improved and sharpened them. The team was skillful at presenting unpalatable messages to either side when necessary, and with very few exceptions their judgments proved accurate. When it was necessary to push, they pushed; when discretion called for them to hold back, they showed restraint."[17]

On the basis of these and other similar cases of mediation by nominally partisan third parties, Zartman and Touval conclude that "mediators do not have to be perceived as impartial in order to be acceptable or influential. Instead, acceptability is determined by power-political considerations—by the expected consequences of acceptance or rejection—not by perceptions of impartiality."[18]

A second distinction may be made between third parties that are relatively powerful and those that are relatively weak. Powerful third parties may be able to take advantage of their resources to promote agreement by making threats or promises to the parties. The powerful third party may be able to manipulate the interests of the parties in dispute to make them overlap, unlike someone who has no resources to introduce into the negotiations. It may be easier for a powerful third party to induce concessions by compensating the state that makes concessions with rewards provided outside of the negotiations or by providing guarantees that will make it difficult or impossible for the other party to exploit those concessions. For example, at the Camp David negotiations the United States offered military aid to Israel to help it defend itself against any Egyptian breach of the accords, while also providing additional assurances about more direct U.S. military aid should the fundamental security interests of Israel ever be threatened. On the other hand, there is frequently a danger that such powerful third parties may attempt to influence the outcome of the negotiation to serve their own national interests rather than the interests of the disputing parties. Indeed, some Israeli leaders were suspicious of U.S. Secretary of State Henry Kissinger's mediation after the 1973 Middle East war, believing that he sought concessions from Israel more in order to assure a continuous supply of oil to the United States and its allies than out of concern for Israeli security.[19]

Conversely, there are some arguments in favor of selecting third parties not so much on the basis of their power, but more on the basis of their moral or legal standing in the international community or by their widespread support from the major members of the international community as reflected in decisions made by international organizations. Power to manipulate an outcome may often be less important than the ability to facilitate the search process and help the parties arrive at efficient, mutually profitable agreements. This attribute may often accompany impartiality, though the two are not necessarily linked. However, together these two attributes of the third party both limit the kinds of intervening roles it can play, while removing any fear by the disputants that the third party will try to manipulate the outcomes for its own advantage. However, third parties that are less powerful will need to achieve sufficient status in the eyes of the parties so that their mediation will be taken seriously. This status may be based on some kind of moral authority (the pope's mediation of the Beagle Channel dispute between Chile and Argentina), on political position (the role of U.N. Secretary General Perez de Cuellar in mediating an end to the war between Iran and Iraq in 1988), on legal status (a famous international jurist or diplomat such as Count Bernadotte of Sweden in the Arab-Israeli conflict), or upon a record of past successful mediation (Gunnar Jarring in the Middle East).

A distinction has frequently been made between various kinds of third-party roles, including good offices, conciliation, arbitration, and mediation. The major distinction, however, falls between arbitration and mediation, since both good offices and conciliation may be viewed as special forms of mediation. The key difference between arbitration and mediation is that arbitration is a procedure in which the third party is asked to render a judgment about the settlement of the conflict, whereas in mediation the third party is requested to help the parties to the dispute reach agreement between themselves.

Arbitration may take the form of binding or nonbinding decisions. Binding arbitration is the procedure most frequently identified with the traditional legal settlement of disputes. International courts such as the International Court of Justices in the Hague, Netherlands, are often introduced to arbitrate disputes. In this instance, the arbitrator listens to the arguments of the two sides and then renders a decision that is binding on the parties, usually because they have agreed in advance to accept the decision issued by the arbitrator or because the arbitration is undertaken by a legal organ, such as a court, to which the parties have agreed in principle to submit their disputes. In the most general form of binding arbitration, this decision may favor the proposal of either of the two parties or fall somewhere in between. Since the arbitrator is empowered to impose a decision on the parties to a dispute, the very threat of taking a case to arbitration may provide the necessary incentive for the parties to reach an agreement between themselves. Thus, arbitration has the advantage of rendering a solution to the dispute that is relatively independent of the power of either disputant, and it may be an especially useful approach to conflict settlement when there are tight deadline pressures or when there are more or less objective criteria by which to judge a fair solution. This is useful for cases such as those that involve a dispute over the interpretation of principles of international law or when it entails technical issues such as disputes about pollution or financing.

On the other hand, conventional arbitration has several distinct disadvantages. It takes the strictly bargaining nature of the negotiation for granted, and seeks to find a solution somewhere within the bargaining space identified by the parties to the dispute. It usually precludes the possibility of seeking novel, inventive solutions to the problem that may upgrade common interests rather than settle between conflicting interests. In the jargon of bargaining theory, it is usually restricted primarily to settling claims for value rather than in creating value. Furthermore, there may be a natural tendency for arbitrators to look for fifty-percent solutions that more or less split the differences between the two parties. As noted in chapter 5, however, this kind of solution tends to give a larger share of the gains to the party with the most extravagant claims, while providing a disadvantage to the party that came to the negotiation with more reasonable claims. Or, alternatively, both parties may try to make extreme claims in order to seek unilateral advantage only to find that the effect of playing the same game is to move both sides toward extreme and rigid positions that are hard to reconcile. Following a single-play Prisoners' Dilemma logic, each seeks to make tough demands in order to gain a unilateral advantage from the fifty-percent solution. When both do this simultaneously, the negotiators move further apart and become more rigidly entrenched in these extreme positions. This kind of behavior can naturally have a chilling effect on negotiations.

In order to try to overcome some of these disadvantages of the typical model of arbitration, one may employ what Stevens has called final offer arbitration.[20] In this method, both parties must submit to the arbitrator their best and final offer. In this case, the arbitrator must choose one or the other of the two offers presented, and is not permitted to choose any other solution between these two offers. This procedure gives the two parties the greatest incentive to make the most reasonable offer possible. If one party makes an extreme offer while the other makes a reasonable one, then the arbitrator is most likely to select the latter. In this way, the procedure will usually benefit the reasonable party and cause the party that seeks extreme unilateral gains to lose. In most cases, this procedure may actually force both parties toward such reasonable offers that they may approach convergence even before the arbitrator must decide. Indeed, the entire logic of the situation, in which each party tries to be just a little more reasonable than the other, may involve such complex strategic calculations that the two parties actually prefer to return to bilateral negotiations in an effort to resolve their differences quickly. As Pruitt and Rubin conclude: "disputants often prefer to reach agreement on their own rather than take their chances on the third-party's judgment. Final-offer arbitration, then, is a procedure designed to create so aversive a situation that disputants will reach agreement of their own accord rather than expose themselves to the vagaries of the final-offer procedure."[21]

Arbitration may also be nonbinding, in that the arbitrator's judgment is simply a recommendation to the parties for a settlement. While this may not be as successful in overcoming some conflicts as binding arbitration, it also reflects the reality that decisions that are clearly unacceptable to one of the parties, even if taken by an arbitrator, are not likely to be implemented. Yet if the decision is in the form of a recommendation that each party accepts voluntarily, they are more likely to feel a real commitment to fulfill the terms of that agreement. The advantages of arbitration stem from the fact that it takes the actual decision about a settlement out of the hands of the disputants. The fact that it represents, in at least some form, an imposed solution usually makes it less satisfactory than an agreement that the parties have reached themselves. It is largely for this reason that mediation is increasingly becoming the preferred third-party role in many conflicts, including international ones.

A third strategy, that has largely been tried in domestic legal settings and not in international relations, is to pursue mediation for a specified period of time, and then, if the parties have not yet reached agreement themselves, the mediator may become an arbitrator and render a judgment about the conflict. Usually the approaching deadline and the threat of arbitration forces the parties to reach a solution themselves rather than losing control of the solution and putting it completely into the hands of the arbitrator. Although this might be a promising avenue for further investigation in international negotiations, at present the most frequently utilized third-party role is mediation alone, where the third party aids the disputants to reach agreement themselves. Therefore, the remainder of our discussion will focus on mediation.

Mediation is often presented as a process in which a third party seeks to help resolve the underlying causes of a conflict as opposed to settling a specific dispute. In such a situation, John Burton and his followers have distinguished between disputes, defined as situations that are negotiable, and conflicts, which cannot be negotiated because they "relate to ontological human needs that cannot be compromised."[22] These latter conflicts require analytical problem solving with the following steps, according to Burton: "First there must be a careful analysis of the parties and issues. Second it is necessary to bring those two parties whose relationships are most affected into a facilitated interactive situation in which relationships are analyzed in depth. Other parties and issues are dealt with in due course in the same way. At this stage no proposals are entertained, nor is there any bargaining or negotiation. When there is an agreed definition of the problem, and a full assessment of the costs of existing policies based on a knowledge of responses to the denial of human needs, there can be exploration of positive outcomes."[23]

Burton and his followers argue that conflict resolution requires mediators to do more than resolve specific cases of conflicts. Their task is enlarged to include removing the underlying sources of the conflict and creating conditions for cooperative relationships to develop.[24] The presence of a third party may enhance the likelihood that fundamental resolution of deep-seated conflicts may occur, but it may also be useful and effective even in assisting the more mundane process of finding negotiated solutions to problems and disputes that often set actors in international relations into conflict with one another.

At a minimum, the introduction of a mediator turns a bilateral negotiation into a trilateral one. As Touval and Zartman have noted, in this case, "the outcome of the contest may be determined by the formation of a coalition of two against one."[25] The parties may try to win over the mediator to support their side in the dispute and garner a winning coalition. The mediator will presumably try to resist being brought into such a partisan coalition for fear of endangering his or her position of neutrality. However, at times, especially in asymmetrical negotiations, the mediator may believe that it is desirable to throw weight behind the weaker party in order create a level playing field.

Of course, the kind of mediator—whether neutral or partisan, powerful or powerless—will affect the kind of mediating roles that the mediator can play. The multiple roles that a mediator can play may be presented along a continuum ranging from relatively modest roles, that might best be played by relatively weak and neutral mediators, to roles that entail a much higher level of involvement and that probably only can be performed by powerful and perhaps even partisan mediators. Altogether, I would suggest that there are five major kinds of roles that mediators can play in international negotiations.

The first role is the mediator as process facilitator. This kind of mediator generally tries to create conditions that are conducive to reaching agreement. In the traditional jargon of international law, this procedure is often referred to as the provision of good offices. Good offices mediation means that a mediator offers services to the disputants to help them negotiate in an environment that is conducive to reaching agreement. This kind of mediator usually pays especially close attention to the atmospherics of negotiations, including providing good facilities, a workable schedule, and a pleasant environment in which to work. Providing a venue for the parties to meet and the logistical support for their negotiations may be an important feature of the work of the facilitator.

The facilitator may also play a modest role in trying to improve communications among the disputants. For example, the facilitator may listen to the positions of both sides and try to determine whether or not available bargaining space exists. In this way, the process facilitator helps to separate negotiable from nonnegotiable issues. Thus, he or she helps to set the agenda for the negotiations, influences which issues will be tackled, and, among the issues to be discussed, influences the order in which they will be taken up. Thus, the facilitator may arrange to deal with issues first that are easier to settle, leaving tough issues to the end. When bargaining space has been located on particular issues, he or she may help to clarify the range of that space and help the parties locate a fair agreement somewhere in the center. If bargaining space does not exist, he or she may try to suggest ways of creating bargaining space, such as possible linkages and tradeoffs between nonnegotiable issues that, when combined, may produce negotiable packages of issues. Or, if that fails, he or she may at least try to help find face saving ways to end the negotiation with as little residual hard feeling as possible. He or she may try to perform various facilitative leadership roles, including those suggested previously in chapter 8. If inspiration is required, he or she may try to become an affect leader who encourages and exhorts the negotiators to reach agreement, such as by warning them of the dire consequences of their failure to reach agreement. Or he or she may become a task leader by trying to turn more emotional disputes into business-like discussions focused directly on the issues, discouraging resort to rhetoric and name-calling and insisting on efficient procedures for the conduct of the negotiations.

In short, the process facilitator exerts little direct influence on the parties or on the substance of the agreement; his or her role rather is restricted to improving the process so that the parties can reach agreement and deal with disagreement in as amiable and business-like of an atmosphere as possible.

The second role is the facilitator of communication, compromise, and convergence. This mediating role is employed most often in negotiations occurring within the general framework of traditional bargaining. It may be recalled here that the major problems encountered in concession-convergence bargaining tend to involve impasses resulting from the reluctance of either party to make the first concessions or from their desire to make the first and firmest commitments. This may be due to the breakdown of communications between the parties or it may result from a fear of having concessions exploited by the other party. In order to avoid appearing weak or an easy victim of exploitation, each party tries to appear firm and unbending, often making premature or excessively rigid commitments to unreasonable positions. The role of the mediator, then, is to facilitate mutual and simultaneous flexibility. This mediator may begin by attempting to clarify the fundamental interests of the two parties as well as their limits to acceptable agreement (their BATNAs); that is, the mediator may have to provide the channels to help the parties to communicate basic information that normally needs to be shared for negotiations to be successful, but where full and open sharing of information may otherwise produce fears of possible exploitation. Most often this may be done through improving face-to-face communications, but there may be circumstances in which it is better to keep the parties separated and for the mediator to serve as the major channel of direct communications between them. The latter method was used by U.S. Secretary of State Henry Kissinger after the 1973 Middle East war. Kissinger engaged in a shuttle diplomacy between Israel and Egypt and between Israel and Syria, since in both cases the intense hostilities following the war made direct, interpersonal communications likely to lead to an exchange of rhetoric and retribution rather than to constructive negotiations.

Once communications lines have been opened, the next obstacle may often be the mutual fear of making initial concessions, which will likely be perceived by others as a sign of weakness. This often leads the party that makes the first concession to become an object of exploitation where others try to take advantage of this perceived weakness by toughening their demands. The typical consequence of these joint behaviors is that both parties become rigidly attached to their positions. In order to overcome this fear of making initial concessions, the mediator may try to create a private agreement to announce simultaneous concessions, or at least to assure each party that their concessions will be reciprocated promptly. The mediator may convey unofficial and conditional word of a willingness to concede between the two parties, or may withhold information about concessions made by one party until counterconcessions have been elicited from the other. Thus, for example, during his step-by-step diplomacy between Israel and Syria in 1974, Henry Kissinger secured a series of Israeli concessions from the Israelis that would have returned most of the Syrian city of Quneitra to their control, but he held back some of these concessions so that he would be sure of having additional ones available to deliver on later trips. He found that a partial presentation of Israeli concessions was sufficient to obtain at least some counterconcessions from the Syrians, and he wanted to have additional concessions available in order to further induce Syrian flexibility in subsequent stages of the negotiations.[26]

Once mutual concessions have begun, the mediator tries to facilitate a process of reciprocal (or tit-for-tat) changes in positions, leading toward convergence. The mediator tries to see that neither party exploits concessions of the other by responding to flexibility with intransigence. She or he may try to convey concessions by one party to the other as if they were proposals of the mediator rather than concessions extracted from the opponent. This may help the conceding party save face, and it may make the proposals easier to accept than if they appeared to be coming from the opponent. Thus, for example, in the shuttle diplomacy in the Middle East, Kissinger presented Egyptian President Sadat with a map of the Sinai desert showing the disengagement line proposed by Israel as if it were his own proposal, thereby gaining the acceptance of the Egyptian leader. Sadat found it a good deal easier to concede to the U.S. secretary of state than to concede to the Israeli enemies.

Thus, the mediator may encourage softer bargaining styles by both parties, especially frequent and reciprocal concessions, and may try to dissuade both from making inflexible commitments. In short, the facilitator of communications, concessions, and convergence tries to see to it that parties engaging in a traditional bargaining process use flexible means to achieve integrative benefits from mutually acceptable agreements, rather than seeking individual gain at the expense of the other through predominantly distributive bargaining.

The third mediating role is that of facilitator of cognitive change. Rather than trying to persuade the parties to change their positions along an issue dimension, in this case the mediator tries to induce the parties to change their preferences themselves through seeing the problem in a new light. This kind of mediation is likely to be most important in those negotiations where stalemate seems to be caused more by different perceptions of the same issues, misunderstandings, or other psychological or personality factors, rather than by conflicts of interest. Of course, even where there are conflicts of interest, the mediator may help the parties to reframe the issues so that the conflict seems less stark or where it is no longer an insuperable obstacle to agreement. Within the traditional terminology of international law, this kind of mediation is often referred to as conciliation, a process in which the mediator tries "to modify the parties' images of each other and to influence them to make concessions by clarifying to each his opponent's views and the bargaining situation that both face."[27]

The primary objective of the facilitator of cognitive change is to create a problem-solving atmosphere in the negotiations within which creative search can take place to look for new solutions to the problem. This mediator will encourage the participants not to deal with one another as opponents, but rather as members of a group seeking solutions to common problems. In order to do this, the mediator may assist the parties in identifying one another's real, underlying interests by distinguishing between these and largely rhetorical positions or posturing. Conceptually, this requires that the parties believe that they are not mutual opponents, but that the enemy is the joint problem that must be solved. Rather than perceiving one another in the inverted mirror image format so often associated with interpersonal conflict, they should see one another as partners in trying to work together to solve a problem that threatens the interests of both.

This may require a substantial cognitive change for the parties immersed in long-standing conflicts to step out of the mode of perceiving one another as enemies and instead viewing each other as partners. Their hostile and angry feelings toward one another must be converted into more constructive motivations to work together rather than against one another. Psychological pressures toward consistency will almost always induce individuals who perceive one another as personal enemies to see their positions and interests as being incompatible as well. Once these emotional and evaluative components of their images change, their need to maintain consistency with their cognitive beliefs may help them see the possibility that they share joint interests with one another. This kind of cognitive change may be extremely hard for a mediator to bring about, especially when conflicts have existed for a long period of time and when they take on a deep, emotional intensity. Yet in many conflict situations this cognitive change may be sufficient to open the way for agreement where none seemed to exist previously.

Finally, this mediator may assist the parties to develop empathy for one another, to try to understand the conflict from each other's point of view. In this instance, the parties must not only recognize the possibility that they have some shared interests, but they must also gain some appreciation for the private interests of the other as well; they must realize that a stable agreement cannot be reached unless and until the other party's fundamental interests are realized and protected. Thus, it is necessary to get into the shoes of the other person, or even into his or her political or bureaucratic role, to see why the other person perceives the world the way she or he does. As noted in chapter 8, one technique for developing this kind of empathy is role reversal, in which parties explain the positions and interests of one party to the satisfaction of the other. Or one may act out the role of the other party in a simulated negotiation exercise to try to understand her or his position better.

As Christopher Mitchell has pointed out, there are a cluster of third-party intervention techniques known as problem-solving workshops, in which techniques such as role reversal and other problem-solving methods may be tried. These typically involve trying to get parties to a dispute engaged in private, informal interactions in which they explore their conflicts, try to reconceptualize them as a shared problem, and then seek to identify solutions that will provide alternatives to coercion by generating a kind of self-sustaining cooperative relationship between the parties. Usually these workshops have a number of characteristics in common, summarized by Mitchell as follows:

> They are seen as processes through which informal, powerless, and—usually—academic third parties can affect the course of protracted and deep-rooted conflict, by providing parties to such conflicts with opportunities to interact in an analytical rather than coercive manner as well as giving scholarly insights into the parties' mutual predicament. The main thrust of the use of such innovative approaches has always tended to be the practical one of bringing about positive, conflict-reducing effects on conflictual relationships, which have resisted the efforts of those using more traditional means of reducing or resolving conflicts, such as formal negotiation, mediation, or conciliation.[28]

However, negotiators are generally reluctant to engage in such workshops or try exercises like role reversal, especially since they are afraid of revealing information that might be exploited by the other, or of granting some degree of legitimacy to the positions advocated by the other. This is usually an unwarranted concern, however, since successful role reversal does not require that one come to agree with all of the beliefs and negotiating positions of the other party. It is just necessary for one to understand those positions accurately in terms that are meaningful to the other. However, trying to step inside the shoes of the other may lead to the belief in various quarters that one has gone over to accept those views as true and good. Domestic audiences, especially bureaucratic and political opponents, may perceive role reversal as the equivalent of selling out to the enemy. And the other side may believe that once its positions have been understood, the first party will automatically come to agree with those positions. Therefore, the party may act as if there are no longer any differences, and may pocket the understanding expressed by the other side as if she or he had won the debate.

However, the fact that one understands the position of another, and maybe even empathizes with it within the context of the other's position, does not mean that one accepts this understanding as the exclusive basis of an agreement. One may understand the other party's position and continue to disagree with it. In other words, role reversal does not hope to eliminate disagreements, only reduce misunderstandings. However, the failure to make this distinction often causes negotiators to resist participating in any kind of role reversal or problem-solving exercise for fear of being trapped into admitting the legitimacy of the opponent's point of view.

In order to resolve this inherent dilemma of role reversal, the mediator may serve as a neutral referee in such an exercise. If the mediator can encourage the parties to reverse roles, and oversee this process to assure that neither side takes advantage of the other, then it might actually be of some practical value to the negotiators in clarifying their real differences. The mediator can keep the distinction between understanding and acceptance clear in the minds of both parties, and may see to it that neither party attempts to take advantage of improved understanding to obtain a tactical advantage in bargaining. If the parties are able to engage in role reversal as a purely informal and unofficial activity under the guidance of the mediator, they may gain greater insight into one another's positions without fear of exploitation. Once each understands the issue differently, especially as it is viewed by the other, then problem-solving techniques of conflict resolution become easier to adopt, and the conflicts become easier to resolve on their intrinsic merits without the interference of extraneous emotional fears and hostility or cognitive misperceptions and misunderstandings.

Of course, the reluctance of actual negotiators to engage in the kinds of techniques that are likely to promote fundamental cognitive and attitudinal change makes it difficult to evaluate the effectiveness of these approaches in resolving actual international conflicts. Thus, while there are good theoretical reasons to believe that these approaches may be desirable, especially when undertaken by a third party, and there is some, albeit limited, experimental evidence to support these arguments, there is scant concrete evidence from the real world of international relations.

Perhaps the best example of the use of these kinds of techniques in recent international relations may be found in the mediation by Norway, especially by Foreign Minister Johan Jørgen Holst, between Israel and the Palestine Liberation Organization (PLO) over the disputed territories of the Gaza and West Bank. These negotiations were conducted in secret to prevent opposition from developing internally within either party, and they generally took place in the Norwegian countryside. In the words of Foreign Minister Holst, the discussions took place in an atmosphere "conducive to human contact, conviviality, and solidarity of effort":

> Furthermore, the talks involved a small group of highly professional and skilled people who developed a degree of collegiality and common commitment to a common end, which enabled the participants to become friends and view the problem of either side as shared problems. Both sides recognized that they were engaged in two interacting levels of negotiations: the direct negotiations between the parties at the tables in Norway, and the negotiations between the parties and their respective masters at home. The interplay of the two levels sometimes caused frustration, irritation, and suspicion, but it also contributed to confidence building through a process of intense interaction and mutual understanding of a shared predicament.[29]

The process employed by Holst and his Norwegian colleagues illustrates how informal, problem-oriented work out of the glare of publicity can help parties such as Israel and the PLO, locked for decades in one of the most bitter disputes of the second half of the twentieth century, modify their images of one another and of their predicament so as to enhance mutual understanding. On the basis of their new understanding of their joint problem, they were able to build sufficient confidence to enable them to take the risks that were necessary to begin to resolve their intense, deeply rooted conflict.

A fourth mediating role is the formulator, someone who will help the parties to invent new solutions to their problems. As Touval and Zartman suggest: "Redefining the issues in conflict, or finding a formula for its resolution or management is the key to its termination, with the parties frequently needing help in finding a solution hidden in the morass of bad relationships or in constructing a solution from the pieces of the conflict itself. *The mediator as a formulator* helps the two parties help themselves, by tactful, sympathetic, accurate, straightforward prodding and suggestion."[30]

Arthur Lall, an experienced Indian diplomat, has suggested that

third-party intervention is most likely to take the form of proposing solutions to the dispute when the parties find that their dispute has become so emotionally charged that face-to-face negotiations are not only
doomed to fail, but may even enhance mutual hatred. Beyond this threshold of emotional involvement these psychological blocks make it difficult or impossible for the parties to propose constructive solutions
themselves: "Particularly when national emotions are strongly aroused
. . . the best solution—direct discussions between the parties—becomes
impracticable. In those circumstances a mediator, conciliator, or good
officer becomes more than an intermediary. He takes on the substantive
function of a maker of proposals or suggestions."[31]

Under these conditions the mediator may function by encouraging
the parties to brainstorm, to seek novel ways of looking at the problem.
He or she may also listen carefully to the parties as they describe their
vital interests and basic needs, and then the mediator may take the initiative to propose new solutions that may satisfy those needs and interests. He or she attempts to work within the formula creation stage of
negotiations as identified by Zartman and Berman, and may even propose formulas intended to bridge the differences between parties to a
negotiation. The mediator may persuade the parties to negotiate different issues within the same negotiation as a package rather than sequentially, one-by-one. The mediator may try to influence the substantive
agenda of the negotiations. As Pruitt and Rubin have observed, two principles should affect how a third party seeks to structure a negotiation
agenda: "One is that the sequence should run from more general to more
specific issues if at all possible—or from formula to detail, in Zartman's
. . . terminology. This allows the parties to develop a road map before
setting out on the difficult trip through the welter of specific issues. The
other is that, when there is a choice, easier issues should be tackled earlier in the agenda. Success on these issues generates a running start, a
kind of momentum that should carry over to the more intractable later
issues and make them seem more amenable to problem solving."[32]

The process through which the mediator develops and proposes
formulas may take the form of identifying ways to aggregate issues,
creating new packages of issues through trade-offs, suggesting ways to
disaggregate or fractionate issues in order to find negotiable agreements
that may not be evident at first glance, or inventing formulas based on
an altogether new way of looking at the problem under negotiations. In
all of these cases, the mediator is actively inventing a new formula, proposing new options not previously considered by either party. Unlike
the three previous mediating roles, the mediator is no longer a more or
less passive third party trying to help the two parties to the conflict find
their own solution to the problem. Rather the mediator has become sufficiently active so as to take the initiative in proposing solutions to the

problem. After listening to the two parties and learning about their needs and interests, the mediator tries to advance solutions that will satisfy both sets of needs and interests to the fullest extent possible under the circumstances. The mediator will then try to persuade both parties to accept the proposed solution to their dispute. He or she becomes an advocate for a specific solution, and tries to persuade the parties in noncoercive ways to accept the proposed solution. Furthermore, the mediator is no longer concerned solely or primarily with the process of negotiation; rather he or she plays a role here in responding to the content of the negotiations and shaping the substance of the eventual agreement.

One interesting variant of this latter role occurs when the mediator serves as the drafter of what Fisher has called a "single-negotiating-text."[33] Fisher notes that this sort of strategy was used by U.S. President Jimmy Carter and Secretary of State Cyrus Vance when mediating between Israeli Prime Minister Menachem Begin and Egyptian President Anwar Sadat at Camp David in 1978. In this procedure, the mediator keeps the parties separated, except for social activities. After listening to both sides separately, the mediator then drafts a proposed text of agreement that he submits to the two parties for their criticism. As Fisher notes: "It is much easier for a party to criticize a draft than it is to make a concession."[34] Furthermore, it is easier to make a concession in private to the mediator than it is to concede openly to the other side. The mediator then listens to these criticisms, redrafts the agreement, and resubmits it to the two parties for their comments and criticisms. This process continues over and over again until the two parties are finally able to agree on the same text, a process that required twenty-three different drafts in the Camp David negotiations. Once the draft has been accepted by both sides, then they may meet face-to-face to formally embrace the final document.

This approach may often be superior to the typical negotiating process in which each party proposes a text, and then each must make concessions to the other in order to resolve the differences between the two. Once a text has been written down it is harder for a party to concede, so separate texts usually tend to create rigidity in negotiations. By contrast, when the mediator proposes that the two parties work on one joint text from the beginning, the negotiation no longer focuses on how to reconcile two competing drafts, but rather turns into a exercise in drafting a common text that serves the interests and needs of both parties. Where there are specific disagreements, alternative texts may be inserted between brackets to be resolved at a later stage in the negotiations. However, this should not be done too frequently, as a single text full of bracketed alternatives may be almost as divisive as working from two completely separate texts, and each bracketed item may become a subject for distributive bargaining in the later stages of the negotiation. The single text approach is most likely to be effective when the mediator takes the initiative in drafting a proposed solution and tries to persuade both to accept his draft, while being sensitive to their criticisms and responding accordingly through redrafting of the proposal. And in response to these mediating efforts, it is typically easier for the disputing parties to be flexible in the conduct of the negotiation.

A fifth and final role for the mediator is that of manipulator, which requires that the mediator use leverage and introduce "resources of power, influence, and persuasion that can be brought to bear on the parties to move them to agreement."[35] This is a role that can only be played by a powerful mediator, and is more likely to be played by a partisan mediator or one who has an interest at stake in the outcome of the negotiations. In this case, the mediator becomes an active participant, almost assuming the role of another party to the negotiations. This active participation may take many forms. The manipulative mediator may be in a special position to be able to (1) control the timing and sequencing of concessions and other negotiating moves; (2) control information available to the parties; (3) exert a direct influence to move the negotiations forward in directions favored by the mediator; and (4) manipulate the international environment in ways that may affect the outcome of the negotiations.

First, the mediator may affect the timing of negotiations by deciding when conditions are ripe to open negotiation and how long negotiations will last. The mediator may establish deadlines that require the parties to reach agreement within a fixed period of time. Deadlines, of course, create pressure for rapid agreement. If they are imposed too early in the process, they may make a negotiation seem intractable and force negotiators to give up before a serious effort has been made to find agreement. Or even if agreement is found, deadlines frequently cause parties to reach outcomes that are inefficient or suboptimal in the sense that, with more time, the parties might have found better agreements that would have produced more positive benefits for both. At the same time, negotiating without deadlines may allow talks to continue almost indefinitely. Neither party may feel pressure to make concessions or invent and propose new solutions to their problem; both may hold out, hoping that the other will concede before they do. However, when good solutions appear to the mediator to be within sight, the imposition of a deadline may facilitate wrapping up an emerging agreement rather than delaying in the hopes for a better or even a perfect result. The mediator may affect the outcome by utilizing this power to open and close negotiations, and control the sequence of interactions in between.

Second, the manipulative mediator may be in a special position to be able to control information. By setting oneself in the position of influencing the flow of communications between the parties, the mediator may be able to add or subtract information about the issues under negotiation that may influence the outcome. The mediator may also use secrecy to prevent domestic or other international pressures from being brought to bear that might influence the outcome. Thus, the Algerian mediation between the United States and Iran over the hostage crisis in 1980–81 was kept secret from both publics, where domestic pressures might have prevented the negotiations from succeeding.

Third, mediators may influence the preferences of the parties to the dispute directly, raising the costs of nonagreement or increasing the rewards of agreement. In both cases, this may cause the point of minimum acceptable agreement, or the BATNA, to change in ways that favor reaching agreement. The mediator may offer threats and promises, sticks and carrots, in order to manipulate the preferences of the conflicting parties in such a way as to create overlapping bargaining space and the possibility of agreement. The mediator may engage in actions that make the status quo even more unacceptable to the disputing parties, thereby pressuring them to come to agreement. Or the actions may be directed solely against one party that appears to be hindering progress. For example, in support of Kissinger's Middle East mission, U.S. President Gerald Ford threatened to reassess U.S. Middle East policy and cut off military and economic aid to Israel in a letter sent to Israeli leaders on 21 March 1975 unless Israel showed greater flexibility in negotiations with Egypt.[36] The fact that the mediating country possesses substantial resources means it will be perceived as having the capability to provide rewards to the parties if they reach agreement on terms advocated by the third party or carry out punishments if they fail to agree. Alternatively, pressure may be exerted indirectly, through parties outside the negotiations. For example, the mediator may exert pressure on an ally of one of the parties, as Kissinger did in 1974 when he sought to put pressure on Syria through contacts with President Boumedienne of Algeria, a radical leader of the Arab states.[37] Even more indirectly, Kissinger reportedly channeled aid through the Central Intelligence Agency to the Kurdish rebels in Iraq, which in turn reduced Iraqi capability to interfere with a Syrian settlement with Israel.[38]

Fourth, the mediator may try to manipulate the external environment in order to enhance the prospects for agreement. For example, in order to promote moderation on the part of Egypt in the negotiations with Israel in 1973–75, Kissinger tried to strengthen the two pillars of moderation in the region, King Faisal of Saudi Arabia and the Shah of Iran. Furthermore, the 1973 Arab-Israeli War had enhanced Arab solidarity, at least for the short run, and that in turn increased Saudi Arabian influence (and indirectly U.S. influence) over Egypt and Syria after the war. Kissinger hoped that King Faisal and the Shah would exert a positive influence on Egypt and Syria, and promise them support from within the region in order for the governments of President Sadat and President Hafez al-Assad to be able to take the risks required in making peace with Israel.[39] Thus, a powerful mediating state not only can influence the parties to the negotiation directly, but it can also affect and even modify the structure of the international environment in ways that may promote agreement when it serves the larger interests of the mediator.

In summary, I have indicated that there are many different roles that a mediator can play in assisting parties to resolve conflicts, ranging from relatively passive roles like the facilitator to very active and involved roles like the manipulator. In virtually all cases, third parties can be especially helpful in directing negotiations away from a zero-sum conflict model toward a more problem-solving orientation. Mediation theory is not really different from the larger theories of negotiation within which it is imbedded, but it does suggest an important tool that may be used to affect the process and to make better use of the tools already available to diplomats in bilateral negotiations. When stalemates result especially from emotional hostility, misunderstanding, misperception, and a dearth of new ideas, the third party may be able to assist the disputants to overcome impasses and resolve their differences successfully and creatively.

Considering its potential utility in overcoming impasses, it may be somewhat surprising that third-party involvement is not utilized more often in international negotiations. Although many successful efforts at mediation have been employed in recent years to reduce or resolve burning international conflicts, there still remains something of a stigma attached to introducing an outsider into an international dispute. This may be especially the case when one party has more capabilities than the other or when one has less to lose from a stalemate (such as when it benefits from the continuation of the status quo); the party with the upper hand may prefer to avoid creating the level playing field that a third party may favor, but from which its opponent may benefit more. The desire to seek greater relative gains in comparison with the other party may override the desire to find solutions that will provide even higher absolute benefits for both parties. Since a third party can generally enter a dispute only when both disputants agree, this may lead a party that believes that it can win from distributive bargaining to refuse to accept a third party.

Often the only way to overcome this striving for greater relative gains compared to the opponent is the overwhelming likelihood that stalemate will produce significant mutual losses. It is for this reason that the stalemate must frequently endure for a long time and also begin to hurt the more powerful or status-quo party, as well as the weaker and more revisionist party, before the former will agree to accept third-party intervention. Unfortunately, this often causes conflicts to become even more bitter and opportunities for resolution of the conflict to become more difficult to uncover or even to be missed altogether. Even if the conflict is eventually resolved in a satisfactory way, at a minimum both parties may suffer substantial costs due to the lengthy stalemate.

Insofar as the parties to conflicts recognize that they are essentially caught in situations with cross pressures toward cooperation and conflict with their opponents, they may also come to recognize the essential validity of the lessons of the repeated Prisoners' Dilemma. By maintaining stalemate, they create situations where both parties lose over the long run. At the same time, they may not be capable of advancing toward mutually beneficial positions for fear that one of them will take advantage of the temptations inherent in that situation to seek unilateral benefit at the expense of the other, in effect to win the negotiation. Sometimes the introduction of a third party may be one of the most effective and efficient ways of enabling the parties to make this transition from an essentially competitive, zero-sum orientation toward a more cooperative, positive-sum orientation, even while operating as always within the essentially mixed motive nature of international negotiations. By reducing the likelihood, however, that one party can exploit the other and seek unilateral gains, third parties may play an increasingly important role in enabling parties involved in international disputes to upgrade common interests and seek more mutually beneficial solutions to the problems that confront them in our highly interdependent international system.

Chapter 13

Multilateral Negotiations

In this chapter, I relax the assumption that negotiations are taking place primarily between two parties, perhaps with a third party as a go-between. Instead I am going to look at negotiations that are truly multilateral in scope. Multilateral negotiations involve three or more essentially independent parties with at least three different sets of interests and preferences about the outcome. The parties seek a general solution to their problem that more or less applies to all. As John Gerard Ruggie has noted, the adjective multilateral refers to institutional forms of interaction where the goal is the coordination of behavior "among three or more states on the basis of generalized principles of conduct."[1]

Although all multilateral negotiations will be considered together, there are important qualitative differences between different kinds of multilateral negotiations. On the one hand, multilateral negotiations may involve only relatively small groups of states negotiating together, perhaps coming from a single region of the globe as was the case in the Central American peace negotiations among the five states of that region. On the other hand, multilateral negotiations may entail participation by large numbers of states from all regions of the globe. The large global conferences organized by the United Nations, such as the 1992 conference in Rio de Janeiro on the Environment and Development, serve as typical examples. Clearly the size and diversity of background of the participants in these large global conferences and the difficulty of reaching consensus among the 180 states belonging to the United Nations (as of 1993) create negotiations that are quite different in character from more limited and focused negotiations among a smaller number of parties. Despite this distinction, most multilateral negotiations share certain features in common that distinguish them from bilateral negotiations, and I shall concentrate on some of these distinctive features in this chapter.

It is important to note at the outset that the topic of multilateral negotiations is one of the least developed areas in negotiation theory. Although a vast literature has developed in recent decades on theories

244

of bilateral negotiations, much of which has been surveyed in the previous chapters, many of the assumptions underlying contemporary negotiation theories do not work well in the multilateral case. Thus, the majority of work on multilateral negotiation has taken the form of anecdotal case studies. This is particularly unfortunate since so many negotiations at the international level are multilateral in scope and so many essential issues can be dealt with best in a multilateral context. Therefore, it is essential that negotiation theorists devote greater attention to developing better theories about the distinctly multilateral aspects of the negotiation process.

Although a great deal of attention has been devoted to the growing frequency of multilateral negotiations in recent years, there is nothing new about multilateral negotiations in history. In the early nineteenth century the Congress of Vienna, and the concert system that it created, provides a classic example of multilateral diplomacy that lasted more or less intact for several decades and continued to influence international relations virtually up to the beginning of World War I. After World War II and the onset of the cold war, attention of the international community seemed to shift more toward negotiations between the nuclear superpowers and their blocs, and the attention of theorists of international negotiation also focused on this centrally important bilateral case. Yet, at the regional level, and within all forms of international organizations, multilateral negotiations have been playing an increasingly important role in the last several decades and deserve still greater attention within the post-cold-war international context.

This chapter will explore the essential differences between multilateral negotiations and the bilateral norm. In some cases, it will suggest that there are real differences of fundamental structure between these two categories of negotiations, whereas in other cases the differences are largely matters of degree. In all instances, this chapter highlights the differences between the two forms of negotiation, perhaps at the risk of overstating them, and then suggests some of the ways in which multilateral negotiations may be managed to produce agreements that purport to serve the collective interests of most or all of their participants.

SOME DISTINCTIVE FEATURES OF MULTILATERAL NEGOTIATIONS

Complexity

As indicated in the previous chapters, most theories of bilateral negotiation focus upon two relatively rational actors who have different (if not always inverse) preferences in a mixed motive situation, and seek to resolve those differences through bargaining. Even in the more sophisticated approaches, when two parties engage in various forms of problem-solving behavior, perhaps with the aid of a third party, the relationship involves essentially a single two-way dialogue between the parties. Unfortunately, the situation is often much more complex when we turn to the analysis of multilateral negotiations. Indeed, since Winham's treatment of multilateral negotiations in 1977, complexity has generally been considered to be the defining characteristic of multilateral negotiations.[2] The fact that there are many parties and issues naturally enhances complexity. There are numerous aspects to this complexity.

First, the identification of appropriate criteria for evaluating an outcome becomes much more complicated in the multilateral case. It is often hard enough for two parties to identify the range of available bargaining space on any given issue and locate a point that may serve as a fair and optimal solution, even though that may be depicted in two-dimensional space. This is especially serious when there are multiple issues and/or multiple outcomes, which can lead to multiple preferences about which outcomes are favored. With the inclusion of each additional party holding different preferences with respect to the outcome, one must add an additional dimension in n-dimensional space to the simple bargaining model. Although such points might be theoretically possible to calculate mathematically if all of the preferences could be quantified, most international negotiators do not operate in this fashion. They usually find it increasingly difficult to conceive of solutions that are universally acceptable, optimal, and fair at the same time. As the number of dimensions increases within which solutions must be located, these factors become increasingly difficult for even the most sophisticated set of negotiators to visualize. Beyond three dimensions, it is no longer possible to depict the graph in Euclidean space, and consensus becomes increasingly difficult to locate. In the technical language of game theory, this may mean that there is no "Condorcet" winner, that is one outcome that dominates all others in the sense that in a series of pairwise comparisons it always wins and is never defeated by any other alternative.[3] Thus, there may be no clear solution that satisfies the preferences of all parties simultaneously.

The result is often that multilateral negotiations proceed in a trial and error fashion, employing an inductive search strategy as negotiators grope about and float trial balloons concerning various possible agreements until finding one that seems acceptable to most parties. And when such a consensus is found, it is typically more difficult to persuade negotiators to continue the process further in search of superior (in the sense of approaching Pareto-Optimality) or fairer, more equitable solutions than is the case in bilateral negotiations. The tendency to "satisfice"[4] noted above may prevail even more than in the bilateral case as a method to arrive at agreement.

A second element of complexity is found in the difficulty of arriving at a decision rule. In bilateral negotiations, it is obvious that the assent of both parties is always required to reach agreement. Yet, in many multilateral negotiations, this decision rule is not quite so obvious, especially since it may breed stalemate with regard to all but the most innocuous decisions. Parties to multilateral negotiations usually find themselves confronted with a procedural tradeoff between efficiency, the ability to reach agreement rapidly and with minimal rancor, and fairness or legitimacy, meaning a recognition by all participants that their interests and views have been taken into account in the eventual decision. Obviously, efficiency tends to suggest simple rules such as majority rule or even domination of multilateral organizations by powerful hegemons that can essentially dictate solutions to the group. These kinds of systems are reflected, for example, in the weighted voting procedures of the World Bank or the International Monetary Fund, where voting is apportioned primarily in relation to a country's financial contribution to the organization. Conversely, fairness suggests that a greater emphasis should be given to basic principles such as the sovereign equality of states and the belief that no state should be forced to accept a decision that goes against its national interests. This belief is enshrined in principles such as the "one state, one vote" rule in the U.N. General Assembly, where all states have equal voting power regardless of their size or capabilities.

An alternative voting procedure to "one state, one vote" was decided upon in the negotiations over the Montréal Protocol on ozone emissions in 1990, taking into account both the principle of majority rule and the need to gain acceptance across different groups of states. There it was agreed that North-South differences would be overcome by a complicated voting formula that would assure that the basic interests of neither bloc were overruled: decisions required a two-thirds majority vote of the entire conference, but also a simple majority in both the group of states from the North and from the South.[5]

Perhaps the most common decision rule in multilateral negotiations throughout history has been the attainment of consensus. Consensus, however, may convey several different meanings. Often multilateral negotiations seek absolute unanimity. But as the number of participants grows larger and larger, unanimity becomes increasingly difficult to achieve, making this an extremely inefficient procedure. There is also an important question about fairness when one small microstate such as San Marino might be able to block agreements supported by the entire remaining membership of large international conferences, such as the Conference on Security and Cooperation in Europe (CSCE) or the United Nations. It was largely for this reason that the CSCE developed in 1991 a procedure known as "consensus minus one" for responding to gross violations of CSCE principles and commitments, whereby the body of thirty-four states (later enlarged to fifty-three) could act against one of its members without its consent in the event of significant violations.[6] And it was, of course, for this reason that the U.N. charter provided that security measures could be adopted by the U.N. Security Council with the vote of seven of its original eleven members (later changed to nine out of fifteen when the council was enlarged), including all of its five permanent members, thereby requiring unanimous consent only of the five great powers.

These cases illustrate that the definition of consensus may be broadened to include more than a formal principle of unanimity. Consensus may be defined as a generally understood, but subjective point beyond which a sufficient number of relevant parties to a negotiation have to agree for a decision to be taken. This may differ from negotiation to negotiation or even from issue to issue within the same negotiation, but it implies that the parties can recognize intersubjectively when a sufficient consensus has been reached within the group. As Miles Kahler has suggested: "Under the opaque exterior of consensus undoubtedly lie rules of thumb not only concerning the degree of consensus that must be achieved but also concerning which of the parties must be included—rules of thumb often based on the formal voting rules. One suspects that most institutions have a tip point at which a large majority becomes a consensus, a rough marker at which the bandwagon begins to roll."[7]

Another similar decision rule is that which prevails in the negotiation of international agreements and treaties. While there is no formal requirement for unanimity, states may opt to ratify or reject any given outcome; therefore, when the participation of certain states is required to make an agreement effective and meaningful, the consent of all important states is essential. For example, in the negotiations on the Law of the Seas Treaty, more than 150 countries tried to arrive at a consensus about a codified regime to cover the legal issues pertaining to the world's oceans. Had the treaty been opposed by landlocked countries such as Austria or Bolivia, there probably would have been few significant consequences for the success of the treaty, and the regime could have moved ahead largely unaffected. However, despite the adherence of 117 countries when the treaty was opened for signature in 1982, the fact that the treaty was not accepted by four important states—Venezuela, Turkey, Israel, and the United States—made the regime a good deal less meaningful than had these important countries with long sea coasts and extensive maritime activities participated.[8] The point at which such agreements have enough support to proceed with signature and ratification is one of judgment by the participants. In the case of the Law of the Seas, it is likely that the negotiations would have been extended had the opposition by the United States been foreseen in advance, but a change in administrations and the arrival of President Reagan in the White House largely accounted for a shift in the position of the United

States from support to opposition.

This kind of judgment is typical of the uncertainty and ambiguity that often surrounds the fundamental decision rule in multilateral negotiations about when to cease negotiating and when to ask each participant to accept or reject the agreement as it stands. In other words, Iklé's classic three-fold choice—to continue negotiations, reach agreement, or break off negotiations[9]—may become much more complex in the multilateral than in the bilateral case.

Although complexity may help to explain why bilateral bargaining theory is not adequate to deal with most multilateral negotiations, it does not really suggest in a more positive vein what in fact constitutes the different characteristics of multilateral negotiations. This is perhaps one of the reasons for the frequent temptation to conclude that systematic theory cannot be readily applied to multilateral negotiations, and for the consequent tendency to revert largely to individual case studies to analyze multilateral negotiations. If complexity is the defining characteristic of multilateral negotiations, then the key to making the multinational process tractable is to simplify the process in order to make it more efficient at reaching acceptable agreements. As Zartman notes: "Multilateral negotiation is not merely complexity reduction: it is the management of complexity," a process involving "reduction (simplification) to make complexity comprehensible, structuring to make it manageable, and direction to produce a result."[10] Just because theory development is more difficult in the case of multilateral compared to bilateral negotiations is no reason to abandon the effort to develop theory. Rather, we must try to identify some of the specific characteristics of complexity, analyze them systematically, and try to identify ways to simplify and manage the complexities inherent in the process to produce meaningful outcomes.

Coalitions and the Reduction of Bargaining Space

A model of two-dimensional bargaining space in a single-issue, five-party negotiation is depicted in figure 13.1. It is important to note that the parties' preferences regarding the outcome may be curvilinear as well as linear. However, the same principle applies here as in the bilateral case, assuming that an agreement must be based upon unanimous consensus rather than a majority or other voting formula: agreement can be achieved only in that space where all actors perceive that they will receive positive benefits from an agreement relative to their next best alternative in the absence of an agreement. It may be observed that the range of bargaining space is typically reduced dramatically in the case of multilateral negotiations, since the agreement must serve the simultaneous interests of many parties, not just two.

However, if the parties recognize the dimensions of the bargaining space, they may realize that agreement essentially requires that the two parties with the narrowest positions (*A* and *C* in figure 13.1) agree between themselves. If these two parties can agree, then those with broader ranges of acceptable agreement will usually find their solution acceptable as well. In this instance, the multilateral negotiation could quickly reduce to a bilateral negotiation between *A* and *C*, in a relatively restricted bargaining space, with the other three parties being more or less content to accept whatever agreement those with the most difficult positions reach. This format works best when the negotiations essentially concern a single issue.

The typical treatment by most game theorists of multilateral nego-

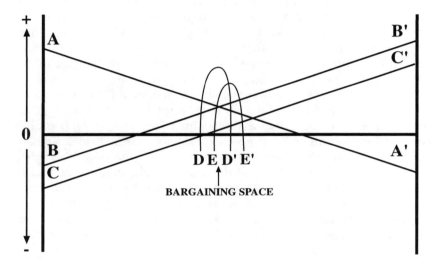

Figure 13.1 A Model of Multilateral Bargaining

tiations emphasizes the central role of coalitions, which in turn may cause some features of the negotiation to resemble the bilateral case. Figure 13.1 suggests the presence of three such natural coalitions, consisting of *A* standing alone, *B* and *C* forming a second group, and *D* and *E* forming a third coalition. The nature of coalition formation is most likely to depend on the decision rule in a negotiation, especially whether an agreement requires a majority decision or consensus.

If the decision rule is based on majority voting, on the one hand, then the actors will tend to form two coalitions in an attempt to achieve victory for their preferred position. Rather than engaging in traditional bargaining, one set of actors may seek to form a coalition large enough to assure victory, so that one no longer needs to negotiate with the other party. States may form what Riker has called minimum winning coalitions as they try to garner enough support to be assured of winning the vote without having to spread the spoils of victory too widely.[11] The key member of the coalition is the one whose addition to the group is necessary for the coalition to win.[12] This sort of strategic behavior, however, is best associated with legislative bodies and has relatively little in common with what we normally think of as negotiation.

On the other hand, if a decision requires a consensus, then a primary function of coalition formation may be to simplify debate. Raiffa argues that multilateral negotiations will frequently see the participants group together in coalitions, usually forming two blocs; the ensuing negotiations may then require two phases. First, the members of each coalition must negotiate together to establish their own common preferences. Next they will tend to bargain with the other coalition in a fashion not all that different from bilateral negotiations.[13] This adds a significant element of complexity, however, since the two phases are often intertwined in complicated ways, and since the coalitions are often unstable as a result of the different preferences represented within each bloc. Coalitions may break down, shift, and reform in the course of a single negotiation. Therefore, this kind of analysis, based on the theory of N-person games, does not yield the same kind of stable solutions to the bargaining problem as those generally obtained from two-person, non-zero-sum game theory, upon which most conceptions of bilateral negotiations are based.

For example, in the negotiations on Mutual and Balanced Force Reductions (MBFR) in Europe, later called Conventional Forces in Europe (CFE), twenty-two states eventually participated. However, they came to the negotiations as members of mutually opposed alliances, namely NATO and the Warsaw Treaty Organization. Often the most strenuous negotiations took place within the two alliances, especially within NATO, since the Soviet Union was largely able to dominate decision making within the Warsaw Pact. Prior to virtually all formal negotiating sessions involving the full set of participants, each alliance met in Vienna to prepare a joint statement and agree on positions to take in the upcoming negotiations. Thus, in many respects the formal interbloc negotiations were essentially bilateral despite the formal participation of twenty-two sovereign states. However, extending the metaphor of the two-level game, this was in effect a three-level game involving two alliances negotiating with one another, interstate negotiation within each alliance, and domestic negotiations within each member state.

The nature of these coalitions often had a significant effect on the character of the negotiations, frequently complicating them a great deal. For example, spontaneous reactions to the arguments of the other side were virtually impossible since each coalition had to meet to discuss in advance how to reply to previous statements by the other bloc. Modifications of negotiating positions would often take months to materialize, since these would have to be submitted first to national capitals and then would have to be negotiated within each coalition. This meant for NATO that all policy decisions had to be made at NATO headquarters in Brussels before the alliance could take any initiative or modify its position in any way in the negotiations in Vienna.[14] At a minimum this slowed the negotiation process down a great deal. In addition, it often meant that negotiating positions advanced in Vienna tended already to be reduced to a lowest common denominator of agreement among members of each alliance, leaving the two alliances with the necessity of trying to find common ground between the already greatly reduced bargaining space established by each coalition. The coalition member with the most restrictive position tends to define the position of the coalition, as frequently occurred in MBFR when the Federal Republic of Germany or occasionally the United States set the limits to acceptable bargaining space for the entire NATO alliance throughout most of the period from 1973 through 1979.

In short, even if multilateral negotiations can be reduced to an essentially bilateral character through the formation of two coalitions, unless those coalitions are extremely unified (such as when both are dominated by a single, hegemonic state), the negotiations will still be a good deal more complex than in a simple two-party bilateral negotiation.

Furthermore, in multilateral international negotiations the coalitions do not necessarily reduce to two, as one would anticipate in a "winner-take-all" voting system. Coalitions may form to simplify negotiations, but they do not necessarily revert to two party negotiations. For example, most negotiations within the U.N. framework throughout the cold-war period involved at least three coalitions, loosely held together by ideological considerations: (1) the industrialized, capitalist bloc; (2) the socialist bloc; and (3) the nonaligned states or Group of 77. Within most global negotiations under U.N. auspices during this period, minimal demands of ideological conformity usually made the appearance of only two coalitions something of a rarity. With the end of the cold war after 1989, global negotiations may become even more fragmented as the three relatively stable coalitions of the bipolar international system are transformed or disappear altogether. While the reduction of the number of parties through coalition formation may simplify the process to some extent, as long as more than two coalitions are formed, many of the complexities of multilateral negotiations will inevitably come into play.

The presence of coalitions may, however, be used to construct agreement through a process of coalition-building. In this way, like-minded parties may form a core coalition and then seek to expand by adding other coalitions with similar, though not identical, interests. As the coalition enlarges, the core coalition may have to modify its positions somewhat in order to make them acceptable to other coalitions with different interests. At the same time, the bandwagon effect may make joining the growing core coalition attractive to others who expect to receive favors from the eventual dominant coalition. Finally, the most intransigent group may find itself isolated and faced with an unattractive choice between undermining an agreement supported by a substantial majority of the group or acceding to the interests of the newly created grand coalition.

This may be illustrated by the process of coalition building employed in the opening meeting of the Uruguay Round of GATT in Punte del Este, Uruguay, in September 1986. Prior to that meeting, in prenegotiations at the GATT headquarters in Geneva, the United States had advocated adding to the GATT agenda a negotiation on trade in services, as opposed to the traditional GATT focus on trade in manufactured goods. At first the United States was largely alone in its desire to see this item take a prominent position in the new GATT agenda, and a group of ten developing countries led by India and Brazil was adamantly opposed to adding this issue to the agenda.

The United States began by seeking the support of its most natural allies, the European Community and Japan, two parties that also had expanding service economies. Then this coalition quietly sought the support of a group of nine small industrialized countries, led by the Swiss representative Pierre-Louis Girard. Prior to any formal joining of these two coalitions, however, this group of nine began meeting with a group of moderate developing countries, headed by the Colombian representative Filipe Jaramillo. This coalition became known as the café au lait group because of this joint Colombian-Swiss leadership. At this point the overall GATT included three major coalitions—the large, developed countries; the café au lait group; and the hard-line developing countries. The next move involved enlarging the core coalition by uniting the group of large developed countries and the large group of moderates from both North and South, leaving the hard-line developing countries isolated when the parties arrived at Punte del Este.

The negotiations in Uruguay were characterized by tough bargaining on the part of the United States and the Brazil/India group. The United States began by establishing a firm deadline for the negotiations and by threatening to force a vote if a consensus, the normal GATT decision-making rule, had not been achieved prior to that deadline. The Brazil/India group was faced with a difficult choice: walking out if the United States forced a vote that it could probably win with the support of the large coalition it had helped to create, or seeking a compromise that would allow them to remain within the GATT framework. The United States was faced with a choice between trying to find a formula that could produce a consensus, or forcing a vote and making the hard liners choose between two unacceptable positions. With the assistance of Uruguayan Foreign Minister Enrique Iglesias, a compromise was found in which services would be separated from the other GATT negotiations, as the hard liners wanted, but in which the new negotiations on services would take place in parallel with the other GATT negotiations at the GATT headquarters in Geneva and using the GATT secretariat. In other words, the hard liners found themselves confronted with a large opposing coalition, and under these circumstances they chose to join that coalition with a face-saving compromise rather than walk out of the GATT. Finally, a coalition of the whole was formed and a consensus was achieved. In this instance, four major coalitions had to be brought together around a single consensus agreement achieved through a process of building the grand coalition one segment at a time.[15] Rubin and Swap contend: "The . . . GATT talks seem to have been driven not by negotiation but by group process. It is not the staking out of positions, from which concessions are subsequently made, that best characterizes the work that takes place in multilateral encounters. Building group consensus, through the dynamics of group process, is the key feature."[16]

In summary, this case illustrates effectively the principle that the complexity introduced into negotiations by the presence of many parties with different interests requires first that these interests be aggregated in coalitions, and second that coalition-building take place until a sufficient consensus is reached to consummate agreement.

Crosscutting Cleavages

An additional feature of negotiations with more than two parties or coalitions and multiple issues is that the lines of division within the group may fall along different cleavages. Students of comparative politics have long compared the structure of socioeconomic and political cleavages in different societies according to whether all such cleavages tend to coincide and reinforce one another, or the extent to which they fall along different lines and crosscut one another as depicted in figure 13.2.[17] In comparative politics it has often been noted that the former tends to be characteristic of two-party legislatures, whereas the latter pattern is found more often in countries with multiparty legislatures. By analogy, we may logically assume that multilateral negotiations will frequently witness crosscutting cleavages, in contrast to the reinforcing cleavages that generally characterize bilateral negotiations. In negotiations with two or more issues, the parties may find that they are divided differently depending on the nature of the issue under negotiation. For example, in many global negotiations during the cold-war period certain security issues tended to divide the globe along East-West lines, whereas economic issues divided more along North-South lines.

This distinction carries important implications for the nature of the negotiation process. With reinforcing cleavages, since most conflicts fall along the same line of division, the conflicts tend to be rather intense and take on features of a zero-sum game, psychologically if not necessarily in reality; indeed, the negotiations tend to polarize. Therefore, the traditional bargaining model is more likely to be applicable, insofar as it emphasizes mutual concession-making along a single line of conflict. By contrast, crosscutting cleavages add complexity because actors may find that their enemy on one issue is their ally on others. This complicates the negotiation, so that simple concession-convergence bargaining becomes virtually impossible; there is no single dimension along which parties may converge. At the same time, conflicts that do exist tend to be muted, since they are often offset by cooperative interests shared with the same party on other issues.[18] These considerations are hypothesized to have several consequences for the dynamics of the negotiation process.

First, this element of shared cooperative interests that cuts across lines of division may enhance the prospects for integrative bargaining rather than the distributive bargaining more typical of traditional bilateral negotiations.[19] Negotiations would be expected to be characterized less by overt conflicts of interest and more by an effort to solve problems jointly. Within the Law of the Seas negotiations, for example, a number of interests were shared by participants that cut across normal lines of cleavage in international politics. As a consequence, these negotiations frequently adopted a problem-solving rather than a conflictual, bargaining approach—especially as different interests also provided a framework for making tradeoffs and constructing package agreements.[20]

Second, coalitions, even if informal, may be used strategically by one party (A) to get another party (B) with which it has common interests to intervene with a third party (C) with which B may have closer relations than A. If two parties find themselves in a highly conflictual relation, their bargaining may be attenuated by common ties that they both have with a third party in the negotiations. Thus, for example, the negotiation between the United States and Vietnam to end the war in Southeast Asia was influenced by the fact that the United States and the Soviet Union had common interests in achieving a strategic arms agreement. This, in turn, made it possible for the United States to use that common interest with the Soviets to encourage them to pressure their Vietnamese allies into reaching a negotiated settlement with the United States. Although the United States and North Vietnam had few joint interests, the fact that another party that was involved had some overlapping interests with both enabled it occasionally to serve as a go-between in these negotiations. And as the Soviet interlocutor became somewhat less effective, the U.S. National Security Advisor, Henry

A) Reinforcing Cleavages

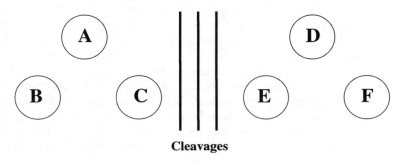

Cleavages

B) Crosscutting Cleavages

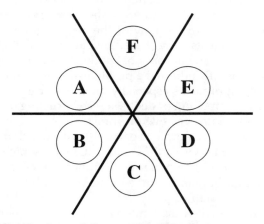

Figure 13.2 Models of Reinforcing and Crosscutting Cleavages

Kissinger, sought to open contacts with the Peoples' Republic of China in 1971 and bring them into the negotiations, at least as an indirect party.

Kissinger visited Beijing for the second time in November 1971, and shortly thereafter the Chinese government invited North Vietnamese Prime Minister Pham Van Dong to Beijing for consultations. When he came in November of that year, according to Seymour Hersh, Mao Tse-tung told the North Vietnamese Prime Minister an old Chinese parable: "If the handle of your broom is very short, you cannot wipe out a spider high on the wall of a closet. So you must allow it to stay." This apparent effort to persuade the North Vietnamese to give up their goal of wiping away the government of President Thieu fell largely on deaf ears, as Pham Van Dong reiterated his belief that the North Vietnamese broom was in fact long enough "to sweep all of these dogs out of Vietnam."[21] Despite the initial rebuff, however, reduced support to the North Vietnamese from both the Soviet Union and China, both seeking closer ties with the United States, encouraged the North Vietnamese to moderate some of their toughest positions in their negotiations in Paris. Kissinger was able to take advantage of this trilateral diplomacy to advance U.S. goals within the Paris negotiations.

Third, the complex system of overlapping interests and coalitions may enhance the prospects for trade-offs compared with bilateral negotiations. This is especially important in multilateral negotiations where it is possible to create a multiparty system of tradeoffs, called circular barter by Touval and Rubin. In this instance, "if party A desires something from party B, and B can be compensated by a resource that is possessed by C, and C can benefit from some other action of D, and D can be paid off by A—a circular barter can take place."[22] They illustrate this process with an example from the 1954 Geneva negotiations on the withdrawal of France from Indochina. In these multilateral negotiations, the Soviet Union and the United States participated along with the major direct parties to the conflict. Touval and Rubin suggest that the French sought concessions from the Vietnamese communists. In exchange the French offered to modify their position on the proposed European Defense Community (EDC), a French proposal that would have brought a rearmed Germany into a European defense network composed of the major countries of Western Europe. Although the EDC was of no concern to the Vietnamese, it was perceived as threatening by the Soviets, both because it sought to rearm their major enemy from World War II within a closely knit network among the core Western European members of NATO. Therefore, the defeat of the EDC in the French National Assembly could be viewed as a compensation provided by France to the Soviet Union in Europe in exchange for Vietnamese concessions that would facilitate a face-saving French departure from Southeast Asia. Presumably the circle was closed when the concessions by the Vietnamese communists were in turn compensated by Soviet guarantees of aid to their fellow communists who maintained power in the northern zone of Vietnam.

All of these hypotheses suggest that, in spite of their greater complexity, there also exist in multilateral negotiations techniques and levers for reaching agreement that are not generally found in the bilateral case. Not surprisingly, one of the key objectives of many of these mechanisms is to try to simplify the negotiations and make them operate as much as possible without masking the issues and problems, in a similar fashion to bilateral negotiations. At the same time, certain characteristics of multilateral negotiations offer distinctive advantages that may be felicitous. The fact that multilateral negotiations are frequently characterized by overlapping and divergent rather than polarized lines of conflict implies that conflict will often be less intense. While mutually beneficial solutions to problems may be difficult to locate, once they are discovered there is less likely to be intense opposition from parties that may have other linked issues on which they seek to achieve agreement. Therefore, integrative formulas are more likely to be available, providing of course that they can be discovered in the midst of the complexity that typically surrounds these negotiations. Therefore, the dynamics of that discovery process form an essential aspect of any multilateral negotiation.

THE GROUP DYNAMICS OF MULTILATERAL NEGOTIATIONS

A critical aspect of any multilateral negotiation is the process by which the parties seek to discover formulas that may suggest integrative solutions to the problems that they face. As I have already suggested, the kinds of issues usually posed by multilateral negotiations are likely to require integrative solutions, as opposed to conflict and bargaining relationships that are more likely to dominate in bilateral situations. The group is more likely to approach the issues by trying to solve common problems rather than by trying to win in a conflict of wills. Thus, the problem-solving orientation of analysts such as Fisher and Ury, while clearly relevant to bilateral negotiations, is likely to be more readily adaptable to multilateral negotiations.

As Zartman and Berman have suggested, this process tends to involve a diagnostic phase in which the sources of the problem are explored, followed by the identification of a formula.[23] This may be contrasted with bilateral negotiations where the issues and lines of conflict are frequently well defined, and solutions may emerge through a process of bargaining in which both parties make concessions until their positions converge at some midpoint. Negotiations such as those between the two nuclear superpowers on arms control often seem to be most successful when processes of mutual reciprocity in bargaining can be established.[24] Such a process, although often less than an ideal procedure for reaching agreement in bilateral negotiations, is usually completely unsatisfactory for coping with the complexity of multilateral negotiations.

Therefore, one of the most effective means for overcoming the complexity inherent in multiple positions is to examine the interests of all parties whose assent is necessary to achieve agreement in the search for a formula that will embrace their essential interests. All of the parties must perceive that the benefits of agreement exceed whatever costs may also ensue. Such formulas, however, do not emerge out of thin air. I have already indicated that they may entail a lengthy and sometimes apparently fruitless search process before they can be identified. Usually a formula is discovered through a diagnosis of underlying causes of the problem and a search for multiple potential solutions until a mutually satisfactory one is discovered. In this search and discovery process, the dynamics of the group interaction are likely to be especially important. Some of these different aspects of group dynamics that might affect the process include:

1. The formation of "in-groups" and "out-groups" among the participants and the creation of group identity and common intersubjective understandings.

2. The pattern of sociometric interactions, especially communications linkages, which develop among the participants.

3. Development of leadership, both of an affective and task-oriented nature.

4. The institutional context within which many multilateral negotiations take place.

"In-groups" versus "Out-groups"

Social psychologists have suggested that individuals' sense of identity as a member of a group tend to extend outward until some threshold is crossed, beyond which point individuals are perceived to belong to a different group. Across this subjective threshold, it is no longer a relationship among "us," but between "us" and "them." Group identities may be based on many sources of commonness, such as membership in the same institutional structure, living in the same location, sharing common attitudes and beliefs, belonging to the same ethnic group, believing in the same religion, speaking the same language, mutual friendship and respect, or perceived similarity in other important attributes. Inside this threshold a process of psychological assimilation tends to occur, in which the ideas, values, and attitudes expressed by other members of the "in-group" tend to be integrated with one's own. Thus, the perceived psychological distance between an individual and other members of the group may seem to shrink. By contrast, beyond that threshold a process of differentiation tends to make members of one group disassociate themselves from the beliefs and values of the "out-group." In this case, the psychological distance separating oneself from others actually seems to expand, and existing cleavages may appear to widen. One form of the latter process is ethnocentrism, favoring the "in-group" over the "out-group." And, of course, widespread ethnocentrism tends to breed conflict between opposing groups.

Within the "in-group" common values tend to be developed, and the group may construct its own collective definition of the situation within which the group members find themselves. They may develop intersubjective understandings among themselves, in the sense that their belief systems tend to merge and they tend to interpret reality within the same basic sets of frames or interpretative lenses. This development of common cognitive maps or social constructs that are shared by group members may reinforce their identity as belonging to the same group and being excluded from other groups. These provide a common filter through which all members of the group perceive the same reality. These feelings of identification and belonging may interact with and even supersede simple calculations of interest when it comes to making decisions about membership in coalitions. The patterns of cleavages that develop within a multilateral forum may be affected by these kinds of fundamental beliefs about belonging rather than by, or in addition to, the strategic calculations of the kind typically predicted within a game theoretic or other rational choice framework.

For example, in negotiations within the U.N. Conference on Trade and Development (UNCTAD), the members of the industrialized, capitalist states of the West and the Group-of-77 states of the South each tended to develop a group vision of the issues that became increasingly differentiated and conflictual. Throughout the negotiation process on the so-called New International Economic Order in the decade of the 1970s, it became apparent that the West and the South shared little in common between themselves about the requirements for economic and political development, while within each group a substantial consensus emerged. The West remained committed to a liberal and open economic order based on the competitive principles of market economics; the South became focused on issues of both political and economic equity in a global system where growth seemed to make the rich richer, while keeping the rest of the world locked in poverty. These two groups were fundamentally committed to the intervention of governments and international institutions not only in domestic markets, but in the international economic system as a whole in order to bring about global economic redistribution and greater equity in the system. Both sides collectively developed these common beliefs and principles, and held to them with such tenacity that agreement became virtually impossible. Without fundamental conceptual changes in these cohesive worldviews of the two sides, common interests were extremely difficult to locate

260

and agreement consistently appeared illusive. Thus, it should come as little surprise that the UNCTAD negotiations on the New International Economic Order from 1974 through 1977 produced little or nothing in the way of concrete agreement, and left a residue of bitterness in North-South relations that lasted for many years afterwards.[25]

As this case illustrates, the dynamics of group interaction may exert considerable impact on the formation and stability of groups composed of like-minded parties, affecting whether or not a multilateral negotiation becomes divided into a set of independent and even competing groups or becomes more unified into a single, interdependent group identity. When social bonds are created among all participants in a conference through perception of common group memberships, conflicts usually become readily amenable to solution; problems may be solved through joint exploration for mutually beneficial results. When social bonds are broken, however, and when individuals deviate from the group norms, several things usually take place: "First, the group tries to persuade the deviate to come around to the majority position, to enter the warm confines of the group, to accept the group's protective embrace (in exchange for recanting); second, if and when efforts at persuasion fail, the group moves to isolate, ostracize, or forcibly extrude the deviate."[26] In other words, the breaking of social bonds may cause an international conference to fragment into "in-groups" and "out-groups," conflicts may tend to escalate, and negotiations will tend to become trapped into distributive bargaining.

For these reasons, coalition formation in multilateral negotiations may be a double-edged sword. As noted above, the reorganization of a multilateral body into a relatively small number of coalitions tends to simplify the negotiation process. On the other hand, this process of forming a small number of groups is likely to be accompanied by an increasing differentiation among groups. Coalitions may establish internal cohesion through negative reference to other coalitions, the "out-groups." The coalition formation process may break down some social bonds, thereby intensifying conflicts among members of opposing coalitions.[27] These conflicts may create obstacles to the coalition-building process if they prevent members of different coalitions from setting aside their differences in order to achieve some common goal.

By contrast, multilateral negotiations like those on environmental issues are most likely to produce results when the parties stay focused on the common problem, for which all seek a joint solution, rather than on those issues (such as assigning responsibility for environmental pollution or arguing about who should pay for the cleanup of pollution) that are likely to divide them into competing groups. Once they become segregated into groups, the processes of assimilation and differentiation are likely to drive each group closer together internally and separate the groups increasingly from one another externally. When this happens, a problem-solving orientation toward negotiation can be more difficult to realize, coalition-building becomes more difficult to achieve, and stalemate is far more likely to ensue.

Sociometric Interactions

A multilateral conference may be viewed as a communications net in which information flows back and forth through multiple channels, among delegates, and between the conference secretariat and the various delegations. Each of these parties may still calculate their interests individually, but, as Caporaso suggests, in this kind of setting "individual intentionality is embedded in social relations in which communication, shared beliefs, norms, and identity commitments are present."[28] These communications networks become the transmission belts through which the parties to a negotiation exchange ideas, share knowledge and technical information, discuss issues jointly, and seek to persuade others of the rightness of each party's own position. Several different network structures are possible, and these may influence how decisions get made within the conference.

One common structure is a hierarchical one. In this model, one single actor—perhaps the conference's secretary general or other presiding officer, or perhaps one powerful and important state—stands at the top of the communications hierarchy. All communications flow from the individual delegations to the top, and from the group leader back down to the individual members. In this network, one member has extraordinary control over the information available to all parties, and that one member also serves as the filter for all information allowing only what it wants to be distributed to others to pass back down the hierarchy. This particular structure may also simplify the negotiation process, since one party alone is in possession of the information necessary to set the agenda for negotiations, define the range of bargaining space, and suggest formulas to serve as a basis for agreement.

This kind of structure has often been suggested to create stability dictated by the dominant role of the hegemonic actor. This organizational pattern is "most conducive to the development of strong international regimes whose rules are relatively precise and well obeyed."[29] Although hegemonic interaction patterns may simplify the negotiation process and create a kind of stability in the results, there are also good reasons to believe that it is not necessarily conducive to the attainment of good results. There is little search in such a process for optimal solutions to common problems, since one party both defines the problem and limits the options available to deal with the problem. Furthermore, this structure is unlikely to produce agreements that will be perceived as fair, since the hegemonical actor will be in a position to control out-comes that meet its own particular interests without full regard for the needs and interests of the other parties. Finally, such an agreement is likely to remain stable only so long as the hegemonical actor retains its position relative to the other parties on a continuing basis after the agreement enters into force.

An example of such a conference might be the Monetary Conference held at Bretton Woods, New Hampshire, in 1944 to establish the postwar international monetary regime and specifically the International Monetary Fund (IMF). Due to the extensive economic influence of the United States at a time when all other major financial powers were suffering greatly due to the damage from World War II, and thus due to the central role of the dollar as the world's reserve currency, the United States was able to dominate the process. Prior to the multilateral conference at Bretton Woods, the United States held a series of bilateral meetings with Great Britain, France, and Canada, thus retaining its central position in the communications network as the only country that was fully ac-quainted with the position of the other participants. Although forty-four countries eventually participated in this multilateral conference, includ-ing the Soviet Union, the final document reflected understandings that the United States had negotiated on a bilateral basis with its various partners, especially Great Britain. The IMF was largely the creation of U.S. Treasury Secretary Henry Morgenthau. Under the terms of the weighted voting procedure, the United States received 33 percent of the overall vot-ing power in IMF decisions, followed by Great Britain with 16 percent of the votes. Although this percentage declined over the years, the United States retained throughout an effective veto power over IMF decisions.

Due to the special requirements of postwar recovery, the Bretton Woods regime was not fully instituted until 1959, and for more than a decade it maintained a system of explicitly mandated and fixed exchange rates among the major countries of the Western world, and procedures for consultation when parties felt that exchange rates needed to be modi-fied. This system endured more or less in tact until the United States suspended the convertibility of the dollar into gold in 1971.[30] Once the United States was no longer able to serve effectively as the sole banker of the world, the agreement that had been adopted in a conference cen-tering around U.S. economic dominance also collapsed. Once the eco-nomic hegemony of the United States began to crumble, so too did the monetary regime that was founded upon that very hegemony.

A variant on the negotiation dominated by a single hegemon is a structure that has been dubbed minilateralism. Instead of a single hegemon, the process may be dominated by a core group of states that cooperate with one another to assure efficient decision making in larger multilateral fora. As Snidal observes, in this situation "collective action has taken up where hegemonic power left off."[31] This minilateral cooperation may support multilateral norms, but more often it supports the interests of a dominant group of states rather than a single hegemon. It may represent a midpoint between completely hierarchical and completely egalitarian structures. Kahler has suggested that many of the postwar global economic institutions were in fact dominated by this kind of small-group minilateralism among the major industrial states, although he also suggests that this order has come under increasing challenge from a new multilateralism in which large-group collaboration has actually proven successful.[32]

A third common sociometric structure is one in which multiple nodes are found that serve as linking points for numerous actors, arranged in either a hierarchical or a nonhierarchical fashion. This is a common framework in global conferences, where numerous groups of states caucus together on a regional basis. Each caucus or group becomes a tightly linked communications network, and a great deal of the communications within the conference as a whole may transpire primarily among caucus groupings rather than among individual participants. These groups tend to share information with one another and shape the perceptions, interests, and negotiating positions of their fellow members as they confront the negotiation.

For example, the Conference on Security and Cooperation in Europe tended to be grouped—in its initial negotiations between 1973 and 1975 in both Helsinki and Geneva—around numerous, overlapping communications nodes. Three of these were mutually exclusive groupings of the major blocs found in the cold-war European system—namely NATO, the Warsaw Pact, and the neutral and nonaligned group. However, these were overlapped by nine members of the European Community (especially on economic issues), the Berlin Group (the four wartime allies: the United States, Great Britain, France, and the Soviet Union, that all had special responsibilities for the status of Berlin and Germany), the Mediterranean Group (emphasizing the need to maintain contact with states of the Middle East and North Africa that did not belong to CSCE, but that played an important role in the future of the Mediterranean region), the Nordic caucus (including three NATO members and two neutral countries), and the secretariat. Each of these groups caucused frequently and played various roles in the negotiations, although they also varied a great deal in terms of internal hierarchy, purpose, and homogeneity.[33] They tended to try to reach common positions on those issues about which they held common interests, although sometimes they remained united only with respect to certain specific issues. Nonetheless, special and private communications took place within each of these caucuses, and the resulting positions were generally shared with other conference members only when differences within each caucus had been resolved. This pattern also differed a great deal from the communications linkages in the concurrent negotiations on Mutual and Balanced Force Reductions where the negotiations were controlled by two tightly organized, mutually exclusive, and hierarchical alliances—NATO and the Warsaw Pact.

A fourth model is the "hub-and-spoke" configuration in which one actor stands at the center of a relatively nonhierarchical communications pattern, and all other parties communicate with one another primarily through that center. This differs from the first pattern described above in that the central actor does not stand in a position of hegemony over and above the other members, but rather at the center as a sole node of a fairly egalitarian sociometric structure. In international negotiations this model may most often be evident in those conferences where a professional secretariat plays a central role. For example, in many routine negotiations that take place within the framework of the General Agreement on Tariffs and Trade (GATT), which are often highly technical in nature, a central secretariat in Geneva stands at the center of communications and information flows. This pattern seldom prevails in formal meetings of the GATT where other patterns of caucus groups are likely to appear as illustrated above with regard to the Uruguay Round prenegotiations and opening meeting. Instead, this is a common pattern of interaction in the informal negotiations over the day-to-day operation of the GATT system where virtually all communications are directed and processed through the GATT headquarters staff in Geneva.

Group Leadership

Of the many aspects of group dynamics, group leadership would seem to be of especially great significance. Without effective leadership, the group may easily get bogged down in the complexity of the issues and multiplicity of interests that must be reconciled. A formula must be found that somehow embraces these multiple interests, that locates the small area where the interests of many parties can be satisfied or even upgraded simultaneously. While this may emerge out of the cacophony of group interaction, it is more likely to emerge if the formula can be articulated clearly and succinctly by an individual group leader who commands respect from all parties. As Rubin and Swap emphasize, an effective leader can "create a sense of 'transcendence'" through the introduction of superordinate goals that bridge "existing bases of conflict or competition in order to reach the goal of increased cooperation. The deliberate introduction of such a superordinate goal increases group cohesiveness."[34] Group leadership, of course, is seldom relevant in bilateral negotiations where the two parties are at least nominally symmetrical. By contrast, in a group setting it may be the single most important factor in breaking through the confusion and complexity to identify a formula around which the group may rally.

The literature on small group dynamics has identified two distinctly different leadership styles, both of which may be significant in multilateral negotiations.[35] The first is affective leadership where the leader tries to inspire or even frighten the parties to reach agreement through appeal to emotional symbols. Rather than focusing on the terms of the agreement itself, the affective leader may dramatize the benefits of agreement or the dangers of failure in order to move the negotiation forward. Such a leader seeks to instill in group members a determination to find a solution and sell a formula once it has been discovered.

By contrast, an instrumental or task leader tends to be very business-like and rational, seeking to establish an orderly process of diagnosis and search. This leader may attempt to uncover the fundamental interests of the parties and identify the available bargaining space within which agreement can be reached. Once a potential solution has been discovered, reluctant parties must then be persuaded that an agreement based on the formula will serve their interests better than stalemate or abandonment of negotiations. Also, a task-oriented leader may rely upon expertise rather than personal or national capabilities to assert a leadership role. An expert may even serve as a broker to help a group achieve consensus. For example, in the negotiations on the 1985 Vienna Convention on the Protection of the Ozone Layer and on the 1987 Montréal Protocol on the same issue, the executive director of the U.N. Environmental Programme, Mostafa Tolba, served as an active mediator and representative of a group of mostly developing countries that were not present in discussions among the minilateral group that dominated these discussions.[36] This is the kind of leadership role that may frequently be played by technical experts from functionalist international organizations or other institutions where the task leadership role stems from technical expertise rather than personal characteristics of the individual.

Leaders are most likely to be effective when they can combine task- and affect-oriented skills in their leadership roles. An effective leader must possess strong analytical skills to discover a potential formula, as well as be persuasive in order to convince others to accept the formula. In most cases, of course, the role of the leader is not to impose his or her own formula on the other parties, but rather to be in a position to listen to and understand the multiple interests represented in the negotiation, discover where those interests overlap, and then articulate a formula that will succeed in reconciling the competing interests and upgrading the common interests. As noted above, a special function of the leader may be to identify superordinate goals that transcend the existing conflicts, and persuade all parties that these goals do indeed supersede their differences. Social psychologists have long argued that such superordinate goals can overcome group conflicts and help create cooperation in order to achieve higher levels of joint benefits.[37]

It is also possible to distinguish a number of different kinds of leadership roles. For example, Underdal has identified three kinds of leadership: (1) those who act through unilateral action; (2) those who utilize coercive means; and (3) those who use instrumental leadership. The unilateral leader takes the initiative to resolve conflicts, and leads by demonstration of personal example or through persuasion. Coercive leaders utilize carrots and sticks to manipulate others to follow them, and their success is in large part a function of the resources that they can mobilize to support their threats and promises. Finally, instrumental leaders seek to identify ways to achieve common goals, and they are influential either because they can persuade others to accept the specific solutions that they propose on the basis of their technical evaluation of the problem or because of their ability to convince others of their overall competence to solve problems. [38] Underdal also argues that successful multilateral negotiations generally require the presence of some combination of all leadership styles, although the relative importance of each may vary from case to case. But in general, he concludes that the "optimal mix of leadership modes [in multilateral negotiations] must include some version of instrumental leadership and (at least) one of the two power based modes (coercion or unilateral action)."[39]

Whatever style is pursued, the leader must aid the parties to discover overarching goals and formulas that enable those goals to be realized. One technique that the group leader may employ to do this is to draft what Fisher calls a single-negotiating-text, a process also discussed in the preceding chapter. In this approach, the group leader functions in a role similar to that of a mediator by listening to the interests of all parties and then drafting a text that seems to embrace all of those interests. The parties may then criticize and modify this text until the formula is refined to meet their essential interests. Rather than making concessions to one another, the parties criticize a draft agreement produced by the group leader, an easier task that is less likely to produce bitterness and acrimony.[40] A single text proposed by a group leader may greatly facilitate the negotiation process by reducing the complexity that so often seems to impede or disrupt multilateral negotiations.

For example, in the negotiations leading up to the Esquipulas II accords in Central America in 1987, Costa Rican President Oscar Arias performed this kind of leadership role. President Arias traveled throughout his region to speak with the leaders of Guatemala, Honduras, El Salvador, and Nicaragua who would have to agree upon a regional peace plan. He also sought to gain outside support in the United States and Western Europe. Out of this he developed a plan that soon became named after him, based on the simultaneous implementation of three principles in all five countries: (1) cease-fires in all civil conflicts; (2) amnesties for all parties; and (3) prohibition against the use of neighboring territories by insurgents and regular armies. He first persuaded the foreign ministers of the five countries to accept these principles in a meeting on 31 July 1987 in Tegucigalpa, Honduras. He then pushed the other four heads of states to sign an agreement based on these principles in Guatemala City on 7 August 1987. In order to achieve this, he had to get the two parties with the most difficult positions, Honduras and Nicaragua, to bridge their differences. Thus, Arias both played a conceptual role in the development of a formula based on mutual benefits, and played the role of a group leader by encouraging, cajoling, and pressuring the parties to accept that formula. He was awarded the Nobel Peace Prize in 1987 for his efforts at leading the Central American states to agree on a positive-sum outcome that brought an end to a decade-long conflict both within and across the borders of most states in that region. The Arias Plan had, in effect, become a single negotiating text around which the regional leaders could negotiate an agreement in Esquipulas II in less than two full days of intense negotiations.[41]

The role of leadership, and the legitimacy that others assign to that role, may emerge as a consequence of a great many different factors, including the resources of the country the leader represents, the individual's personality or intellectual skills that make him or her especially appropriate for this role, a widespread perception of neutrality or fairness in approaching the issues, and/or occupying a formal position of special significance, such as the U.N. secretary general or the secretary general of a particular conference. The leader may also exert influence on the process in many different ways, including manipulation of the process through the resources that he or she commands, articulation of solutions on the basis of a careful analysis of the problem, creating a business-like and constructive atmosphere for negotiations, or through the use of persuasion and appeals to the fears and aspirations of the parties. In short, there are many different kinds of leaders that emerge within negotiations for different reasons, who play many diverse kinds of roles. While there is considerable variation in leadership role and style, the emergence of effective leadership that can develop a positive-sum package out of conflicting interests is hypothesized to be a common denominator for success in the vast majority of multilateral international negotiations.

Institutional Context

Frequently, multilateral negotiations take place within multilateral institutions such as the United Nations, GATT, the Conference on Security and Cooperation in Europe, and the Organization of American States. This contrasts with most bilateral negotiations that are generally ad hoc and focused on specific issues or relationships, such as a border dispute, exchange agreements, or debt relief for a specific country. When multilateral negotiations occur within an established institutional context, this means that the parties approach a negotiation with a sense of participation in a ongoing process of interaction that has a history and a sense of direction. A negotiation is no longer solely a discrete interaction to solve a specific problem, but rather it occurs within the context of enduring rules, procedures, and norms that are generally shared by other institutional members. While the parties may have divergent interests on specific issues, they still approach those divergent interests within the framework of a continuing institutional structure.

Within this institutional context, collective group identities may take shape. As James Caporaso notes, institutions offer "an environment in which socialization and learning can occur."[42] Within this environment, cognitive change may take place as individual members adapt their beliefs and interests to those of other group members. They share information, which may be especially important for negotiations on technical issues such as the environment, trade, or arms control. From this information sharing, they may learn of new ways to approach problems and resolve differences. They may also learn to trust others as they understand the fundamental interests that undergird their behavior over a period of sustained interactions. Finally, again as Caporaso notes, institutions encourage states to adhere to multilateral norms: "In the institutional approach, norms are not treated as utilities (or as second-order utilities) but as prescriptions lying outside of preference structures. The content of norms has less to do with what agents want concretely than with how they ought to behave in certain situations and what goals they ought to pursue. The U.N. prohibition on the use of force to acquire territory, people, or resources is a norm. It proscribes the use of force for these ends, even though such ends are represented in the preference schedules of some decision makers."[43]

Furthermore, these norms and shared beliefs within institutions are acquired through the historical development and evolution of institutions. They become part of the shared and collective memory of institutional members, and they are generally not questioned in the same direct way that positions based on individual interests may be brought under critical review. They serve to limit the range within which debate may occur in a multilateral negotiation, and sometimes may provide shared assumptions around which larger and more interest-based agreements may be constructed.

In short, the institutional context does not eliminate the essential premise of our analysis that negotiations occur in mixed motive situations where common and conflicting interests are present simultaneously. On the other hand, it does remind us that the preservation of the institutional structures and norms may be one of those common interests that binds the group together and sometimes enables it to overcome more concrete conflicts of interest on specific issues. By providing an overall framework within which conflicts of interest may be discussed, debated, and negotiated, the institutional context may also place some restraints on the intensity of those conflicts of interest and provide some countervailing pressures to offset the will of individual states to resist agreements that would seem to restrict their sovereign prerogatives or impinge upon their individual interests.

CONCLUSIONS REGARDING THEORIES OF MULTILATERAL NEGOTIATIONS

In summary, multilateral negotiations have long presented a stumbling block for negotiation theorists because of their inherent complexity. That very same complexity has also plagued negotiators who have frequently found multilateral negotiations highly frustrating and too often tending toward lowest-common-denominator agreements with little substantive content. Yet both from a theoretical and a prescriptive point of view, getting a handle on multilateral negotiations requires that the process be simplified and rendered manageable through several distinct processes.

One means of doing so is to note the formation of coalitions among participants in the negotiations that may reduce the number of essential actors in a large international conference. Whether coalitions act as a bloc, or whether they explicitly or implicitly designate a bloc leader to speak on their behalf, the number of effective different parties may be reduced substantially through the process of coalition formation. In the extreme, the number of coalitions may reduce to two, in which case the negotiation becomes essentially bilateral. But even if three or more coalitions remain, the number of essentially independent parties to the negotiation is likely to be reduced substantially. When the number of coalitions is reduced, the number of parties that need to be brought along to achieve agreement is also reduced. Thus, the reduction of the number of completely independent actors through coalition formation also lays the groundwork for the construction of even larger supracoalitions that may eventually achieve consensus around a solution to the problems under negotiation. Coalition-building is one of the most frequent processes for achieving agreement in multilateral negotiations.

Second, when there are three or more parties or coalitions of parties, one may take advantage of the presence of crosscutting rather than reinforcing cleavages. These diverse patterns of difference may make it possible to tradeoff settlement of issues in dispute between two parties in exchange for their cooperation on other issues. Or it may make it possible to design multiple, linked tradeoffs or circular barter. In other words, complexity may itself introduce opportunities for creative problem solving, for advantageous use of issue aggregation and packaging, and other techniques to find common interests that may not be so readily apparent in the more direct clash between two opposing parties.

Finally, by virtue of the fact that multilateral negotiations in effect operate as groups, often within an institutional context, certain aspects of group dynamics may affect the ability of multiparty negotiations and conferences to overcome complexity and find agreement. Patterns of mutual exploration and learning may appear, and the context provided by historically developed institutional norms may restrain conflicts of interest or promote agreement on the basis of shared beliefs and norms of behavior. But perhaps the most important of these group factors is leadership, the emergence of one or a few group leaders (individuals or countries) who can inspire the group to find collective solutions to their common problems. This leadership may be a function of the hegemonical power position of a single actor, in which case that party's position within the group of participants may give it a particularly influential role. However, group leadership may also flow from expertise and the ability to command respect, produce new and attractive ideas, and articulate effective solutions to the group's problems. That is, as interdependence theorists have long emphasized, leadership within a group should not necessarily be equated with domination or exploitation of the weak by the strong:

> . . . leadership is based on action to induce other states to help stabilize an international regime. Leading states forego short-run gains in bargaining in order to secure the long-run gains associated with stable international regimes. Large states are most likely to make such short-run sacrifices, because they are likely to be major beneficiaries of the regime and they can expect their initiatives to have significant effects on world politics. Yet for such leadership to be sustainable under non-hegemonic conditions, other states must cooperate somewhat. . . . Cooperation by middle-level states, however, will depend in turn on the legitimacy of the regime—the widespread perception that it is indeed in the interests of all major parties.[44]

In other words, leadership that is directed toward securing agreements on international regimes widely perceived as serving common interests may make it possible to find agreement, even in large group negotiations and in spite of the complexity and confusion that inevitably surrounds multilateral and conference diplomacy.

While a good deal of theory building and research still needs to be done in order to gain a clearer understanding of multilateral negotiations, substantial progress now appears to be underway in gaining some systematic understanding of this complex process. As multilateral negotiations continue to flourish in a increasingly interdependent and multilateral international system, it is extremely likely that negotiation theorists will find it essential to devote increasing attention to this area, which still remains one of the least understood aspects of theorizing about international negotiations.

SOME GENERAL THEORETICAL CONCLUSIONS

We have now completed an extensive survey of many different dimensions of negotiation theory. I started with a simple game theoretic model of two unitary, symmetrical, and rational actors bargaining with one another about a single issue arrayed along a simple continuum. This kind of model lends itself readily to deductive inferences about the kinds of agreements that are likely to be reached, provided that one accepts a large number of simplifying assumptions. All of the simplifications associated with this model render it largely inappropriate as a general model for a process as complex as international negotiations. This simple model is quite parsimonious, and it suggests some useful axioms upon which a more nuanced and sophisticated theory of negotiations may be based.

The construction of that more complex theory, however, required relaxing one by one many of the simplifying assumptions of the game theoretic model, and the introduction of new sets of factors that influence the negotiation process and affect the outcome of that process. With the addition of each new set of factors, the model became progressively less parsimonious, but it has also expanded its ability to explain a wider set of phenomena associated with the negotiation process and a wider range of negotiations of the kind frequently found in international relations.

In part 3, I have looked successively at the impact of asymmetries between the negotiating parties, the role of individual and cultural factors in conditioning the behavior of negotiators, the domestic politics and bureaucratic struggles entailed in formulating negotiating positions and backstopping negotiators, the dynamics of the interaction process within the negotiations themselves, the influences exerted on negotiations by the relations among the parties and other international events outside the negotiations, the role of third parties that seek to aid in finding negotiated settlements, and the impact of multilateral negotiations and the dynamics of large global conferences. Obviously, not all of these considerations are necessary to explain every particular negotiation, and the outcomes of some negotiations may be accounted for efficiently with reference to only one or a few of the dimensions analyzed in this book.

Yet the development of a theoretical framework broad enough to account for the wide varieties of behaviors that occur in diverse kinds of international negotiations taking place in different situations requires a sacrifice of parsimony and high predictive power in favor of flexibility and breadth of explanation. This is an unavoidable tradeoff in the construction of theory in the social sciences, and I have clearly and explicitly opted here in favor of broad explanation under many different conditions rather than in support of narrow, but parsimonious explanation.

Furthermore, theoretical propinquity would tend to argue in favor of trying to identify the relative impact that each of these many factors has on the outcome of negotiations, hopefully even suggesting how each of these sets of factors interacts with the others. Unfortunately, this is impossible at our present stage of theoretical development, and perhaps will always remain an unsolvable problem. Indeed, the relative importance of each of the set of factors discussed in the chapters in part 3 will depend almost entirely on the context, issues, composition, and other aspects that may be unique to each and every specific negotiation. My goal has not been to develop a rigid, if coherent, theory that would account equally well for the relationship between process and outcome in all negotiations in general. Indeed, that is impossible unless we reduce the level of explanation to very simple and general factors that will provide little in terms of explanatory or predictive power for the wide variety of negotiations that occur in international relations. Such an approach would be of virtually no prescriptive value to practitioners of international negotiations.

What I have tried to do here is construct a flexible framework for the analysis of international negotiations, which acknowledges that the applicability of any given set of explanatory considerations will depend largely on the particular features of any specific negotiation. I have also tried to identify factors that are sufficiently ubiquitous in international negotiations that they will be of some value in helping to explain outcomes in most negotiations and are sufficiently general so that the most important variables required to explain any particular negotiation should have been considered within this framework. It is my hope that this somewhat eclectic account of the many factors that may affect international negotiations is sufficiently rich to be able to capture the most important explanations for a wide range of different kinds of international negotiations. Of course, this also means that the utilization of this framework to explain any particular negotiation will inevitably require the analyst to pick and choose those features of the framework that are most relevant for that specific case. This framework does not readily provide a simple set of concepts that may be applied in a more or less mechanistic fashion to any single negotiation. Rather, it seeks to present a series of guideposts, a checklist of essential categories and questions one may wish to pose in order to explain how the negotiation process links interdependent parties with different preferences to the results of any particular international negotiation.

In order to illustrate how these concepts may be applied to a particular negotiation, I shall examine in part 4 one such negotiation in the Eighteen Nation Disarmament Conference (ENDC) in 1962–63 that led to the agreement on the Partial Nuclear Test Ban Treaty. Although this case study will not consider all of the many factors mentioned in the previous chapters of this book, it will hopefully illustrate how concepts presented above may be applied flexibly and selectively according to the requirements of the case at hand.

Part 4

Application of the Theoretical Framework to the Test Ban Negotiations

Chapter 14

An Analysis of the Test Ban Negotiations

In this chapter, I shall apply relevant analytical concepts identified in parts 2 and 3 of this book to analyze the negotiation process in the partial test ban case, as summarized in chapter 2. My goal here is to demonstrate that the theoretical constructs provide a rich framework for explaining how many factors interacted to produce the outcome achieved in Moscow in July 1963 when the Partial Nuclear Test Ban Treaty was initialed. This is intended to suggest how a broad and eclectic theoretical framework can draw one's attention to the essential factors that explain the results of an important international negotiation. Similarly, the degree to which this framework helps us analyze the case may also serve as a partial validation of the theoretical construct as well. Obviously no single case can confirm a theory. But to the extent that a theoretical or analytical construct can be applied successfully to elucidate more and more cases, our confidence in the utility and validity of that theoretical approach grows. If this book inspires its readers to apply these constructs to a large variety of cases, then the theoretical framework presented may be simultaneously strengthened and adapted to fit a wider range of negotiation situations.

Therefore, in this chapter I shall present some of the major analytical components of a comprehensive negotiation framework one at a time in an effort to explain how the negotiation process on the test ban issue unfolded and resulted in the agreement achieved in Moscow in 1963. I will not follow exactly the same order in which these considerations were presented earlier, but I shall attempt to indicate how all aspects of the framework were relevant to the outcome and how they must be brought together to achieve a comprehensive understanding of the results obtained in Geneva and Moscow. But first I shall recapitulate briefly the main events of the test ban negotiations as presented in chapter 2.

THE PARTIAL TEST BAN NEGOTIATIONS: A BRIEF SUMMARY

The partial test ban negotiations took place over a five-year period from July 1958 through July 1963. At times these negotiations occurred in a bilateral format between the two superpowers; at other times they took place in a multilateral setting such as the Eighteen Nation Disarmament Conference (ENDC) from March 1962 through June 1963; and most often they occurred in a trilateral format such as when the United Kingdom joined the two superpowers in the final conference in Moscow in July 1963.

The negotiations were characterized by substantial bursts of progress alternating with periods of stalemate or even drawing apart. The early conferences of experts made a great deal of progress on technical issues, only to find that the political and diplomatic representatives were not so eager to reach agreement. The negotiations were also frequently affected by external events such as when the shooting down by the Soviet Union of a U-2 spy plane from the United States in 1960 was followed by a significant deterioration of the negotiations. This hostility continued through the Berlin crisis of 1961 and the Cuban missile crisis of 1962. In the aftermath of the Caribbean crisis in late 1962, substantial progress was made to narrow the differences between the sides on the issue of on-site inspections and seismographic stations on the territory of the nuclear states. But misunderstandings and diplomatic *faux pas* seemed to intervene to prevent the final attainment of an agreement on a comprehensive nuclear test ban in all environments.

It was only in the renewed cooperative atmosphere, which became apparent with Kennedy's June 1963 speech at American University, that real progress became evident. However, progress at attaining agreement also required a significant redefinition of the scope of the proposed treaty. At this time the two parties picked up on an abortive Anglo-American attempt in August 1962 to fractionate the issue, separating out the difficult issue of underground nuclear explosions from those in other environments—the atmosphere, oceans, and outer space. By that time it had become evident that the United States and Great Britain were firmly opposed to any ban on underground tests that did not include the right to intrusive on-site inspections of Soviet territory, while the Soviet Union was unalterably opposed to any significant number of intrusive inspections of their territory. Therefore, the logical conclusion was to fractionate the issue and reach agreement prohibiting the testing of nuclear weapons in those environments in which on-site inspections were not necessary to detect a violation, while permitting nuclear weapons testing to continue and even to expand underground. This compromise also carried the additional political advantage that it enabled advocates of continued arms tests in all nuclear powers to achieve their main objective while removing the threat of atmospheric contamination due to nuclear testing that had been a major source of political opposition.

The Partial Nuclear Test Ban Treaty, initialed in Moscow on 25 July 1963 and signed there on 5 August 1963, represented the first postwar agreement on arms control between the cold-war rivals. The long and difficult negotiations culminated in an important and enduring agreement that brought an end to atmospheric nuclear weapons testing among the three nuclear powers in 1963, and for the first time slowed the nuclear arms race between these hostile states. It marked an important turning point in Soviet-American relations and ushered in the first era of East-West détente. The lessons drawn from this important negotiation may have profound significance for understanding how states negotiate in a tense international environment over issues of life and death for their states and their entire population.

GOALS, INTERESTS, POSITIONS, AND BATNAS

The dilemma that the test ban negotiations posed for all three nuclear superpowers was that it entailed taking risks if one state should halt nuclear testing while the other continued, yet it also entailed risks associated with the continuation of nuclear testing and the resulting unimpeded rush of the nuclear arms race between the two superpowers. Throughout the negotiations there was a great deal of uncertainty in the minds of policy makers and negotiators about which of these two sets of risks was greater, and there was also a substantial division within each country about the relative balance of these risks. I shall turn to the domestic divisions over how to assess these risks later. For the moment I shall deal with the way in which the national leadership of both nuclear superpowers tended to handle these tradeoffs and alternate risks.

At the most general level it is likely that it was in the interest of both nuclear superpowers to slow the nuclear arms race, if this could be done without a serious risk of falling behind in nuclear weaponry. The development of intercontinental ballistic missiles in the late 1950s had made the nuclear arms race all the more dangerous due to the capability of delivering nuclear weapons virtually instantaneously. Both nuclear powers possessed this capability, and there was no known defense against it. The possibility of mutual annihilation through nuclear war had become a reality by 1961. Furthermore, as both sides rushed to close perceived missile gaps, the costs of the arms race itself were also increasing: the arms race entailed increasingly burdensome financial costs and dramatically increased the risks entailed in nuclear war, where modern delivery systems could wreak untold destruction anywhere on earth within a matter of minutes. Finally, public opinion was only beginning to become aware of the dangers of nuclear testing for the environment. In particular, high levels of a radioactive isotope, Strontium 90, a product of the fallout from nuclear testing, were entering the food chain and becoming especially concentrated in milk. This set off considerable alarm among the general public about the safety of basic foods that had long been taken for granted. Thus, both parties, especially the United States, had a distinct interest in reducing the atmospheric pollution produced by nuclear testing.

At the same time, the frequent debates over the missile gap made it quite clear that both sets of national leaders feared falling behind the other in the nuclear arms race. The rapidly changing nature of military technology made the military balance seem to be extremely sensitive to technological innovations, the kind of innovations that might be produced through a program of nuclear testing. To forego these advances while the other moved ahead seemed to spell disaster. In some sense, there were four broad possible interactive outcomes to the arms race, which both sides seemed to rank order more or less identically as follows from most desirable to most abhorrent:

1. Win the arms race and achieve strategic superiority over the other, thereby gaining political dominance as well.

2. Cease the arms race, have both countries disarm, and coexist peacefully.

3. Continue a balanced competition through the arms race, resulting in a tense stalemate at high cost to both parties.

4. Lose the arms race and become strategically inferior relative to the other and hence become dominated by them.

With respect to the test ban, each side had roughly two choices: to continue testing or cease testing. If these two choices are arrayed in a two-by-two game matrix, we can see in figure 14.1 that the result is a classic Prisoners' Dilemma outcome. As Christer Jönsson observes, the two sides both seemed to reason more or less as follows:

> If I continue testing, I may preclude lagging behind my opponent in weapons development and I might even come out ahead. On the other hand, continued testing promises to be costly in terms of absorbing resources that could be used elsewhere, and it does not safeguard me against a technological breakthrough by my opponent. These drawbacks probably outweigh the possible gains in security derived from continued testing.
>
> If, however, I cease testing and my opponent continues, I

shall be worse off, because then my opponent will reap the gains of new weapon developments while I lag behind. A mutual agreement to stop testing would alleviate the economic burden and also the fear of technological breakthrough. In addition, it might make it harder for other states to acquire and try out nuclear weapons.[1]

		USSR	
		Compete	Disarm
USA/UK	Compete	3, 3	1, 4
	Disarm	4, 1	2, 2

Figure 14.1 The Test Ban as a "Prisoners' Dilemma"

There is a stable outcome to this game in which both parties prefer to continue testing, producing the third preference for both. Perhaps the most important impact of the Cuban missile crisis was to reverse the rank-order between outcomes 3 and 4. Suddenly a continued arms race seemed to both Kennedy and Khrushchev to carry a very high risk of nuclear annihilation, an outcome even worse than losing the arms race. This was indicated in part by Khrushchev's hasty retreat from Cuba and by Kennedy's frequent observation that the risks of a violation of a test ban agreement were considerably outweighed by the dangers of an unfettered arms race. This change in the preference ordering was further strengthened by the mutual fear of nuclear proliferation, especially by China. Both countries wanted to place considerable pressure upon potential new members of the nuclear club not to test and develop these weapons. As the Chinese program advanced, however, and as both parties became aware that the Peoples' Republic of China was on the verge of testing a nuclear weapon, their interest in a test ban also strengthened.

When priorities 3 and 4 are reversed as in figure 14.2, the game changes from a Prisoners' Dilemma to Chicken. Chicken has no stable or dominant solution, but it does provide some hope that the two parties can agree on mutual restraint, in which case each receives their second preferred outcome—peaceful coexistence. As the game changed, the interests of both parties favored a more cooperative, if not terribly

USSR

		Compete	Disarm
	Compete	4, 4	1, 3
USA/UK	Disarm	3, 1	2, 2

Figure 14.2 The Test Ban as "Chicken"

stable, solution to the arms race in general and the issue of nuclear testing in particular.

At the same time, avoiding the outcome of losing the arms race remained unattractive in both games; indeed, it was the least preferred outcome in the Prisoners' Dilemma and the third preference of both in Chicken. Therefore, each side retained a BATNA in which it wished to avoid an outcome where the other could take advantage of a test ban agreement to achieve or act upon a clear strategic advantage. For the United States and Great Britain, this meant avoiding an uninspected ban that the Soviet Union might violate to achieve significant technological gains while the West was frozen into inaction. Somewhat less evident to Western analysts at the time, though probably clearer from the vantage point of thirty years later, is that a major Soviet concern may well have been that the West would learn how far the Soviet Union trailed in the strategic arms race. Although the Soviets were the first to launch an earth satellite in 1957, it did not take long for the United States to achieve a clear quantitative and qualitative lead in the capability to deliver nuclear weapons over long distances. It was probably in an effort to compensate for this American leap forward in strategic missile delivery systems that the Soviets installed their medium-range missiles in Cuba in 1962. Having lost that advantage when those missiles were withdrawn from Cuba, however, the Soviets found themselves surrounded by U.S. medium-range missiles and threatened by intercontinental-range missiles based in the United States. Their one hope of staving off this threat was to maintain what we now know to have been the myth of Soviet superiority in strategic weapons. To have opened their territory to widespread on-site inspections in 1963 risked revealing this situation, which the Soviets had every reason to believe the West would seek to exploit. Therefore, preserving the maximum secrecy for their strategic programs remained a top Soviet priority, making their resistance point in the negotiations one in which they would allow few and preferably no on-site inspections of their military facilities under a test ban agreement.

In summary, the United States, United Kingdom, and Soviet Union had a common interest, at least by 1963, in achieving a test ban treaty in order to slow the arms race and the proliferation of nuclear weapons to so-called "nth countries"—particularly France and China. They also felt under common pressure from world public opinion and from their own publics at home to cease the atmospheric pollution that inevitably accompanied nuclear weapons tests above ground. Yet at the same time the West feared that the Soviet Union might exploit an uninspected ban to gain strategic superiority, so they insisted on on-site inspections as part of a comprehensive test ban. On the other hand, the Soviet Union probably feared revealing to its enemies its relative strategic inferiority. If the West were permitted extensive on-site inspections, they might have become aware of Soviet strategic weakness and taken advantage of their superiority politically or perhaps even militarily. Therefore, out of a sense of security, the Soviet Union opposed on-site inspections to verify a test ban treaty. These two BATNAs narrowed the bargaining space considerably, leaving open only the option for a test ban in those environments where the ban could be verified without on-site inspections. Therefore, the outcome of a partial ban on nuclear weapons tests in the atmosphere, outer space, and under water was a logical result of the essential perceived interests of the two parties, their minimum acceptable positions, and the range of bargaining space within which they could strike an agreement.

THE STRUCTURE OF THE NEGOTIATIONS: POWER AND NUMBER OF PARTIES

In some ways the nuclear test ban negotiations combined features of bilateral negotiations between two relatively symmetrical parties, bilateral negotiations with a third party, and multilateral negotiations. In the period prior to 1962 the negotiations were formally trilateral, though in reality they were essentially bilateral. That is, the United States and the United Kingdom acted in tandem throughout most of these negotiations, and U.S. leadership remained dominant throughout.[2] Even the Ten Nation Disarmament Conference involved essentially members of NATO and the Warsaw Pact face-to-face against one another. Furthermore, for all practical purposes there were few significant disparities between these two alliances or even between the two superpowers in terms of power and ability to influence the outcome of the negotiations.

Beginning in 1962, however, the ENDC became formally multilateral, although elements of bilateralism were retained. The United States and the Soviet Union were cochairs. This meant that they each selected their own allies to participate and they had to agree upon the eight non-aligned nations that made up the balance of the membership. Furthermore, the eight nonaligned countries often acted together as a bloc, trying to mediate between the two cold-war alliances. In this respect, the ENDC approximated a model of bilateral negotiations with a third-party mediator.

However, it is also important to note that the two alliances were not always perfectly cohesive. On the Soviet side, the four allies—Bulgaria, Czechoslovakia, Poland and Romania—generally followed the alliance position closely. On the Western side, the British generally seemed to be more eager to reach an agreement than their American allies. For example, the British were especially reluctant to resume atmospheric nuclear testing in 1962, and it was with great reluctance that British Prime Minister Macmillan agreed with President Kennedy in their meeting in Bermuda in December 1961 to allow the United States to test on Christmas Island, a British possession in the Pacific where they had previously tested nuclear weapons. This difference in tone reached its peak in Moscow when Ambassador Harriman held strongly to the U.S. position about language of the withdrawal clause that Soviet Foreign Minister Gromyko opposed. According to Harriman's own account, a threat by Harriman to walk out if the Soviets did not accept the withdrawal clause led Lord Hailsham to telegram Prime Minister Macmillan, suggesting that Harriman was being excessively tough with Gromyko. Macmillan then asked the British ambassador in Washington to speak with President Kennedy about this, though Washington continued to support Harriman's decision to "sit tight" on the issue.[3] This was not necessary, however, as Gromyko came forth with a compromise proposal the following day that broke the deadlock and essentially paved the way for agreement on the language contained in the withdrawal clause. With this exception, however, the British generally followed the American lead. Although of lesser significance, Canada also often acted independently of its allies as well, to the point where the Indian ambassador, Arthur Lall, often referred to it as "the ninth nonaligned country."[4]

Viewed in the larger context, these subtle differences between the British and Canadian positions and those of their American allies were really quite minor, and the negotiation remained essentially a bilateral East-West dialogue. The major structural feature of the negotiations was provided by the eight nonaligned countries, which tried to serve as third-party mediators throughout the sixteen months during which the ENDC discussed the test ban issue. The eight nonaligned countries—Brazil, Burma, Ethiopia, India, Mexico, Nigeria, Sweden, and the United Arab Republic—were quite diverse in their orientations, though they usually tried to act as a unified bloc in Geneva. Indeed, there was a certain tacit division of labor among them.

The only significant technical expertise in the group on nuclear issues was provided by Sweden. Led by Ambassador Alva Myrdal, the Swedes were readily able to produce technical information provided by their defense, university, and research institutes that specialized in military, arms control, and seismological issues. The Swedish delegation assumed the role of task-oriented leader of the nonaligned group, trying to find technical solutions that would bridge the gap between the two antagonists. A very different role was played by Mexico. Under the leadership of Ambassador Luis Padilla Nervo, a former president of the U.N. General Assembly, Mexico became the affect leader of the group. Ambassador Padilla Nervo continually reminded the negotiators of their responsibilities to the human race and the future of the planet, engaging in extensive rhetoric dramatizing the importance of their task. Finally, a classic diplomatic role of formal mediator was often played by the Indian delegation under the leadership of Ambassador Arthur Lall. Lall, however, was also strongly influenced by Indian domestic politics, and especially by the goals of his patron, Defense Minister Krishna Menon.

The eight nonaligned countries generally acted as neutral mediators, without access to significant resources. Although several—including Brazil, India, and Sweden—were potential nuclear proliferators, none had the military or economic resources to threaten in any significant way the interests of either bloc. Furthermore, they clearly had an agreement among themselves not to compromise their neutrality in any way. Thus, when the Eight Nation Memorandum was accepted by both East and West, but interpreted in diametrically opposite terms, none of the eight nations was willing to offer any additional interpretation of the memorandum that might have helped to clarify their intentions. Once the two interpretations of the intentionally ambiguous document were clearly stated in Geneva, any further interpretation by the eight nonaligned countries would have necessarily favored either the NATO or Warsaw Pact interpretation of the document. Thus, they refused to compromise their neutrality, even at the price of allowing their attempt to overcome the deadlock itself become the source of stalemate within the ENDC.

The primary role played by the eight nonaligned countries was that of a facilitator of communication, compromise, and convergence, although they may be considered to have made a half-hearted effort to serve as a formulator of new agreements. This latter role was played only at the beginning of the ENDC, through the Eight Nation Memorandum. Here they attempted to identify the BATNAs of the two parties and, with the assistance of some creative ambiguity, to identify a formula for on-site inspections by invitation that they hoped would satisfy both parties. They believed that it would serve the Western need to have specific provisions for on-site inspections, while preserving a veto against espionage on the part of the Soviet Union. While they realized that this would not constitute the obligatory inspections favored by the West, they felt that by giving parties an obligation to issue invitations in the event of suspicion they would put sufficient pressure on them to comply. And they further felt that the refusal to invite inspectors when requested by the International Commission would virtually constitute an admission of guilt on the part of the party refusing these inspections. Therefore, they hoped that this formula might overcome the impasse.

When it became evident, however, that each of the superpowers interpreted the Eight Nation Memorandum as a vindication of their own prior positions, the eight nations gave up any further attempts to formulate new solutions. Rather, over the next several months, they urged the parties to make concessions that would bring them closer together along the lines suggested by their formula. Furthermore, the fact that the three nuclear powers almost immediately created a tripartite subcommittee to discuss the test ban issue under the ENDC auspices throughout 1962 seemed to indicate a lack of enthusiasm upon the part of the big three for the mediating role of the nonaligned. Therefore, the eight nonaligned found it increasingly important to try to appeal over the heads of the delegations of these three countries to world public opinion, especially in opposing the resumption of nuclear testing by the United States or the Soviet Union.

The eight nonaligned countries continued to search for possible ways of overcoming the stalemate between the nuclear powers. It was the nonaligned that first began to disaggregate the issues, at least in public, and emphasize the special risks associated with atmospheric testing of nuclear weapons. Indeed, it was the Brazilian delegate who, on 25 July 1962, noted that all of the obstacles to agreement seemed to concern only the issue of underground nuclear tests, whereas there did not seem to be any important obstacles to an agreement banning atmospheric tests. He further noted that the role of the nonaligned was not to serve as arbitrators, but rather as conciliators that would use persuasion to try to promote consensus and create confidence on the part of the nuclear powers. He then concluded with the first public suggestion within the ENDC of what in fact became the disaggregated formula around which an agreement was eventually achieved: "Why, then, not concentrate our efforts on this question of atmospheric and outer space tests which are the most dangerous, actually and potentially, and the ones which have a most disturbing effect on mind, body and nerves? Why not, along the lines of the eight-nation joint memorandum, further explore the possibility of an agreement on the question of control of atmospheric and outer space tests and, at the same time, start a discussion on the adequate methods of detection and identification of underground tests?"[5]

Within a few weeks, all eight of the nonaligned countries began to support this position in one way or another. The proposal was especially reinforced by the Swedish Ambassador Alva Myrdal on 1 August by producing an impressive inventory of meteorological and seismographic facilities around the world that could facilitate monitoring nuclear weapons tests. Swedish support for an atmospheric test ban was conveyed to President Kennedy by Ambassador Arthur Dean at a White House meeting on the next day, and the president's advisors began to consider alternatives to the comprehensive proposal thus far supported by U.S. negotiators.[6] When the United States and the United Kingdom introduced their two draft treaties on 27 August 1962 it seemed natural that the eight nonaligned countries would have supported the second draft of a partial ban with a good deal of enthusiasm. However, the rapid Soviet rejection of the partial ban proposal made it difficult for the nonaligned nations to support the partial ban while still maintaining their neutrality.

The result was that the eight nonaligned nations played a somewhat less active role on the test ban issue from that time on. Following the Cuban missile crisis in October, it was obvious to almost everyone that the test ban negotiations were in effect held hostage to the broader lines of Soviet-American relations. Thus, once they had helped to clarify the options, the nonaligned countries had only a very limited role to play in these negotiations. Their direct influence on the negotiations throughout 1963 was very limited, and it appears that they played virtually no role in arranging for the Moscow conference in July 1963 or for influencing the negotiating process that took place there among the three nuclear weapons states.

Power asymmetry was largely absent as a factor in these negotiations, with one possible exception. Following the Cuban missile crisis the Soviet Union probably felt that it was falling into an increasingly inferior position in terms of the capability to deliver nuclear weapons over long ranges. As the American missile development program rapidly sped up in the early 1960s, it was likely evident to Soviet military leaders that they were falling further behind the United States in intercontinental ballistic missiles and in their ability to station nuclear missiles within easy striking range. This sense of inferiority may have had an impact on the opposition frequently expressed to a test ban by Soviet military leaders. As noted previously, it probably also contributed to the absolute opposition by the Soviet military to allowing any on-site inspections of their military facilities that might have put into doubt their bluff of nuclear superiority. The Americans and British appear not to have been fully aware of this emerging asymmetry, and failed to exploit it significantly in the negotiations. But this may have been a significant factor in complicating the ability of the two sides to agree upon the kind of verification machinery that would have been necessary to achieve a comprehensive test ban agreement.

THE IMPACT OF INDIVIDUAL BEHAVIOR

In this section I shall turn our attention to the role of individual negotiators from the three nuclear powers in these negotiations. For the most part, these were highly constrained and formal negotiations with relatively little room for individual personality or images to exert dramatic effects on the negotiations. The complex combination of scientific/technical issues and complicated political issues also meant that individual roles were also diminished in overall importance. Yet in the final analysis, political will to achieve an agreement also turned out to be an important factor in these negotiations, and it is for this reason that much of this section will be devoted to the roles of the two superpowers leaders, John F. Kennedy and Nikita S. Khrushchev.

John F. Kennedy

When President Kennedy entered office in January 1961 he was strongly committed to achieving a nuclear test ban agreement. However, the first major decision that he faced on this issue concerned the resumption of nuclear testing. A combination of pressures emanating from the Atomic Energy Commission, the weapons laboratories, and the Department of Defense was strongly advocating an end to the moratorium on nuclear tests and a resumption of these tests. Kennedy's early response was to try to postpone a decision on the resumption of testing to allow the process of negotiations in the Ten Nation Disarmament Committee to try to overcome the impasse. However, Kennedy's optimism about the test ban issue declined throughout 1961. His commitment to maintaining a moratorium while negotiations were underway began to weaken after his encounter with Khrushchev in Vienna in June, after which he permitted preparations for a new round of nuclear tests without authorizing the actual implementation of those tests. His hopes for agreement declined even further following the Berlin crisis in August when he saw that the Soviet leader appeared to be testing his resolve after the encounter in Vienna. Thus, on 30 August he authorized the resumption of underground nuclear tests and permitted preparations to get underway for resuming atmospheric tests. When the Geneva Conference on the Discontinuance of Nuclear Weapons Tests dissolved following a desultory session on 29 January 1962, President Kennedy's personal ability to resist the pressures of those who wanted to resume testing was at a low point. Yet, as Glenn Seaborg makes clear, the president remained firmly committed, perhaps more than ever, to the goal of obtaining a nuclear test ban: "He [Kennedy] appeared, in private, to be considerably more in favor of accepting risks and making compromises in order to achieve a test ban than either he or U.S. negotiators ever allowed themselves to be in public. The president's public position was in all likelihood constrained by the realities of American politics, particularly by what the U.S. Senate, through its leadership, had given notice it would be likely to accept."[7]

Even when he decided to resume atmospheric nuclear testing, Kennedy rationalized it on the grounds that it would provide an additional incentive for the Soviets to negotiate seriously on the nuclear test ban.[8] Nuclear testing became a kind of bargaining chip that Kennedy tried to manipulate, both to satisfy demands of domestic constituencies, on the one hand, and lever the Soviets toward a more serious negotiating position, on the other.

The major attitudinal turning point for Kennedy, however, came in the aftermath of the Cuban missile crisis. At first sight it would appear that Soviet behavior in this crisis might have reinforced Kennedy's increasingly hostile image of the Soviet Union, built up through a series of setbacks in Vienna, Berlin, and then in Cuba. Had Kennedy been the kind of cognitively rigid personality that rejects ambiguity and insists on simplicity and absolute consistency, it is probable that this would have been the outcome. Yet instead Kennedy recognized the opportunity as well as the threat inherent in the Caribbean crisis. At the very end of the crisis, on 28 October 1962, he wrote to Khrushchev: "perhaps now, as we step back from danger, we can make some real progress in this vital field. I think that we should give priority to questions relating to the proliferation of nuclear weapons . . . and to the great effort for a nuclear test ban."[9]

Throughout the next several months, Kennedy appeared to follow a two track diplomatic style. In the official negotiations and in many public statements, he took a fairly hard line, perhaps largely to assuage his critics in Congress and in those agencies of the government that were opposed to a test ban. At the same time, he increasingly utilized back channel and track two diplomacy to try to bring Khrushchev around toward his position. He relied on individuals such as Norman Cousins to make personal contact with Khrushchev and convey messages about the test ban issue to and from the Soviet leader. Then Kennedy went public in June 1963 with his speech at American University, that, unlike most of his other speeches, was written without soliciting any input or advice from the usual government agencies.[10] He sought instead to hold out an olive branch to the Soviets without having to balance this with the usual threats or warnings of nuclear destruction that normally accompanied any such overtures. This, he felt, was clearly a time to present an unambiguous and undiluted appeal to the Soviet interest in slowing the nuclear arms race.

Kennedy's personal commitment to success in these negotiations was further indicated by the way in which he personally managed the negotiations from that moment forward. Ambassador Harriman's instructions for the Moscow negotiations were hammered out in White House meetings in which the president participated along with his top advisors. While Kennedy participated in drafting instructions, he also told his emissary that his primary responsibility was to achieve an agreement within general guidelines, without any specific instructions on tactical details. Thus, he left the tactical aspects of the negotiations up to Harriman, a highly experienced diplomat. Once Harriman went to Moscow, Kennedy insisted that all communications with Washington be directed through the White House in order to prevent various government agencies from interfering in the process. Once he made a strong commitment to achieve an agreement, Kennedy did everything within his power as president to see to it that the negotiation process would not be complicated by excessive attention to domestic bureaucratic or political concerns. And he also placed a good deal of faith in the diplomatic savvy of Averell Harriman to carry out the negotiations and produce the result that he wanted to achieve. There can be little doubt that this commitment to realize a test ban agreement made at the highest political level in Washington and implemented by a skilled negotiator was an important factor in the successful negotiations in Moscow.

Nikita S. Khrushchev

If Kennedy's role and personal belief system was important to the outcome of the test ban negotiations, the personal role of Khrushchev on the Soviet side was at least as great, if not even greater. Following Stalin's death in 1953, there was a substantial period during which a struggle for power took place within the Kremlin. It was not until 1958 that Khrushchev was in full command of the Soviet government, following the ouster of the so-called antiparty group and his replacement of Nikolai Bulganin as premier. Khrushchev's major priority after achieving full control was to improve the efficiency of agricultural production, but this required a relaxation of international tensions so that he could allocate resources away from the military and heavy industry, the so-called "metal eaters," and toward the agricultural and consumer sectors of the economy. Thus, initially within the Soviet government, he began to advocate negotiations on a nuclear test ban along with Anastasia Mikoyan, one of his strongest supporters within the leadership circles. Khrushchev publicly declared his support for a test ban in his address to the 21st Party Congress in January 1959, even though this effort seemed to receive little support from elsewhere within the high levels of the Soviet political system.

Following his visit to the United States in the fall of 1959, Khrushchev became an even more eager advocate of a nuclear test ban, which he suggested could be completed at the Paris Summit scheduled for May 1960. His support for such a test ban with the West was founded upon his belief that there were sober and realistic elements in the West with whom he could make contact and who would be eager to negotiate an agreement with him, in spite of the opposition of certain monopoly capitalists who still wanted to gain financial profit from the arms race. As Christer Jönsson has pointed out, Khrushchev was among the first Soviet leaders to develop a dual perception of the United States rather than the typical Soviet stereotype of the United States as an implacably hostile enemy of communism and the Soviet Union. This somewhat more cognitively complex image recognized that the United States was both a partner and an enemy, depending on which faction of the American elite one was speaking about.[11] This dual image was based on a more sophisticated appraisal of domestic divisions within the American polity than was generally found in Soviet commentary about the West. It also reflected a certain tolerance for the ambiguity inherent in superpower relations during the cold war, where the two sides represented ideological opponents that could each destroy the other completely. This very fact also gave them a common interest in avoiding that disastrous final outcome.

Khrushchev's optimism about a test ban declined considerably, however, after the shooting down of the U-2 spy plane and the failure of the Paris Summit in May 1960. Not only did this mean that a valuable opportunity to conclude a test ban agreement had been missed, but it also meant that Khrushchev's opposition from hard liners within his own government increased as a result of this new evidence about American espionage efforts against the USSR. Thus, Khrushchev was forced to beat a hasty retreat on many foreign policy fronts. Jönsson observes: "Khrushchev's dilemma was that whereas he saw détente with the West as necessary for his pro-consumer program, to pursue détente unambiguously in the wake of the U-2 incident would have exposed him to charges of being 'soft on capitalism.' And the summer of 1961 saw a series of militant Soviet moves: a one-third increase of the military budget, suspension of the 1960 troop cut, erection of the Berlin wall, and resumption of nuclear testing."[12]

Following the U-2 incident and then the Vienna Summit one year later, Khrushchev began to become increasingly preoccupied with the German issue. Furthermore, he found himself pressured into giving in to those who wanted to resume nuclear testing, even while negotiations on a test ban were taking place in Geneva. Nonetheless, the Soviet leader continued to advocate a test ban quietly throughout this period, without any apparent support from within the leadership circles of the Kremlin. As with Kennedy, Khrushchev seemed to gain renewed vigor in his advocacy of a test ban following the Cuban missile crisis in October 1962. In his case, however, this came at a time of great domestic weakness and an intense foreign challenge from the Chinese. His surrender in the Caribbean played into the hands of his hard-line domestic opponents, especially Mikhail A. Suslov and Frol R. Kozlov, whose role will be discussed more fully in the next section, as well as into the hands of his harsh critics among the Chinese leaders. Kozlov especially seemed to be on the ascendancy in the spring of 1963 when he was suddenly taken ill in April. This allowed Khrushchev to reassert himself as the dominant leader of the Soviet Union. From that time on the Soviet leader resumed his efforts at establishing détente with the West and pursuing the conflict with the Chinese communist leadership, having apparently recognized that he could no longer regain their support under any reasonable conditions.[13]

At about this time Khrushchev also began to engage in track two diplomacy with Kennedy through intermediaries such as Norman Cousins. He especially emphasized openly how recent events had embarrassed him in his relations with his domestic opponents, especially the unofficial offer by the U.S. ambassador in Geneva in late 1962 to accept two to three on-site inspections, which was subsequently disavowed by the U.S. government. Khrushchev purposely went outside official channels to plead with Western leaders to give him a face-saving way to achieve an agreement, which would not require the kind of public humiliation that he had experienced in the wake of the Cuban missile crisis. He also acknowledged that the political factions that he and his allies saw in the West were also mirrored in his own government, and he stressed the need for factions on both sides that favored a test ban to meet at a propitious moment when their efforts could not be contradicted by their opponents. Thus, there was a kind of mirror image created in which leaders on both sides recognized that there was considerable internal division within both nuclear superpowers, in contrast to the images of many members in both governments who perceived the other side as a monolithic, unitary actor. Even though Khrushchev achieved sufficient power after Kozlov's illness to bring the Soviet government to accept a partial rather than a comprehensive test ban, his support apparently remained thin throughout the entire negotiations. Indeed, even at the signing of the treaty, Khrushchev was accompanied only by his closest allies within the Politburo—Leonid Brezhnev, Andrei P. Kirilenko, and Nikolai I. Podgorny.

Thus, it might be reasonable to conclude that the test ban agreement was achieved in part because of Khrushchev's personal support for it within the Soviet leadership. At least for a brief period of time he was able to gain ascendancy on this issue, and he was willing to risk his personal position by defying his opponents in order to achieve this important arms control agreement with the West. Khrushchev appeared himself at the Moscow negotiations on several occasions, and it was perhaps fortunate that they took place on his own territory where he was better able to assert his authority over his own negotiators without interference. With the assistance of his loyal foreign minister, Andrei Gromyko, he was able to achieve a personal triumph viewed in the context of the substantial internal opposition.

During the final phase of the test ban negotiations, the leaders of both nuclear superpowers seemed to be personally in charge of the test ban negotiations. Although the bureaucracies and the many diplomats that had participated in the previous negotiations had defined the issues and identified the major options, in the end the personal role of the two world leaders seems to have been an important one in achieving the final breakthrough in Moscow in July 1963.

BUREAUCRATIC AND POLITICAL CONSTRAINTS
ON THE NEGOTIATIONS

Although Kennedy and Khrushchev appear to have been very influential in the final stages of the test ban negotiations, up until that point the negotiations appear to have been very much mired in the bureaucratic and political competition that was going on in both nuclear powers. Most negotiating positions presented in Geneva, and many relevant actions that took place outside the negotiations, reflected the outcome of extensive bureaucratic and political bargaining in both major countries. In this section I shall examine these domestic influences on both sets of negotiators and indicate how they constrained the range of possible options around which an agreement could be fashioned.

The United States

In the U.S. government there were several key groups that were generally opposed to a nuclear test ban treaty, at least on terms that were negotiable with the Soviet Union. These included the Atomic Energy Commission (AEC) and the weapons laboratories under its jurisdiction, the Joint Chiefs of Staff and the uniformed military forces under their command, and conservative members of Congress from both parties.

The Atomic Energy Commission and the weapons labs under its authority were active opponents of a test ban agreement throughout the entire period of negotiations. The AEC had opposed Eisenhower's test moratorium, and stressed throughout that time the importance of nuclear weapons tests for at least two different purposes. The first was for the development of new weapons technologies, including enhanced radiation warheads (later referred to as the neutron bomb), smaller warheads required for multiple warhead (or MIRV'd) missiles, and nuclear explosives that could be utilized in an antiballistic missile program. Second, the AEC insisted on the importance of proof testing existing weapons in order to determine the reliability of weapons stationed with active nuclear units of the armed forces. The AEC also had a strong institutional interest, namely that a test ban would make it difficult to retain highly qualified nuclear scientists and maintain updated laboratories; in the event that testing had to be resumed, the U.S. nuclear program might be greatly delayed in starting up again. Under the leadership of Glenn Seaborg during the Kennedy administration, the AEC officially came closer to the main administration position at least at the top level, although opposition continued from the weapons labs in the field (led by Dr. Edward Teller, a famous nuclear scientist and the so-called father of the H-bomb). In addition, throughout the negotiations the AEC tried to protect the Plowshares program for peaceful nuclear explosions, a position on which it was successful up until the final stages of the Moscow negotiations when Plowshares was abandoned in order to get the Soviets to accept the Western provisions on withdrawal from the treaty.

Second, the Joint Chiefs of Staff and even many on the civilian side in the Department of Defense tended to oppose a test ban agreement. They also presented several major arguments, generally stressing their belief that the test ban would enable the Soviets to achieve significant military advantages. Perhaps the most consistent argument of the military leadership was that the United States needed to maintain a substantial lead over the Soviet Union in nuclear weaponry in order to offset what at the time was perceived to be a significant inferiority, especially numerically, of NATO troops on the ground in Europe. If a test ban agreement cut into the American advantage in nuclear weaponry, then it would also reduce U.S. security. The joint chiefs were mostly concerned about possible Soviet cheating on the test ban agreement, through which they feared the Soviets could gain advantages in nuclear weaponry that the United States could not match because of the agreement. Some even went so far as to argue that the Soviet test series in the fall of 1961 had enabled them to gain a significant advantage in nuclear weapons technology, which only continued testing by the United States could close.

Opposition to the test ban by the joint chiefs continued all the way through the Senate hearings on the treaty's ratification. Although the joint chiefs had not been able to block the negotiation of the treaty, they did insist on a series of very stringent conditions in return for their reluctant support for the treaty before the Senate, many of which appeared to negate the intent of the treaty itself. These included a commitment to an aggressive series of underground nuclear tests, the maintenance of modern laboratory facilities with a highly professional scientific staff prepared to resume atmospheric testing at any time, and continuous research on improving the technology and intelligence activities for detecting violations of the treaty. Certainly these conditions had a serious deleterious effect on the ability of the United States to agree to a comprehensive nuclear test ban treaty for many decades to come.

Third, members of the Senate on both sides of the aisle expressed considerable concern about the test ban agreement. For the most part, these objections tended to echo those of the weapons labs and the military, combined with a general distrust of and hostility toward the Soviet Union. Senate opposition was led on the Republican side by Barry Goldwater of Arizona and on the Democratic side by Henry Jackson of Washington. In addition, Christopher Dodd, a Democrat from Connecticut, criticized U.S. concessions on the comprehensive test ban extensively in a Senate speech in February 1963, and in May he cosponsored with Senator Hubert Humphrey of Minnesota a Senate resolution calling for a partial nuclear test ban in the atmosphere and oceans. Although the members of the Senate were not fully integrated into the negotiations themselves, several key members served as liaisons with the Geneva negotiations. Of special importance were Senator Albert Gore Sr., a Democrat from Tennessee, and Senator Bourke Hickenlooper, a Republican from Iowa, who served on two of the key and very different Senate committees responsible for the negotiations—the Foreign Relations Committee and the Joint Committee on Atomic Energy. Both of these senators also served as advisors to the U.S. delegation in Geneva.[14]

Arrayed on the other side of this issue were a number of bureaucratic agencies and political groups that tended to be much more supportive of a test ban agreement. In general, the State Department, from which a significant number of the diplomats actually negotiating in Geneva came, seemed to be supportive of an agreement. Indeed, in at least one case the efforts of Ambassador Arthur Dean to expedite the process by revealing a BATNA still being debated within bureaucratic circles in Washington almost caused the complete breakdown of the negotiations, since this error led Khrushchev to accuse Kennedy of acting in bad faith. This would seem to illustrate an extreme example of the boundary role conflict, but one in which the negotiator actually overstepped his boundaries and created havoc for the negotiations for some time to come.

In addition, Senate and administration supporters of arms control led a fight to create the Arms Control and Disarmament Agency, which was officially established in September 1961 as a primary center for developing policy and negotiating agreements in this field. Led by William C. Foster during this period, it rapidly began to play a significant role in integrating different bureaucratic positions on arms control and managing the negotiations within the U.S. government.

Finally, support for an agreement began to grow within general public opinion, especially among environmentally conscious citizens, who in some ways played an early role in the creation of a significant environmental lobby in the United States. Because these individuals and groups focused primarily on the threat of radioactive fallout from atmospheric tests, they also tended to influence the eventual focus of the agreement around a ban on atmospheric as opposed to underground testing. As early as 1957 a Gallup poll revealed that 63 percent of the U.S. population polled favored a test ban, and even though most of the public was not actively engaged on this issue, this did provide a favorable reservoir of support for advocates of a test ban agreement.

On balance, then, the forces arrayed against the treaty seemed at least as powerful as those that supported it within the United States. Throughout most of the negotiations these opposing forces held a rough balance in determining the U.S. negotiating position, which combined elements of carrots and sticks, but which continued to insist upon inspection provisions clearly unacceptable to the Soviet Union. The final shift in favor of a test ban would seem to be accounted for primarily by the reaction of the public and especially of the American president to the Cuban missile crisis and the fear of nuclear holocaust that it engendered. In the final analysis, it was President Kennedy himself who threw the weight of his office behind a partial test ban, combined with a shift in support in the Senate in that same direction, which seemed to tip the bureaucratic balance in Washington in favor of negotiating the treaty. Yet the uncertain basis of his support would seem to account for Kennedy's insistence on controlling the negotiation process in Moscow personally, keeping his bureaucratic and political opponents almost entirely out of the process, and then for his subsequent concessions, especially to the joint chiefs, in order to assure a favorable vote and eventual ratification of the treaty in the Senate.

The Soviet Union

Just as President Kennedy and the U.S. negotiators in Geneva were constrained by bureaucratic and political forces at home, so were Premier Khrushchev and his test ban negotiators. Khrushchev's major sources of domestic opposition were two-fold. First, there were his ideological opponents within the Presidium of the Supreme Soviet, Mikhail A. Suslov and Frol R. Kozlov. Although Khrushchev had removed many of his opponents in the so-called antiparty group, these two ideological purists remained close to the center of power and were a threat to Khrushchev throughout most of his tenure. These two opposed Khrushchev's dual image of political divisions within the United States, insisting that monopoly capitalism in the United States was united in its desire to promote the arms race and international tensions. In 1960, in a reorganization of the upper levels of the Communist Party apparatus, these two managed to strengthen their positions and have some of Khrushchev's allies demoted. After the U-2 incident they both became powerful forces in the Soviet bureaucracy and claimed that American actions substantiated their image of implacable American hostility as opposed to Khrushchev's more nuanced, differentiated, and cognitively complex view. The result was that Khrushchev's public statements toward the United States became more hostile and his statements on the test ban negotiations became more negative and militant. Suslov and Kozlov both argued that a test ban was irrelevant in the absence of an agreement on General and Complete Disarmament (GCD), and they began to emphasize the desirability of moving forward on Soviet proposals on GCD within the Eighteen Nation Disarmament Conference in 1962. This contrasted with Khrushchev's efforts to reach agreement on the more limited, but also more negotiable, test ban treaty. As noted above, it was only Kozlov's illness in the spring of 1963 that neutralized this source of opposition to Khrushchev's arms control policies.

The second major source of domestic opposition was the military-heavy industry organizations, often referred to as the "metal-eaters." Although Khrushchev had attained power with the aid of Marshal Georgi Zhukov and the military, he dismissed his military leader in October 1957. However, Zhukov left behind a professional and independent military organization that continued to resist excessive pressure from the party or bureaucratic leadership. His replacement as defense minister, Marshall Rodion Malinovsky, continued to be an important source of opposition to Khrushchev on arms control matters, as well as on policy toward agriculture and consumer goods. Throughout their period of ascendancy from the U-2 incident until the aftermath of the Cuban missile crisis in late 1962, the military effectively opposed any consideration of arms control options that would open Soviet territory to any significant on-site inspections. As noted above, this may have been especially accounted for by fears in high level military circles that extensive inspections of Soviet military facilities might reveal their military weaknesses, which could then be exploited by what they perceived to be an aggressive opponent. Furthermore, it appears to have been the military that largely prevailed on Khrushchev to resume nuclear testing during this period. They feared that they were falling rapidly behind the West in nuclear technology and that only through an extensive testing program could they close the widening gap. They also tended to insist that the nuclear testing issue be closely linked to agreements upon GCD, probably intended largely to prevent any agreement since such full-scale disarmament hardly seemed realistic in the political atmosphere of the early 1960s.

Even as Khrushchev regained control of policy making in the security domain in 1963, Marshal Malinovsky expressed doubts about a test ban. First, he insisted that the West would be unlikely to accept any such agreement, and second he proposed that the ban apply not only to the testing, but also to the manufacture of nuclear weapons,[15] an addition certain to make a prophesy of Western rejection come true. Even after the treaty was initialed in Moscow, it was either ignored altogether or dismissed by leading Soviet military journals.

Support for the test ban within the Soviet bureaucratic and party circles was limited, but it certainly did exist. Soviet scientists were often effective proponents of a test ban agreement. For example, Andrei Sakharov and Igor Kurchatov, both nuclear physicists, appealed to Khrushchev to stop nuclear testing as early as November 1958. They had also succeeded in gaining permission for Soviet scientists to participate in the Pugwash meetings, a form of track two diplomacy among scientists from many countries who explored technical and political issues related to the test ban at some length. Sakharov in mid-1962 also became a significant proponent of a test ban restricted to the atmosphere, outer space, and under water, and the proposal for creating black boxes to monitor seismic activity also originated within the Soviet scientific community. A second source of support for a test ban came from the academics and intellectuals associated with the foreign affairs institutes in Moscow. These individuals, especially those belonging to the prestigious Institute for the Study of the USA and Canada of the USSR Academy of Sciences, largely promoted a differentiated view of the U.S. domestic political system, especially noting the dichotomy between realists and "madmen" within the American political system.[16] According to these analysts, apparent inconsistencies and shifts in American policy on the test ban were largely accounted for by the domestic divisions within the U.S. government rather than by some imperialist plot to deceive the Soviet Union.

In addition to the intelligentsia, Khrushchev also had some support for the test ban negotiations from within the Central Committee and its Presidium, especially from Anastasia Mikoyan, Leonid Brezhnev, and Nikolai Podgorny (the latter two were elevated to secretaries within the Presidium in June 1963 apparently replacing the ailing Frol Kozlov). Foreign Minister Andrei Gromyko seemed to remain loyal to Khrushchev throughout this period, but his enthusiasm for a test ban, at least in public, was often more muted than his boss. For example, when addressing the Supreme Soviet on 24 April 1962 Gromyko gave only lukewarm support to a test ban agreement, which he assigned a low priority at least in comparison with GCD.[17] But, after the Cuban missile crisis, Gromyko told the Supreme Soviet that U.S. behavior during the crisis reflected the influence of both aggressive and sane elements within the U.S. government, but he concluded that after the crisis it appeared that "restraint and a sober approach in the end won the upper hand."[18] In the Moscow negotiations themselves, Gromyko aggressively pursued his efforts to obtain a nonaggression pact associated with the test ban agreement, perhaps in order to respond to military critics. He rapidly abandoned this position when the West insisted that this could not be negotiated as part of a test ban treaty, but might be taken up at a later date. He negotiated constructively with Harriman to work out a tradeoff between the Soviet and Anglo-American positions on a withdrawal clause and peaceful nuclear explosions. This tradeoff involved getting the West to drop the latter in exchange for the Soviet acceptance of the essential elements of the provisions for withdrawing from the treaty in event of a violation or other major threat to the national interests of the parties. During the final negotiations, he apparently worked in close harmony with General Secretary Khrushchev to reach the desired agreement.

Throughout the test ban negotiations there was a constant conflict within the Soviet government between supporters and opponents of a test ban treaty, and the relative strength of these competing forces tended to vary during different phases of the negotiations. Jönsson concludes his analysis of the relationship between internal struggles within the Soviet Union and their policy in the test ban as follows: "changes in Soviet negotiating behavior at Geneva seem to be correlated with changes in the success and influence of the different groupings in internal Soviet bargaining. The 1960–62 period of intransigent Soviet behavior in the Geneva negotiations coincided with the ascendancy of the orthodox groupings' having reservations in regard to a test ban and an 'enemy' image of the United States. Conversely, the initial (1958–60) and final (1963) periods of more flexible and conciliatory Soviet behavior at Geneva concurred [sic] with greater reformist influence."[19]

In short, for both the United States and the Soviet Union there was strong domestic opposition to a test ban treaty that continually constrained national leaders and those who represented them in formal negotiations. Agreement on the Partial Nuclear Test Ban Treaty was possible in July 1963 only after these opposition forces had been partially offset internally, and even then the kind of agreement that could be achieved was significantly constrained by domestic opposition. If Kennedy had agreed to a comprehensive ban with provisions for only a few or no on-site inspections of Soviet territory, he would have faced strong opposition from the military, the intelligence community, and the nuclear weapons laboratories. This opposition probably would have been sufficient to prevent him from obtaining the necessary "advice and consent" from a two-thirds majority in the Senate, which is necessary before a treaty may be ratified. Similarly, if Khrushchev had accepted extensive and intrusive inspections of Soviet test facilities as a condition of a comprehensive ban, he would have faced strong and unified opposition from his military and ideological opponents. Had Khrushchev followed up his retreat in Cuba in October 1962 with such significant concessions to the West on the test ban issue, there is a very good chance that he would have been removed from office in the summer of 1963, instead of in the fall of 1964 when his opponents were able to amass sufficient strength to overthrow this always vulnerable leader.

Therefore, this mutual veto by domestic forces over a ban on underground nuclear tests made it politically impossible to agree on a comprehensive test ban. The BATNAs of both sides with regard to a comprehensive test ban were effectively set by domestic forces, and these BATNAs did not overlap; there was no available bargaining space within which a comprehensive test ban could be negotiated. However, agreement on a comprehensive test ban was not possible at that time not primarily for technical reasons, but more for bureaucratic and political reasons. Both Kennedy and Khrushchev were forced to be content with a partial ban on testing in the atmosphere, under water, and in outer space only. They were unable to achieve the comprehensive ban on nuclear testing that both seemed to want but neither could convince their domestic opponents to accept on terms that were acceptable to the other. Domestic constraints, therefore, contributed significantly to an explanation not only of the timing of an agreement, but also of the nature of the compromise that was eventually struck to make agreement possible.

PROCESS AND INTERACTIONS IN THE TEST BAN NEGOTIATIONS

In contrast to most of the issues discussed thus far, the interaction processes in the test ban negotiations have been subjected to a variety of empirical analyses using quantitative data to look for consistent patterns. Given the theoretical arguments presented in chapter 7, it should come as no surprise that much of the research has examined the issue of reciprocity between the two nuclear power blocs throughout these negotiations. The general finding has been that, although these negotiations have been characterized by frequent oscillations between convergence and divergence, both phenomena have evidenced substantial reciprocity. That is, to a large degree, both the United States/United Kingdom and the Soviet Union displayed considerable responsiveness in reacting to the converging and diverging behaviors of the other.

Typically, quantitative studies of the negotiation process have been based upon a categorical content analysis system.[20] In such a procedure, texts of negotiations are coded into categories of negotiation behavior, and the frequency of such behaviors is then tracked over time. The first such analysis of the test ban negotiations was conducted by Lloyd Jensen, who examined the overall pattern of interaction in the test ban negotiations from the opening of the Conference on the Discontinuation of Nuclear Weapons Tests in 1958 though the Moscow Conference of July 1963.[21] Jensen coded behaviors into two broad categories. First, he coded concessions, defined as any movement by one party toward the position of the other. Second, he measured the frequency of retractions, defined as any movement away from the position of the other. Within the theoretical framework of concession-convergence bargaining, Jensen was able to trace the progress of convergence and divergence between the United States and the Soviet Union throughout the six-year history of the partial nuclear test ban negotiations.

Jensen found that the test ban negotiations were characterized by what he described as an approach-avoidance conflict. This is a psychological concept typically found in situations in which an individual has a desired goal, but must experience some pain or suffering in order to reach that goal. This creates a significant ambivalence toward approaching the goal, so that the individual tends to draw back and retreat as the goal is approached, then tends to try again, to draw back again, in a cycle that is broken when the desire for the goal eventually overcomes the fear of pain. Jensen found that the test ban negotiations were characterized by such an ambivalence, including a general tendency to accommodate one another during the Experts Meetings and the Conference on the Discontinuation of Nuclear Weapons Tests, followed by retreat after the U-2 incident in 1960, followed by a new period of mutual approach throughout much of 1962, then by a new period of divergence after the Cuban missile crisis and the misunderstanding about on-site inspections in late 1962, and eventually concluding when the final obstacles were overcome in Moscow in July 1963.

Jensen explained this pattern of approach and avoidance in several ways. For one thing, the last concessions often have to be made on the most difficult issues that threaten one's vital interests and might force one to go below a resistance point or BATNA. Therefore, these last concessions are more difficult to make than earlier ones where less essential interests are at stake. Second, concessions early in the negotiations can be made largely for symbolic purposes, but they also seem somewhat unreal in the sense that there is little danger that they will immediately be accepted and form the basis for an agreement. Thus, there is relatively little risk that one will actually have to live with these concessions, since agreement still seems far off into the future. By contrast, the final concessions might actually lead to agreement, so that they usually contain a very definite element of reality; they are likely to be part of a concrete agreement with which both parties will have to live in the immediate future. Both parties may tend to back away from one another as they approach the final concessions that could actually enable them to reach agreement. This approach offers a great deal of insight into why negotiations sometimes become stalemated just when agreement otherwise seems to be in sight, so that the momentum that may be building toward agreement may actually stall as agreement seems near. It does not, however, explain why and how those final obstacles are overcome in order to consummate an agreement.

This author and several associates have undertaken an intensive analysis of the negotiation process just in the Eighteen Nation Disarmament Conference from March 1962 through June 1963. The entire verbatim transcripts of these negotiation were coded in a more intensive system called Bargaining Process Analysis.[22] The coding system included a number of broad categories: (1) substantive behavior or changes in offers and demands, included the specific categories of (a) the initiation of new proposals, (b) accommodations or concessions to the preferences of the other party, and (c) retractions of previous proposals or concessions; (2) strategic or bargaining behavior, including (a) commitments to firm positions, (b) threats of punishment or the removal of rewards, and (c) promises of rewards or removal of punishments; (3) task behavior, based largely on the work of Robert Bales on general group interactions,[23] including (a) asking questions, (b) providing answers to the questions of others, (c) agreeing, and (d) disagreeing with statements of fact made by the other; and (4) affective or emotional behavior, including expressions of (a) positive and (b) negative affect. Using these categories, the behaviors of the three nuclear powers—the United States, United Kingdom, and the Soviet Union—were tracked throughout the fifteen months (the ENDC was in recess throughout January in 1963) during which the ENDC took place, with data aggregated on a monthly basis.

The interactions among the three nuclear states within the ENDC were reported by Hopmann and King.[24] They dichotomized the negotiation process variables into hard (frequent use of retractions, commitments, threats, and disagreements) and soft (frequent initiation of new proposals and use of concessions, promises, and agreements) categories. They found quite high and significant correlations between these negotiating behaviors within the ENDC. For the interactions between the Soviet Union and the combined behaviors of the United States and the United Kingdom, the simultaneous correlation reached .77; for the United States and the Soviet Union alone it was .68; and for the United Kingdom and the Soviet Union alone it was .84. These very high correlations seemed to suggest that the nuclear powers' positions in the ENDC moved together in a reciprocal, tit-for-tat fashion. Their positions tended both to converge and diverge at more or less the same time. In the same analysis, Hopmann and King also examined the mediating role of the perceptions of the individual negotiators in an effort to determine what effect their individual attitudes and beliefs might have on the negotiations. These perceptual variables were also measured through content analysis procedures designed to tap attitudes that the representatives of the three countries expressed toward one another. Overall these perceptual variables were found to have little impact on the negotiating behavior, and paled in comparison with the overt interactions when it came to accounting for the high level of reciprocity exhibited in these negotiations.

These findings suggest that the partial test ban negotiations were characterized by substantial reciprocity between the United States and the United Kingdom, on the one hand, and the Soviet Union, on the other hand. This applied in both the positive and the negative direction. Moderate levels of cooperative behavior were followed by virtually uniform hard bargaining immediately following the Cuban missile crisis in November and December 1962. This hard behavior continued through early 1963, but soft behaviors began to increase in the spring of 1963, reaching a high for the period analyzed in June 1963 after Kennedy's American University speech and the agreement to send negotiators to Moscow to work out the final details of a test ban agreement. At this point, a process of tacit reciprocity became much more explicit as positive moves by each side were openly reciprocated by positive countermoves.

The central role of the reciprocity factor was further confirmed in a follow-up study by Hopmann and Smith.[25] When comparing the effects of external events and negotiator attitudes with the reciprocity within the negotiations, using a multiple regression statistical procedure, they found that the most significant factor accounting for the negotiating behavior of both the United States and the Soviet Union was the behavior of the other toward itself. The behaviors of each of the superpowers toward the other significantly accounted for their negotiating behavior, and this interactive variable consistently accounted for the largest percentage of the variance in the negotiating behavior of each of these two states. Furthermore, it was the only variable that made a consistently significant impact on negotiating behavior out of a number of variables considered in this study. But, going beyond the issue of evaluating the size of impacts, Hopmann and Smith also examined the role of perceptions in mediating between the one party's behavior and the other's response. They found, for example, that when the American negotiators perceived the Soviet actions as being softer, they became tougher in their negotiating behavior. There were some exceptions to the complete mirror model, though, in that conciliatory Soviet gestures were sometimes exploited rather than reciprocated by the United States. It is likely that Soviet suspicion of this kind of Western exploitation of their cooperative actions was partly responsible for the toughened Soviet positions in the early months of 1963.

A subsequent study by Hopmann and King, using an expanded

coding procedure, found that this reciprocity within the ENDC was actually concentrated primarily in the period after the Cuban missile crisis, from November 1962 through June 1963.[26] In this study, the authors found that the bargaining behaviors of the two sides were weakly negatively correlated between 21 March and 1 November 1962, but in the ENDC sessions from 6 November 1962 through the Moscow conference of 25 July 1963 the correlation changed to a highly significant, positive .72. The authors concluded: "After the Cuban crisis there appeared to be a greater effort by the two superpowers to coordinate their mutual behaviors and to respond in a reciprocal way, in both forward movement and intransigence, to one another's changes in behavior. This may well have been one of the most significant effects of the Cuban missile crisis upon these negotiations."[27]

The dynamics of this process might at first sight appear to confirm the arguments of the concession-convergence bargaining model of negotiations rather than the problem-solving models that, as I noted in chapter 6, have become dominant in the theoretical literature on negotiations in recent years. A qualitative evaluation of the negotiations, however, reveals some aspects of problem solving in the approach taken to the partial test ban negotiations. This is most evident in the process of disaggregation, which took place on both the domestic and the interactive level. The critical requirement for a breakthrough in these negotiations was that all of the parties had to recognize clearly that they confronted an absolute stalemate over their most highly valued goal, namely a comprehensive and verifiable test ban agreement. Once it became apparent to the parties that the monitoring of underground testing required the West to insist upon verification procedures that were clearly unacceptable to the Soviet Union, it became necessary to disaggregate the issue into its components in the search for a partial agreement on those parts of the issue where the parties possessed overlapping bargaining space.

What resulted was a search process both for ways to overcome the impasse on a comprehensive ban and seek optimal and mutually acceptable alternatives to a comprehensive ban (in case that proved impossible). It was in this search process, as already noted, that the nonaligned members of the ENDC proved to be most helpful, especially countries such as Brazil and Sweden, in suggesting the possibility of an uninspected ban on testing in the atmosphere, outer space, and under water. It soon became evident that this option was probably optimal, perhaps even preferable to a comprehensive ban, in terms of domestic political and bureaucratic considerations in the United States. Thus, the United States and the United Kingdom were able to develop and propose an alternative formula to the comprehensive ban in August 1962. However, at that time other aspects of the process seemed to be out of synchronization, and domestic opposition within the USSR probably prevented Khrushchev from responding positively to such a proposal.

This case suggests that a formula can be recognized without being mutually accepted, and that a process of convergence may have to occur before that formula can become the basis for agreement. This is especially true in a case such as the test ban negotiations where two broad formulas were available. Thus, the reciprocal search for a formula to consummate a comprehensive ban went forward after the Cuban missile crisis, even though it was badly complicated by the misunderstanding conveyed to the Soviets by the American representative on the details for implementing that formula. In the end, the inability to agree upon the details itself demonstrated convincingly the unattainability of the comprehensive formula to the negotiators, and, combined with Khrushchev's expanded authority by late spring of 1963, made it possible for the Soviets to accept the alternative formula. In some sense the formula for the eventual agreement was struck when Khrushchev announced his acceptance of the ban on nuclear testing in the atmosphere, outer space, and under water in East Berlin on 2 July 1963. That meant that all that needed to be accomplished in the Moscow negotiations was to dismiss the comprehensive formula once and for all, and negotiate the details on the basis of the partial formula, a set of details that were far less complicated than would have been the case had agreement been reached on a comprehensive ban.

This analysis would seem to suggest that the newer problem-solving models of negotiation are not altogether inconsistent with the older concession-convergence models of bargaining, at least in the test ban case. Formulas arose and were dismissed as the interaction process failed to produce agreement on details, and the final formula was largely adopted due to the relative ease with which details could be agreed upon. Thus, Zartman and Berman note the following regarding the relationship between the formula and the detail phases of their model: "Not only are the two phases blurred around the edges, there can also be movement back and forth from one to the other. Many analyses of the phases have been faulted for neglecting the possibility of backtracking. In negotiation, backtracking is a constant possibility; therefore negotiators must be aware that if they and their opponents cannot turn their formula into an agreement on details they must go back to reformulate a framework that works. The settlement of details is a formula's only test and can be accomplished only on a trial and error basis."[28]

Another obvious distinction that must be noted here is between the descriptive/explanatory role of theory, on the one hand, and the prescriptive role of theory, on the other. Much of the argument on behalf of problem solving, especially that of Anatol Rapoport, Howard Raiffa, and Roger Fisher and William Ury, is put forward in order to demonstrate its prescriptive superiority over more traditional bargaining models such as those of Thomas Schelling and others working within game theory and economic theory traditions. Their argument seems to be that problem solving will not only produce agreement more often and more efficiently than traditional bargaining, but that it will also produce normatively better agreements.

This should not be interpreted to mean, however, that all of the desirable features of problem solving must be applied in order to get agreement as an outcome in all negotiations. Even if problem solving is a normatively superior method for producing positive-sum results in negotiations, most actual negotiators may be using traditional bargaining methods most of the time, either out of political necessity or lack of knowledge of any alternative perspective. This appears to have been largely the case for the test ban negotiations. While there was a search for a mutually acceptable formula in the test ban negotiations, many of the other features of the problem-solving approach were notably absent.

For example, King has analyzed the coded transcripts of the test ban negotiations in search for the use of procedures such as role reversal and bilateral focus, both of which would have required the negotiators to look at the same issue from the other's perspective.[29] He concluded, however, that debates within the test ban negotiations were largely competitive rather than cooperative. The parties only rarely engaged in the kind of bilateral focus and role reversal activities proposed by Rapoport, that is defining the issues from the other's perspective, exploring the overlapping regions of validity, and seeking similar interests. In fact they generally tended to present their own positions unilaterally, discussed the other's position in order to attack it, and emphasized the differences rather than the similarities in their positions; hardly ever did they express positive affect toward one another in the negotiations.

Therefore, it appears that the test ban negotiations exhibited only the most basic aspects of problem-solving negotiations, namely the identification of BATNAs and the search for a mutually acceptable formula. Agreement seems to have been reached in spite of the failure of the parties to engage frequently in brainstorming, role reversal, exploration of mutual benefits, reconceptualization of the fundamental issues, or the search for objective criteria. And the process of reaching agreement seems to have been characterized by frequent use of strategic bargaining behaviors such as commitments, threats, and promises. These kinds of soft and hard bargaining behaviors have generally been disparaged by theorists such as Roger Fisher and William Ury, who argue on behalf of principled negotiations rather than positional bargaining.

One may, of course, argue that this incomplete utilization of the tools of contemporary negotiation theory accounts for the failure of the parties to reach a more optimal agreement on a comprehensive test ban, and there are certainly credible arguments that could be advanced to support this assertion. However, on balance it seems more likely that the comprehensive agreement was blocked by incompatible interests as defined by powerful domestic actors within both superpowers rather than by the failure of the negotiators to invent a creative solution to a difficult problem. Indeed, the most appropriate characterization of the partial test ban negotiations would seem to reinforce the general argument of Zartman and Berman that negotiations often precede through trial and error search processes until a mutually beneficial agreement is discovered, even if it represents only a lowest common denominator of agreement. As suggested in chapter 6, this may take place either through an aggregation of issues previously seen as disparate or, as in the case of the test ban negotiations, through the disaggregation of issues previously seen as inextricably linked until overlapping interests can be discovered on a subset of the original issue under negotiation. Thus, whatever normative judgment one makes about what might have hypothetically been the best process for negotiating the test ban issue, empirically the test ban negotiations seem to conform more or less to a model of trial and error search, combined with concessions/retractions and convergence/divergence in bargaining over details until finally the process of discovery revealed a formula that would work for all three nuclear countries—both in terms of producing a mutually beneficial agreement and in terms of satisfying critical domestic interests. The process, in summary, was important to the outcome, but that process cannot be separated altogether from a consideration of the fundamental needs and interests of the negotiating parties.

THE IMPACT OF THE INTERNATIONAL ENVIRONMENT

As suggested in chapter 11, an international negotiation is inherently a subprocess of the larger international environment within which it is imbedded. Thus, the negotiation process may be significantly affected by the interactions occurring within the larger international context. This was certainly the case in the nuclear test ban negotiations where the Cuban missile crisis especially exerted a significant impact not only on the test ban negotiations, but on the entire course of East-West relations as they had evolved up until that point during the cold-war period.

Quantitative analysis, similar to that discussed above, has also been employed to evaluate the relationship between the interactions among the three nuclear powers in the test ban negotiations and their behavior within the negotiations. Hopmann and King analyzed responsiveness to internal and external factors in the 1962–63 rounds of the partial nuclear test ban negotiations.[30] This study examined interactions among the United States, United Kingdom, and Soviet Union outside and inside the negotiations. Interactions within the ENDC were coded using the Bargaining Process Analysis system described above. Outside interactions were coded from chronologies of events in the *New York Times Index* (for the United States), *Keesing's Contemporary Archives* (for the United Kingdom), and the *New Times* (for the Soviet Union). These events were coded along a continuum ranging from cooperation to competition as defined by Corson,[31] and aggregated on a monthly basis in terms of the ratio of cooperative to competitive interactions.

Hopmann and King used a correlational analysis among the variables, that showed a continuous sequence of mutual interactions among the nations inside and outside the negotiations. In addition to the high level of reciprocity within the negotiations noted above, there were also generally high correlations between interactions outside (either conflictual or cooperative) and inside (either hard or soft bargaining) the negotiations. U.S. behaviors within the ENDC were correlated with their responses to their actions outside the negotiations at .74, using a decaying-lag model in which the greatest impact was exerted by the present month, followed by a decreasing impact for behaviors in the two previous months. Soviet behaviors inside and outside the negotiations toward the two Western allies were correlated at .57, whereas British behaviors correlated at .68, using the same decaying-lag model in both cases. All of these relationships were statistically significant with less than a .05 probability of erroneously accepting a false hypothesis. More interesting, however, is the relative impact of the internal and external stimuli on the parties' responses. Using partial correlations, the authors found that the United States responded most strongly to external events in a decaying lag model, while the British and Soviet negotiators responded most clearly to the other's negotiating behavior in the same month.[32]

A further study using the same data by Hopmann and Smith,[33] but using a multiple regression statistical model, found that the major factor affecting the negotiating behavior of both the United States and the Soviet Union was the behavior of the other toward it within the negotiations, as noted above. However, the behavior of the United States was also significantly influenced by the external actions of the Soviet Union. On the other hand, the Soviets were significantly influenced only by the behavior of the United States in Geneva.

As noted above, Hopmann and King looked specifically at the impact of the one dramatic external event that occurred during the ENDC negotiations, namely the Cuban missile crisis.[34] Using a quasi-experimental design that distinguishes between patterns before and after the missile crisis in late October 1962, they found that this critical event had a significant impact on the course of the negotiations. Comparing the general level of interactions before and after the Cuban missile crisis, they found that the Soviet behavior became significantly more positive in the aftermath of the crisis; there were less significant differences in American behavior, largely due to some important positive moves made by the United States prior to the crisis, especially in their proposals of August 1962.[35] The authors concluded that the Cuban missile crisis may have been one important catalytic factor in accounting for the successful completion of the test ban negotiations: "Perhaps most importantly, the behaviors of the United States and the Soviet Union within these negotiations became more symmetrical and reciprocal in the aftermath of the Cuban missile crisis. Thus, each nation tended to respond to the behaviors of the other in a more or less tit-for-tat fashion. Furthermore, this positive reciprocity in the aftermath of the Cuban crisis included a general mutual increase in positive affect expressed toward one another, in a reduction of attacking arguments, and in forward movement in positions on the issues under negotiation."[36]

In research with negotiations in a complex setting it is impossible to control the independent effects that different explanatory variables may have on the outcome of an international negotiation. Therefore, Hopmann and Walcott have also explored the impact of a crisis on a simulated negotiation under controlled conditions, structured to replicate in a limited way the issues in the test ban negotiations.[37] The results from these laboratory studies could then be compared with the parallel studies by Hopmann/King and Hopmann/Smith discussed earlier. A simulation based on the ENDC negotiations was repeated twenty-four times under three different conditions: a malign condition (a news bulletin announcing the onset of a crisis similar to the one over missiles in Cuba), a benign condition (a bulletin announcing a tension-reducing agreement on economic and political issues), and a neutral condition in which no intervention occurred. Differences among the conditions showed that the malign condition (compared to both the benign and neutral conditions) produced more hostility in mutual perceptions, more hard relative to soft tactics, more commitments, more negative relative to positive affect, a higher ratio of disagreements to agreements on substantive issues, and fewer overall agreements. On the other hand, no differences were obtained between the benign and neutral conditions. The direction of these effects suggests that high conflict environments hinder negotiations, but that lower stress environments do not necessarily enhance performance (compared to a neutral, control condition). Tension reduction was not a necessary precondition for agreements in the simulation runs.

Several results from the Hopmann and King study reinforced the simulation findings. As indicated previously, coded levels of tension in external interactions correlated significantly in the hypothesized direction with indices of negotiating behavior and perceptions. Unlike the laboratory results, however, lower levels of tension (compared to the benign condition) were related to more positive perceptions and softer bargaining tactics (for the Western nations); this relationship became stronger as they approached the agreement. Thus, as expected, the Cuban missile crisis of October 1962 exerted a dampening effect on the test ban negotiations in the short run. However, when President Kennedy announced a coordinated set of measures to reduce tensions in his address at American University on 10 June 1963, and Khrushchev reciprocated with tension-reducing responses of his own, a positive cycle of reduced tensions and greater cooperation within the test ban negotiations followed immediately thereafter. Therefore, there can be little doubt that the outcome of the test ban negotiations was significantly influenced by the détente in East-West relations that began in the aftermath of the brush with nuclear war in the Caribbean in October 1962.

CONCLUSION

In reviewing the negotiations leading up to the Partial Nuclear Test Ban Treaty of 1963, some of the many levels of explanation identified in the comprehensive negotiation framework were found to combine with one another to account for the outcome reached in Moscow in July 1963, while some other factors played only a minor role in these particular negotiations. Of course, many of these less important factors would probably take on much more significant roles in other negotiations.

Overall, the basic axioms of negotiation theory were satisfied by this case. Agreement took place within a narrow range of bargaining space that was available between the Western allies, the United States and Great Britain, and the Soviet Union. All parties clearly perceived that they were better off with agreement than with their next best alternative, which seemed to be continued atmospheric nuclear testing. Both the United States and the Soviet Union avoided agreements that might have violated their minimum criteria for an acceptable agreement, which for the United States would have occurred with a ban on underground tests without provisions for a significant number of on-site inspections and which for the Soviet Union would have occurred had they accepted large numbers of foreign inspectors into their territory, especially in militarily sensitive areas.

Far less significant in accounting for this outcome was the role of individuals. Indeed, individual negotiators in Geneva seemed to act largely as representatives of their governments back home, with little discretionary authority. Their perceptions and attitudes seemed to exert little influence on the process. The only individuals who seemed to exert a significant impact on the process were the two heads of state, Nikita Khrushchev and John F. Kennedy. Both received a significant scare during the missile crisis in the Caribbean, both took personal command of their relationship, and both made special efforts thereafter to reduce tensions with their adversary. Similarly, power asymmetry was largely irrelevant to this negotiation, as this was a negotiation essentially between the two most powerful states on the globe that possessed huge nuclear weapons arsenals. However, the rapid spurt in the race in intercontinental missiles that the United States made during this period may have affected the negotiations by making the Soviets both more desirous of slowing the arms race and more reluctant to reveal their inferiority openly. Finally, this was essentially a bilateral negotiation in structure between East and West, although the nonaligned members of the ENDC did exert some influence, especially during the early months of the ENDC negotiations. By the end, however, their influence had waned, and the three nuclear states were the only parties whose assent was essential to reach agreement.

This review would indicate, however, that the three most important influences on the outcome of the test ban negotiations were domestic bureaucratic and political influences, the international environment, and the negotiation process itself. Domestic factors on both sides sharply narrowed the range of acceptable agreements and necessitated a negotiation process that allowed the parties to wait for domestic conditions to ripen, especially in the Soviet Union after the U-2 fiasco. This negotiation entailed a complex search process for possible solutions that would fall within the limited bargaining space made available to the negotiators by these domestic constraints. The final ban on testing in the atmosphere, outer space, and under water both satisfied the environmental concerns about nuclear testing within the domestic constituency, especially in the United States, and eliminated the need for on-site inspection, which the Soviets resisted for internal reasons. Thus, the U.S. Congress began to support a partial ban at the same time that Soviet Premier Khrushchev freed himself of domestic challenges to his authority within the Politburo, so that agreement became possible on a limited ban in the summer of 1963.

At the same time, it is unlikely that leaders in the United States or the Soviet Union would have searched so long and hard, and battled so effectively to overcome domestic opposition to a test ban, had it not been for the great scare created by the Cuban missile crisis. Prior to that time, the prospect of nuclear war seemed to be unreal, and the arms race, while a wasteful drain of resources, did not seem to carry any cataclysmic dangers. All of that changed after October of that year. Both Kennedy and Khrushchev, who had led their countries in crisis bargaining in October 1962, also took a personal interest in the test ban negotiations and assumed a leadership role in them after the events in the Carribbean. Both came to believe that nuclear war was both more likely and more dangerous than they had ever thought before. While the events in Cuba, combined with some rather poor communications between Soviet and American negotiators in late 1962, served to complicate negotiations in the immediate aftermath of the crisis, by spring and summer of 1963 a process of reciprocal initiatives to reduce tensions seemed to get underway, both within general East-West relations and within the test ban negotiations themselves.

After the Cuban crisis, the test ban negotiations became more reciprocal. Greater mutual responsiveness between the competing cold-war states produced greater predictability and reduced uncertainty. A vicious cycle of spiraling arms races and increased tensions was at least temporarily reversed, and a different cycle of détente and progress in arms control negotiations took over. Although part of this was reflected in mutual concessions leading toward convergence, it also entailed a disaggregation of issues into their component parts and a complex search for a formula that could be politically acceptable to the domestic constituencies in both countries. Through both the ups and downs of the next several months, the negotiating positions of the United States and the Soviet Union became intimately tied to one another. This mutually recognized interdependence, the acceptance of a shared fate that depended on their joint decisions rather than on any unilateral decision, more than anything created a negotiation process that moved toward agreement on a partial test ban in the atmosphere, outer space, and under water. On 25 July 1963, when the Partial Nuclear Test Ban Treaty was initialed in Moscow, the United States, the United Kingdom and the Soviet Union took the first step back from the arms race, eloquently described by President Kennedy in the following words: "According to the ancient Chinese proverb, 'A journey of a thousand miles must begin with a single step.' My fellow Americans, let us take that first step. Let us, if we can, get back from the shadows of war and seek out the way of peace. And if that journey is one thousand miles, or even more, let history record that we, in this land, at this time, took the first step."[38]

Chapter 15

Conclusion: Theory and Practice of International Negotiation

The Partial Nuclear Test Ban Treaty negotiation was, of course, just a single important step in the history of postwar East-West relations. The analysis of the preceding case study has demonstrated some ways in which a theoretical framework like that developed in this book can help to explain the impact of the negotiation process on the outcomes of a particular negotiation. Furthermore, the case itself has provided important evidence in support of some of the theoretical arguments advanced throughout this book. However, we need many more case studies in order to refine and deepen the theoretical framework presented throughout the preceding pages, to give us greater confidence in its utility, or to suggest adaptations and elaborations where the framework falls short. Many important features of the negotiation framework were not particularly relevant to this case study, especially those aspects concerning third-party roles and complex multilateral negotiations. Furthermore, these negotiations were characterized more by reciprocal concessions and convergence than by creative problem solving, even though the disaggregation of the issues producing a partial agreement may be viewed as incorporating some features of the problem-solving approach. Therefore, the full exploration of the value of such a comprehensive framework depends upon its ability to assist analysts in explaining and interpreting a larger number of cases of international negotiations. Fortunately, there is a growing body of case studies appearing in the literature of international relations that could be analyzed in light of this framework.[1]

At the same time, we cannot wait for a finished theory of negotiations before we try to apply what we already know to ongoing negotiations. Even with the end of the cold war, conflict and violence have not disappeared from the face of the earth; if anything they may be even more frequent now that the imminent threat of escalation to all-out war between the nuclear superpowers no longer exerts its paradoxical restraint upon the behavior of individuals, groups, and states. Conflict is unavoidable in a complex world, but large-scale violence and death is avoidable if people understand that no single person, group, or state may control events through unilateral action. Joint decision making is an essential feature of the contemporary international system. Whenever human relations entail joint decision making, and whenever the results need to reflect the interdependence of those decisions, negotiation is a necessary part of the process for resolving conflicts—preferably before rather than after erupting into violence. It is important to translate what we now know about negotiations on a systematic basis into the daily practice of international diplomacy. A sophisticated understanding of the negotiation process is important not only for the sake of producing elegant theory, but also because better theory can be a guide to more constructive action.

Diplomacy has always been based upon theory about negotiations, but usually that theory has been implicit, unarticulated, and untested; its logical consistency and support with empirical evidence have usually remained unexamined or even unquestioned. An important task of theory is to aid in systematic understanding by making explicit what is usually left implicit. That is precisely what I have tried to do in this book, namely to draw out explicit theoretical underpinnings of our understanding of negotiation, evaluate their logical consistency and integrity, and examine them in the light of empirical evidence, both from systematic and quantitative evidence and comparative, qualitative case studies. The result is a theoretical framework for analyzing negotiations that is far from being firmly established, but which is at least founded upon a series of logically coherent axioms consistent with a wide variety of empirical evidence. This kind of imperfect theory, still in a state of development, unfortunately does not provide an unambiguous guide for practitioners of international negotiations; it cannot completely replace the intuitions of the experienced negotiator. But it can supplement and bring out into the open the assumptions of even the most experienced artisans of international diplomacy. In addition, it can serve as a guide for action based on general and explicit understandings of the key relationships that affect the negotiation process, rather than on a series of hunches that may turn out to be misleading or even wrong. The difficulties seasoned diplomats have had in mediating and resolving the conflicts that erupted in the early 1990s in the wake of the breakup of the Soviet Union and Yugoslavia have certainly demonstrated that experience alone is not an adequate guide to good diplomacy, and that a more rigorous and systematic underpinning for the behaviors of diplomats and negotiators is required.

This book has attempted to draw together some of the major strands of negotiation theory as it has evolved to date, and suggest some directions that still need to be taken to strengthen that theory, especially if it is to serve as a reliable basis for action. It is the continuing task of scholars to build upon this existing knowledge and try to improve our understanding of the negotiation process. And it is the responsibility of all who participate in the game of international politics to apply what we know already in order to improve the process of negotiating peaceful and mutually beneficial solutions to those conflicts that continue to divide human beings on this planet.

Notes

NOTES TO CHAPTER 1

1. Robert O. Keohane and Joseph S. Nye, *Power and Interdependence*, 2d ed. (Glenview, Ill.: Scott, Foresman, 1989), especially 24–29.

2. Bernard Brodie, ed. *The Absolute Weapon* (New York: Harcourt, Brace, 1946), 76.

3. Keohane and Nye, 254.

4. For a systematical analysis of the impact of the Cuban missile crisis and the Partial Test Ban Treaty on the overall pattern of Soviet-American relations, see P. Terrence Hopmann and Timothy D. King, "From Cold War to Détente: The Role of the Cuban Missile Crisis and the Partial Nuclear Test Ban Treaty," in *Change in the International System*, eds. Ole R. Holsti, Randolph M. Siverson, and Alexander L. George (Boulder: Westview Press, 1980), 163–88.

NOTES TO CHAPTER 2

1. In addition to the secondary sources cited below, the analysis presented in this chapter, and in chapter 14, is based upon extensive interviews undertaken by the author on a background basis with many of the participants in the test ban negotiations, and a reading and coding of the complete verbatim transcripts and all supporting documents produced by the Eighteen Nation Disarmament Conference from its opening in March 1962 through June 1963, up to the opening of the Moscow conference on the test ban. The majority of this research was carried out at the Palais des Nations in Geneva where the negotiations took place. The author is grateful to the University of Minnesota and the office of the Carnegie Endowment for International Peace, formerly located in Geneva, for their support of this research.

2. U.S. Arms Control and Disarmament Agency, *Documents on Disarmament, 1945–59* (Washington, D.C.: U.S. Government Printing Office, 1960), 1091.

3. Harold Karan Jacobson and Eric Stein, *Diplomats, Scientists, and Politicians: The United States and the Nuclear Test Ban Negotiations* (Ann Arbor: University of Michigan Press, 1966), 171.

4. Ibid., 231.

5. U.N. Document, ENDC/SC.1/PV.1, 9.

6. U.N. Document, ENDC/28, 16 April 1962.

7. Glenn T. Seaborg, *Kennedy, Khrushchev, and the Test Ban* (Berkeley: University of California Press, 1981), 162.

8. U.N. Document, ENDC/PV.61, 36.

9. U.N. Document, ENDC/59, 27 August 1963.

10. U.N. Document, ENDC/SC.1/PV.24, 22.

11. Seaborg, 176.

12. Ibid., 179.

13. Ibid. Seaborg quotes Warren Heckrotte on the U.S. delegation to the ENDC as saying that "irrespective of what Dean thought he said, Kuznetsov's report was a correct appraisal of what he thought he had been told." This slightly ambiguous statement has been clarified in personal interviews between this author and two individuals who were close to these negotiations. Both the late Professor Hans Morgenthau of the University of Chicago, a frequent consultant to the U.S. Arms Control and Disarmament Agency, and the late Herbert "Pete" Scoville, at the time deputy director of the CIA for Science and Technology, have indicated that Ambassador Dean revealed to Kuznetsov (without authorization) a bottom-line proposal that had not yet been agreed upon in Washington. The proposal presented by Ambassador Dean during a meeting at the Soviet mission to the United Nations in New York was evidently under discussion within the U.S. government at the time, but had not been officially accepted. The proposal would have reduced the Western quota for on-site inspections to three to four per year.

14. Norman Cousins, "Notes on a 1963 Visit with Khrushchev," *Saturday Review* 7 (November 1964): 21.

15. Seaborg, 185.

16. Ibid., 191.

17. Jacobson and Stein, 447.

18. Seaborg, 209.

19. Address by President Kennedy at American University, June 10, 1963, *Documents on Disarmament 1963*. (Washington, D.C.: United States Arms Control and Disarmament Agency, 1964), 217.

20. Arthur M. Schlesinger, *A Thousand Days: John F. Kennedy in the White House* (Boston: Houghton Mifflin Co., 1965), 904.

21. Seaborg, 227.

22. Ibid., 245–46.

23. Ibid., 246.

24. This account of the Moscow negotiations is based largely on Ibid., 235–53, and Jacobson and Stein, 454–58.

Notes to Chapter 3

1. Thucydides, *The Peloponnesian War* (New York: Random House, 1951), 331.

2. Fred Charles Iklé, *How Nations Negotiate* (New York: Frederick Praeger, 1964), 3–4.

3. I. William Zartman, *The 50% Solution* (Garden City, N.Y.: Doubleday, Anchor, 1976), 7.

4. Richard E. Walton and Robert B. McKersie, *A Behavioral Theory of Labor Negotiations* (New York: McGraw-Hill, 1965), 3.

5. Roger Fisher, "What Is a 'Good' U.S.-Soviet Relationship—And How Do We Build One?" *Negotiation Journal* 3, no. 4 (October 1987): 319.

6. This categorization is similar to one presented by Arild Underdal, "The Outcomes of Negotiations," in *International Negotiation: Analysis, Approaches, Issues*, ed. Victor A. Kremenyuk (San Francisco: Jossey-Bass, 1991), 100–15. However, Underdal presents five categories; the last of these, "distance from opening positions," will be treated later in this book as one among several criteria for

determining the fairness or inequality of the distribution of the benefits. I treat it here as a subset of the outcome distribution.

7. See Ernst B. Haas, "International Integration: The European and the Universal Process," *International Organization* 15, no. 4 (Autumn 1961), reprinted in *International Political Communities* (Garden City, N.Y.: Doubleday, Anchor, 1966), 96.

8. Underdal, 110.

9. See works such as Roger Fisher and William Ury, *Getting to Yes: Negotiating Agreement Without Giving In*, 2d ed. (New York: Penguin, 1991); I. William Zartman and Maureen Berman, *The Practical Negotiator* (New Haven: Yale University Press, 1982); and John W. Burton, *Conflict and Communication: The Use of Controlled Communication in International Relations* (New York: Free Press, 1969) for some of the most prominent examples of works that promote a particular framework or strategy for resolving international conflicts.

NOTES TO CHAPTER 4

1. Oran R. Young, "Strategic Interaction and Bargaining," in *Bargaining: Formal Theories of Negotiation*, ed. Oran R. Young (Urbana: University of Illinois Press, 1975), 5.

2. Anatol Rapoport, *Two Person Game Theory* (Ann Arbor: University of Michigan Press, 1969), 18–21.

3. Ibid., 60.

4. I shall not take up time here explaining the mathematics involved in the solution of this simple game. Interested readers may consult Ibid., 70–73.

5. R. Duncan Luce and Howard Raiffa, *Games and Decisions* (New York: John Wiley, 1957), 90–94.

6. This discussion and diagram are based on Rapoport, 96–101.

7. Richard E. Walton and Robert B. McKersie, *A Behavioral Theory of Labor Negotiations* (New York: McGraw-Hill, 1965), 5.

8. Ibid., 4.

9. See John F. Nash, "The Bargaining Problem," *Econometrica* 18 (1950), 155–62; and John F. Nash, "Two-Person Cooperative Games," *Econometrica* 21 (1953): 128–40.

10. Young, 32.

11. While it may be fairly easy to find positive-sum solutions on trade issues, this may not be so easy on other issues such as territorial or ethnic disputes, where parties may have a more rigidly conflictual definition of the situation. In issues of civil war, such as those between Bosnian Serbs and Muslims, Azeris and Armenians in Nagorno-Karabakh, or Eritreans and Ethiopians in the Horn of Africa, positive-sum solutions may seem few and far between. Nonetheless, I will discuss in subsequent chapters ways in which one may at least attempt to shift from zero-sum to positive-sum thinking, even in the apparently most intractable international conflicts.

NOTES TO CHAPTER 5

1. Thomas C. Schelling, *The Strategy of Conflict* (Cambridge, Mass.: Harvard University Press, 1960).

2. Ibid., 5.

3. Hans J. Morgenthau, *Politics Among Nations*, 4th ed. (New York: Alfred Knopf, 1967), 521.

4. Schelling, 5.

5. Kenneth N. Waltz, *The Theory of International Politics* (Reading, Mass.: Addison-Wesley, 1979), 209.

6. Martin Staniland, "Getting to No: The Diplomacy of the Gulf Conflict, August 2, 1990–January 15, 1991, Part I: Background to the Conflict" (Washington, D.C.: Pew Case Studies in International Affairs, Case 449, Part 1, 1992), 14.

7. Ibid.

8. Roger Fisher and William Ury, *Getting to Yes: Negotiating Agreement Without Giving In*, 2d ed. (New York: Penguin, 1991), 100.

9. Richard E. Walton and Robert B. McKersie, *A Behavioral Theory of Labor Negotiations* (New York: McGraw-Hill, 1965), 4.

10. Ibid., 5.

11. James K. Sebenius, "Negotiation Analysis," in *International Negotiation: Analysis, Approaches, Issues*, ed. Victor A. Kremenyuk (San Francisco: Jossey-Bass, 1991), 209–11.

12. Fred Charles Iklé, *How Nations Negotiate* (New York: Frederick A. Praeger, 1964), 59–60.

13. Schelling, 24.

14. Ibid., 28.

15. V. Edwin Bixenstine and Kellogg V. Wilson, "Effects of Level of Cooperative Choice by the Other Player on Choices in a Prisoner's Dilemma Game, Part II," *Journal of Abnormal and Social Psychology* 67 (1963): 139–47.

16. Sebenius, 210–11.

NOTES TO CHAPTER 6

1. Anatol Rapoport, *Fights, Games, and Debates* (Ann Arbor: University of Michigan Press, 1960), 247.

2. I. William Zartman and Maureen R. Berman, *The Practical Negotiator* (New Haven: Yale University Press, 1982).

3. Louis Kriesberg, "Introduction: Timing Conditions, Strategies, and Errors," in *Timing the De-escalation of International Conflicts*, eds. Louis Kriesberg and Stuart J. Thorson (Syracuse: Syracuse University Press, 1991), 23–24.

4. Zartman and Berman, 66.

5. Ibid., 9.

6. Ibid., 87.

7. Ibid., 95.

8. Ibid., 93.

9. Roger Fisher, *International Conflict for Beginners* (New York: Harper and Row, 1969), 90–95.

10. Ibid., 94–95.

11. Roger Fisher, "Playing the Wrong Game?" in *Dynamics of Third Party Intervention: Kissinger in the Middle East*, ed. Jeffrey Z. Rubin (New York: Praeger, 1981), 99–100.

12. Ibid., 112.

13. George Caspar Homans, *Social Behavior: Its Elementary Forms* (New York:

Harcourt, Brace & World, 1961), 62.

14. Zartman and Berman, 9.

15. Ibid., 147.

16. Ibid., 191.

17. Roger Fisher and William Ury, *Getting to Yes: Negotiating Agreement Without Giving In*, 2d ed. (New York: Penguin, 1991).

18. Ibid., 13.

19. Ibid., 60.

20. Ibid., 79.

21. Ibid., 42.

22. Ibid., 12.

23. Thomas Schelling, *The Strategy of Conflict* (Cambridge, Mass.: Harvard University Press, 1960), 54–58.

24. Ibid., 22.

25. Dean G. Pruitt and Steven A. Lewis, "The Psychology of Integrative Bargaining," in *Negotiations: Social-Psychological Perspectives*, ed. Daniel Druckman (Beverly Hills: Sage, 1977), 183–84.

26. Dean G. Pruitt and Jeffrey Z. Rubin, *Social Conflict: Escalation, Stalemate, and Settlement* (New York: McGraw Hill, 1986), 153.

27. John W. Burton, "Conflict Resolution as a Political Philosophy," in *Conflict Resolution Theory and Practice: Integration and Application*, eds. Dennis J. D. Sandole and Hugo van der Merwe (Manchester, U.K.: Manchester University Press, 1993), 59.

28. Robert O. Keohane and Joseph S. Nye, *Power and Interdependence*, 2d ed. (Glenview, Ill.: Scott, Foresman, 1989), 24–29.

Notes to Chapter 7

1. R. Duncan Luce and Howard Raiffa, *Games and Decisions* (New York: Wiley, 1957), 65–68.

2. Richard E. Walton and Robert B. McKersie, *A Behavioral Theory of Labor Negotiations* (New York: McGraw-Hill, 1965), 41–44.

3. Roger Fisher and William Ury, *Getting to Yes: Negotiating Agreement Without Giving In*, 2d ed. (New York: Penguin, 1991), 99–102.

4. Anatol Rapoport, *Fights, Games, and Debates* (Ann Arbor: University of Michigan Press, 1960), 242.

5. Inis L. Claude Jr., *Power and International Relations* (New York: Random House, 1962), 6.

6. Hans J. Morgenthau, *Politics Among Nations*, 4th ed. (New York: Alfred Knopf, 1967), 26.

7. Joseph S. Nye Jr., *Bound to Lead: The Changing Nature of American Power* (New York: Basic Books, 1990), 260.

8. I. William Zartman, "Reality, Image, and Details: The Paris Negotiations, 1969–73," in *The 50% Solution*, ed. I. William Zartman (Garden City, N.Y.: Doubleday, Anchor, 1976), 393–98.

9. Peter M. Haas, "Introduction: Epistemic Communities and International Policy Coordination," *International Organization* 46, no. 1 (Winter 1992): 2.

10. Wm. Mark Habeeb and I. William Zartman, *The Panama Canal Negotiations* (Washington, D.C.: Johns Hopkins Foreign Policy Institute, 1986), 39–41.

11. J. David Singer, "Inter-Nation Influence: A Formal Model," *American Political Science Review* 57 (1963): 420–30.

12. Ibid., 421.

13. James K. Sebenius, "On 'Offers that Can't Be Refused,'" *Negotiation Journal* 8, no. 1 (January 1992): 49–57.

14. Fisher and Ury, 97.

15. Ibid., 100.

16. See L. S. Shapely, "A Value for N-Person Games," in *Contributions to the Theory of Games, II*, eds. H. W. Kuhn and A. W. Tucker (Princeton: Princeton University Press, 1953), chap. 17, 307–17.

17. John Nash, "Non-Cooperative Games," *Annals of Mathematics* 54 (1951): 286–95.

18. Fisher and Ury, 106.

19. Wilfred L. Kohl and Carol W. Rendell, "OPEC and the World Oil Market: The March 1983 London Agreement" (Washington, D.C.: Pew Case Studies in International Affairs #123, 1991), 38–39.

NOTES TO CHAPTER 8

1. See Max H. Bazerman and John S. Carroll, "Negotiator Cognition," in *Research in Organizational Behavior*, eds. L. L. Cummings and Barry M. Staw, vol. 9 (Greenwich, Conn.: JAI Press, 1987), 268.

2. The most important works in this tradition include Theodore M. Newcomb, "An Approach to the Study of Communicative Acts," in *Small Groups: Studies in Social Interaction*, eds. A. Paul Hare, Edgar F. Borgatta, and Robert F. Bales (New York: Alfred A. Knopf, 1955), 149–63; Leon Festinger, *A Theory of Cognitive Dissonance* (Stanford: Stanford University Press, 1957); Fritz Heider, *The Psychology of Interpersonal Relations* (New York: John Wiley and Sons, 1958); Robert B. Zajonc, "The Concepts of Balance, Congruity, and Dissonance," *Public Opinion Quarterly* 24, no. 2 (Summer 1960): 280–96; Milton J. Rosenberg and Robert P. Abelson, "An Analysis of Cognitive Balancing," in *Attitude Organization and Change*, eds. Carl I. Hovland and Milton J. Rosenberg (New Haven: Yale University Press, 1960); Charles E. Osgood, "Cognitive Dynamics in the Conduct of Human Affairs," *Public Opinion Quarterly* 24, no. 2 (Summer 1960): 341–65. It has been applied to international relations by Ole R. Holsti, P. Terrence Hopmann, and John D. Sullivan, *Unity and Disintegration in International Alliances* (New York: John Wiley and Sons, 1973), chap. 3 and appendix B; and to labor-management negotiations by Richard E. Walton and Robert B. McKersie, *A Behavioral Theory of Labor Negotiations* (New York: McGraw-Hill, 1965), chaps. 6–7.

3. Jean Piaget, "Principal Factors Determining Intellectual Evolution from Childhood to Adult Life," in *Organization and Pathology of Thought*, ed. D. Rapoport (New York: Columbia University Press, 1951), 186.

4. Heider, 201.

5. Ibid., 195.

6. Milton Rokeach, *The Open and Closed Mind* (New York: Basic Books, 1960).

7. O. J. Harvey, David E. Hunt, and Harold M. Schroder, *Conceptual Systems and Personality Organization* (New York: John Wiley and Sons, 1961), 82.

8. Ibid., 22.

9. See Philip E. Tetlock, "Integrative Complexity of American and Soviet Foreign Policy Rhetoric: A Time-Series Analysis," *Journal of Personality and Social Psychology* 49, no. 6 (December 1985): 1565–85.

10. Ibid., 1566.

11. Ibid., 1567.

12. Ralph K. White, *Nobody Wanted War: Misperception in Vietnam and Other Wars* (New York: Doubleday, Anchor, 1970) 319.

13. Ole R. Holsti, "Crisis Decision Making," in *Behavior, Society, and Nuclear War*, eds. Philip E. Tetlock, Jo L. Husbands, Robert Jervis, Paul C. Stern, and Charles Tilly, vol. 1 (New York: Oxford University Press, 1989), 36.

14. See especially Harold H. Kelley, "Attribution Theory in Social Psychology," in *Nebraska Symposium on Motivation*, ed. D. Levine, vol. 15 (Lincoln: University of Nebraska Press, 1967); Lee Ross, "The Intuitive Psychologist and His Shortcomings: Distortions in the Attribution Process," in *Advances in Experimental Social Psychology*, ed. Leonard Berkowitz, vol. 10 (New York: Academic Press, 1977), 173–220; and Richard Nisbett and Lee Ross, *Human Inference: Strategies and Shortcomings of Social Judgment* (Englewood Cliffs, N.J.: Prentice-Hall, 1980).

15. Christer Jönsson, "Cognitive Theory," in *International Negotiation: Analysis, Approaches, Issues*, ed. Victor A. Kremenyuk (San Francisco: Jossey-Bass, 1991), 230.

16. Ross, 179.

17. Nisbett and Ross, 5.

18. Ibid., 6.

19. Robert Axelrod, "Decision for Neoimperialism: The Deliberations of the British Eastern Committee in 1918," in *Structure of Decision: The Cognitive Maps of Political Elites*, ed. Robert Axelrod (Princeton: Princeton University Press, 1976), chap. 4, 77–95.

20. G. Matthew Bonham, Christer Jönsson, Stefan Persson, and Michael J. Shapiro, "Cognition and International Negotiations: The Historical Recovery of Discursive Space," *Cooperation and Conflict* 22, no. 1 (1987): 1–19.

21. Bazerman and Carroll, 247–88.

22. Ibid., 282. Italics in original.

23. Daniel Kahneman and Amos Tversky, "Prospect Theory: An Analysis of Decision Under Risk," *Econometrica* 47 (March 1979): 263–91; and Amos Tversky and Daniel Kahneman, "The Framing of Decisions and the Psychology of Choice," *Science* no. 211 (January 1981): 453–58.

24. Ibid., 260. Italics in original.

25. Ibid., 274.

26. Jeffrey Z. Rubin, "Psychological Approach," in *International Negotiation: Analysis, Approaches, Issues*, ed. Victor A. Kremenyuk (San Francisco: Jossey-Bass, 1991), 222–23.

27. Bazerman and Carroll, 275.

28. Jönsson, 241.

29. Robert F. Bales, *Interaction Process Analysis: A Method for the Study of Small Groups* (Reading, Mass.: Addison-Wesley, 1950), 51.

30. Sidney Verba, *Small Groups and Political Behavior: A Study of Leadership* (Princeton: Princeton University Press, 1961), chap. 6.

31. Bales, 138–39

32. Recent arguments in the general theory of international politics recently have tended to use this dichotomy as the basis for distinguishing between neoliberals (that prefer absolute gains) and neorealists (that focus more on relative gains). See, for example, the review of this debate by Robert Powell, "Absolute and Relative Gains in International Relations Theory," *American Political Science Review* 85 (December 1991): 1303–20. However, I am using this distinction here to refer to different individual psychological orientations or predispositions toward the world in general, and not in an attempt to describe or explain the basic structural logic of international relations. Of course, the possible relationship between the psychological orientations of individual scholars and their interpretation of the operation of the international system may not be totally independent.

33. Janice Gross Stein, "International Co-operation and Loss Avoidance: Framing the Problem," in *Choosing to Co-operate: How States Avoid Loss*, eds. Janice Gross Stein and Louis W. Pauley (Baltimore: Johns Hopkins University Press, 1993), 30.

34. Ibid., 18.

35. Ibid., 19.

36. Ibid., 31.

37. Theodore W. Adorno, et al., *The Authoritarian Personality* (New York: W. W. Norton, 1950), 46.

38. Muzafer Sherif and Carl I. Hovland, *Social Judgment* (New Haven: Yale University Press, 1961), 128–29.

39. Daniel J. Levinson, "Authoritarian Personality and Foreign Policy," *Journal of Conflict Resolution* 1, no. 1 (March 1957): 37–47.

40. See Pierre Casse and Surinder Deol, *Managing Intercultural Negotiations* (Washington, D.C.: SIETAR International, 1985), 64–65, 79–80.

41. Ibid., 53.

42. Harry C. Triandis, *The Analysis of Subjective Culture* (New York: John Wiley and Sons, 1972), 3–5.

43. Raymond Cohen, *Negotiating Across Cultures* (Washington, D.C.: U.S. Institute of Peace Press, 1991), 8.

44. Glen Fisher, *International Negotiation: A Cross-Cultural Perspective* (Yarmouth, Maine: Intercultural Press, 1980), 8.

45. Raymond Cohen, "An Advocate's View," in *Culture and Negotiation: The Resolution of Water Disputes*, eds. Guy Olivier Faure and Jeffrey Z. Rubin (Newbury Park, Calif.: Sage Publications, 1993), 22.

46. Fisher, 56–57.

47. Harry C. Triandis, et al., "Individualism and Collectivism: Cross-Cultural Perspectives on Self-Ingroup Relationships." *Journal of Personality and Social Psychology* 54, no. 2 (February 1988): 323–38.

48. Cohen, *Negotiating Across Cultures*, 23.

49. Ibid., 24.

50. Cohen, "An Advocate's View," 35–36.

51. I. William Zartman and Maureen R. Berman, *The Practical Negotiator* (New Haven: Yale University Press, 1982), 226.

52. Winfried Lang, "A Professional's View," in *Culture and Negotiation: The*

Resolution of Water Disputes, eds. Guy Olivier Faure and Jeffrey Z. Rubin (Newbury Park, Calif.: Sage Publications, 1993), 44–45.

53. Ibid., 46.

54. This framework is based on Wilbur Schramm, "How Communication Works," in *The Process and Effects of Mass Communication,* ed. Wilbur Schramm (Urbana: University of Illinois Press, 1954), 3–26.

55. Cohen, *Negotiating Across Cultures,* 20.

56. Newcomb, 149.

57. Kendall O. Price, Ernest Harburg, and Jack M. McLeod, "Positive and Negative Affect as a Function of Perceived Discrepancy in ABX Situations," *Human Relations* 28, no. 1 (February 1965): 99.

58. White, 284.

59. See Carl R. Rogers, *Client-Centered Therapy* (Boston, Mass.: Houghton Mifflin, 1951).

60. Anatol Rapoport, *Fights, Games, and Debates* (Ann Arbor: University of Michigan Press, 1960), 286–88.

61. This approach is most identified with John W. Burton, *Conflict and Communication: The Use of Controlled Communication in International Relations* (New York: Free Press, 1969); Leonard W. Doob, ed., *Resolving Conflict in Africa: The Fermeda Workshop* (New Haven: Yale University Press, 1970); and Herbert C. Kelman and Stephen P. Cohen, "The Problem-Solving Workshop: A Social-Psychological Contribution to the Resolution of International Conflicts," *Journal of Peace Research* 13, no. 2 (1976): 79–90. An excellent review of this literature may be found in Barbara J. Hill, "An Analysis of Conflict Resolution Techniques: From Problem-Solving Workshops to Theory," *Journal of Conflict Resolution* 26, no. 1 (March 1982): 109–38.

62. Hill, 130.

63. Kelman and Cohen, 83.

NOTES TO CHAPTER 9

1. Stephen D. Krasner, *Defending the National Interest* (Princeton: Princeton University Press, 1978), 35.

2. Herbert Simon, *Models of Man: Social and Rational* (New York: John Wiley and Sons, 1957), 198. Italics in original.

3. Arthur Lall, *Modern International Negotiation: Principles and Practice* (New York: Columbia University Press, 1966), 344.

4. Fred Charles Iklé, *How Nations Negotiate* (New York: Frederick A. Praeger, 1964), 59–60.

5. Richard C. Snyder, H. W. Bruck, and Burton Sapin, *Foreign Policy Decision-Making* (Glenview, Ill.: Free Press of Glencoe, 1962).

6. Richard E. Walton and Robert B. McKersie, *A Behavioral Theory of Labor Negotiations* (New York: McGraw-Hill, 1965), 283.

7. Robert L. Kahn, "Organizational Theory," in *International Negotiation: Analysis, Approaches, Issues,* ed. Victor A. Kremenyuk (San Francisco: Jossey-Bass, 1991), 149.

8. Robert Putnam, "Diplomacy and Domestic Politics: The Logic of Two-Level Games," *International Organization* 42, no. 3 (Summer 1988): 428–60.

9. Ibid., 436.

10. Ibid., 442.

11. See P. Terrence Hopmann, "The Changing International Environment and the Resolution of International Conflicts: Negotiations on Security and Arms Control in Europe," in *Timing the De-Escalation of International Conflicts*, eds. Louis Kriesberg and Stuart J. Thorson (Syracuse: Syracuse University Press, 1991), 47–49; and Strobe Talbott, *Deadly Gambits: The Reagan Administration and the Stalemate in Nuclear Arms Control* (New York: Alfred A. Knopf, 1984), 43–51.

12. See Dean G. Pruitt, "Negotiation Between Organizations: A Branching Chain Model," *Negotiation Journal* 10, no. 3 (July 1994): 217–30; and Dean G. Pruitt, "Comments on Flexibility in Inter-Organizational Negotiation," paper presented at the conference on "Negotiation Flexibility" of the Processes of International Negotiation Project, International Institute of Applied Systems Analysis, Laxenburg, Austria, 16–17 March 1992.

13. Simon, 198.

14. Pruitt, "Comments," 2.

15. Pruitt, "Negotiation," 227.

16. Kahn, 153. See also J. Stacy Adams, "The Structure and Dynamics of Behavior in Organizational Boundary Roles," in *Handbook of Industrial and Organizational Psychology*, ed. Marvin D. Dunnette (Chicago, Ill.: Rand McNally, 1976), 1175–99.

17. Walton and McKersie, 283–302.

18. Daniel Druckman, "Boundary Role Conflict: Negotiation as Dual Responsiveness," in *The Negotiation Process: Theories and Applications*, ed. I. William Zartman (Beverly Hills: Sage, 1978), 109.

19. Talbott, 118.

20. Ibid., 128.

21. Ibid., 144.

22. Walton and McKersie, 298.

23. Ibid., 299.

24. Talbott, 137.

25. Ibid., 147.

26. Pruitt, "Comments," 3. Underlining in original.

27. Talbott, 118.

28. Hopmann, 53–54.

29. Putnam, 454.

30. Kahn, 155–56.

31. Robert O. Keohane, *After Hegemony: Cooperation and Discord in the World Political Economy* (Princeton: Princeton University Press, 1984), 115–16.

NOTES TO CHAPTER 10

1. Harold H. Saunders, "The Pre-Negotiation Phase," in *International Negotiations: Art and Science*, eds. D. B. Bendhamane and J. W. McDonald (Washington, D.C.: Foreign Service Institute, U.S. Department of State, 1984), 47–56.

2. Jo L. Husbands, "The Conventional Arms Transfer Talks: Negotiation as Proselytization" Paper presented to the American Political Science Association, Washington, D.C., 1979.

3. Saunders, 47–56.

4. Janice Gross Stein, "Getting to the Table: The Triggers, Stages, Functions, and Consequences of Prenegotiation," in *Getting to the Table: The Process of International Prenegotiation*, ed. Janice Gross Stein (Baltimore: Johns Hopkins University Press, 1989), 257.

5. Brian W. Tomlin, "The Stages of Prenegotiation: The Decision to Negotiate North American Free Trade," in *Getting to the Table: The Process of International Prenegotiation*, ed. Janice Gross Stein (Baltimore: Johns Hopkins University Press, 1989), 22–26.

6. Husbands.

7. I. William Zartman and Maureen R. Berman, *The Practical Negotiator* (New Haven: Yale University Press, 1982), chap. 3.

8. Johan Jørgen Holst, "Reflections on the Making of a Tenuous Peace," *Brown Journal of World Affairs* 1, no. 2 (Spring 1994): 2.

9. Ibid., 4.

10. Saadia Touval and I. William Zartman, "Introduction: Mediation in Theory," in *International Mediation in Theory and Practice*, eds. Saadia Touval and I. William Zartman (Boulder: Westview Press, 1985), 16.

11. P. Terrence Hopmann and Daniel Druckman, "Henry Kissinger as Strategist and Tactician in the Middle East Negotiations," in *Dynamics of Third Party Intervention: Kissinger in the Middle East*, ed. Jeffrey Z. Rubin (New York: Praeger, 1981), 208–9.

12. Ernst B. Haas, "International Integration: The European and the Universal Process," in *International Political Communities* (Garden City, N.Y.: Doubleday Anchor, 1966), 96.

13. Zartman and Berman, 82–85.

14. See B. M. Bass, "Effects on Subsequent Performance of Negotiators of Studying Issues or Planning Strategies Alone or in Groups," *Psychological Monographs* no. 614 (1966); and Daniel Druckman, "Prenegotiation Experience and Dyadic Conflict Resolution in a Bargaining Situation," *Journal of Experimental Social Psychology* 4, no. 4 (October 1968): 367–83.

15. Robert Axelrod, *The Evolution of Cooperation* (New York: Basic Books, 1984), 13.

16. Ibid., 20.

17. Ibid., 31.

18. Anatol Rapoport and Albert M. Chammah, *Prisoner's Dilemma: A Study in Conflict and Cooperation* (Ann Arbor: University of Michigan Press, 1965).

19. Warner Wilson, "Reciprocation and Other Techniques for Inducing Cooperation in Prisoner's Dilemma Game," *Journal of Conflict Resolution* 15, no. 2 (June 1971): 167–95.

20. D. Michael Kuhlman and Alfred F. J. Marshello, "Individual Differences in Game Motivation as Moderators of Preprogrammed Strategy Effects in Prisoner's Dilemma," *Journal of Personality and Social Psychology* 32, no. 5 (November 1975): 922–31.

21. Svenn Michael Lindskold, Russell Bennett, and Marc Wayner, "Retaliation Level as a Foundation for Subsequent Conciliation," *Behavioral Science* 21, no. 1 (January 1976): 13–18.

22. Stuart Oskamp, "Effects of Programmed Strategies on Cooperation in the Prisoner's Dilemma and Other Mixed-Motive Games," *Journal of Conflict Resolution* 15, no. 2 (June 1971): 242.

23. V. Edwin Bixenstine and Jacquelyn W. Gaebelein, "Strategies of 'Real' Others in Eliciting Cooperative Choice in a Prisoner's Dilemma Game," *Journal of Conflict Resolution* 15, no. 2 (June 1971): 164.

24. S. S. Komorita and John Mechling, "Betrayal and Reconciliation in a Two-Person Game," *Journal of Personality and Social Psychology* 6, no. 3 (July 1967): 349–53. Other moderating variables are discussed by Morton Deutsch, *The Resolution of Conflict: Constructive and Destructive Processes* (New Haven: Yale University Press, 1973), 347.

25. Axelrod, 38–39.

26. Roger Fisher, "What is a 'Good' U.S.-Soviet Relationship—and How Do We Build One?" *Negotiation Journal* 3, no. 4 (October 1987): 326.

27. This term was coined by Joseph V. Montville and William D. Davidson, "Foreign Policy According to Freud," *Foreign Policy* 1981–82, 145–47.

28. John W. McDonald, "Further Exploration of Track Two Diplomacy," in *Timing the De-escalation of International Conflicts,* eds. Louis Kriesberg and Stuart J. Thorson (Syracuse: Syracuse University Press, 1991), 202–3.

29. Dean G. Pruitt and Jeffrey Z. Rubin, *Social Conflict: Escalation, Stalemate, and Settlement* (New York: McGraw-Hill, 1986), 158–59.

30. Charles E. Osgood, *An Alternative to War or Surrender* (Urbana: University of Illinois Press, 1962).

31. Charles E. Osgood, "GRIT for MBFR: A Proposal for Unfreezing Force-Level Postures in Europe," *Peace Research Review* 8, no. 2 (1979): 77–92.

32. Pruitt and Rubin, 163.

33. Ibid., 163–64.

34. William Rose, *U.S. Unilateral Arms Control Initiatives: When Do They Work?* (Westport, Conn.: Greenwood Press, 1988), 153–56.

35. S. Lindskold, B. Betz, and D. S. Walters, "Transforming Competitive or Cooperative Climates," *Journal of Conflict Resolution* 30 (1986): 113.

36. Martin Patchen, "Strategies for Eliciting Cooperation from an Adversary: Laboratory and Internation Findings," *Journal of Conflict Resolution* 31, no. 1 (March 1987): 182.

37. Ibid., 183.

38. See Lewis F. Richardson, *Statistics of Deadly Quarrels* (Pittsburgh: Boxwood Press, 1960) and Lewis F. Richardson, *Arms and Insecurity* (Pittsburgh: Boxwood Press, 1960).

39. Anatol Rapoport, *Fights, Games, and Debates* (Ann Arbor: University of Michigan Press, 1960), 20–21.

40. Otomar J. Bartos, *Process and Outcome of Negotiations* (New York: Columbia University Press, 1974), 76.

41. Ibid., 38.

42. Ibid., 143.

43. Ibid., 144–45.

44. P. Terrence Hopmann and Theresa C. Smith, "An Application of a Richardson Process Model: Soviet-American Interactions in the Test Ban Negotiations, 1962–1963," in *The Negotiation Process: Theories and Applications,* ed. I. William Zartman (Beverly Hills: Sage, 1978), 173.

45. John G. Cross, "Negotiation as a Learning Process," in *The Negotiation Process: Theories and Applications,* ed. I. William Zartman (Beverly Hills: Sage, 1978), 45.

46. Erika Apfelbaum, "On Conflicts and Bargaining," in *Advances in Experimental Social Psychology*, ed. Leonard Berkowitz, vol. 7 (New York: Academic Press, 1974), 133.

47. Alan Coddington, *Theories of the Bargaining Process* (Chicago, Ill.: Aldine, 1968), 14–15.

48. Daniel Druckman, "Stages, Turning Points, and Crises: Negotiating Military Base Rights, Spain and the United States," *Journal of Conflict Resolution* 30, no. 2 (June 1986): 327–60.

49. Teresa M. Amabile, *The Social Psychology of Creativity* (New York: Springer-Verlag, 1983), 192.

50. Pruitt and Rubin, 151–53.

51. Ibid., 153.

52. Amabile, 191–92.

53. Fisher, 324.

54. Ibid., 326.

NOTES TO CHAPTER 11

1. See A. F. K. Organski and Jacek Kugler, *The War Ledger* (Chicago: University of Chicago Press, 1980), 19–22.

2. Kenneth N. Waltz, *Theory of International Politics* (Reading, Mass.: Addison-Wesley, 1979), 111.

3. Gordon A. Craig and Alexander L. George, *Force and Statecraft: Diplomatic Problems of Our Time*, 2d ed. (New York: Oxford University Press, 1990), 250.

4. Ibid., 262.

5. J. David Singer, *Deterrence, Arms Control, and Disarmament* (Columbus: Ohio State University Press, 1962), 173–76.

6. P. Terrence Hopmann and Daniel Druckman, "Henry Kissinger as Strategist and Tactician in the Middle East Negotiations," in *Dynamics of Third Party Intervention: Kissinger in the Middle East*, ed. Jeffrey Z. Rubin (New York: Praeger, 1981), 198–202, 206–9.

7. Inis L. Claude Jr., *Swords Into Plowshares: The Problems and Progress of International Organizations*, 2d ed. (New York: Random House, 1963), 298.

8. See, for example, Roger Hilsman, *To Move A Nation: The Politics of Foreign Policy in the Administration of John F. Kennedy* (Garden City, N.Y.: Doubleday, 1967), 228–29.

9. Saadia Touval and I. William Zartman, "Introduction: Mediation in Theory," in *International Mediation in Theory and Practice*, eds. Saadia Touval and I. William Zartman (Boulder, Colo.: Westview Press, 1985), 16.

10. Geoffrey Blainey, *The Causes of War* (New York: Free Press, 1973), 245.

11. Seymour M. Hersh, *The Price of Power: Kissinger in the Nixon White House* (New York: Summit Books, 1983), 442.

12. Gary Geipel, "The Nixon Administration and Vietnam: A Case Study in Negotiation and War Termination" (Washington, D.C.: Pew Case Studies in International Affairs #337, 1988), 53–54.

13. Henry Kissinger, *The White House Years* (Boston: Little, Brown, 1979), 1173.

14. Charles F. Hermann, "Some Issues in the Study of International Crisis," in *International Crises: Insights from Behavioral Research*, ed. Charles F. Hermann (New York: Free Press, 1972), 10.

15. Oran R. Young, *The Intermediaries: Third Parties in International Crises* (Princeton: Princeton University Press, 1967), 10.

16. Hermann, 13.

17. See reviews in P. Terrence Hopmann and Charles Walcott, "The Impact of External Stresses and Tensions on Negotiations," in *Negotiations: Social-Psychological Perspectives*, ed. Daniel Druckman (Beverly Hills: Sage, 1977), 301–23; and Daniel Druckman, *Human Factors in International Negotiations: Social-Psychological Aspects of International Conflict* (Beverly Hills: Sage Professional Papers in International Studies, #02–020, 1973).

18. See R. S. Lazarus and S. Folkman, *Stress, Appraisal, and Coping* (New York: Springer-Verlag, 1984); and S. Levine and H. Ursin, *Coping and Health* (New York: Plenum, 1980).

19. Ole R. Holsti, "Crisis Decision Making," in *Behavior, Society, and Nuclear War*, eds. Philip E. Tetlock, Jo L. Husbands, Robert Jervis, Paul C. Stern, and Charles Tilly, vol. 1 (New York: Oxford University Press, 1989), 28.

20. Ibid., 30.

21. See Ralph K. White, *Nobody Wanted War* (Garden City, N.Y: Doubleday Anchor, 1970), 319–20.

22. Holsti, "Crisis Decision Making," 30.

23. Ibid., 31–32.

24. See James G. Blight and Andrew W. Lynch, "Negotiation and the New World Disorder," *Negotiation Journal* 8, no. 4 (October 1992): 351–52.

25. Graham T. Allison, *Essence of Decision: Explaining the Cuban Missile Crisis* (Boston: Little, Brown, 1971). 4–5.

26. Barry M. Staw, Lance E. Sanderlands, and Jane E. Dutton, "Threat-Rigidity Effects in Organizational Behavior: A Multilevel Analysis," *Administrative Science Quarterly* 26, no. 4 (December 1981): 501–24.

27. H. Wilensky, "Intelligence, Crisis, and Foreign Policy: Reflections on the Limits of Rationality," Berkely: University of California mimeo cited in Holsti, "Crisis Decision Making," 18.

28. Ibid., 21.

29. Otomar J. Bartos, *Process and Outcome of Negotiations* (New York: Columbia University Press, 1974), 121.

30. I. William Zartman and Maureen R. Berman, *The Practical Negotiator* (New Haven: Yale University Press, 1982), 195.

31. CBS News, "Conversation with President Kennedy," 3, cited in Ole R. Holsti, *Crisis Escalation War* (Montréal, Québec: McGill-Queen's University Press, 1972), 192–93.

NOTES TO CHAPTER 12

1. Jeffrey Z. Rubin, "Introduction," in *Dynamics of Third Party Intervention: Kissinger in the Middle East*, ed. Jeffrey Z. Rubin (New York: Praeger, 1981), 5.

2. Saadia Touval and I. William Zartman, "Introduction: Mediation in Theory," in *International Mediation in Theory and Practice*, eds. Saadia Touval and I. William Zartman (Boulder: Westview Press, 1985), 16.

3. I. William Zartman and Saadia Touval, "Conclusion: Mediation in Theory and Practice," in *International Mediation in Theory and Practice*, eds. Saadia Touval and I. William Zartman (Boulder: Westview Press, 1985), 254.

4. Arthur Lall, *Modern International Negotiation* (New York: Columbia University Press, 1966), 90.

5. Roger Fisher, "Playing the Wrong Game?" in *Dynamics of Third Party Intervention: Kissinger in the Middle East,* ed. Jeffrey Z. Rubin (New York: Praeger, 1981), 97.

6. Oran R. Young, *The Intermediaries: Third Parties in International Crises* (Princeton: Princeton University Press, 1967), 309.

7. Ibid., 81.

8. Indar Jit Rikhye, "Critical Elements in Determining the Suitability of Conflict Settlement Efforts by the United Nations Secretary General," in *Timing the De-escalation of International Conflicts,* eds. Louis Kriesberg and Stuart J. Thorson (Syracuse: Syracuse University Press, 1991), 71.

9. Lall, 100.

10. Saadia Touval, *The Peace Brokers: Mediators in the Arab-Israeli Conflict, 1948–1979* (Princeton: Princeton University Press, 1982), 26.

11. Ibid., 140–41.

12. Thomas Princen, "International Mediation—The View from the Vatican," *Negotiation Journal* 3, no. 4 (October 1987): 348–49.

13. See, for example, Elmore Jackson, *Meeting of Minds* (New York: McGraw-Hill, 1952), 125–29.

14. Fisher, 97.

15. Ibid., 97.

16. See Gary Sick, "The Partial Negotiator: Algeria and the U.S. Hostages in Iran," in *International Mediation in Theory and Practice,* eds. Saadia Touval and I. William Zartman (Boulder: Westview Press, 1985), 49–53.

17. Ibid., 50.

18. Zartman and Touval, "Conclusion," 255.

19. See Matti Golan, *The Secret Conversations of Henry Kissinger: Step-by-Step Diplomacy in the Middle East* (New York: Quadrangle, 1976) 151–56.

20. Carl M. Stevens, "Is Compulsory Arbitration Compatible with Bargaining?" *Industrial Relations* 5, no. 2 (February 1966): 38–52.

21. Dean G. Pruitt and Jeffrey Z. Rubin, *Social Conflict: Escalation, Stalemate, and Settlement* (New York: McGraw-Hill, 1986), 181.

22. John W. Burton, "Conflict Resolution as a Political Philosophy," in *Conflict Resolution in Theory and Practice: Integration and Application,* eds. Dennis J. D. Sandole and Hugo van der Merwe (Manchester, U.K.: Manchester University Press, 1993), 55. Burton and his followers tend to make a clear distinction between disputes and conflicts, on the one hand, and conflict settlements and resolutions on the other hand. Disputes can be settled through ordinary negotiation, usually without a third-party intervention, whereas conflicts require a complex process of conflict resolution that almost always requires the active intervention of a third party as mediator and facilitator. I do not make such a sharp distinction between the two, since it seems that the settlement of many superficial disputes may be aided by third parties, and on occasion direct negotiations without an intermediary may actually be successful in resolving underlying conflicts. At the same time, I do agree with the general thrust of Burton's criticism that the two are not fully interchangeable, and that generally the role of a mediator is far

more crucial in the resolution of deep conflicts with strong emotional underpinnings than in the case of more superficial disputes over concrete interests.

23. Ibid., 59.

24. Ibid., 60.

25. Touval and Zartman, "Introduction," 10.

26. P. Terrence Hopmann and Daniel Druckman, "Henry Kissinger as Strategist and Tactician in the Middle East Negotiations," in *Dynamics of Third Party Intervention: Kissinger in the Middle East,* ed. Jeffrey Z. Rubin (New York: Praeger, 1981), 214.

27. Touval, *The Peace Brokers,* 4.

28. Christopher R. Mitchell, "Problem-Solving Exercises and Theories of Conflict Resolution," in *Conflict Resolution in Theory and Practice,* eds. Dennis J. D. Sandole and Hugo van der Merwe, (New York: Praeger, 1981), 78.

29. Johan Jørgen Holst, "Reflections on the Making of a Tenuous Peace," *The Brown Journal of World Affairs* 1, no. 2 (Spring 1994): 5.

30. Touval and Zartman, "Introduction," 12.

31. Lall, 99.

32. Pruitt and Rubin, 174–75.

33. Fisher, 107–10.

34. Ibid., 108.

35. Touval and Zartman, "Introduction," 12.

36. Hopmann and Druckman, 217.

37. Ibid., 214–15.

38. Ibid., 215.

39. Ibid., 200–2.

Notes to Chapter 13

1. John Gerard Ruggie, "Multilateralism: The Anatomy of an Institution," *International Organization* 46, no. 3 (Summer 1992): 574.

2. Gilbert R. Winham, "Negotiation as a Management Process," *World Politics* 30, no. 1 (1977): 87–114.

3. For an elaboration of this problem and an exploration of its implications for multilateral negotiation theory, see Bruce Bueno de Mesquita, "Multilateral Negotiations: A Spatial Analysis of the Arab-Israeli Dispute," *International Organization* 44, no. 3 (Summer 1990): 317–40.

4. See Herbert F. Simon, *Models of Man: Social and Rational* (New York: John Wiley, 1957), 198.

5. Richard Elliot Benedick, *Ozone Diplomacy: New Directions in Safeguarding the Planet* (Cambridge, Mass.: Harvard University Press, 1991), 178.

6. U.S. Congress, Commission on Security and Cooperation in Europe, "The Conference on Security and Cooperation in Europe: An Overview of the CSCE Process, Recent Meetings and Institutional Development," February 1992, 22.

7. Miles Kahler, "Multilateralism with Small and Large Numbers," *International Organization* 46, no. 3 (Summer 1992): 705.

8. James K. Sebenius, *Negotiating the Law of the Sea* (Cambridge, Mass.: Harvard University Press, 1984), 9.

9. Fred Charles Iklé, *How Nations Negotiate* (New York: Frederick A. Praeger, 1964), 59–60.

10. I. William Zartman, "The Elephant and the Holograph: Toward a Theoretical Synthesis and a Paradigm," in *International Multilateral Negotiation: Approaches to the Management of Complexity,* ed. I. William Zartman (San Francisco: Jossey-Bass, 1994), 220.

11. William H. Riker, *The Theory of Political Coalitions* (New Haven: Yale University Press, 1962), 32–33.

12. Christophe Dupont, "Coalition Theory: Using Power to Build Cooperation," in *International Multilateral Negotiation: Approaches to the Management of Complexity,* ed. I. William Zartman (San Francisco: Jossey-Bass, 1994), 155.

13. Howard Raiffa, *The Art and Science of Negotiation* (Cambridge, Mass.: Harvard University Press, 1982), 273–74.

14. For further discussion of this aspect of these negotiations, see P. Terrence Hopmann, "Bargaining Within and Between Alliances on MBFR," Carlisle Barracks, Penn.: U.S. Army War College, Strategic Studies Institute, 1978.

15. This account is based largely on David M. Kennedy, "Launching the Uruguay Round: Clayton Yeutter and the Two-Track Decision," Washington, D.C.: Georgetown Institute for the Study of Diplomacy, Pew Case Studies in International Affairs #144, 1988; and Gilbert R. Winham, "The Prenegotiation Phase of the Uruguay Round," in *Getting to the Table: The Processes of International Prenegotiation,* ed. Janice Gross Stein (Baltimore: Johns Hopkins University Press, 1989).

16. Jeffrey Z. Rubin and Walter C. Swap, "Small Group Theory: Forming Consensus Through Group Processes," in *International Multilateral Negotiation: Approaches to the Management of Complexity,* ed. I. William Zartman (San Francisco: Jossey-Bass, 1994), 147.

17. Robert A. Dahl, "Some Explanations," in *Political Opposition in Western Democracies,* ed. Robert A. Dahl (New Haven: Yale University Press, 1966), 369.

18. Karl W. Deutsch and J. David Singer, "Multipolar Power Systems and International Stability," *World Politics* 16, no. 3, (April 1964): 390–406.

19. Richard E. Walton and Robert B. McKersie, *A Behavioral Theory of Labor Negotiations* (New York: McGraw-Hill, 1965), 4–5.

20. Sebenius, 69–70.

21. Seymour M. Hersh, *The Price of Power: Kissinger in the Nixon White House* (New York: Summit Books, 1983), 442.

22. Saadia Touval and Jeffrey Z. Rubin, "Multilateral Negotiation: An Analytical Approach," Harvard Law School, Program on Negotiation, Working Paper Series 87–5 (July 1987): 18.

23. I. William Zartman and Maureen R. Berman, *The Practical Negotiator* (New Haven: Yale University Press, 1982), chaps. 3 and 4.

24. The literature supporting this generalization has been reviewed in Daniel Druckman and P. Terrence Hopmann, "Behavioral Aspects of Negotiations on Mutual Security," in *Behavior, Society, and Nuclear War,* eds. Philip E. Tetlock, Jo L. Husbands, Robert Jervis, Paul C. Stern, and Charles Tilly, vol. 1 (New York: Oxford University Press, 1989), 85–173.

25. Robert L. Rothstein, *Global Bargaining: UNCTAD and the Quest for a New International Economic Order* (Princeton: Princeton University Press, 1979), especially 276–79.

26. Rubin and Swap, 137.

27. Dean C. Pruitt and Jeffrey Z. Rubin, *Social Conflict: Escalation, Stalemate, and Settlement* (New York: McGraw-Hill, 1986), 68–70.

28. James A. Caporaso, "International Relations Theory and Multilateralism: The Search for Foundations," *International Organization* 46, no. 3 (Summer 1992): 612.

29. Robert O. Keohane, "The Theory of Hegemonic Stability and Changes in International Economic Regimes, 1967–1977," in *Change in the International System,* eds. Ole R. Holsti, Randolph M. Siverson, and Alexander L. George, (Boulder: Westview Press, 1980), 132.

30. Robert O. Keohane and Joseph S. Nye, *Power and Interdependence: World Politics in Transition,* 2d ed. (Glenview, Ill.: Scott, Foresman, 1989), 78–82.

31. Duncan Snidal, "The Limits of Hegemonic Stability Theory," *International Organization* 39, no. 4 (Autumn 1985): 612.

32. Kahler, 703.

33. John J. Maresca, *To Helsinki: The Conference on Security and Cooperation in Europe 1973–1975* (Durham, N.C.: Duke University Press, 1985), 18–22.

34. Rubin and Swap, 136.

35. Sidney Verba, *Small Groups and Political Behavior: A Study of Leadership* (Princeton: Princeton University Press, 1961), chaps. 5–7.

36. Kahler, 700.

37. See the evidence on this produced in the so-called "Robbers' Cave experiments" by Muzafer and Carolyn W. Sherif, *Groups in Harmony and Tension,* (New York: Harper Brothers, 1953).

38. Arild Underdal, "Leadership Theory: Rediscovering the Arts of Management," in *International Multilateral Negotiation: Approaches to the Management of Complexity,* ed. I. William Zartman (San Francisco: Jossey-Bass, 1994), 183–91.

39. Ibid., 192.

40. Roger Fisher, "Playing the Wrong Game?" in *Dynamics of Third Party Intervention: Kissinger in the Middle East,* ed. Jeffrey Z. Rubin (New York: Praeger, 1981), 107–8.

41. This case is further developed in P. Terrence Hopmann, "Negotiating Peace in Central America," *Negotiation Journal* 4, no. 4 (October 1988): 361–80.

42. Caporaso, 625.

43. Ibid., 625.

44. Keohane and Nye, *Power and Interdependence* 231.

NOTES TO CHAPTER 14

1. Christer Jönsson, *Soviet Bargaining Behavior: The Nuclear Test Ban Case* (New York: Columbia University Press, 1979), 23–24.

2. Glenn T. Seaborg, *Kennedy, Khrushchev, and the Test Ban* (Berkeley: University of California Press, 1981), 236

3. Harriman's account is reported in Ibid., 246–47.

4. Harold Karan Jacobson and Eric Stein, *Diplomats, Scientists, and Politicians: The United States and the Nuclear Test Ban Negotiations* (Ann Arbor: University of Michigan Press, 1966), 359.

5. ENDC/PV.61, 34–37 found in *Documents on Disarmament, 1962,* vol. 2 (July–December), Washington, D.C.: U.S. Arms Control and Disarmament Agency, 1963, 695–96.

6. Seaborg, 167.

7. Ibid., 129.

8. Ibid., 139.

9. Ibid., 176.

10. Theodore Sorenson, *Kennedy* (New York: Harper and Row, 1965), 730–31.

11. Jönsson, 152–61.

12. Ibid., 164.

13. Personal communication with Ambassador Oleg Troyanovsky, interpreter and aid to Khrushchev at that time, and Sergei N. Khrushchev, son of the former Soviet leader, 23 April 1993, Providence, R.I.

14. Jacobson and Stein, 476.

15. Jönsson, 197.

16. Ibid., 153.

17. Ibid., 177.

18. Ibid., 201–2.

19. Ibid., 207.

20. For a general evaluation of the use of content analysis in research in international relations, see Ole R. Holsti, *Content Analysis for the Social Sciences and Humanities* (Reading, Mass.: Addison-Wesley, 1969). For an application to negotiations, see Daniel Druckman with the collaboration of P. Terrence Hopmann, "Content Analysis," in *International Negotiation: Analysis, Approaches, Issues,* ed. Victor A. Kremenyuk (San Francisco: Jossey-Bass, 1991), 244–63.

21. Lloyd Jensen, "Approach-Avoidance Bargaining in the Test Ban Negotiations," *International Studies Quarterly* 12, no. 1 (1968): 152–60.

22. Charles Walcott and P. Terrence Hopmann, "Interaction Analysis and Bargaining Behavior," in *The Small Group in Political Science: The Last Two Decades of Development,* ed. Robert T. Golembiewski (Athens: University of Georgia Press, 1978).

23. Robert F. Bales, *Interaction Process Analysis: A Method for the Study of Small Groups* (Cambridge, Mass.: Addison-Wesley, 1950), 8–9.

24. P. Terrence Hopmann and Timothy King, "Interactions and Perceptions in the Test Ban Negotiations," *International Studies Quarterly* 20, no. 1 (March 1976): 105–42.

25. P. Terrence Hopmann and Theresa C. Smith, "An Application of a Richardson Process Model: Soviet-American Interactions in the Test Ban Negotiations 1962–1963," in *The Negotiation Process: Theories and Applications,* ed. I. William Zartman (Beverly Hills: Sage, 1978), 149–74.

26. P. Terrence Hopmann and Timothy D. King, "From Cold War to Détente: The Role of the Cuban Missile Crisis and the Partial Nuclear Test Ban Treaty," in *Change in the International System,* eds. Ole R. Holsti, Randolph M. Siverson, and Alexander L. George (Boulder: Westview Press, 1980), 163–88.

27. Ibid., 176.

28. I. William Zartman and Maureen R. Berman, *The Practical Negotiator* (New Haven: Yale University Press, 1982), 147.

29. Timothy D. King, "Role Reversal Debates in International Negotiations: The Partial Test Ban," paper presented at the annual convention of the International Studies Association, Toronto, Canada, 1979.

30. Hopmann and King, 1976, "Interactions and Perceptions," 105–42.

31. Walter H. Corson, *Measuring Conflict and Cooperation Intensity in East-West Relations: A Manual and Codebook* (Ann Arbor: University of Michigan, Institute for Social Research, 1970).

32. Hopmann and King, "Interactions and Perceptions," 139.

33. Hopmann and Smith, "An Application of a Richardson Process Model," 149–74.

34. Hopmann and King, "From Cold War to Détente," 163–88.

35. Ibid., 178–79.

36. Ibid., 184.

37. P. Terrence Hopmann and Charles Walcott, "The Impact of External Stresses and Tensions on Negotiations," in *Negotiations: Social-Psychological Perspectives,* ed. Daniel Druckman (Beverly Hills: Sage, 1977).

38. John F. Kennedy, "Radio-Television Address, July 26, 1963," *Documents on Disarmament, 1963* (Washington, D.C.: U.S. Arms Control and Disarmament Agency, 1964), 257.

NOTES TO CHAPTER 15

1. Of particular note here are the Pew Case Studies in International Affairs, that contain a wide range of cases on negotiations, especially useful for presentation in an instructional format. The Pew Cases are available through the Pew Case Study Center at the Georgetown University Institute for the Study of Diplomacy, Washington, D.C., 20057–1052.

Index